BUSINESS ETHICS

A Stakeholder and Issues Management Approach

SECOND 2 EDITION

JOSEPH W. WEISS

BUSINESS ETHICS
A Stakeholder and Issues Management Approach

SECOND EDITION

JOSEPH W. WEISS
Bentley College

The Dryden Press
Harcourt Brace College Publishers
Fort Worth   Philadelphia   San Diego   New York   Orlando   Austin   San Antonio
Toronto   Montreal   London   Sydney   Tokyo

Publisher	George Provol
Acquisitions Editor	John Weimeister
Product Manager	Lisé Johnson
Developmental Editor	Tracy Morse
Project Editor	Kathryn Stewart
Art Director	Scott Baker
Production Manager	Eddie Dawson

Battelle Press Chart, appearing in text on page 114: Courtesy of Battelle Press and William Hitt, *Ethics Are Leadership: Putting Theory into Practice.* Columbus, OH: Battelle Press, 1990, pp. 138–74.

ISBN: 0-03-024747-0

Library of Congress Catalog Card Number: 97-69301

Address for Orders
Harcourt Brace College Publishers, 6277 Sea Harbor Drive, Orlando, FL 32887
1-800-782-4479

Address for Editorial Correspondence
The Dryden Press, 301 Commerce Street, Suite 3700, Fort Worth, TX 76102

Web-site address
http://www.hbcollege.com

THE DRYDEN PRESS, DRYDEN, and the DP Logo are registered trademarks of Harcourt Brace & Company.

Printed in the United States of America

7 8 9 0 1 2 3 4 5 6   066   9 8 7 6 5 4 3 2 1

The Dryden Press
Harcourt Brace College Publishers

The Dryden Press Series in Management

Anthony, Perrewé,
and Kacmar
*Strategic Human Resource
Management*
Second Edition

Bereman and Lengnick-
Hall, Mark
*Compensation Decision
Making: A Computer-
Based Approach*
Second Edition

Bergmann, Scarpello,
and Hills
*Compensation Decision
Making*
Second Edition

Boone, Kurtz
Contemporary Business
Eighth Edition

Bourgeois
*Strategic Management:
From Concept to
Implementation*

Bracker, Montanari,
and Morgan
*Cases in Strategic
Management*

Brechner
*Contemporary
Mathematics for Business
and Consumers*

Calvasina and Barton
*Chopstick Company: A
Business Simulation*

Costin
*Readings in Total Quality
Management*

Costin
*Managing in the Global
Economy: The European
Union*

Costin
*Economic Reform in Latin
America*

Costin
*Management Development
and Training: A TQM
Approach*

Costin
*Readings in Strategy and
Strategic Management*

Czinkota, Ronkainen,
and Moffett
International Business
Fourth Edition

Czinkota, Ronkainen,
Moffett, and Moynihan
Global Business
Second Edition

Daft
Management
Fourth Edition

Daft, Marcic
*Understanding
Management*
Second Edition

DeSimone and Harris
*Human Resource
Development*
Second Edition

Foegen
Business Plan Guidebook
Revised Edition

Gatewood and Feild
Human Resource Selection
Fourth Edition

Gold
*Exploring Organizational
Behavior: Readings, Cases,
Experiences*

Greenhaus and Callanan
Career Management
Second Edition

Higgins and Vincze
*Strategic Management:
Text and Cases*
Fifth Edition

Hodgetts
*Modern Human Relations
at Work*
Sixth Edition

Hodgetts and Kroeck
*Personnel and Human
Resource Management*

Hodgetts and Kuratko
*Effective Small Business
Management*
Sixth Edition

Holley and Jennings
*The Labor Relations
Process*
Sixth Edition

Holt
*International Management:
Text and Cases*

Jauch and Coltrin
*The Managerial Experience:
Cases and Exercises*
Sixth Edition

Kindler and Ginsburg
Strategic & Interpersonal
Skill Building

Kirkpatrick and Lewis
Effective Supervision:
Preparing for the 21st
Century

Kuratko and Hodgetts
Entrepreneurship: A
Contemporary Approach
Fourth Edition

Kuratko and Welsch
Entrepreneurial Strategy:
Text and Cases

Lengnick-Hall, Cynthia,
and Hartman
Experiencing Quality

Lewis
Io Enterprises Simulation

Long and Arnold
The Power of Environmental
Partnerships

Morgan
Managing for Success

Ryan, Eckert, and Ray
Small Business: An
Entrepreneur's Plan
Fourth Edition

Sandburg
Career Design Software

Vecchio
Organizational Behavior
Third Edition

Walton
Corporate Encounters:
Law, Ethics, and the
Business Environment

Weiss
Business Ethics: A
Stakeholder and Issues
Management Approach
Second Edition

Zikmund
Business Research Methods
Fifth Edition

PREFACE

Read any major newspaper or business journal, and you will find an event, crisis, or issue that raises ethical questions about a corporation's activities. Questions are quickly asked: "Who is right? Who is wrong? Who stands to gain or lose? Who is hurt or liable? Who should pay for the damages? Who should have acted responsibly? Will justice be served?"

Students and professionals need straightforward frameworks to help sort out complex issues and make ethical decisions about their own actions and organizations in which they work and observe in the wider society. The second edition of *Business Ethics: A Stakeholder and Issues Management Approach* was created as a first course in business ethics and was written with the following four goals in mind:

1. To examine relationships among business, government, and other institutions and stakeholders;

2. To present stakeholder and issues management frameworks as practical methods for identifying and evaluating newsbreaking events in the business world;

3. To present concepts and studies regarding business and society and ethics in a straightforward, "reader friendly" way; and

4. To offer practical guidelines for making ethical decisions in real time.

The second edition provides questions and discussions that encourage the reader's participation in the decision-making process. Ethical decision making involves a person's own value judgments as well as those of observed individuals and groups. This textbook helps readers understand their own ethical decision-making styles and assumptions and use learned concepts to observe the ethical premises of executives and stakeholders in organizations.

A PROACTIVE APPROACH

Although business ethics issues change daily, classic ethical principles remain constant. This textbook shows that contemporary business topics can be analyzed by using traditional ethical principles in a stimulating way. The reader is put in the decision maker's seat with thought-provoking cases and discussion questions that ask "What would you do if you had to decide a course of action?" Readers will also be able to examine changing ethical issues and business problems as they appear in the *Wall Street Journal*, *60 Minutes*, *20/20*, the *New York Times*, *Business Week*, and other news media.

STAKEHOLDER AND
ISSUES MANAGEMENT ANALYSIS

Stakeholder and issues management methods are presented early in Chapter 2 to help identify and examine ethical dilemmas and problems in businesses, our own organizations, and in the six case studies included in this textbook. Stakeholder analysis is one of the most comprehensive, orienting approaches for identifying issues, groups, strategies, and outcomes (potential or realized) in complex ethical dilemmas. Issues management and crisis management can also be used with a stakeholder analysis. The nature of the situation or problem determines which approach is more useful. Stakeholder analysis is presented here as a starting point for mapping the "who, what, when, where, why, and how" of ethical problems that involve organizations and their constituencies.

FEATURES OF THE BOOK

Throughout the text, the presentation is clear and understandable: principles, concepts, and examples are written to minimize jargon and maximize meaning. The content is intended to contribute to courses in these areas: introduction to business, business law, business and society, and business policy.

Additional features of this textbook include the following:

❏ A new case section that includes six real-company, up-to-date cases. Each case presents students with current ethical dilemmas for them to discuss and solve.

❏ An expanded Chapter 7 now includes a section on global capitalism.

❏ Japanese and U.S. cultural decision-making approaches that affect ethical outcomes are discussed using a contemporary approach for examining international moral issues regarding competitiveness.

❏ Discrimination and sexual harassment are presented from management and third-party unbiased perspectives.

❏ Mini case examples are presented within each chapter.

❏ A focused approach is used with concrete examples when examining controversies in business ethics such as privacy issues on the Internet, AIDS in the workplace, managing in other cross-cultural contexts, sexual harassment, and other issues in the workplace.

OBJECTIVES OF THE BOOK

❏ To introduce basic ethical concepts, principles, and examples that enhance the understanding and use of ethical precepts and frameworks in solving moral dilemmas;

❑ To introduce the stakeholder and issues management methods as strategic and practical ways for mapping corporate, group, and individual relationships so readers can understand and apply ethical reasoning in the marketplace and in workplace relationships;

❑ To expand readers' awareness of what constitutes ethical and unethical practices in business at the individual, group, organizational, and multinational levels; and

❑ To instill a confidence and competence in the readers' ability to think and act according to moral principles as they create, manage, and study stakeholder relationships in their own worlds, at the national and international levels.

STRUCTURE OF THE BOOK

Chapter 1 defines business ethics and familiarizes the reader with examples of ethics in business practices, levels of ethical analysis, and what can be expected from a course in business ethics.

Chapter 2 introduces the stakeholder and issues management methods for studying social responsibility relationships at the individual employee, group, and organizational levels. These methods provide for and encourage the incorporation of ethical principles and concepts from the entire book.

Chapter 3 contains a discussion of the "micro-level" approach to ethical decision making: moral principles and concepts derived from both classical and more contemporary ways of thinking and acting ethically are presented. Individual styles of moral decision making are also discussed in this section. Although this section is a micro-level approach, these principles can be used to examine and explain corporate strategies and actions as well. (Executives, managers, employees, coalitions, government officials, and other external stakeholder groups are also individuals.)

Chapter 4 presents the corporation as stakeholder and discusses contemporary moral and conceptual issues that organizations face in stakeholder relationships. It also addresses the nature of corporations as moral actors and environments.

Chapter 5 presents ethical issues and problems that firms face with external consumers, government, and environmental groups. The question "How moral can and should corporations be and act in commercial dealings?" is examined.

Chapter 6 addresses the individual employee stakeholder and examines the kinds of moral issues and dilemmas individuals face in the workplace.

Chapter 7 aggregates the level of analysis to domestic and multinational corporations (MNCs) and discusses ethical issues between MNCs, host countries, and other groups. International variations of capitalism are presented. Ethics and industrial competitiveness within and between nations are also discussed, using the United States and Japan as examples.

Chapter 8 outlines emerging ethical issues that employees, managers, corporations, and multinational stakeholders must manage into the rapidly approaching twenty-first century.

CASES

Six new cases have been added to the text. These include the following:

1. Dow Corning Corporation and Silicone Breast Implants
2. The "Pentium Chip Crisis": Intel's Pentium Chip Problem
3. Women in Public Accounting (and Other Professions): Gender and Workplace Obstacles
4. Trouble in Paris: Euro Disney's Experiment
5. General Motors versus the Media, *Dateline NBC*
6. Some Don't Like It So Hot: *Stella Liebeck* vs. *The McDonald's Corporation*

ACKNOWLEDGMENTS

This textbook has been in the making throughout several years of teaching MBA students. I would like to thank them for their questions, challenges, and class contributions that stimulated the research, cases, and presentation of this text. I also thank my colleagues with whom I have met and worked over the years in the Academy of Management and the Organizational Behavior Teaching Society. Their suggestions are reflected in the book. I also thank colleagues and administrators at Bentley College who contributed resources, ideas, and motivation for executing the writing of the text. Kathy Rusiniak, my graduate assistant, helped enormously with the first edition. Vinamra Daga and Angela Ding, Bentley College MBAs, helped make the second edition possible with their research and writing assistance. Kristin Galfetti helped with the original research and construction of discussion questions. I recognize and extend thanks to those who reviewed and offered valuable revision suggestions, including Robert Giacalone, University of Richmond; John James, University of Florida; Susan Jarvis, University of Texas-Pan American; Dr. Lisa Newton, Fairfield University; Joan Ryan, Lane Community College; and William Wines, Boise State University.

CONTENTS IN BRIEF

CONTENTS

BUSINESS ETHICS AND THE CHANGING ENVIRONMENT

1.1 AN INTEGRATIVE FRAMEWORK

Organizations are embedded in and interact with multiple changing local, national, and international environments. As Figure 1.1 illustrates, these environments include the *economic, political, legal, technological, demographic* and *social,* and *governmental/regulatory* environments.

This framework shows an integrative, dynamic set of relationships between the environments and industries of organizations. Forces in and from each of these environments affect the performance and operations of industries, organizations, and jobs. As we approach the twenty-first century, the *economic environment* is shifting into a more global, international context of trade, markets, and cross-industry and organizational alliances. Large and small U.S. companies are expanding business and products overseas. Companies must learn how to market products to different nationalities, more so now than ever before. This framework can be used as a starting point to identify trends, issues, opportunities, and ethical problems which a company and/or industry may encounter from one or more of the external environments. We briefly introduce changes in the following environments which can affect organizations, their operations, and socially responsibility issues which may consequently face owners, managers who must respond to these influences.

Technologically, the advent of the Information Age, facilitated by Internet and telecommunications innovations, is also changing markets, the ways business is conducted, and jobs. Online technologies are part of corporate practices. Corporations are becoming more "virtual." Privacy and surveillance issues emerge in the workplace.

Politically, the fall of communist regimes and the rise of different forms of capitalism are also changing trading and business partners. National and organizational borders and boundaries are blurring. Understanding how different country and business cultures operate has become a requirement for professionals in the global economy.

Many *governmental and regulatory* laws and procedures also are changing. The Federal Drug Administration, for example, reconsiders the required market approval time for new drugs sought after by life-threatened patients with deadly diseases. Acquired immunodeficiency syndrome (AIDS) was not seriously encountered as a disease in the United States until the 1980s. Also, how and to what extent are U.S. antitrust laws to be enforced in a fiercely competitive global marketplace?

Legally, questions and issues must be addressed concerning product liability laws. How much and to what extent should companies be punished and made to pay lawyers and their clients who suffer from unsafe products? Should a limit exist? Who decides?

Demographically, the workforce has become more diverse. Employers and employees are faced with issues such as sexual harassment, discrimination, and effects of downsizing on morale, productivity, and plant closings.

■ FIGURE 1.1

ENVIRONMENTAL DIMENSIONS AFFECTING
INDUSTRIES, ORGANIZATIONS, AND JOBS

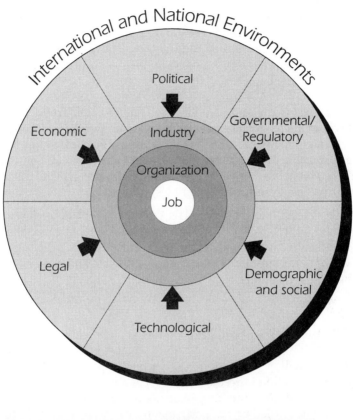

SOURCE: Copyright © Joseph W. Weiss, Bentley College, Waltham, MA, 1997.

This book addresses **issues** that have emerged from organizations', managers', and employees' interactions in the context of changing environments. It focuses in particular on the **social responsibility** and ethical (or unethical) practices of different individuals, groups, institutions, agencies, and organizations that interact in business transactions. The text presents methods that will enable you to identify, track, and evaluate major issues corporations and their affected constituencies (or stakeholders) must strategically manage in the marketplace or in courts: for example, the smoking controversy, AIDS in the workplace, same-sex marriage policies in companies, product safety regulation, the role of the media in reporting objective corporate crises and issues, advertising to minors and minorities, global competition, and antitrust laws, to name only a few.

BUSINESS ETHICS: AN AWAKENING

Recent business crises and scandals have had societal, even global, consequences and have awakened the interest of media, government, and public group stakeholders in business ethics. The following sample of recent business crises indicates that business has not been conducted "as usual" between business leaders and their stakeholders, outside and inside firms. Here are several examples:

❏ The savings-and-loan scandals cost taxpayers more than an estimated $200 to $500 billion. The scandals involved irresponsible and unethical actions by governmental and business professionals in a variety of occupations who exceeded their mandates and responsibilities. Who should pay? Taxpayers?

❏ Union Carbide's gas leak in Bhopal, India, resulted in 2,000 deaths and more than 200,000 injuries. The company still faces lawsuits. Would reactions have been the same if this had happened in the United States?

❏ The Manville Corporation filed for bankruptcy as a strategy to gain court protection for remaining solvent and for avoiding paying millions in liability suits to thousands of asbestos claimants, many of whom have died or are permanently disabled. Who is liable? Who should pay?

❏ Carl Icahn, T. Boone Pickens, Irwin Jacobs, and other corporate raiders have bought, sold, and restructured corporations for quick profit at the cost of local jobs and even of national long-term economic interests. Companies are continually acquired, merged, downsized, and transformed by changing owners and shareholders. Should corporations be bought, sold, and restructured as a competitive strategy? Who wins? Who loses in this game?

Inside corporations, moral issues and problems are also under greater scrutiny:

❏ Corporations are increasingly implementing sexual harassment programs as more women enter the workplace and as complaints grow; the U.S. Supreme Court has ruled to protect employees from such harassment at work. How should managers deal with issues of sexual harassment at work?

❑ AIDS in the United States and in the workplace is a serious problem. It is estimated that 1 percent of the U.S. health care budget was spent on AIDS in 1991. This estimate continues to increase as the decade advances, although there was a slight decline in the increase of the HIV virus between 1994 and 1996. To what extent is company management responsible for screening and educating employees about AIDS? Should certain professionals and employees be required to be tested for AIDS?

These crises and other moral issues in the workplace involve business leaders, managers, and employees as invested **stakeholders.** Business leaders are seeking ethical principles and guidelines to understand and manage these and other legal and moral dilemmas.

Although business ethics is not new, a renewed and growing interest in the subject is occurring. Major corporations such as Johnson & Johnson, Boeing, General Mills, GTE, Hewlett-Packard, Xerox, and others have created ethics codes, instituted social responsibility audits, and included ethics in their training. A 1990s follow-up survey of *Fortune* 500 industrial firms and 500 service corporations by Bentley College's Center for Business Ethics showed that 46 percent of the 244 firms responding were expanding efforts to incorporate ethics into their companies—this compares to 19 percent of companies surveyed in 1984. In this same study, 49 percent of companies surveyed also had adopted some form of ethics training, compared to 35 percent in 1984; 91 percent reportedly had a written code of ethics, compared to 75 percent in 1984. Nearly 87 percent of those surveyed in 1990 believed the public is more aware of ethical issues in business, and 84 percent listed "being a socially responsible corporation" as a main goal in their ethics program, as compared to 27 percent who said increased profit is a main goal.

The *Wall Street Journal, Business Week, Forbes, Fortune, Business Horizons,* and other business journals frequently feature surveys and articles on ethical issues that range from global dumping to sexual harassment. Moreover, nationally accredited business schools require business ethics topics in their curriculum. Ethics is now included in accounting, business policy, strategic and international management, law, and organizational theory and behavior courses.

1.2 BUSINESS ETHICS: A STAKEHOLDER APPROACH

Schools of business administration have moved over the past 25 years from teaching the basic principles useful in operations management, to the quantitative models applicable in the functional departments, to the computer systems needed for the technical areas, to the competitive concepts required for strategic planning. In the next five years I forecast that these schools will move even further to the ethical principles required for stakeholder commitment. (Hosmer 1991, 50–51)

We present a *stakeholder approach* and *issues management frameworks* in this book for understanding and studying a corporation's responses, moral responsibilities, and obligations toward the individuals, groups, and institutions it serves. A stakeholder approach is also critical to meet what Sethi, Namiki, and Swanson have called "the Management Challenge." In their book *The False Promise of the Japanese Miracle* (1984) they note six areas that determine the success or failure of an enterprise: financial, manufacturing, human resource, management, marketing, and strategic management. They stated:

> To this must be added a seventh area: the management of external relations—that is, business-government relations and dealing with other external constituencies. For in a hostile external environment, sociopolitical factors often have as much, if not more, impact on a firm's performance as the economic and market factors. (Sethi et al. 1984)

The stakeholder approach and issues management frameworks are explained in detail in Chapter 2. For purposes of introduction, note at the outset that the stakeholder approach views a corporation's ethical responsibilities in terms of its moral and economic obligations to the stakeholders (that is, constituencies) with whom it does business. Corporations are dependent to a large extent on their stakeholders to execute business goals successfully in society. A corporation's stakeholders include its stockholders, customers, suppliers, employees worldwide, political and environmental groups that influence its transactions, unions, and international governments. Corporations also depend on and are obligated to each of their constituencies in different ways to achieve their combined aims. They are primarily obligated economically to their stockholders; however, a stakeholder approach argues that if a company does not meet its moral, social, political, and legal obligations to its other stakeholders, it cannot function effectively or serve its shareholders fairly and justly in a democratic social system.

The stakeholder approach addresses these types of ethical dilemmas for individuals, managers, and corporations. It is an approach that provides (1) a pragmatic means of understanding the social and moral obligations of a business to each of its stakeholders and stockholders; (2) a method for mapping the complex relationships between a focal stakeholder and other constituencies; (3) a method for identifying strategies each stakeholder can use for interacting with moral responsibility toward others in crises, critical incidents, or ethical dilemmas; and (4) a way to "keep score" and assess the moral responsibility and responsiveness of focal and other key stakeholders to each other. In complex and ambiguous ethical situations, right and wrong decisions are not always clear. A stakeholder approach enables decision makers to clarify relationships, strategies, and events in order to describe and evaluate their moral options for addressing specific issues with justice, fairness, and equity for all stakeholder interests.

The moral role of managers from a stakeholder perspective is also not limited to purely economic, scientific, or profit motives. Society has evolved to such a point of complexity that business owners and managers must understand their moral obligations and their interdependencies with governments, consumers, the media, and a host of external constituencies in order to succeed in their stakeholder relationships. As one author noted:

> The ethical manager will be realistic about both the situation and the roles and functions of business, government and other institutions in dealing with it. He will also bear in mind the long-term interest of the persons and communities which he affects, having the courage to place those interests above his own short-term preoccupations. He will see his problems in the context of all of their relationships, employing his skills as a generalist to help produce appropriately systemic solutions.

Before this approach is explained in greater detail in Chapter 2, let us return to defining and clarifying the following topics: business ethics, levels of ethical analysis, myths about business ethics, reasons why ethical reasoning is required in business, the nature of ethical reasoning in business, and whether business ethics can be taught or trained.

1.3 WHAT IS BUSINESS ETHICS?

Business ethics is the art and discipline of applying ethical principles to examine and solve complex moral dilemmas. Business ethics asks, "What is right and wrong? good and bad?" in business transactions. Ethical "solutions" to business problems may have more than one "right" alternative, and sometimes no "right" alternative may seem to be available. Logical and ethical reasoning are therefore required for understanding and thinking through complex moral problems in business situations.

Although no one "best" definition of business ethics exists, the consensus is that business ethics requires reasoning and judgment based on both principles and beliefs for making choices that balance economic self-interests against social and welfare claims.

Laura Nash (1990, 5) defined business ethics as "the study of how personal moral norms apply to the activities and goals of commercial enterprise. It is not a separate moral standard, but the study of how the business context poses its own unique problems for the moral person who acts as an agent of this system." Nash stated that business ethics deals with three basic areas of managerial decision making: (1) choices about what the laws should be and whether to follow them; (2) choices about economic and social issues outside the laws' domain; and (3) choices about the priority of one's self-interest over the company's.

For defining business ethics, it is also helpful to see how working professionals identify a wide range of issues they experience in their professions and organizations. In an international survey of 300 companies worldwide, more than 80 percent of chief executive officers (CEOs) and senior managers stated the following as the top ethical issues facing businesses (Baumann 1987):

Employee conflicts of interest	91%
Inappropriate gifts	91
Sexual harassment	91
Unauthorized payments	85
Affirmative action	84

Also, in a national *Wall Street Journal* survey (1990, A1) of 1,400 working women, the following unethical practices were reported as occurring most frequently in business:

❏ Managers lying to employees

❏ Expense-account abuses at high levels

❏ Office nepotism and favoritism

❏ Taking credit for others' work

The same study reported that the most unethical behavior happens in the following areas:

Government	66%
Sales	51
Law	40
Media	38
Finance	33
Medicine	21
Banking	18
Manufacturing	14

Other examples of questionable ethical activities that involve and also affect corporations include the following (Gordon 1990, 93):

❏ Receiving or offering kickbacks

❏ Stealing from the company

❏ Firing an employee for whistle-blowing

❏ Padding expense accounts to obtain reimbursements for questionable business expenses

❏ Divulging confidential information or trade secrets

❑ Terminating employment without giving sufficient notice

❑ Using company property and materials for personal use

These reported ethical issues in business suggest that any useful definition of business ethics must address social and economic problems in the workplace, including relationships among professionals at all organizational levels and between corporate executives and external groups.

1.4 LEVELS OF BUSINESS ETHICS

Business ethics, then, is not simply a personal or an individual matter. Business ethics operates at multiple levels and perspectives. This section reviews two illustrations of the levels of analyzing ethical dilemmas in business. Because business leaders—and other invested business parties—must manage a wide range of stakeholders, inside and outside of organizations, understanding the different levels of stakeholders facilitates our understanding of the complex relationships among the participants involved in ethical business dilemmas.

Carroll (1993, 110–12) discusses addressing business ethical issues at five levels. Figure 1.2 illustrates these as *individual, organizational, association, societal,* and *international* levels.

Understanding moral dilemmas by identifying the level(s) at which moral issues originate and influence different stakeholder interests can help clarify the decision of what action to take. Also, as the film *Wall Street* illustrates, individual motivation and morality (or immorality) are linked to the organization, industry, and society. The themes of individual greed and unlimited ambition in the film were based on beliefs that brokerage firms (in the 1980s) could be vehicles for pursuing illegal activity: buying and selling stocks based on inside information to gain individual wealth. The view in the film that U.S. society rewards individual wealth above all else is controversial but intriguing.

Ethical questions at the *individual level* address issues such as whether to cheat on an expense account, to call in sick when one is not, to accept a bribe, to follow one's conscience over an administrative order, to report a sexual harassment incident, or, as in the film *Wall Street*, to sacrifice legality for individual wealth. If an ethical issue involves or is limited to individual responsibilities, then a person must examine his or her own ethical motives and standards before choosing a course of action. (Chapter 3 deals with ethical individual stakeholder principles.)

At the *organizational level,* ethical issues arise when, for example, a person or group is pressured to overlook wrongdoings of his or her peers in the interest of company harmony or when an employee is asked to perform an unethical or illegal act to earn a division or work unit profit. In the film *Wall Street,* the brokerage firm director praised Bud, the young

■ FIGURE 1.2

BUSINESS ETHICS LEVELS

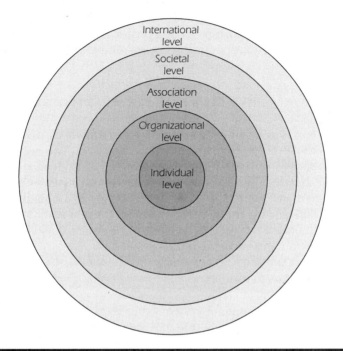

SOURCE: S. A. M. Advanced Management. Reprinted with permission, *SAM Advanced Management Journal*, vol. 43, no. 3, summer 1997, Society for Advancement of Management, Texas A&M University—Corpus Christi, College of Business, 6300 Ocean Drive, FC111, Corpus Christi, Texas 78412 USA.

employee, when he succeeded and fired him when he was caught for insider trading. If an ethical issue arises at the organizational level, the organizational member(s) should examine the firm's policies, procedures, and ethics code—if one exists—before making a decision.

At the *association level,* an accountant, lawyer, medical doctor, or management consultant may refer to his or her professional association's charter or ethics code for guidelines on conducting business before, for example, advising a client to deduct questionable items for tax purposes, offering a plea bargain, risking harmful side effects from ordering a prescription, or advising a client to acquire a company that conducts illegal business transactions.

At the *societal level,* the laws, norms, customs, and traditions govern the legal and moral acceptability of behaviors. Business activities acceptable in Italy may be immoral or illegal in the United States. The 1977 Foreign Corrupt Practices Act (FCPA) made it illegal for a U.S. company or its officials to bribe foreign government officials and politicians. However, business customs in some countries in the Middle East and Asia, as well as in certain other Mediterranean societies, include grease payments and bribery as acceptable negotiating tactics. It is advisable to consult with knowledgeable and trustworthy contacts in a foreign country to understand the legal and moral codes of conduct before doing business there.

At the *international level*, an example of an ethical issue would be whether an employee should work for or accept the policy of a company doing business with a government that supports apartheid when U.S. social values and laws do not support racial discrimination. Ethical issues at this level can be more difficult to resolve, since a mix of cultural, political, and religious values often is involved in a decision. Constitutions, laws, and customs should be consulted to understand what are and are not acceptable practices with regard to a particular decision.

As shown, these levels can and often do overlap. Thus it is helpful to identify all the ethical level(s) when confronting a moral issue and to ask whose values, beliefs, and economic interests are at stake in the decision. Does a moral basis or guide—an authority—exist for making decisions about this issue? Whose authority is more legitimate? Chapter 2 builds on these levels by explaining how to construct a stakeholder map that more specifically identifies interest groups at each of the levels discussed here.

The second and related illustration of levels, a set of three ethical business perspectives, is offered in Figure 1.3. These levels also include the *person* and the *organization* and add a dimension referred to as the *system*.

These ethical perspectives are shown here because they distinguish among the domains of the national, political, economic, cultural, religious, and business "systems" in relationship to the person and the firm. When an individual is identifying or confronting a particular ethical dilemma, these perspectives force the decision maker to ask, "What are the values, customs, and mores of the *country?* Of the political and

■ **FIGURE 1.3**

A FRAMEWORK FOR CLASSIFYING ETHICAL LEVELS

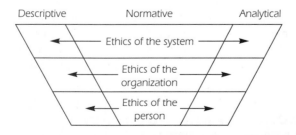

SOURCE: Reproduced with permission of The McGraw-Hill Companies, John B. Matthews, Kenneth E. Goodpastor, and Laura L. Nash. 1985. *Policies and persons: A casebook in business ethics.* New York: McGraw-Hill, 509.

business system? Of my organization? What are my individual values? How congruent or incongruent are these ethical perspectives in my deciding a course of action for a given moral dilemma?"

In Chapter 2, the stakeholder and issue management approaches are presented as methods to assist decision makers in their identification of different interest groups who hold economic, political, social, and moral "stakes" or interests in particular business and ethical outcomes. That chapter also will discuss how to rank and evaluate the importance and effects of different economic, political, and moral stakes on a decision. International groups' stakes frequently enter into ethical conflict, as the earlier example illustrates, and when U.S. corporations operate across national borders, deciding whose stakes should prevail in a difficult moral dilemma is often not easy. As is discussed in Chapter 7, the U.S. practice of **capitalism** differs from that of Japan. Recently, ethical conflicts have surfaced over these differences at the system level. This author maintains that a stakeholder analysis can help resolve such conflicts by clarifying who the stakeholders are and what their stakes entail.

To this point business ethics and different levels of analysis for examining ethical dilemmas have been defined. Before the nature of ethical reasoning is discussed, let us turn to four common myths about business ethics, since these continually surface in discussions and arguments regarding this subject.

1.5 MYTHS ABOUT BUSINESS ETHICS

Not everyone agrees that ethics is a relevant or necessary subject for business education or dealings. Although this book does not advocate or promote a particular ethical position or belief system, it argues that ethics *is* relevant to business transactions for reasons presented throughout the text. However, certain myths persist about business ethics, which I will discuss here and refute, along with other business ethicists.

A **myth** is "a belief given uncritical acceptance by the members of a group, especially in support of existing or traditional practices and institutions" (*Webster's* 1947). Myths regarding the relationship between business and ethics, in this discussion, do not represent truth but, instead, popular and unexamined notions. The four myths presented in Figure 1.4 are refuted in the following discussion. Which myths have you accepted as unquestioned truth? Do you agree that the following myths are indeed myths?

FIRST MYTH: "ETHICS IS A PERSONAL, INDIVIDUAL AFFAIR, NOT A PUBLIC OR DEBATABLE MATTER."

This myth holds that individual ethics is based on personal or religious beliefs and that one decides what is right and wrong in the privacy of

■ FIGURE 1.4

MYTHS ABOUT BUSINESS ETHICS

1. Ethics is a personal, individual affair.
2. Business and ethics don't mix.
3. Ethics in business is relative.
4. Good business means good ethics.

one's own conscience. This myth has its notable advocates. For example, Milton Friedman (1970, 33), a well-known economist, views ethics as not suitable for business professionals to address or deal with seriously or professionally, since they are not equipped or trained to do so.

Although it is true that individuals must and do make moral choices in life, including in business affairs, it is also true that individuals do not operate in a vacuum. Individual ethical choices are most often made and influenced in discussions, conversations, and group contexts. Individuals rely on organizations and groups for meaning, direction, and purpose. Moreover, individuals are integral parts of organizational cultures, which have norms, values, rules of conduct, and standards to govern what is acceptable and unacceptable. Therefore, to argue that ethics related to business issues is only or mainly a matter of personal or individual choice is to belittle the role organizational culture plays in shaping and influencing members' attitudes, perceptions, and behavior.

One survey (Posner and Schmidt 1984) showed that 60 percent to 70 percent of managers in U.S. firms claimed they felt pressure to sacrifice their personal moral integrity for corporate goals. Another study (Carroll 1975) found that the lower a manager is in a hierarchy, the greater the pressures he or she perceives toward unethical behavior. This evidence strongly suggests that business cultures and organizational pressures powerfully influence individual ethical choices and decisions. This is not to say that individual ethical decisions are not important; they are. The argument here is that business ethics is not primarily or only a private affair. It also can be a societal, organizational, or international affair, since business ethical decisions also involve these influential levels.

SECOND MYTH: "BUSINESS AND ETHICS DO NOT MIX."

This popular myth (DeGeorge 1986) holds that business practices are basically amoral (not necessarily immoral), since businesses operate in a free market. This myth also asserts that management is based on scientific, not religious or ethical, principles.

Although this myth might have thrived in an earlier industrializing U.S. society and even during pre-Vietnam 1960s America, the myth has eroded over the past two decades given widespread accounts of bribery, kickbacks, unsafe products, oil spills, toxic dumping, air and water pollution, improper use of public funds, and the savings and loan scandals. The international and national basis for an infatuation with a purely scientific understanding of U.S. business practices, in particular, and of a value-free marketing system has been undermined by these events. As one saying goes, "A little experience can inform a lot of theory."

The ethicist Richard DeGeorge has noted that the myth that business is amoral *is* a myth because it ignores the business involvement of all of us. Business is a human activity, not simply a scientific one, and as such can be evaluated from a moral perspective. If everyone in business acted amorally or immorally, as a pseudoscientific notion of business would suggest, businesses would collapse. Employees would steal from employers; employers would fire employees at will; contractors would openly violate obligations; and chaos would prevail. DeGeorge also noted that business and society share the same U.S. values: rugged individualism in a free-enterprise system, pragmatism over abstraction, freedom, and independence. When business practices violate these American values, society and the public are threatened or harmed.

Finally, the belief that businesses operate in "free markets" is debatable. Although the value or desirability of the concept and principles of a "free market" is not in question, practices of certain firms in free markets are. At issue are the unjust methods of accumulation of and noncompetitive uses of wealth and power in the formation of monopolies and oligopolies (that is, small numbers of firms dominating the rules and transactions of certain markets). AT&T before the breakup is an example of how one powerful conglomerate could dominate and control the market. The U.S. market environment can be characterized best as a "mixed economy" based on, but not limited to or explainable only by, free-market mechanisms. Mixed economies rely on governmental policies and laws for control of deficiencies and inequalities. For example, protective laws are still required, such as those governing minimum wage, antitrust situations, layoffs from plant closings, and instances of labor exploitation. In such mixed economies where injustices thrive, ethics is a viable and lively topic.

THIRD MYTH: "ETHICS IN BUSINESS IS RELATIVE."

This is one of the more popular myths, and it holds that no right or wrong way of believing or acting exists. Right and wrong are in the eyes of the beholder.

The claim that ethics is not based solely on absolutes has some truth to it. However, to argue that all ethics is relative contradicts everyday experience. For example, the view that because a person or society believes something to be right makes it right is problematic when examined. Many societies believed in and practiced slavery; however, in most contemporary individuals' experiences, slavery is historically and morally wrong. When these individuals and firms do business in societies that promote slavery, does that mean the individuals and firms also must condone and practice slavery? Also, an employee may steadfastly believe that working overtime violates his or her beliefs in holding to an eight-hour day. This may be true for that person, but it may harm the work group's and company's goals and needs in specific instances. Should the individual quit whenever a few weeks of overtime are required? The simple logic of relativism, as we discuss again in Chapter 3, gets complicated when seen in daily experience. Also, if ethical relativism were carried to its logical extreme, no one could argue or disagree with anyone about moral issues, since each person's values would be right and true for him or her. Ultimately, this logic would state that no right or wrong exists apart from an individual's or society's principles. How could interaction, communication, transactions, and negotiations be completed if ethical relativism were carried to its limit?

FOURTH MYTH: "GOOD BUSINESS MEANS GOOD ETHICS."

The reasoning here (Stone 1975) is that executives and firms that maintain a good corporate image, practice fair and equitable dealings with customers and employees, and earn profits by legitimate, legal means are de facto ethical. Such firms, therefore, would not have to be concerned explicitly with ethics in the workplace. Just do a hard, fair day's work, and that has its own moral goodness and rewards.

The faulty reasoning underlying this logic is that ethics does not provide solutions to technical business problems in marketing, accounting, finance, research and development, and the like. Moreover, as Rogene Buchholz (1989, 28) argued, no correlation exists between "goodness" and material success.

Lisa Newton (1986, 249) and Buchholz (1989, 25) also argue that "excellent" companies and corporate cultures have created and pursued values and concern for people in the workplace that exceed the profit motive. In these cases, excellence seems to be related more to customer service, to maintenance of meaningful public and employee relationships, and to corporate integrity than just to the profit motive.

The point is that ethics is not something value-added to business operations; it is integral, necessary, and central to managing successfully. A more accurate logic from business experience would suggest that "good ethics means good business." This is more in line with observations from successful companies that are ethical first and also profitable.

Finally, Michael Hoffman and Jennifer Moore (1995, 13) ask, "What happens, then, if what should be ethically done is not the best thing for business? What happens when good ethics is not good business?" They continue:

> The ethical thing to do may not always be in the best interests of the firm. . . . We should promote business ethics, not because good ethics is good business, but because we are morally required to adopt the moral point of view in all our dealings with other people—and business is no exception. In business, as in all other human endeavors, we must be pre-pared to pay the costs of ethical behavior. The costs may sometimes seem high, but that is the risk we take in valuing and preserving our integrity.

As indicated here, many logical problems occur with these myths about business ethics. In many instances, these myths hold simplistic and even unrealistic notions about ethics in business dealings. In the follow-ing sections, the discussion about the nature of business ethics continues by exploring two questions: (1) "Why use ethical reasoning in business?" and (2) "What is the nature of ethical reasoning?"

1.6 WHY USE ETHICAL REASONING IN BUSINESS?

Ethical reasoning is required in business for at least three major reasons:

1. Many times, laws are insufficient and do not cover all aspects or "gray areas" of a problem (Stone 1975). For example, should the Manville Corporation have paid millions to asbestos claimants if that would have bankrupted the firm? Or should that company (as it did) have legally declared bankruptcy and faced ethical reaction from the media and the public? Many legal actions may be unethical and cause pain and physical or economic harm to others. What rules or guidelines can people turn to in these situations when laws are not enough?

2. Free-market and regulated-market mechanisms do not effectively inform owners and managers about how to respond to complex crises that have far-reaching ethical consequences. For example, should companies, as American Cyanamid did in the late 1970s, legally prohibit pregnant women from working in toxic areas to protect their unborn fetuses, even though the firm's policy had the effect of pressuring several women into unemployment or choosing sterilization? Later, in the 1980s, the firm faced unanticipated discrimination charges and lawsuits from several interest groups. In 1991, the Supreme Court ruled in a six-to-three vote that such "fetal protection" policies are a form of sex bias prohibited by civil rights law. American Cyanamid may have acted legally in the 1970s, but did it act

ethically? What reasoning and guidelines help us answer questions when or before enacted laws provide authoritative guidelines?

3. A third argument holds that ethical reasoning is *necessary* because complex moral problems require "an intuitive or learned understanding and concern for fairness, justice, due process to people, groups and communities" (Carroll 1993). Company policies and procedures are limited in scope and detail in covering human, environmental, and social costs of doing business. On what grounds or reasoning did the U.S. Congress vote to allow President Bush to use his authority to declare war on Iraq? Were ethics and moral principles involved? The point here is that law, formal policy, and written procedures may not be sufficient in certain situations to enable those who must act to do so with clear, unquestionable authority. Ethics plays a role in business because laws are often absent or insufficient to guide morally complex decisions.

THE NATURE OF ETHICAL REASONING IN BUSINESS

In addition to the reasons discussed so far, LaRue Hosmer offers five major characteristics of ethical problems that also show the complexity of managerial ethics and point out the nature of ethical reasoning (Hosmer):

1. *Most ethical decisions have extended consequences.* Managerial decisions, actions, and results have consequences that extend beyond their control and beyond the organization into society. For example, bribes change governmental processes. Pollution affects environmental health. All the consequences and effects should be considered before decisions are made.

2. *Most ethical decisions have multiple alternatives.* Simple yes or no choices do not adequately characterize the many alternatives that exist and that should be considered for decisions such as "Should a manager pay a bribe?" and "Should a factory pollute the air?"

3. *Most ethical decisions have mixed outcomes.* As noted in the second point for alternatives, outcomes are not unambiguous; they have social benefits and costs as well as financial revenues and expenses associated with the ethical choices.

4. *Most ethical decisions have uncertain consequences.* Unanticipated and unknown consequences can follow ethical choices.

5. *Most ethical decisions have personal implications.* Such decisions can affect the lives and careers of the decision makers. Individual costs and benefits, in addition to financial and social ones, are associated with most alternatives in ethical decisions.

Hosmer's approach to using ethical reasoning in moral dilemmas is to (1) consider different alternatives to the problem, (2) do a legal analysis, and (3) think through a moral analysis, using several ethical principles such as those discussed in Chapter 3.

George Steiner and John Steiner list ten reasons why moral problems are often complex and difficult and require reasoning from ethical principles:

1. *Managers confront a distinction between facts and values when making ethical decisions.* Facts are statements about what is; values are views individuals hold independently from facts. A full description of the facts in business problems does not automatically give a just answer.

2. *Good and evil exist simultaneously, interlocked.* Paraquat, a chemical manufactured by Imperial Chemical Industries in England and Chevron Chemical Company in America, increases crop yield but is toxic to humans and has led to illnesses and deaths in less-developed countries. Should firms export this product to countries that know the effects but still request it?

3. *Knowledge of consequences is limited.* Results that owners and managers sometimes intend to happen often have very different effects on employees and customers. Facts alone often do not justify the negative consequences of intended positive actions.

4. *The existence of multiple corporate constituencies exposes management to competing and conflicting ethical claims.* Tobacco farmers give ethical priority to the tobacco economy in the South, as do stockholders. The Surgeon General's office and the medical establishment argue against harmful effects of smoking. Managers in this industry must weigh these pros and cons when doing business.

5. *Multiple constituencies often use conflicting ethical arguments to justify their claims.* Who is right and who is wrong? Managers must be able to recognize conflicting premises and assumptions in moral arguments. In Niagara Falls, the Love Canal Homeowners Association charged Hooker Chemical with disregard for the health of residents near the canal because, during the 1940s, the company dumped 22,000 tons of highly toxic, carcinogenic chemical wastes. Birth defects, miscarriages, and nerve and respiratory illnesses resulted. Hooker's defense was that the country needed the chemicals. In 1990, health officials declared the area once again inhabitable, and residents are moving back to houses once condemned. Whose interests take precedence and on what grounds?

6. *Ethical standards change over history.* In the 1950s, U.S. firms made payoffs to foreign officials; with the 1977 passage of the Foreign Corrupt Practices Act, bribes and payoffs are illegal. In certain Arab, Asian, African, and Latin American countries, payoffs are still part of doing business. Ethically correct conduct is an elusive goal, and applying ethical standards is an art.

7. *Human reasoning is imperfect.* Well-intentioned managers make mistakes in their ethical judgment. When faced with the temptation for profit

performance, honest managers may compromise their standards, as did Robert Beasley at Firestone Tire and Rubber Company when he embezzled more than $500,000 from a $12.6 million slush fund he managed. He was caught by the Internal Revenue Service (IRS) and served four years in jail.

8. *Ethical standards and principles are not always adequate for resolving conflicts.* No principles can replace human judgment in complex cases.

9. *Twentieth-century [and this author adds twenty-first-century] managers are faced with new ethical problems that exceed traditional concerns such as honesty, charity, and modesty.* Now managers must weigh and balance human life against economic factors in decisions. How should managers balance cancer studies that show that workers and residents exposed to plant emissions risk illness against the costs of emission regulation, inflationary impact, capital investment reduction, and loss of jobs and economic benefits from closed plants?

10. *Managers in large organizations now must deal with ethical complexities.* These include moral problems such as organizational versus public-interest loyalty, preferential hiring of certain classifications of individuals, and peaked performance of individuals before retirement.

Given the complexity of most ethical decisions, it is clear that simple yes and no answers are insufficient. Ethical reasoning should, therefore, help us sort out fact from fiction, assumptions and inferences, alternatives and options, and benefit and cost alternatives to make more informed, responsible moral decisions.

1.7 CAN BUSINESS ETHICS BE TAUGHT AND TRAINED?

Given the complexity and often vague nature of ethical problems and moral dilemmas, the question arises, "Can business ethics, then, be taught or instructed?" This ongoing debated question has no final answer. Studies continue to address the issue. One study, for example, that surveyed 125 graduate and undergraduate students in a business ethics course at the beginning of a semester showed that students did not reorder their *priorities* at the end of the semester on the importance of ten social issues, but they did *change the degree of importance* they placed on the majority of the issues surveyed (Stead and Miller 1988). What, if any, value can be gained from teaching and training ethical principles and their uses in business?

This discussion begins with what business ethics courses *cannot* or should not, in my judgment, do. Ethics courses should not advocate a single set of rules to play by nor offer one best or only solution to specific ethical problems. Given the facts and circumstances of situations, more-desirable and less-desirable courses of action may exist. Decisions will depend on facts, inferences, and rigorous, logical ethical reasoning. Neither should ethics courses or training sessions promise "superior" or absolute ways of thinking and behaving in situations. Rigorous, informed, and conscientious ethical analysis does not mean it is the best or only way to reason moral problems.

Ethics courses and training *can* do the following (Jones 1988–1989):

❑ Provide people with rationales, ideas, and vocabulary to help them participate effectively in ethical decision-making processes

❑ Help people "make sense" of their environments by "abstracting" and selecting ethical priorities

❑ Provide intellectual weapons to do battle with advocates of economic fundamentalism and those who violate ethical standards

❑ Enable employees to act as alarm systems for company practices that will not·pass society's ethical tests

❑ Enhance conscientiousness and sensitivity to moral issues and commitment to finding moral solutions

❑ Enhance moral reflectiveness and strengthen moral courage

❑ Increase people's ability to become morally autonomous ethical dissenters and the conscience of a group

❑ Improve the moral climate of firms by providing ethical concepts and tools for creating ethics codes and social audits

Other scholars argue that ethical training can add **value** to the moral environment of a firm and to relationships in the workplace in the following ways (Hanson 1987):

❑ Finding a match between an employee's and employer's values

❑ Managing the push-back point where one's values are tested by peers, employees, and supervisors

❑ Handling an unethical directive from one's boss

❑ Coping with a performance system that encourages cutting ethical corners

Teaching and training business ethics, then, does not promise to provide answers to complex moral dilemmas, but thoughtful and resourceful business ethics educators can facilitate the development of *awareness* of what is and is not ethical; help individuals and groups realize that their ethical tolerance and decision-making styles decrease unethical blindspots; and enhance curiosity and concern about discussing moral problems openly in the workplace.

Before a summary of this chapter, the following synopsis of Lawrence Kohlberg's (1973) six stages of moral development illustrates a major theory in this field.

STAGES OF MORAL DEVELOPMENT

Kohlberg's three levels with six stages of moral development offer a guide for observing our (and others') level of moral maturity, especially as we engage in different organizational transactions. Whether, and to what extent, ethical education and training contribute to our moral development in later years is not known. Most individuals in Kohlberg's 20-year study reached the fourth and fifth stages by adulthood. Only a few attained the sixth stage. The levels and stages follow:

Level 1: Preconventional Level (Self-Orientation)

Stage 1: Punishment avoidance: avoiding punishment by not breaking rules. The person has little awareness of others' needs.

Stage 2: Reward seeking: acting to receive rewards for oneself. The person has awareness of others' needs but not of right and wrong as abstract concepts.

Level 2: Conventional Level (Others Orientation)

Stage 3: Good person: acting "right" to be a "good person" and to be accepted by family and friends, not to fulfill any moral ideal.

Stage 4: Law and order: acting "right" to comply with law and order and norms in societal institutions.

Level 3: Postconventional, Autonomous, or Principles Level (Universal, Humankind Orientation)

Stage 5: Social contract: acting "right" to reach consensus by due process and agreement. The person is aware of relativity of values and tolerates differing views.

Stage 6: Universal ethical principles: acting "right" according to universal, abstract principles of justice, rights. The person reasons and uses conscience and moral rules to guide actions.

Refer to these stages when you are attempting to resolve a moral conflict at work or in other settings. Observe and identify the level and stage at which the individuals or groups are. At which level and stage are the arguments of those resolving a moral dilemma?

SUMMARY

Business ethics deals with what is "right and wrong" in business decisions, behavior, and policies. Business ethics provides principles and guidelines that assist people with making informed choices to balance economic interests and social responsibilities.

Business ethics operates at several levels: the individual, organizational, association, societal, and international levels. These illustrate the complexity and linkages of ethical decision making in business transactions. This chapter introduces the stakeholder approach to ethical decision making, which identifies constituencies and their claims at these levels of interaction in business environments.

Stakeholders include corporations, managers, individuals, groups, societal institutions, and nations. The stakeholder approach provides a means for mapping complicated relationships between the focal and other stakeholders, a means of identifying the strategies of each stakeholder, and a means for assessing the moral responsibility of all the constituencies.

Four myths often held about business ethics are discussed. Each myth is illustrated and refuted.

Ethical reasoning in business is explained with steps provided to guide decision making. Three reasons why ethical reasoning is necessary in business follow: (1) Laws are often insufficient and do not cover all aspects or "gray areas" of a problem; (2) free-market and regulated-market mechanisms do not effectively inform owners and managers about how to respond to complex crises that have far-reaching ethical consequences; and (3) complex moral problems require an intuitive or learned understanding and concern for fairness, justice, and due process for people, groups and communities. Ethical reasoning helps individuals sort through conflicting opinions and information in order to solve moral dilemmas.

Kohlberg's three levels and six stages of moral development are presented and discussed as means of assisting people with ethical decision making by identifying the basic underlying moral arguments and motivations.

Ethical education and training can be useful for developing a broader awareness of the motivations and consequences of our decisions. Business ethics does not, however, provide superior or universally correct solutions to morally complex dilemmas. Principles and guidelines are provided that can enhance—with case analysis, role playing, and group discussion—a person's insight and self-confidence in resolving moral dilemmas that often have two right (or wrong) solutions.

QUESTIONS

1. What are the environments organizations must manage, survive, and compete in? Identity three recent trends in any of the environments from Figure 1.1, and explain how these trends have ethical consequences for organizations or employees.

2. Why does a renewed interest in business ethics exist?

3. What are three outstanding ethical issues businesses face today?

4. What unethical practices occur most frequently in business?

5. Identify the benefits of using the stakeholder approach in ethical decision making.

6. Which, if any, of the four myths in the chapter do you not accept as a myth?

7. Identify three reasons for using ethical reasoning in business situations.

8. Is the law sufficient to help managers/employees solve ethical dilemmas? Explain.

9. What are some important distinctive characteristics of ethical problems?

10. Briefly describe three or four of the benefits that can be gained from ethics courses and training.

EXERCISES

1. Invent and state your own definition of "business ethics." Do you believe ethics is an important factor in business today? If you were the CEO of a corporation, how would you communicate your perspective on the importance of ethics to your employees, customers, and other stakeholder groups?

2. Conduct your own small survey of five people regarding their opinions on the importance of unethical practices in businesses today. Do your interviewees give more or less importance to economic performance *or* to socially responsible behavior? Summarize your results.

3. You are giving a speech at a Rotary International meeting. You are asked to give an introduction to the members on business ethics. Give an outline of your speech.

4. Explain how a major trend in the environment has affected your profession, job, and/or skills. Be specific. Are any ethical consequences involved, and has this trend affected you?

5. Review Kohlberg's levels and stages of moral development. After careful consideration, briefly explain which stage predominantly, or characteristically, defines your ethical positions and arguments. Explain. Has this stage influenced a recent decision you have made or action you have taken? Explain.

6. You are applying to a prestigious business school. The application requires you to describe an ethical dilemma in your history and how you handled it. Describe the dilemma.

REFERENCES AND SUGGESTED READINGS

Baumann, Mary. 1987. Ethics in business. *USA Today*. The original source for the statistics is the Conference Board.

Bowie, Norman, and Ronald Duska. 1991. *Business ethics*. 2d ed. Englewood Cliffs: Prentice Hall.

Buchholz, Rogene. 1989. *Fundamental concepts and problems in business ethics*. Englewood Cliffs: Prentice Hall.

Carroll, Archie. 1975. Managerial ethics: A post-Watergate view. *Business Horizons* (April): 75–80.

———. 1993. *Business and society: Ethics and stakeholder management*. 2d ed. Cincinnati: South-Western.

DeGeorge, Richard. 1986. *Business ethics*. 2d ed. New York: Macmillan.

Ethics are lacking in business. 1990. *Wall Street Journal,* 21 August, A1.

Freeman, R. E., and D. Gilbert Jr. 1988. *Corporate strategy and the search for ethics.* Englewood Cliffs: Prentice Hall.

Friedman, Milton. 1970. The social responsibility of business is to increase its profits. *New York Times Magazine* (13 September): 33.

Goldsmith, Arthur. 1996. *Business, government, society.* Chicago: Irwin.

Gordon, Judith et al. 1990. *Management and organizational behavior.* Boston: Allyn & Bacon.

Hanson, Kirk O. 1987. What good are ethics courses? *Across the Board* (September): 10–11.

Hoffman, Dr. Michael, and Dr. Robert Frederick. 1989–90. Unpublished summary of survey. Available on request from Bentley College Center for Business Ethics.

Hoffman, Michael, and Jennifer Moore. 1995. *Business ethics: Readings and cases in corporate morality.* 3d ed. New York: McGraw-Hill.

Hosmer, LaRue. 1991. Managerial responsibilities on the micro level. *Business Horizons* (July/August): 49–55.

———.1987. *The ethics of management.* Chicago: Irwin.

Jones, Thomas. 1988–89. Ethics education in business: Theoretical considerations. *The Organizational Behavior Teaching Review* 13, no. 4: 1–18.

Kanter, Elizabeth Ross. 1989. *When giants learn to dance.* New York: Simon & Schuster.

Kohlberg, Lawrence. 1969. State and sequence: The cognitive developmental approach to socialization. In *Handbook of socialization theory and research,* edited by D. A. Gosline. Chicago: Rand-McNally.

———. 1973. The claim to moral adequacy of a highest stage of moral judgment. *The Journal of Philosophy* 70: 630–46.

Matthews, John, Kenneth E. Goodpastor, and Laura L. Nash. 1985. Policies and persons: *A casebook in business ethics.* New York: McGraw-Hill.

Miles, Robert. 1987. *Managing the corporate social environment: A grounded theory.* Englewood Cliffs: Prentice Hall.

Nash, Laura. 1990. *Good intentions aside: A manager's guide to resolving ethical problems.* Boston: Harvard Business School Press.

Newton, Lisa. 1986. The internal morality of the corporation. *Journal of Business Ethics:* 249.

Posner, Barry, and Warren Schmidt. 1984. Values and the American manager: An update. *California Management Review* (spring): 202–16.

Semke, Ron. 1977. Ethics training: Can we really teach people right from wrong? *Training HRD* (May).

Sethi, S., Nobuaki Namiki, and Carl Swanson. 1984. *The false promise of the Japanese miracle.* Boston: Pitman.

Stead, Bette, and J. Miller. Can social awareness be decreased through business school curriculum? *Journal of Business Ethics* 7, no. 7 (July).

Steiner, George, and John Steiner. 1989, 1996. *Business, government, and society: A managerial perspective.* 6th, 8th eds. New York: Random House.

Stone, C. D. 1975. *Where the law ends.* New York: Harper & Row.

Thurow, Lestor. *The future of capitalism.* New York: William Morrow and Company.

Velasquez, Manuel. 1988, 1992. *Business ethics, concepts, and cases.* 2d, 3d eds. Englewood Cliffs: Prentice Hall.

Webster's third new international dictionary of the English language unabridged. Vol. 2 1971. Chicago: Encyclopedia Britannica.

2

A STAKEHOLDER APPROACH, ISSUES MANAGEMENT FRAMEWORKS, AND BUSINESS ETHICS

"A year after the Exxon *Valdez* ripped open its bottom on Bligh Reef [off the Alaskan coast] and dumped 11 million gallons of crude oil, the nation's worst oil spill is not over . . . Like major spills in the past, this unnatural disaster sparked a frenzy of reactions: congressional hearings, state and federal legislative proposals for new preventive measures, dozens of studies and innumerable lawsuits" (Dumanoski 1990). The grounding of the tanker on March 24, 1989, spread oil over more than 700 miles. "The disaster fouled waters and shorelines . . . damaging one of the world's major fisheries and killing more than 36,000 migratory birds including at least 100 bald eagles" (Rawkins 1990). A grand jury indicted Exxon in February 1990. At that time the firm faced fines totaling more than $600 million if convicted on the felony counts. More than 150 lawsuits and 30,000 damage claims were reportedly filed against Exxon, and most were not settled by July 1991, when Exxon made a secret agreement with seven Seattle fish processors Under the arrangement, Exxon agreed to pay $70 million to settle the processors' oil-spill claims against Exxon. However in return for the relatively quick settlement of those claims, the processors agreed to return to Exxon most of any punitive damages they might be awarded in later Exxon spill-related cases.

The charge that the captain of the *Valdez*, Joseph Hazelwood, had a blood-alcohol content above 0.04 percent was dropped, but he was convicted of negligently discharging oil and ordered to pay $50,000 restitution to the state of Alaska and to serve 1,000 hours cleaning up the beaches. Exxon executives and stockholders have been embroiled with courts, environmental groups, the media, and public groups over the crisis. Exxon has paid $300 million to date in nonpunitive damages to 10,000 commercial fishers, business owners, and native Alaskan villages. (In May 1991, Exxon's first-quarter profits were reported at $2.24 billion.)

In 1996 the grand jury ordered Exxon to pay $5 billion in punitive damages to the victims of the 1989 Exxon *Valdez* oil spill. At the time the fish processors had entered the agreement with Exxon, they did not know the Alaskan jury would slap the company with the $5 billion punitive damage award. One of the judges claimed that had the jury known about this secret agreement, it would have charged Exxon with even more punitive damages (McCoy 1996).

2.1 WHY A STAKEHOLDER APPROACH TO BUSINESS ETHICS?

The Exxon *Valdez* incident illustrates the magnitude of problems and issues a large corporation faces in a crisis; this situation provides a window into the combined economic, political, environmental, and moral dimensions of interactions between a corporation and its stakeholders.

Moreover, an incident that begins as an industrial problem can quickly escalate to societal and even international proportions. What method(s) can best be used to understand and evaluate who is right, who is wrong, and what costs must be incurred by whom in resolving issues of justice, rights, and fairness in such complex situations? "Rightness" and "wrongness" are not always easy to determine in moral dilemmas. As Abraham Lincoln stated, "The true role, in determining to embrace or reject anything . . . is not whether it have any evil in it, but whether it have more evil than of good. There are few things wholly evil or wholly good."

The **stakeholder approach** is an analytical way of observing and explaining how different constituencies are affected by and affect business decisions and actions. The stakeholder approach, as applied to the moral management of organizational stakeholders, is based on the view that profit maximization is constrained by justice, that regard for individual rights should be extended to all constituencies of a business that have a stake in its affairs (Bowie and Duska 1991).

Underlying the stakeholder approach is the ethical imperative that businesses are mandated in their fiduciary relationships to their stockholders and shareholders (1) to act in the best interests of and for the benefit of their customers, employees, suppliers, and stockholders and (2) to respect and fulfill these stakeholders' rights (Evan and Freeman 1988). In this chapter, the stakeholder approach is a tool for analyzing complex ethical dilemmas that call for moral (as well as political and economic) judgment, as the Exxon *Valdez* case exemplifies. Chapter 3 presents ethical decision-making principles and criteria that stakeholders can use to make choices and that observers can apply to examine decisions various stakeholders made or can make.

The stakeholder approach, then, is a method for mapping and managing the complex moral relationships between a corporation's strategic activities and those who affect and are affected by such actions (Freeman 1984). Why use a stakeholder approach? The stakeholder approach is a response to the growth and complexity of the modern corporation and to its influence on the environment, the economy, and the public. A more familiar way of understanding corporations is a "stockholder approach" that focuses on financial and economic relationships; however, a stakeholder approach includes moral, political, ecological, and human-welfare interests as well as economic factors. Both approaches inform management about the strategic and ethical status and direction of a company, division, or unit.

This chapter focuses on the stakeholder approach as a means of studying managers' social and moral responsibility strategies, actions, and outcomes toward other stakeholders. The stakeholder approach is a pragmatic way of understanding multiple, competing political, economic, and moral claims of a host of constituencies. The aim here is to familiarize you with the framework so that you can apply it in the classroom and in actual newsbreaking events that appear in the press and in other media. Even though you may not be an executive or manager, the framework can enable you to see and understand more clearly the complex corporate dealings, events, and crises in the immediate environment. And, as will be discussed later in the chapter, the stakeholder analysis can be used in smaller units and groups within a company. In fact, individuals are also stakeholders in organizations. Although this chapter focuses on upper-level and functional area managers as stakeholders who formulate and direct corporate strategy, Chapters 3 and 5 discuss the individual employee and manager as stakeholders. Your first task is to understand the logic and use of the stakeholder approach in general. The text then will discuss how this approach can be used in the moral management of organizational stakeholders, since this is the focus of this textbook. Chapter 3 provides ethical principles you can use to evaluate the moral criteria of strategies managers use when responding to different stakeholders.

In an earlier industrial age, when business owners were concerned more with basic production relationships, people had less need for a framework to understand a company's dealings with a limited number of suppliers and customers. In the present technological and information age, corporate activities affect the public in wide-ranging ways. These activities are under the scrutiny of the media, lobbying groups, and sophisticated consumers who can respond legally, morally, and economically to enterprises. The example of Exxon's oil spill illustrates how that firm's executives had to address a host of groups—and lawsuits—who had a wide range of "stakes" (that is, interests) in how the company handled the incident. The number of constituencies and stakeholders Exxon had to address reflects the complexity of the business environment in the twentieth century.

The Exxon *Valdez* incident also shows that in a pluralistic, democratic society, power is diffused across groups, individuals, organizations, and institutions. In fact, no central or absolute source of authority exists to direct, unify, or evaluate competing interests between a company and its stakeholders, especially in a democratic, pluralist, and capitalist society such as the United States. The governmental and legal systems often play roles in this process, but more often than not these roles operate after the fact. In an open-market system, special interests, lobbyists, and the media are significant forces that influence corporate decisions. In such a complex, pluralistic society, corporate leaders and those who strive to understand and monitor corporate activities need a method that helps them understand and "keep score" on each of their stakeholder's *strategies and power relationships* in crises and events that affect the public and the business. The stakeholder analysis is one approach used for these purposes. Just as important, it is a method that can be used to identify the *moral reasoning* of managers and their stakeholders. Stakeholder *welfare, rights, and responsibilities* can be identified and monitored in given situations. "Issues management" and "crises management" frameworks can also be used with the stakeholder analysis, as we will discuss later in this chapter.

2.2 STAKEHOLDER ANALYSIS DEFINED

The **stakeholder analysis** is a framework that enables users to map and then manage corporate relationships (present and potential) with groups who affect and are affected by the corporation's policies and actions. A stakeholder analysis does not have to result from a crisis situation. It can also be used as a planning method to anticipate actions and reactions to events and policy outcomes. As will be explained, a stakeholder analysis is not limited in its use to large enterprises. One goal of a stakeholder analysis from a firm's perspective is to create "win-win" situations for the business and its stakeholder relationships. Here "win-win" means making moral decisions that are profitable for all constituencies within the constraints of justice, fairness, and economics. In reality, this does not always happen.

STAKEHOLDER ANALYSIS: A STRATEGIC AND MORAL MANAGEMENT PERSPECTIVE

Stakeholder analysis is part of the strategic management activity of a firm. As noted, the analysis can serve a number of purposes. Here, we emphasize using stakeholder analysis to identify and manage social responsibility roles and relationships between a company and its constituents in a given or projected situation that involves exchanges between the firm and external groups. As in the Exxon *Valdez* incident, using a stakeholder analysis forces and opens economic and political relationships into wider legal, moral, and social responsibility issues (and vice versa). For example, the following questions regarding the *Valdez* crisis can be posed: What effect on the judicial system will this extended case have? Why did stakeholders sue Exxon? What are the limits of the tort system in the larger U. S. political system?

The analysis usually begins with economic, political, or ecological issues and then uses social responsibility and ethical decisions when questions of human and social costs and benefits, equity, and justice are raised.

STAKES

A *stake* is any interest, share, or claim a group or individual has in the outcome of a corporation's policies, procedures, or actions toward others. Stakes and claims can be based on legal, economic, social, moral, technological, ecological, political, or power interests. The stakes of stakeholders are not always obvious or explicit. The physical health of a community, for example, may be at stake when a corporation decides to empty toxic waste near residential sites. All stakes—actual and potential—must be identified in the analysis.

Stakes also can be present, past, and future oriented. For example, stakeholders may seek compensation for a firm's past actions, as occurred when lawyers recently argued that certain airlines owed their clients monetary compensation after having threatened their emotional stability when pilots announced an impending disaster (engine failure) that, subsequently, did not occur. Stakeholders may seek future claims; that is, they may seek injunctions against firms that announce plans to drill oil or build nuclear plants in designated areas.

STAKEHOLDERS

A **stakeholder** is "any individual or group who can affect or is affected by the actions, decisions, policies, practices, or goals of the organization" (Freeman 1984, 25). The **primary stakeholders** of a firm include its owners, customers, employees, and suppliers. Also of primary importance to a firm's survival are its stockholders and board of directors. The CEO and other top-level executives can be stakeholders, but in the stakeholder analysis they are generally considered actors and representatives of the firm. **Secondary stakeholders** include all other interested groups, such as the media, consumers, lobbyists, courts, governments, competitors, the public, and society. In the Exxon *Valdez* oil spill, stockholders also had an ecological stake in the economic consequences of how lawsuits were settled against the company; local communities had a stake in their shoreline and wildlife; local, state, and federal courts had stakes in the legality, liability, and future rulings on this and future such incidents; local fishers had a stake in their economic survival; and Congress had stakes in serving the competing interests of oil company lobbyists and the public good.

Stakeholders also have stakeholders. For example, Exxon gas station operators had to face angry clients and neighbors who perceived the company as negligent and unconcerned about the environment. Identifying and managing stakeholders requires understanding the involved groups' motivations and the interests of all their stakeholders. By acknowledging the stakeholders of the stakeholders, we can understand the sources of influence and power for the major interest groups in our analysis.

WHO ARE THE MOST IMPORTANT STAKEHOLDERS?

Who are the most important stakeholders for executive, middle-level, and supervisory managers in America? Figure 2.1 shows the results of a study

THE IMPORTANCE OF VARIOUS ORGANIZATIONAL
STAKEHOLDERS TO MANAGERS[a]

	Supervisory Managers	Middle Managers	Executive Managers
Customers	5.57	6.10	6.40
Myself	6.28	6.29	6.28
Subordinates	6.06	6.30	6.14
Employees	5.93	6.11	6.01
Boss(es)	5.72	5.92	5.82
Co-Workers	5.87	5.82	5.81
Colleagues	5.66	5.78	5.75
Managers	5.26	5.56	5.75
Owners	4.07	4.51	5.30
General Public	4.38	4.49	4.52
Stockholders	3.35	3.79	4.51
Elected Public Officials	3.81	3.54	3.79
Government Bureaucrats	3.09	2.05	2.90

[a]Scale of 1 to 7 (1 = lowest; 7 = highest).

SOURCE: Reprinted from the *California Management Review* 34, no. 3 Copyright 1992 by The Regents of the University of California. Reproduced with permission of The Regents.

that surveyed more than 6,000 managers and asked them to rank whom they considered most important.

Supervisory managers saw themselves as most important, followed by subordinates, employees, and coworkers. Stockholders ranked near the bottom. *Middle managers,* similarly, saw themselves and subordinates as the most important stakeholders, followed by employees and customers. This group also ranked stockholders near the bottom. *Executive managers* ranked customers first and themselves second, followed by subordinates and then employees. The authors of the survey concluded, "The stereotype of managers as running the nation's corporations for the primary benefit of their stockholders does not seem to be borne out by the data" (Posner and Schmidt 1984, 207). It cannot be concluded from these results that managers see themselves as more important than the survival of their company or its profits. These results do suggest, however, that profit may not be the only concern of managers and that other significant stakeholders can influence profitability (Steiner and Steiner 1988).

Similarly, in a *Wall Street Journal* article, "How Do You Spell Success? Executives Dismiss Money as a Measure," a Harrison Conference Services survey reported that executives most wanted *respect* from bosses, peers, and employees. The article quoted executives who stated "support for a charitable foundation," "job satisfaction," "self-respect," and "satisfying stockholders" as other important indicators of success.

Again, profit is important and necessary, but perhaps it is not always the only or the most important indicator of success for executives. They also seem to believe that money is a result—not necessarily a primary cause—of success. These findings taken together strongly suggest that a stakeholder approach, in addition to a stockholder approach, is essential for managing corporate policy and relationships.

2.3 HOW TO EXECUTE A STAKEHOLDER ANALYSIS

Assume you are the CEO working with your top managers in a firm that has just been involved in a major controversy of international proportion. The media, some consumer groups, and several major customers have called you. You want to get a handle on the situation without reverting to unnecessary "firefighting" management methods. A couple of your trusted staff members have advised you to adopt a planning approach quickly, while responding to immediate concerns, in order to understand the "who, what, where, when, and why" of the situation before jumping to many hasty "hows." Your senior strategic planner suggests you lead and participate in a stakeholder analysis. What is the next step?

The stakeholder analysis is a series of steps aimed at the following tasks:

1. Mapping stakeholder relationships
2. Mapping stakeholder coalitions
3. Assessing the nature of each stakeholder's interest
4. Assessing the nature of each stakeholder's power
5. Constructing a matrix of stakeholder moral responsibilities
6. Developing specific strategies and tactics
7. Monitoring shifting coalitions (Frederick et al. 1988)

Each step is described in the following sections. Let us explore each one and then apply them in our continuing scenario example.

STEP 1: MAPPING STAKEHOLDER RELATIONSHIPS

R. Edward Freeman (1984) offered questions that help begin the analysis of identifying the major stakeholders (see Figure 2.2). The first five questions, in particular, offer a quick jump start on the analysis. (Questions 6 through 9 may be used in later steps when you assess the nature of each stakeholder's interest and priorities.)

SAMPLE QUESTIONS FOR "STAKEHOLDER REVIEW"

1. Who are our stakeholders currently?
2. Who are our potential stakeholders?
3. How does each stakeholder affect us?
4. How do we affect each stakeholder?
5. For each division and business, who are the stakeholders, etc.?
6. What assumptions does our current strategy make about each important stake-holder (at each level)?
7. What are the current "environmental variables" that affect us and our stakeholders (inflation, GNP, prime rate, confidence in business [from polls], corporate identity, media image, and so on)?
8. How do we measure each of these variables and their impact on us and our stakeholders?
9. How do we keep score with our stakeholders?

SOURCE: R. Edward Freeman. 1984. *Strategic management: A stakeholder approach.* Boston: Pitman, 242. Reproduced with permission of the publisher.

Let us continue our example with you as CEO. While brainstorming questions 1 through 5 with individuals you have selected in the firm who are the most knowledgeable, current, and close to the sources of the problems and issues at hand, you may want to draw a stakeholder map and fill in the blanks. Note that your stakeholder analysis is only as valid and reliable as the sources and process you use to obtain your information. As a first pass, using only internal staff will get the process going. As more controversial, incomplete, or questionable issues arise, you may wish to go outside your immediate core planning group to obtain additional information and perspective. A general picture of an initial stakeholder map is shown in Figure 2.3.

If you were the CEO of Exxon, your map might resemble the one in Figure 2.4, a hypothetical stakeholder map presented by a student assuming the role of David Glickman, Exxon's public relations executive.

STEP 2: MAPPING STAKEHOLDER COALITIONS

After you identify and map the stakeholders who are directly and indirectly involved with your firm in the specific incident you are addressing, the next step is to determine and map any coalitions that have formed. Coalitions among and between stakeholders form around issues and stakes that they have—or seek to have—in common. Different interest groups and lobbyists sometimes will join forces against a common "enemy." Competitors also may join forces if they see an advantage in numbers. In reference to the Exxon example in Figure 2.4, you would

■ **FIGURE 2.3**

STAKEHOLDERS MAP OF A LARGE ORGANIZATION

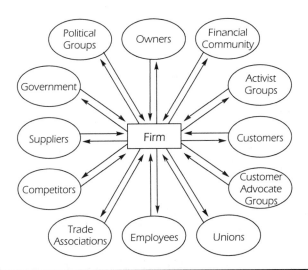

SOURCE: R. Edward Freeman. 1984. *Strategic management: A stakeholder approach*. Boston: Pitman, 25. Reproduced with permission of the publisher.

likely see Alaskan fishers, consumers, and unemployed groups from the crisis form a coalition with lobbyists and political action committees (PACs). Mapping actual and potential coalitions around issues can help you, as the CEO, anticipate and design strategic responses toward these groups—before or after they form.

STEP 3: ASSESSING THE NATURE OF EACH STAKEHOLDER'S INTEREST

Step 3, assessing the nature of each stakeholder's interest, and Step 4, assessing the nature of each stakeholder's power, overlap to some extent. Figure 2.5 is a guide for determining the nature of each stakeholder's interest.

By identifying the "supporters" (active and nonactive or uncommitted) and the active "opposition," as shown in Figure 2.5, we already have begun to assess the relative power of each stakeholder's interests.

In the Exxon example, a hypothetical CEO with his or her staff might determine that supporters in the Exxon *Valdez* oil spill crisis might be some stockholders and employees. The opposition, or those who may seek to further disrupt Exxon operations and its public image, might be

EXXON *VALDEZ* STAKEHOLDER MAP

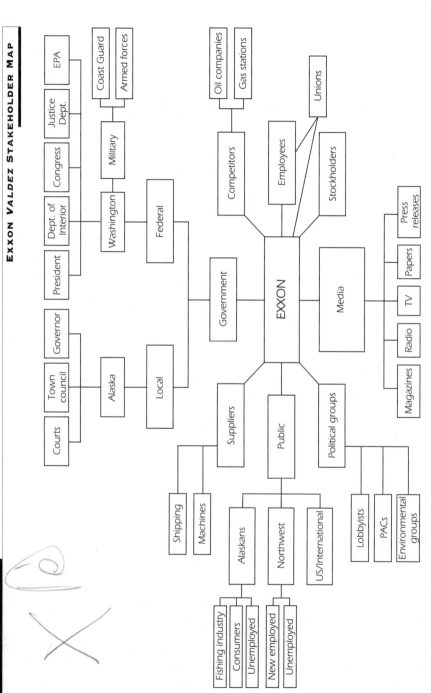

SOURCE: Organizational Behavior Teaching Conference, 1989. Reproduced with permission of David Glickman and Professor Kathryn Rogers, Pitzer College, Claremont, CA.

▪ FIGURE 2.5

	Supporters (Active)	Uncommitted (Nonactive)	Opposition (Active)
	Supporters (Active)	Uncommitted (Nonactive)	Opposition (Active)

Who Are the Stakeholders?
Currently active?
Not active?
Potentially active
For or against?

Actions
What are they doing, e.g., what pressures and procedures are they using, and what actions have they taken to get what they want?
What are the thresholds between their indifference and activism? What could trigger their response? What are their sensitive areas?
What are they asking for; what will they ask for; what do they want—i.e., what are their objectives?

Beliefs
What do their executives believe in? Is their knowledge of us accurate or inaccurate?
What assumptions do they make about us? What assumptions about them are *implicit* to our strategy? How do they think we affect their success, and they ours?
What is their power relative to us? What is our power over them?

How do they measure our performance, and we measure theirs? What do we really want? Are these objectives legitimate? Are they satisfied? Are we satisfied? What do they really want?
How will time and current trends affect their satisfaction, relative power, and activism?

Cooperative Potential
With which of our stakeholders sets are they related or dependent?
What differences are there between them and us, or our other stakeholders? Are these differences fundamental or superficial?
How could they be influenced, and by whom, at what cost?

Stakes
What is their stake in us, and what is our stake in them? How important are these stakes?
What is their real power in our affairs? Is theirs an *equity* interest, or is it economic? Do they seek influence for some other reason?
What power do we have in their affairs?

SOURCE: Kenneth Hatten and Mary Louise Hatten. 1988. *Effective strategic management*. Englewood Cliffs: Prentice Hall, 116. Reproduced with permission of Prentice Hall.

two PACs, three media companies, and so on. By systematically completing the categories in the audit through brainstorming the actions, beliefs, cooperative potential, and stakes of your stakeholders, you as a CEO in crisis force a broader, more objective picture of the situation, the players, and your firm's potential and actual role in the situation.

STEP 4: ASSESSING THE NATURE OF EACH STAKEHOLDER'S POWER

This part of the analysis asks, "What's in it for each stakeholder? Who stands to win, lose, or draw over certain stakes?" Three types of power stakeholders you can use are those with (1) voting power, (2) political power, and (3) economic power (Freeman 1984). For example, owners and stockholders can vote their choices to affect the firm's decisions in the Exxon *Valdez* situation. Federal, state, and local governments can exercise their political power by increasing regulations over shipping firms to avert future oil spills. Consumers can exercise their economic power by boycotting Exxon's products. What other sources of stakeholder power exist?

Figure 2.6 provides a series of short questions that assist in identifying and assessing the power of different groups' stakes. (Note that some of the questions in Figure 2.6 may repeat or overlap earlier probes.)

This part of the analysis forces you to attempt to identify your so-called allies' and opponents' strategies regarding their issues with your firm. It also helps you question your potential strategies toward each stakeholder and asks you to identify the groups you wish to cooperate with, neutralize, or counter over particular issues and claims. For example, in the Exxon *Valdez* incident, the hypothetical CEO might discover that a powerful lobbyist group organizing a lawsuit against Exxon could be neutralized if he or she met with its leaders, learned about its grievances, and negotiated demands; negative press could possibly be averted if the CEO faced the issues directly with two particular stakeholders. Again, this step asks you to assess the nature of each stakeholder's power. This information will enable you to decide later how, when, and who from your firm should respond to these stakeholders.

STEP 5: CONSTRUCTING A MATRIX OF STAKEHOLDER MORAL RESPONSIBILITIES

After you map stakeholder relationships and coalitions and assess the nature of each stakeholder's interest and power, the next step is to determine what responsibilities and moral obligations your company has to each stakeholder. Carroll (1989, 72) constructed a matrix of stakeholder responsibilities. It is a simple depiction to visualize and to draw. Visualize a graph with two axes. The stakeholders (owners, customers, employees,

■ FIGURE 2.6

STAKEHOLDER ANALYSIS

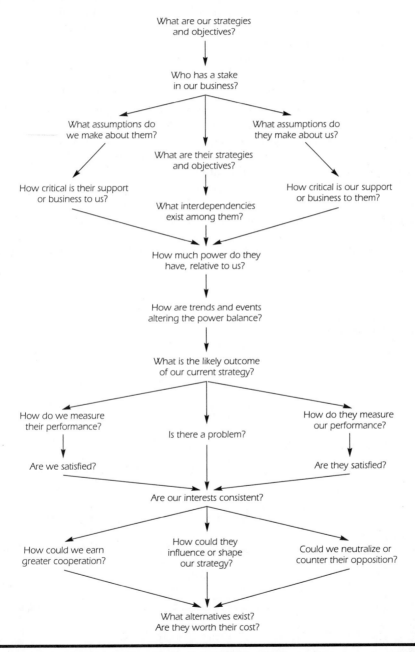

SOURCE: Kenneth Hatten and Mary Louise Hatten. 1988. *Effective strategic management.* Englewood Cliffs: Prentice Hall, 114. Reproduced with permission of Prentice Hall.

community, public, activist groups, and others) are listed down the left-hand column, and the nature of your firm's responsibilities (that is, legal, economic, ethical, and voluntary) to each stakeholder is placed across the top, as shown in Figure 2.7. For example, Exxon's hypothetical CEO might see the firm's *economic responsibility* to the owners (as stakeholders) as preventing as many costly lawsuits as possible. *Legally,* the CEO would want to protect the owners from corporate as well as personal liability and damage. This would entail proactively negotiating disputes outside the courts, if possible, in an equitable way to all. *Ethically,* the CEO could see Exxon advising its owners to show their responsibility by paying to help clean up the shoreline, by establishing policies to prevent another such catastrophe from occurring, by helping compensate Alaskan fishers who lost work, and so on. Chapter 3 explains ethical principles and guidelines that can assist in this type of decision making. *Voluntarily,* for example, the CEO also might advise Exxon's owners to show responsibility by publicly announcing their plans for and roles in resolving the crisis equitably and by offering services and remuneration to affected local communities.

This part of the analysis should continue until you have completed matching the economic, legal, ethical, and voluntary responsibilities you

■ **FIGURE 2.7**

STAKEHOLDER MORAL RESPONSIBILITY MATRIX

Nature of Focal Company Responsibilities

	Legal	Economic	Ethical	Voluntary
Owners	X	X		
Customers				
Employees				
Community interest groups				
Public (citizens at large)				

Stakeholders

have for each stakeholder so that you can develop strategies toward each stakeholder in the situation.

STEP 6: DEVELOPING SPECIFIC STRATEGIES AND TACTICS

Using your results from the preceding steps, you can now proceed to outline the specific strategies and tactics you wish to use with each stakeholder.

First, you will consider whether to approach each stakeholder directly or indirectly. Second, you need to decide whether to do nothing, monitor, or take the offensive or defensive with certain stakeholders. Third, you will determine whether to accommodate, negotiate, manipulate, resist, avoid, or "wait and see" with specific stakeholders. Finally, you will decide what combination of strategies you should employ with each stakeholder.

A useful typology for both identifying and deciding strategies to employ in a complex situation is shown in Figure 2.8 (Savage, Nix, Whitehead, and Blair 1991). This diagnostic typology of organizational stakeholders shows two dimensions, "potential for threat"and "potential for cooperation." Note that stakeholders can move across the quadrants,

■ **FIGURE 2.8**

DIAGNOSTIC TYPOLOGY OF ORGANIZATIONAL STAKEHOLDERS

Stakeholder's Potential for Threat to Organization

		High	Low
Stakeholder's Potential for Cooperation with Organization	**High**	Type 4 **MIXED BLESSING** Strategy: **COLLABORATE**	Type 1 **SUPPORTIVE** Strategy: **INVOLVE**
	Low	Type 3 **NONSUPPORTIVE** Strategy: **DEFEND**	Type 2 **MARGINAL** Strategy: **MONITOR**

SOURCE: G. Savage et al. 1991. Strategies for assessing and managing organizational stakeholders. *The Executive* 5, no. 2 (May): 65.

changing positions as situations and stakes change. As Figure 2.8 illustrates, the ideal strategic situation for the focal corporation is **Type 1,** the **supportive stakeholder**—low potential for threat and high potential for cooperation. Here the strategy of the focal company is to *involve* the supportive stakeholder. Think of both internal and external stakeholders who might be supportive and who should be involved in the focal organization's strategy—employees, suppliers, board members, the parent company, vendors. At the other extreme is **Type 3,** the **nonsupportive stakeholder** who shows a high potential for threat and a low potential for cooperation. The suggested strategy in this situation calls for the focal organization to *defend* its interests and reduce dependence on that stakeholder. A **Type 4** stakeholder is a **mixed blessing**—both a high potential for threat and for cooperation. This stakeholder calls for a *collaborative* strategy. In this situation the stakeholder could become supportive or nonsupportive. Collaborative attempts to move the stakeholder to the focal company's interests is the goal. Finally, **Type 2** is the **marginal stakeholder.** This stakeholder has a low potential for threat to and for cooperation with the organization. Such stakeholders may not be interested in the issues. The recommended strategy in this situation is to *monitor* the stakeholder: "Wait and see"; minimize expenditure of resources, unless and until it moves to a mixed-blessing, supportive, or nonsupportive position.

Again, while you are developing specific strategies, it is important to keep the following points in mind if you are the focal stakeholder:

1. Your goal is to create a win-win set of outcomes, if possible. However, this may mean economic costs to your firm if, in fact, members of your firm are responsible to certain groups for harm caused by or as a consequence of its actions.

2. Ask "What is our business? Who are our customers? What are our responsibilities to the stakeholders, to the public, and to the firm?" Keep your mission and responsibilities in mind as you move forward.

3. Consider what the probable consequences of your actions will be. For whom? At what costs? Over what period? Ask "What does a win-win situation look like for us?"

4. Keep in mind that the *means* you use are as important as the ends you seek; that is, how you approach and treat each stakeholder can be as important as what you do with and to them.

Specific strategies now can be articulated and assigned to corporate staff for review and implementation. Remember, social responsibility is a key variable, as important as the economics and politics of a decision, since social responsibility is linked to the costs and benefits in other areas as well. At this point you can ask to what extent your strategies are just and fair, and you can consider the welfare of the stakeholders affected by your decision. Ethical principles will be discussed in more detail in Chapter 3.

In actual experience, executives use a range of strategies, especially in crisis situations over time, to respond to external threats and stakeholders. Their strategies often are shortsighted and begin in a defensive or reactive mode. For observing and using a stakeholder analysis, it is important to question why executives respond to their stakeholders as they do, especially in threatening situations (for example, the silicon-gel breast implant incidents Dow Corning faced). Again, following the questions and methods in this chapter systematically helps you understand why key stakeholders respond as they do to critical incidents.

STEP 7: MONITORING SHIFTING COALITIONS

Because time and events can change the stakes and stakeholders, you will want to monitor the evolution of the issues as they are affected by media exposure, politics, economics, legal actions, and public reaction. Creating and updating a time line can be helpful. One method is simply to draw a horizontal line on a paper, starting at the beginning of the situation, crisis, or incident and then place points from left to right with abbreviations below or above the line that identify the time (month, day, year, or combination), the major event that occurred, and the key player(s). A vertical time line is illustrated in Figure 2.9, which is a chronology of events in the savings and loan (S & L) crisis. In this illustration, the year is listed on the left-hand column and the corresponding key events on the right. Time lines can help you track decisions in order to maintain perspective and decide prospective strategies.

SUMMARY OF STAKEHOLDER ANALYSIS

You have now completed the basic stakeholder analysis and should be able to proceed with strategy implementation in more realistic, thoughtful, interactive, and responsible ways.

The stakeholder analysis provides a rational, systematic basis for understanding economic, political, social, and moral issues involved in complex relationships between an organization and its constituents. It helps decision makers guide and structure strategic planning sessions and decide how to meet the moral obligations of all stakeholders. The extent the resultant strategies and outcomes are moral and effective for a firm and its stakeholders depends on many factors, including the values of the firm's leaders, the stakeholders' power, the legitimacy of the actions, the uses of available resources, and the exigencies of the changing environment.

■ FIGURE 2.9

TIME LINE OF THE S&L CRISIS, 1980–1990

Year	S&L Failures	Key Events
1980	11	Volker's Fed drives interest rates up to battle inflation, beginning three-year squeeze that left many S&Ls insolvent.
1981	28	Federal Home Loan Bank Board invents regulatory accounting, turning huge losses into "capital," delaying day of reckoning for many years.
1982	63	Congress passes Garn-St. Germain Act, partly deregulating thrifts; several state legislatures totally deregulate the industry.
1983	36	Taggart named California S&L Commissioner.
1984	22	Knapp ousted at American Savings.
1985	31	Energy bust begins, unmasking bad investments by Texas S&Ls; Empire Savings of Mesquite becomes first big failure from reckless lending.
1986	46	Congress fails to adopt Reagan administration plan to raise $15 billion to pay for closing of insolvent S&Ls.
1987	47	Congress adopts watered-down plan to raise $10 billion, but limits spending and protects certain insolvent S&Ls.
1988	205	Bank Board sells many failed thrifts by issuing loans to acquirers; estimated costs: $39 billion. Northeast bust begins.
1989	328	Congress passes sweeping rescue and reregulation legislation, raising $50 billion for more closings.
1990	181	Estimated cost of 1988 deals rises to roughly $70 billion.
1996	100 Pending cases	Estimated costs $130 billion.
Total	998	Estimated total losses: $200 billion.

SOURCE: The *Wall Street Journal,* November 2, 1990, A4 and January 22, 1996, B3. (C) 1990, 1996 Dow Jones & Company, Inc. All rights reserved. Reproduced with permission of the publisher.

2.4 MORAL RESPONSIBILITIES OF AREA EXPERT MANAGERS

One goal of a stakeholder analysis is to force organizational managers to articulate the moral responsibility of their company and of their profession toward their different constituencies. It also focuses the enterprise's attention and moral decision-making process on external events. The stakeholder approach applies internally as well—especially to individual managers in traditional functional areas. These managers "must be seen as the conduit through which they can reach other external stakeholders.

(They may also be an impediment, but even so, in many organizations they remain the major available channels open to stakeholders.)" (The material in this section is based on Freeman 1984.)

Because our concern is to focus on managing moral responsibility in organizational stakeholder relationships, this section will briefly outline some of the general responsibilities of selected functional area managers in order to illustrate moral dilemmas that can arise in their work.

Figure 2.10 illustrates a general functional area manager's stakeholders. The particular functional area can be written in while reading the descriptions discussed next. Note that the same procedures, steps 1 through 7 presented in the stakeholder analysis, also can also be used for this level of analysis.

Traditional functional and expert areas include marketing, research and development (R&D), manufacturing, public relations, and human resource management (HRM). The basic moral dimensions of each of these will be discussed. Several other line and staff functions, such as finance, information systems, planning, and legal, will not be covered here. Even though functional areas are often blurred in emerging network

■ FIGURE 2.10

FUNCTIONAL AREA MANAGER STAKEHOLDERS

SOURCE: R. Edward Freeman. 1984. *Strategic management: A stakeholder approach*. Boston: Pitman, 218. Reproduced with permission of the publisher.

organizational structures and self-designing teams, many of the responsibilities of these managerial areas remain intact. Understanding these managerial roles from a stakeholder perspective helps clarify the pressures and moral responsibilities of these job positions.

MARKETING AND SALES MANAGERS AS STAKEHOLDERS

With increasing frequency, marketing and sales managers interact, directly or indirectly, with customers. Because customers have been recognized as an integral part of most businesses, these managers must create and maintain customer interest and loyalty. They must be concerned with consumer safety and welfare regarding product use while increasing revenue and obtaining new accounts. Many marketing and sales professionals also are responsible for determining and managing the firm's advertising, as well as the truthfulness (and legality) of the data and information they issue to the public about products and services. Thus, they must interact with many of the other functional areas and with advertising agencies, customers, and consumer groups. Moral dilemmas can arise for marketing managers who may be asked to promote unsafe products or to implement advertising campaigns that are untrue or not in the consumer's best interests.

For example, marketing managers at Nestlé, the Swiss conglomerate, were forced to battle criticisms for advertising and selling infant formula in developing countries. The criticisms centered on the company's practice of persuading women to bottle-feed, instead of breast-feed, their infants. Because of impure water, poor health conditions, and illiteracy, women in these countries used the formula improperly. Executives at Nestlé never imagined the international controversy this would cause.

A major moral dilemma for marketing managers is having to choose a profitable decision over a socially responsible one (Abratt and Sacks 1988). The stakeholder analysis helps marketing managers in these morally questionable situations by identifying stakeholders and understanding effects and consequences of profits and services on their lives. Balancing company profitability with human rights and interests is a moral responsibility of marketers.

R&D ENGINEERING MANAGERS AS STAKEHOLDERS

R&D managers and engineers are responsible for the safety and reliability of product design. Faulty products can mean public outcry, which can result in increased public attention, unwanted media exposure, and possible (perhaps justifiable) lawsuits. R&D managers must work with and communicate effectively and conscientiously with professionals in manufacturing, marketing, and information systems; senior managers; contractors; and government representatives, to name a few stakeholders. As studies and reports on the *Challenger* space shuttle disaster illustrate, engineers and managers at the National Aeronautics and Space Administration (NASA) and the cooperating company, Thiokol, had different priorities, perceptions, and technical judgments regarding the "go, no-go" decision of that space launch. Lack of individual role responsibility and lack of critical judgment as well as its expression contributed to the miscommunication and resulting disaster (Werhane 1991).

Moral dilemmas can arise for R&D engineers whose technical judgment and risk assessments conflict with administrative managers seeking profit and time-to-market deadlines. R&D managers thus also can benefit from doing a stakeholder analysis in situations like the *Challenger* launch—before such events occur.

PUBLIC RELATIONS MANAGERS AS STAKEHOLDERS

Public relations (PR) managers must constantly interact with outside groups and corporate executives, especially in an age when media, external relations, and company exposure play such vital roles. PR managers are responsible for transmitting, receiving, and interpreting information on employees, products, services, and the company. The firm's public credibility and image rely on how PR professionals manage stakeholders, since PR people often must negotiate the boundaries between corporate loyalty and credibility with external groups. These groups often use different criteria for measuring success and responsibility than corporate executives use, especially during crises. Moral dilemmas can arise when PR managers must defend or protect company actions or policies that have questionable or known harmful effects on the public or on certain stakeholders. A stakeholder analysis can prepare PR managers and inform them about the situation, the stakes, and the strategies they must address.

MANUFACTURING MANAGERS AND ENGINEERS AS STAKEHOLDERS

Manufacturing managers and engineers are responsible for product safety, quality, and control. R&D professionals design products, and manufacturers produce them. Manufacturers also share in the safety and quality of products after the products leave the factory. Manufacturing managers must communicate with R&D professionals, corporate executives, marketing professionals, customers, and environmental groups, to name a few of their stakeholders. As the *Challenger* space shuttle case suggested, technical engineering manufacturers' perceptions and risk assessments of what constitutes a safe product must be weighed against societal responsibility and safety interests. Often, the moral dilemma the manufacturing engineer faces is whether and how to voice opposing judgments on a product's safety to administrators concerned less with technical safety and more with profit.

HUMAN RESOURCE MANAGERS AS STAKEHOLDERS

Human resource managers (HRMs) are on the frontline of helping other managers recruit, hire, fire, promote, evaluate, reward, discipline, transfer, and counsel employees. Human resource managers negotiate union settlements and assist the government with regulating Equal Employment Opportunity Commission (EEOC) standards. Human resource management professionals must translate employee rights and laws into practice. They also research, write, update, and maintain company policies on employee affairs. They face constant ethical pressures and uncertainties over issues about invasion of privacy and violations of employees' individual and constitutional rights. HRM professionals' stakeholders include but are not limited to employees, other managers and bosses, unions, community groups, government employees, lobbyists, and competitors.

Moral dilemmas can arise for these managers when affirmative-action policies are threatened in favor of corporate decisions to hide biases or protect profits. HRM professionals also straddle the often fine line between the individual rights of employees and corporate self-interests, especially when downsizing, layoffs, reductions in force (RIFs), and other hiring or firing decisions are involved. As industries restructure, merge, downsize, and expand internationally, the HRM's work becomes even more complicated. Human rights versus corporate profit always will be a tightrope these professionals must walk when making decisions.

Expert and functional area managers, then, are confronted with balancing operational profit goals with corporate moral obligations toward stakeholders. These pressures are considered "part of the job." Unfortunately, clear corporate directions for resolving dilemmas involving conflicts over individuals' rights and corporate economic interests generally are not available. Using a stakeholder analysis is a step toward clarifying the issues, stakes, and parties involved in resolving such potential or actual ethical dilemmas. As noted, Chapter 3 presents moral decision-making principles and criteria that can help individuals and managers think through these issues and take responsible actions.

FUNCTIONAL MANAGEMENT STAKEHOLDER ANALYSIS AND MORAL RESPONSIBILITY

Why should individual expert and functional area managers use the stakeholder analysis? First, by thinking in terms of stakeholders, managers can acknowledge and begin to change their perceptual biases, blind spots, and harmful activities that affect the firm's and their unit's operations. The analysis allows them to see and perform their roles and moral responsibilities toward external and internal groups. Second, by seeing how managers in a firm handle their complex stakeholder relationships, individual managers can begin to create value and realize corporate moral and legal obligations toward stakeholders. Third, the basis for increasing the quality of cross-functional communication and integration can be developed. The process and results of the stakeholder analysis can provide a platform for opening corporate communication channels to discuss stressful, unrealistic, or immoral expectations, problems, and pressures that often lead to illegal and unethical activities, such as creating faulty products, price-fixing, cheating, and lying. Finally, by identifying specific stakeholders' responsibilities, expert area managers can begin to see common patterns of pressures, resources, and ethical issues *across the firm.* An enterprise's moral identity and mission can be identified or reinforced. Moreover, managers can begin to think ahead and operate with moral responsibility as they perform their work. These advantages create opportunities for corporate executives to develop and implement meaningful enterprise ethical codes, policies, and procedures that help maintain a moral corporate climate and culture. In addition, costly lawsuits may be avoided.

2.5 EXECUTING A STAKEHOLDER ANALYSIS AS AN OBSERVER

So far this chapter has discussed how to execute a stakeholder analysis from the perspectives of a corporate executive and an individual manager. For an observer or stakeholder outside or inside a company, or for a student who is executing a stakeholder analysis, this technique provides useful information and perspective toward understanding strategic political, economic, and moral relationships. The procedures and steps outlined in section 2.2 are used by observers as well as by corporate members.

Questions and issues that surface when a person is executing a stakeholder analysis as an observer or student include the following:

1. Does the company have to be the focus of the analysis?

2. How detailed do the maps and analysis have to be?

3. What issues are the most important for each stakeholder, and who determines this in a stakeholder analysis?

4. How objective or reliable can the analysis be if those with the primary responsibilities are not directly involved or questioned?

5. Can an analysis be done before or during an event?

6. What difference or value, especially regarding ethics, can a stakeholder analysis add?

In response to the first question, "Does the company have to be the focus of the analysis?" the stakeholder analysis usually focuses primary and secondary strategic relationships around the CEO, the firm's executives, or a key manager. An individual employee stakeholder also can be the focus of an analysis if, at a microlevel, issues relating to employee rights or responsibilities in the workplace are involved. Most often it is a corporation or organization whose planned or unintentional acts command the attention of external groups and the public. Therefore, the actions of the corporation and its key executives toward other stakeholders must be understood. This is especially the case when influential or comprehensive decisions must be made that affect the lives and welfare of many people, as in the Exxon *Valdez* example. This does not mean that other stakeholders, such as functional area managers, are less important or that we as observers also cannot refocus attention around any one of the key positions and strategies.

The second question, "How detailed do the maps and analysis have to be?" can be addressed as follows: (1) Include only enough detail necessary to capture a basic understanding of the *who, what, where, when, why,* and *how* of the relevant stakeholder relations and primary issues; and (2) "KIS"—if the analyzers "keep it simple," the analysis will move along and not get bogged down in too much detail. No absolute rule exists about how detailed the analysis should be. This is a judgment call. A key concern is to have accurate, relevant, and timely information on the topic; the abbreviation of this information on the maps is a tactical matter. Also, factors such as time, effort, and monetary costs constrain one's ability to have all available information on a stakeholder. Good judgment is needed.

Third, "What issues are the most important for each stakeholder, and who determines this in a stakeholder analysis?" A response to this question is also a matter of judgment. Results from issue identification are as valid and reliable as the methods used to collect the data and the collectors' responsibility and conscientiousness in determining the most pertinent issues. Also, having more than one competent and knowledgeable person involved in the analysis and giving feedback during this process will result in a more objective approach and conclusions. If possible, the analyzer should circulate the issue list to those who can help identify key issues. Discretion is necessary, depending on the nature of the topic and the individuals involved.

Fourth, "How objective or reliable can the analysis be if those with the primary responsibilities are not directly involved or questioned?" Obtaining information, impressions, and perspectives from the major stakeholders and players is the primary objective in executing the analysis. However, this is not always possible. As often occurs with pollsters and political consultants in campaigns, stakeholders' strategies and tactics have to be sought from other sources. This task therefore must involve as thorough and comprehensive an indirect investigation as possible. Again, results and inferences are as valid and reliable as the analyzers' methods, expertise, and conscientiousness. The closer they get to the primary sources, the more reliable their information should be.

Fifth, "Can an analysis be done before or during an event?" Yes. Information in these instances is more tentative and variable. The analysis becomes more of a monitoring or prediction report than a completed profile. However, this is frequently the case in a stakeholder analysis. Corporate executives, strategic planners, and PR managers are also usually involved in a critical event before they turn to mapping it. They are not historians. This is one purpose of a stakeholder analysis. It is a type of field action research used for making strategic decisions and determining moral responsibility.

Sixth, "What difference or value, especially regarding ethics, can a stakeholder analysis add?" Having an informed, comprehensive understanding of a corporation's strategic relationships to its stakeholders in a critical incident or event is better than having little or no information at all. And a biased or unreliable picture may hinder the situation. Again, the purpose of the stakeholder analysis as presented here is for a firm to gain a realistic understanding of its strategic socially responsibile relationships, options, and actions toward its constituents so that corporate leaders can act morally in their policy decisions. A stakeholder analysis gathers diverse perspectives and information pertaining to an event. One party's ethical judgments are not taken as absolute in such an analysis. Also, these methods help participants to (1) separate and discriminate among the legal, political, economic, and moral issues and consequences of stakeholder actions and policies; (2) learn to use informed, ethical judgments when determining and managing moral obligations to stakeholders; (3) learn to separate facts from inferences; and (4) learn to evaluate the power, legitimacy, and motivations of organizational stakeholders' positions and strategies.

2.6 STAKEHOLDER ANALYSIS AND ETHICAL REASONING

Because the stakeholder analysis is an analytical method, no prescribed ethical principles or responsibility rules are "built in." Ethical reasoning in the stakeholder analysis means asking, "What is equitable, just, fair, and good for those who affect and are affected by business decisions?" Also, "Who are the weaker stakeholders in terms of power and influence? Who can, who will, and who should help weaker stakeholders make their voices heard and encourage their participation in the decisional process and outcomes?" Finally, the stakeholder analysis requires the focal or principal stakeholders to define and fulfill their ethical obligations to the affected constituencies.

As noted earlier, Chapter 3 explains major ethical principles that can be used to examine individual motivation for resolving an ethical dilemma. Although Chapter 3 focuses on the micro- or individual level of ethical reasoning, the logic underlying the ethical principles also can be extended to a more macro- or policy level, as will be explained.

2.7 ISSUES MANAGEMENT FRAMEWORKS

Managing the environment and moral responsibility in the marketplace for corporations also means managing strategic issues and crises related to advertising and product safety, as well as environmentally related problems. To act morally toward stakeholders in the marketplace, corporate executives and managers should be aware of potentially harmful issues and problems before these evolve into crises. Often at stake in strategic issue management, as well as in crises that suddenly erupt, are human lives, property, environmental damage, the firm's reputation, market share, profits, and sometimes the firm's existence—as was the case with the Manville Corporation in the asbestos lawsuits and with A. H. Robins Company in the Dalkon Shield lawsuits.

This section outlines how issue and crisis management are part of a firm's strategic planning process, which is discussed in detail in Chapter 4. Issue and crisis management are also related topics in the stakeholder analysis. Managing corporate responsibility vis à vis a firm's constituencies—especially groups affected by critical issues and crises stemming from a firm's activities—involves issue and crisis management. Recent examples of industrial crises that threatened the environment and a wide range of stakeholders, and that triggered intense media coverage, include the Exxon *Valdez* oil spill, the Three Mile Island nuclear plant crisis in New York, the *Challenger* space shuttle disaster, and the Union Carbide chemical leak in India. Product crises include the discovery of cyanide in Johnson & Johnson's Tylenol, Ford Pinto's rear gas-tank explosions, injuries blamed on Firestone 500 radial tires, Procter & Gamble's Rely tampon and toxic shock connection, A. H. Robins's Dalkon Shield–related deaths and injuries, and Dow Corning Corporation's recent manufacturing and marketing of the silicone gel used in breast implants. Because of the seriousness and scope of the stakes regarding such extraordinary events, many firms use specific methods and techniques to manage critical issues and crises.

STRATEGIC ISSUES MANAGEMENT

Strategic issues management attempts to (1) detect and address issues that may cause a firm and its stakeholders problems or harm and (2) contain or solve issues that could become potentially damaging crises. Many firms (for example, Monsanto, Sears, and Arco) have hired issues management staff who alert top management about controversial trends that could affect operations.

Managing and controlling issues involves the following steps (derived from a number of sources, including Brown 1979; Buchholz 1982; Carroll 1989; and King 1987), illustrated in Figure 2.11:

1. Environmental scanning
2. Identifying issues
3. Prioritizing issues
4. Analyzing issues
5. Strategizing issue solutions
6. Responding and implementing strategies
7. Evaluating and monitoring strategies

■ **FIGURE 2.11**

ISSUE MANAGEMENT PROCESS

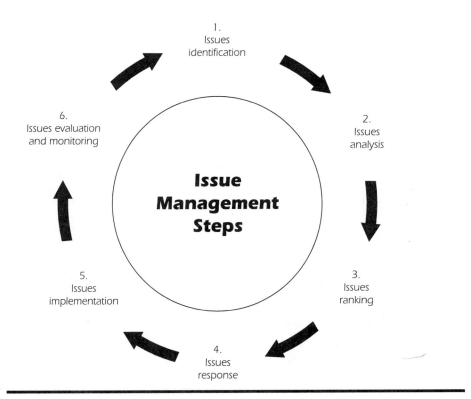

These steps are part of a firm's corporate planning process. In the strategic issues management process, these steps are isolated, and a firm uses its special-issues unit to work on emerging trends as they relate to the specific industry and company. This framework is a first-step, basic approach for mapping issues.

DEVELOPMENTAL LIFE-CYCLE APPROACH

Issues also are believed to follow a developmental life-cycle process. Views differ (for example, see Carroll 1989; Gottschalk 1982; and Mahjon 1986) on the stages and time involved in the life cycle—one source has assigned an eight-year span to an issue's life. It is instructive to understand some of the life-cycle stages suggested for tracking an issue.

A seven-stage issue developmental process follows (see Figure 2.12):

1. A felt need arises (from emerging events, advocacy groups, books, movies).

2. Media coverage is developed (TV articles such as on *60 Minutes, 20/20,* radio).

■ FIGURE 2.12

ISSUE DEVELOPMENTAL PROCESS

Businesses lobby if issues evolve into laws that could affect them → Litigation

Legislation and regulation

Federal government attention — hearings and studies

Businesses gain awareness but take no action →

Leading political jurisdictions (cities, states, counties) adopt policies

Interest group development and growth

Media coverage — public awareness, TV (*60 Minutes, 20/20, Dateline,* news) articles, radio

Felt need — leading events, advocacy, groups, books, movies

Stages in the Issue Developmental Process

Time

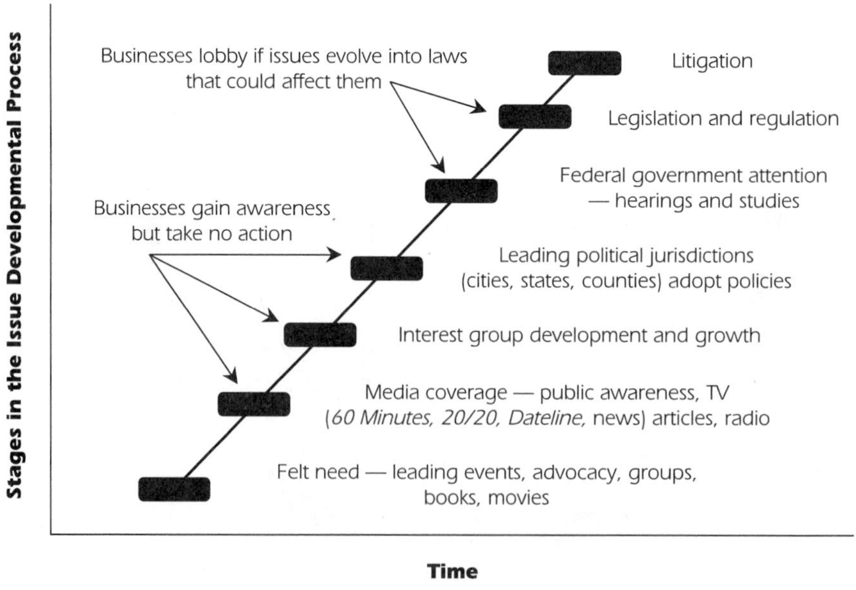

3. Interest group development and growth gains momentum.

4. Policies are adopted by leading political jurisdictions (cities, states, counties).

5. The federal government gains attention (hearings and studies).

6. Issues and policies evolve into legislation and regulation.

7. Issues and policies enter litigation. (Carroll 1989, 489)

Can you think of some contemporary issues that evolved through part or all of these stages? Did an issue change in its perceived importance or danger to society? Did the issue gain or lose public legitimacy as it evolved through the legislative stage? How did the stakes and stakeholders change as the issue evolved?

Thomas Marx (1986) has offered a four-stage issue life cycle. Marx observed that issues evolve from social expectations to social control through the following steps (see Figure 2.13):

1. Social expectation

2. Political issue

3. Legislation

4. Social control

Marx illustrated his framework with the auto-safety belt issue. The four stages of this issue, according to Marx, were reflected by the following events:

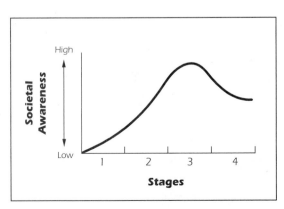

■ **FIGURE 2.13**

AN ISSUE DEVELOPMENT LIFE CYCLE

1. Social Expectations and Awareness
   - Social Discussion and Debate
   - Interest Group Attention
2. Political Awareness
   - Media Attention
   - Legislation Initiated
   - Hearings Held
3. Legislative Engagement
   - Law Passed
   - Legal Involvement
   - Regulations Enacted
4. Social Control and Litigation
   - Compliance Issues
   - Legal Conflict
   - Court Rulings

1. Ralph Nader's book *Unsafe at Any Speed* (1964) created a social expectation.

2. The National Traffic Auto Safety Act and resulting Motor Vehicle Safety hearings in 1966 moved the expectation into the political arena.

3. In 1966, the Motor Vehicle Safety Act was passed, which was later followed by four states adopting required seat-belt use in 1984. This represented the legislation stage.

4. Social control was established in 1967 when all cars were required to have seat belts. Driver fines and penalties, recalls of products, and defects litigation further emphasized the control stage.

Again, selecting an issue in the news and tracing its evolution through these different stages provides a window into the social, political, economic, and legislative functional processes of society. Issues are not static or predetermined commodities. Stakeholder groups' values and interests move or impede an issue's development. To understand how an issue develops or is killed is to understand how power works in a political system.

ISSUES MANAGEMENT AND STAKEHOLDER ANALYSIS

After the issues are prioritized, a stakeholder analysis can be enhanced by asking the following questions (King 1987):

❑ Which stakeholders are affected by the issue?

❑ Who has an interest in the issue?

❑ Who is in a position to exert influence on the issue?

❑ Who has expressed an opinion on the issue?

❑ Who ought to care about the issue?

Issues then can be ranked from highest to lowest in terms of impact on corporate-level operations and the ethical obligations and responsibilities of each stakeholder. An issues management process complements the stakeholder analysis and can be used to anticipate and resolve corporate-related issues and crises. Students of business ethics also can use these frameworks to understand and track newsbreaking incidents that present economic, legal, social, and moral problems for a company and its stakeholders.

At a societal macrolevel, John Naisbitt and Patricia Aburdene (1990) summarized a list of predominant forces and issues in the "extraordinary decade" of the 1990s:

❑ Economic considerations transcend political ones.

❑ Movement toward worldwide free trade is occurring.

❑ The importance of telecommunications is increasing.

❑ A relative abundance of natural resources exists.

❑ Competition for reduced taxes is occurring.

❑ Downsizing of economic output is happening

❑ Containing inflation and interest is a trend across nations.

❑ An Asian consumer boom will continue.

❑ Advancement of democracy and free enterprise will continue.

❑ Obsolescence of war is occurring among major nations.

❑ New attention to the environment will continue.

What moral issues do these trends present to corporations and to us as individual stakeholders? Do any additional issues exist that this list does not identify?

MANAGING CRISIS

In addition to general issues models are "crisis management" frameworks. These frameworks have evolved from the study of how corporations actually responded (and should have responded) to crises. Note that stakeholders and issues approaches also can be part of the crisis management process when events are explained. A crisis is a "turning point for better or worse"; a "decisive moment" or "crucial time"; or "a situation that has reached a critical phase" (Fink 1986, 15). Steven Fink (1986) states that crisis management "is the art of removing much of the risk and uncertainty to allow you to achieve more control over your destiny." Crises, from a corporation's point of view, can deteriorate if the situation escalates in intensity, comes under closer governmental scrutiny, interferes with normal operations, jeopardizes a positive company image or officers' image, and damages a firm's bottom line (Fink 1986, 16). A turn for the worse also could occur if any of the firm's stakeholders were seriously harmed or if the environment was damaged or destroyed.

CRISIS STAGES: FIRST MODEL   Crises, according to one model, consists of four stages: (1) prodromal (precrisis), (2) acute, (3) chronic, and (4) resolution (Fink 1986, 20). Judgment and observation are required to manage these stages. Figure 2-14 illustrates these stages.

The **prodromal stage** is the warning stage. If this stage is missed, the second stage (acute crisis) can rush in, leaving damage control to follow. Clues in this stage must be carefully observed. For example, a clue could be verbal, such as a union leader telling upper management a strike could occur if certain contract conditions are not signed.

The second stage, **acute crisis,** is the occurrence of the actual crisis. Damage has been done at this stage. The point here is to control as much

■ FIGURE 2.14

■ FIGURE 2.14

FOUR CRISIS MANAGEMENT STAGES

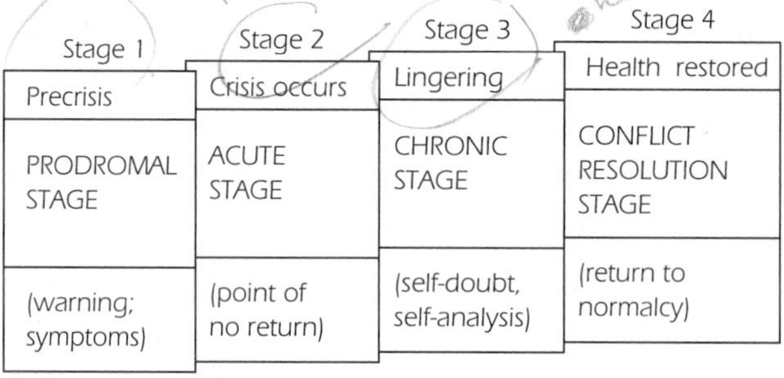

Stage 1	Stage 2	Stage 3	Stage 4
Precrisis	Crisis occurs	Lingering	Health restored
PRODROMAL STAGE	ACUTE STAGE	CHRONIC STAGE	CONFLICT RESOLUTION STAGE
(warning; symptoms)	(point of no return)	(self-doubt, self-analysis)	(return to normalcy)

of the damage as possible. This is most often the shortest of the stages.

The third stage, **chronic crisis,** is the clean-up phase. This is a period of recovery, self-analysis, self-doubt, and healing. Congressional investigations, audits, and interviews occur during this stage. This stage can linger indefinitely, according to Fink (1986). A survey of *Fortune* 500 CEOs found that companies that did not have a crisis management plan stayed in this stage two and a half times longer than those who had plans.

The final stage, **crisis resolution,** is the crisis management goal. The key question here is "What can I do to speed up this phase and resolve this crisis once and for all?" (Fink 1986, 25).

PRODUCT CRISIS MANAGEMENT: SECOND MODEL Matthews, Goodpaster, and Nash (1985) have suggested five phases of corporate social responses to crises related to unsafe products. These phases, as illustrated in Figure 2.15, are (1) reaction, (2) defense, (3) insight range, (4) accommodation, and (5) agency. Not all executives involved in unsafe product crises respond the same to the public, media, and other stakeholders. These phases can be used to examine and evaluate the moral responsibility of corporate responses to crises such as the Firestone radial 500 tire, the Tylenol tampering, the Rely tampon, the Ford Pinto, the Dow Corning silicon-gel issue, and those presently occurring. How and to what extent executives acknowledge responsibility and act morally and economically responsible to their stakeholders in each response stage varies. It is interesting to observe how some executives continue to deny or avoid responsibility in crises that erupt. Knowledge of these stages certainly would be a first step toward corporate awareness.

The **reaction stage** occurs when a crisis has in fact occurred. Management lacks complete information and time to analyze the event thoroughly. A public reaction is required that responds to allegations about

■ FIGURE 2.15

CORPORATE SOCIAL RESPONSE PHASES

REACTION　→　DEFENSE　→　INSIGHT RANGE　ACCOMMODATION　→　AGENCY

the product and the crisis. This stage is important to corporations, since the public, the media, and those stakeholders involved see for the first time who the firm selects as its spokesperson, how the firm responds, and what the message is.

The second stage, **defense,** signals that the company is overwhelmed by public attention. The firm's image is at stake. This stage usually involves the company's recoiling under media pressure. But this does not have to be always a negative or reactive situation.

The third stage, **insight range,** is the most agonizing time for the firm in the controversy. The stakes are substantial. The firm's existence may be questioned. The company must come to grips with the situation under the external circumstances. During this stage, the executives realize and confirm from evidence whether and to what extent their company is at fault in the safety issues of the product in question.

In the fourth stage, **accommodation,** the company either acts to remove the product from market or refutes the charges against the product's safety. Addressing public pressure and anxiety is the task of this stage.

During the last stage, **agency,** the company attempts to understand the causes of the safety issue and to develop an education program for the public.

Observe newspaper and media reports of industrial crises. Apply this model and compare how company executives and spokespersons handle crises. Take special note of how companies respond morally to their different stakeholders. Observe whether companies give more or less attention to consumers, media, and government stakeholders. Use the frameworks in this chapter to help inform your observations and judgments. Develop a time line as the crisis unfolds. Ask who the company chooses as its spokesperson. Inquire how and why the company is assuming or avoiding responsibility.

CRISIS MANAGEMENT RECOMMENDATIONS

A number of suggestions that corporations can follow to respond more effectively to crises are briefly summarized here. More in-depth strategies and tactics can be found in several sources (Matthews, Goodpaster, and Nash 1985; Mitroff, Shrivastava, and Udwadia 1987).

❏ Face the problem; don't avoid or minimize it, and tell the truth.

❏ "No comment" answers imply guilt; take your "lumps" in one big news story rather than in bits and pieces.

❏ Recognize that in the age of instant news, no such thing exists as a secret or private crisis.

❏ Stage "war games" to observe how your crisis plan holds up under pressure. Train executives to practice press conferences, train teams to respond to crises that may affect other functional areas or divisions.

❏ Use the firm's philosophy, motto, or creed to respond to a crisis: For example, "We believe in our customer. Service is our business."

❏ Use the firm's closeness to customers and end-users for early feedback on the crisis to evaluate your effectiveness in responding and addressing the events.

Finally, issues and crisis management methods and preventive techniques cannot be effective in corporations without implementing the following actions: Top management must be supportive and must participate; cross-departmental involvement is needed; the issues management unit must fit with the firm's culture; and output instead of process must be the focus (Wartick and Rude 1986).

SUMMARY

Organizations and businesses in this century have increased in complexity and power. Because of their numerous economic and noneconomic transactions with different groups in the environment, a method is required to understand an organization's moral obligations and relationships to its constituencies.

The stakeholder approach provides an analytical method for determining how various constituencies affect and are affected by business activities. The stakeholder model also provides a means for assessing the power, legitimacy, and moral responsibility of managers' strategies in terms of how they meet the needs and obligations of various stakeholders.

A stakeholder analysis is also a strategic management tool that allows firms to map and manage relationships with constituents in any given or projected situation. An individual or group is said to have a "stake" in a corporation if it possesses an interest, share, or claim in the outcome of that corporation's policies, procedures, or actions. A "stakeholder" is defined as an individual or group who can affect or be affected by the actions, policies, practices, or goals of the organization.

Recent studies have indicated that profits and stockholder approval may not be the most important driving forces behind management objectives. Job enrichment, concern for employees, and personal well-being are also important objectives.

The implementation of a stakeholder analysis involves a series of steps designed to help a corporation understand the complex economic, political, and moral factors involved in its obligations toward constituencies.

The moral dimensions of managerial functional and area expert roles (marketing, research and development, manufacturing, public relations, and human resource management) are discussed from a stakeholder perspective. The stakeholder approach can assist functional area managers in resolving difficulties from conflicts over individual rights and corporate economic objectives. This approach can help managers think through and chart morally responsible decisions in their work and for the corporation and its stakeholders.

The use of the stakeholder analysis by an observer or third party is also presented as a means for understanding social responsibility issues between a firm and its constituencies. Finally, ethical reasoning is discussed as it relates to the stakeholder approach.

Issues and crisis management frameworks are presented to complement the stakeholder analysis. Understanding what the central issues are for a company and how the issues evolved over time can help explain changing stakes and stakeholders. Crisis frameworks are presented for predicting and evaluating an organization's response to emergencies.

QUESTIONS

1. Describe the stakeholder approach and method.

2. Define the term *stakeholder*. Give examples of primary and secondary stakeholders.

3. What changes have occurred since the industrial age that have facilitated the need for a stakeholder approach?

4. What are some of the types of power stakeholders can use to support their positions? Briefly explain these.

5. From the survey cited in the chapter, who do supervisory managers see as the most important stakeholders? Middle managers? Executive managers?

6. Who are the principal stakeholders of area and functional managers in companies? Could teams use a stakeholder approach in their project or business environment? Explain.

7. What are the reasons for encouraging expert area managers to use the stakeholder approach? Would these reasons apply to teams?

8. Identify six common questions that arise when executing a stakeholder analysis. Identify your questions from your use of this method.

9. Give a recent example of a corporation that had to manage a crisis in public confidence. Did the company representative respond effectively or ineffectively to its stakeholders regarding the crisis? What should the company have done differently in its handling of the crisis?

10. Using a framework from the chapter, identify a controversial societal issue(s) and explain how the issue(s) evolved and changed. Predict how the issue(s) *will evolve*. Defend and substantiate your prediction.

EXERCISES

1. Describe a situation in which you were a stakeholder. What were the issues? What were your stakes? What was the outcome? Who won, who lost, and why?

2. Recall your personal work history. Who was your manager's most important stakeholder(s)? Why? Did you agree or disagree?

3. Briefly invent your own corporation. What is the industry? Your environments? Your product or service? Trace through the steps of a stakeholder analysis, and map out a stakeholder relationship. Describe the nature of your firm's responsibilities to each stakeholder.

4. Describe each of the steps used in a stakeholder analysis, and apply this framework to an incident in the news (such as the Exxon *Valdez* oil spill).

5. Choose one of the expert area managers in the chapter. Describe a dilemma involving this function from the news or a recent article. Discuss how a stakeholder model could help a manager develop a resolution in your example.

6. Describe a recent crisis that involved a product. Which crisis management model best applies in an explanation of the crisis and management responses? Why?

REFERENCES AND SUGGESTED READINGS

Abratt, Russell, and D. Sacks. 1988. The marketing challenge: Towards being profitable and socially responsible. *Journal of Business Ethics* 7: 497–507.

Bowie, Norman. 1991. New directions in corporate social responsibility. *Business Horizons* (July/August): 56–65.

Bowie, Norman, and Ronald Duska. 1991. *Business ethics.* 2d ed. Englewood Cliffs: Prentice Hall.

Brown, James. 1979. *This business of issues: Coping with the company's environment.* New York: Conference Board.

Buchholz, Rogene. 1982. Education for public issues management: Key insights from a survey of top practitioners. *Public Affairs Review* 3: 65–76.

———. 1989. *Fundamental concepts and problems in business ethics.* Englewood Cliffs: Prentice Hall.

———. 1991. *Corporate responsibility and the good society: From economics to ecology. Business Horizons* (July/August): *19–31.*

———. 1992. *Business environment and public policy: Implications for management and strategy.* 4th ed. Englewood Cliffs: Prentice Hall.

Business Week. December 23, 1991, 34.

Carroll, Archie B. 1989, 1993. *Business and society: Ethics and stakeholder management.* 1st, 3d eds. Cincinnati: South-Western.

———. 1991. The pyramid of corporate social responsibility: Toward the moral management of organizational stakeholders. *Business Horizons* (July/August): 39–48.

Dumanoski, Diane. 1990. One year later—The lessons of *Valdez. The Boston Globe,* 2 April, 29.

Evan, William, and R. Freeman. 1988. A stakeholder theory of the modern corporation: Kantian capitalism. In *Ethical theory and business,* 3d ed., edited by Tom L. Beauchamp and Norman E. Bowie. Englewood Cliffs: Prentice Hall.

Fink, Steven. 1986. *Crisis management.* New York: AMACOM.

Frederick, William, et al. 1988. *Business and society: Corporate strategy, public policy, ethics.* 6th ed. New York: McGraw-Hill.

Freeman, R. Edward. 1984. *Strategic management: A stakeholder approach.* Boston: Pitman.

Gottschalk, Earl, Jr. 1982. Firms hiring new type of manager to study issues, emerging troubles. *Wall Street Journal,* 10 June, 33, 36.

Hatten, Kenneth, and M. L. Hatten. 1988. *Effective strategic management analysis and action.* Englewood Cliffs: Prentice Hall.

Herkert, Joseph. 1991. Management's hat trick: Misuse of 'engineering judgment' in the *Challenger* incident. *Journal of Business Ethics* 10: 617–20.

How do you spell success? 1990. *Wall Street Journal,* 30 October, A1.

King, William. 1987. Strategic issue management. In *Strategic planning and management handbook,* edited by W. King and D. Cleland. New York: Van Nostrand Reinhold, 256.

McCoy, Charles. 1996. Exxon's secret *Valdez* deals anger judge. *Wall Street Journal,* 13 June, A3.

Mahjon, John. 1986. Issues management: The issue of definition. *Strategic Planning Management* (November): 81–85.

Marx, Thomas. 1986. Integrating public affairs and strategic planning. *California Management Review* (fall): 145.

Matthews, John B., Kenneth Goodpaster, and Laura Nash. 1985. *Policies and persons: A casebook in business ethics.* New York: McGraw-Hill.

———. 1991. Policies and persons: *A casebook in business ethics.* 2d ed. New York: McGraw-Hill.

Mitroff, Ian, Paul Shrivastava, and Firdaus Udwadia. 1987. Effective crisis management. *Academy of Management Executive* 1, no. 7 (November), 283–92.

Naisbitt, John, and Patricia Aburdene. 1990. *Megatrends 2000: Ten new directions for the 1990s.* New York: William Morrow and Company.

Posner, Barry, and Warren Schmidt. 1984. Values and the American manager: An update. *California Management Review* (spring).

Rawkins, Robert. 1990. U.S. indicts Exxon in oil spill. *Miami Herald,* 28 February.

Savage, G., T. Nix, C. Whitehead, and J. Blair, 1991. Strategies for assessing and managing organizational stakeholders, *The Executive* 5, No. 2:61–75. Also found in *Management and the changing environment,* edited by J. Weiss (McGraw-Hill, 1995), 41–55.

Steiner, George A., and John F. Steiner. 1988, 1991. *Business, government, and society: A managerial perspective,* 5th, 6th eds. New York: Random House.

Wartick, Steven, and Robert Rude. 1986. Issues management: Fad or function? *California Management Review* (fall): 134–40.

Weiss, Joseph. 1986. *The management of change: Administrative logics and actions.* New York: Praeger.

Werhane, Patricia. 1991. Engineers and management: The challenge of the *Challenger* incident. *Journal of Business Ethics* 10: 605–16.

3

ETHICAL PRINCIPLES AND DECISION-MAKING GUIDELINES

Ralph Simms, a newly graduated MBA [master of business administration], was hired by a prestigious U.S.-based multinational firm and sent, with minimal training, to open negotiations with a high-ranking Middle Eastern government official. Simms's assignment was to "do whatever it takes to win the contract; it's worth millions to us." The contract would enable Simms's firm to select and manage technology companies that would install a multi-million-dollar computer system for that government. While in the country, Simms was told by the representative government official that Simms's firm had "an excellent chance to get the contract" if the official's nephew, who owned and operated a computer company in that country, could be assured "a good piece of the action." The official told Simms this would remain a confidential matter and closed by saying, "That's how we do business here; take it or leave it." Simms called his superior in Chicago and informed him of what had happened. Simms was told, "Take it! But use your best judgment on how to handle the details."

Complex ethical dilemmas in business situations usually involve tough choices that must be made among conflicting and competing interests. Should Ralph Simms move to close the lucrative deal or not? Is the official offering him a bribe? Is the official's request legal? Is it ethical? Is this a setup? Would Ralph be held individually responsible if something went wrong? Who is going to protect him should legal complications arise? How is Ralph supposed to negotiate such a deal? (He wasn't taught that in a management class.) What does Ralph stand to win and lose if he does or does not accept the official's offer? Finally, what *should* Ralph do to act morally responsible in this situation? What is the right action to take? These are the kinds of questions and issues this chapter will address. No obvious or easy answers may exist, but specific principles and guidelines can help you identify and think through issues that underlie ethical dilemmas. The aim here is to present ethical principles and guidelines that can help you evaluate—as shown in Figure 3.1—your own and others' moral responsibilities when resolving ethical dilemmas.

The stakeholder analysis in Chapter 2 illustrated how to map and plan social responsibility strategies between corporate managers and external stakeholders. This chapter introduces and summarizes fundamental ethical principles and decision rules to use when making difficult moral decisions in complex business transactions. It intentionally does not offer exhaustive explanations of ethical principles or the philosophical reasoning underlying these principles. That is beyond the scope of the book, and such material can be found in the citations and other philosophical works. Our aim, however, is to simplify, and briefly present a summary of, major ethical principles and guidelines that can be applied in a stakeholder analysis framework— that is, a decisional context that involves business settings. This section begins by presenting ethical reasoning at the individual level. The ethical reasoning processes, principles, and decision rules also are applicable at the corporate-policy and group levels.

■ FIGURE 3.1

INTENDED EFFECTS OF BUSINESS ETHICS EDUCATION ON STAKEHOLDER BELIEF SYSTEMS AND DECISIONS

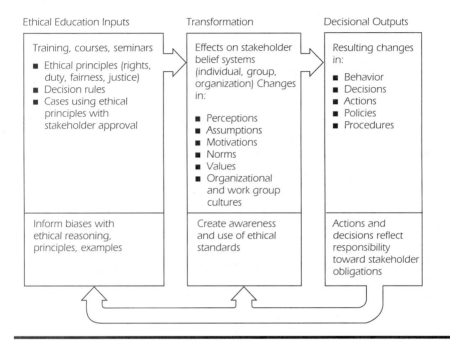

3.1 DECISION CRITERIA FOR ETHICAL REASONING

A first step in addressing ethical dilemmas is to identify the problem(s) and related issues. This is particularly necessary for a stakeholder approach, since the problems and issues depend on who the stakeholders are and what their stakes entail. Before specific ethical principles are discussed, let us begin by considering important decision criteria for ethical reasoning. How would you, as you read these, apply the criteria to Ralph Simms's situation?

Laura Nash (1981, 78–90) presents 12 questions to ask yourself during the decision-making period to help clarify ethical problems:

1. Have you defined the problem accurately?

2. How would you define the problem if you stood on the other side of the fence?

3. How did this situation occur in the first place?

4. To whom and to what do you give your loyalty as a person and as a member of the corporation?

5. What is your intention in making this decision?

6. How does this intention compare with the probable results?

7. Whom could your decision or action injure?

8. Can you discuss the problem with the affected parties before you make your decision?

9. Are you confident that your decision will be as valid over a long period as it seems now?

10. Could you disclose without qualm your decision or action to your boss, your chief executive officer, the board of directors, your family, or society as a whole?

11. What is the symbolic potential of your action if understood? if misunderstood?

12. Under what conditions would you allow exceptions to your stand?

These 12 questions can help individuals openly discuss and articulate the responsibilities necessary to solve ethical problems, Nash states. Sharing these questions can facilitate group discussions, build cohesiveness and consensus around shared points, serve as an information source, uncover ethical inconsistencies in a company's values, help a CEO see how senior managers think, and increase the nature and range of choices, she notes. The discussion process is cathartic, Nash says.

To return briefly to the opening case, if Ralph Simms considered the first question, he might, for example, define the problem he faces from different levels or perspectives (as Chapter 1 illustrated). At the *organizational level,* his firm stands to win a sizable contract if he accepts the government official's conditions. Yet his firm's image and reputation could be jeopardized in the United States if indeed this deal turned out to be a scandal, if a controversy arose among competitors, or if the media covered the events in a critical way. At the *societal level,* the issues are complicated. In this Middle Eastern country, this type of bargaining might be acceptable. In the United States, however, Ralph could have problems with the Foreign Corrupt Practices Act. Is this a bribe? And is Ralph acting officially on behalf of his company or as an individual? At the *individual level,* Ralph must decide if his values and conscience can tolerate the actions and consequences this deal involves. He also must consider the economic, political, social, and moral costs and benefits he will incur from his company if he decides to accept or reject this assignment. Ralph must decide to whom his loyalty belongs in this situation, as a person and as an employee. Whom could his decision potentially injure? As you can see, these questions can serve to help Ralph clarify his goal of making a decision and the prices he is willing or not willing to pay.

Manuel Velasquez (1988, 32–43) also offers criteria that can be used in ethical reasoning and that help systematize and structure our arguments:

1. Moral reasoning must be logical. Assumptions and premises, both factual and inferred, used to make judgments should be known and made explicit.

2. Factual evidence cited to support a person's judgment should be accurate, relevant, and complete.

3. Ethical standards used in a person's reasoning should be consistent. When inconsistencies among one's ethical standards in an argument or decision are discovered, one or more of the standards must be modified.

If Ralph Simms were to use Velasquez's criteria, he would articulate the assumptions underlying his decision. If Ralph, for example, chose to accept the government official's offer, he might say he assumed it was not a bribe; that even if it were a bribe, he assumed he will not get caught; and that even if he or his company did get caught, he would be willing to incur any penalty individually—including loss of his job. Moreover, Ralph would want to obtain as many facts as he could about both the U.S. laws and the Middle Eastern country's laws on negotiating practices such as the one he will accept. He also would gather information from his employer and check the accuracy of the information against his decision. Finally, Ralph would be consistent in his standards. If he chooses to accept the foreign official's conditions, he must be willing to accept additional contingencies consistent with those conditions. He would not, for example, midway through helping the official's nephew obtain part of the contract, suddenly decide that these actions were wrong and "unethical" and then back out. Ralph must think through these contingencies *before* he makes a decision.

Finally, a simple but powerful question can be used throughout your decision-making process of solving ethical dilemmas: "What is my motivation for choosing a course of action?" Examining individual motives, and separating these from known motivations of others, provides clarity and perspective. Ralph, for example, might ask, "Why did I agree to negotiate with the official on his terms? Was it for money? To keep my job? To impress my boss? For adventure?" Ralph also might ask whether his stated motivation from the outset will carry his commitments through the entire contracting process.

MORAL RESPONSIBILITY

A major aim of ethical reasoning is to gain a clearer and sharper logical focus on problems in order to act in morally responsible ways. Velasquez (1988) states that individuals are morally responsible for their actions and the harmful effects of their actions when (1) they knowingly and freely acted or when they caused the act to happen when that act was morally wrong or hurtful to others, and (2) when they knowingly and freely *failed* to act or prevent a harmful act that, also, was morally wrong for a person to have failed to do or prevent from happening. Although no universal definition of what constitutes a morally wrong act exists in absolute terms, it is suggested that an act and the consequences of an act are morally wrong if physical or emotional harm or damage is done to another as a result of the act committed. Again, the degree of harm and the two Velasquez conditions just mentioned also must be considered.

Two conditions that eliminate a person's moral responsibility for causing injury or harm are *ignorance* and *inability* (Velasquez 1988). A person, however, who intentionally prevents himself or herself from understanding or knowing that a harmful action will occur is still responsible. Also, a person who negligently fails to inform himself or herself about a potentially harmful matter still may be responsible for the resultant action. Of course, some mitigating circumstances can excuse or lessen a person's moral responsibility in a situation. Velasquez (1988) describes such circumstances as (1) based on the level of seriousness or lack of seriousness of a wrongful act, (2) those that show a person is uncertain about his or her knowledge of a wrongdoing, (3) those that cause a person difficulty if he or she avoids doing an act, and (4) those that affect the degree a person caused or helped cause a harmful injury. As we know from court trials, proving intent or motive for an alleged illegal act is not an easy matter. Similarly, the extent a person is morally irresponsible for complicated harmful actions also can be difficult to determine. For example, was the captain of the Exxon *Valdez* morally responsible individually for the resultant harm done to the Alaskan coastline and the local economies? Are the savings and loan officers individually morally responsible for the billions their institutional investment failures cost taxpayers? What principles and standards can we, as well as judges and juries, use to establish moral responsibility for ourselves and others?

In the following sections, five fundamental ethical principles that can be used in our ethical reasoning for choosing particular alternatives and justifying difficult decisions and actions are explained and discussed. The principles are (1) relativism, (2) utilitarianism, (3) universalism, (4) rights, and (5) justice. Then four social responsibility modes and four individual styles of ethical reasoning will be presented. Finally, some "quick ethical tests" are provided that you also may use to clarify ethical dilemmas. Note at the outset that this discussion does not go into great depth or philosophical detail. The sources cited provide a fuller discussion for those interested.

Once more, no single principle may be sufficient to help you or a manager make tough ethical decisions. The intent here is to inform and develop your repertoire of ethical concepts by presenting ethical guidelines and reasoning examples so that you may have a range to choose from when thinking through moral problems. It is hoped your resultant decisions, actions, and policies reflect fairness, justice, and responsibility toward those you serve as well as toward your own interests. While reading the following sections, think of different levels of stakeholders and of situations where stakeholders such as individuals, students, managers, owners, suppliers, competitors, government regulators, and interest groups might apply these principles in their actions.

Ethical relativism holds that no universal standards or rules can be used to guide or evaluate the morality of an act. What is right for you may be wrong for me. This view argues that people set their own moral standards for judging their actions. Only the individual's self-interests and values are relevant for judging his or her behavior. This form of relativism also is referred to as **naive relativism.**

If Ralph Simms from the opening case were to adopt the principle of ethical relativism for his decision making, he might, for example, choose to accept the government official's offer in order to promote his own standing in his firm. He might reason that his self-interests would be served best by making any deal that would push his career ahead. On the other hand, Simms also could use ethical relativism to justify his rejection of the offer. Simms might say that any possible form of such a questionable negotiation is against his beliefs. The point behind this principle is that individual standards are the basis of moral authority.

The logic of ethical relativism also extends to cultures. **Cultural relativism,** as the position is called, argues, "When in Rome, do as the Romans do." What is morally right for one society or culture may be wrong for another. Moral standards vary from one culture's customs, belief systems, and value structure to another. Cultural relativists would argue that firms and business professionals doing business in a country are obliged to follow that country's laws and moral codes. A criterion relativists would use to justify their actions would be "Are my beliefs, moral standards, and customs satisfied with this action or outcome?"

The benefits of ethical and cultural relativism are that these principles recognize the distinctiveness of individual and social values, customs, and moral standards. These views take seriously the conscientiousness and unique belief systems of individuals and societies. Social norms and mores are seen in a cultural context.

However, ethical and cultural relativism lead to several problems. First, these views indicate an underlying laziness (Steiner and Steiner 1988). Individuals who justify their morality only from their personal beliefs without taking into consideration other ethical principles may use the logic of relativism as an excuse for not having or developing moral standards that can be argued and tested against other claims, opinions, and standards. Second, this view contradicts everyday experience. Moral reasoning is developed from conversation, interaction, and argument. What I believe or perceive as "facts" in a situation may or may not be accurate. How can I validate or disprove my ethical reasoning and moral judgments if I do not communicate, share, and remain open to change my own standards? Third, ethical relativists can become absolutists. That is, individuals who claim their moral standards are right—regardless of whether others view the standards as right or wrong—can be closed to outside influence and thus accept only their beliefs as true. Also, what if my beliefs conflict with yours? Whose relativism is right then? Who decides and on what grounds? In practice, ethical relativism does not effectively or efficiently solve complicated conflicts involving many parties. These require tolerating doubts and permitting our observations and beliefs to be informed.

Finally, cultural relativism suffers from the same problems as those listed so far. Although it is important to observe and respect the values and moral customs of all cultures, especially since business professionals are increasingly operating across national boundaries, we must still not be lazy or blindly absolute or divorce ourselves from rigorous moral reasoning or laws aimed at protecting individual rights and justice. As Freeman and Gilbert (1988, 36) ask, "Must American managers in Saudi Arabia treat women as the Saudis treat them? Must American managers in South Africa treat blacks as the white South Africans treat them? Must white South Africans treat blacks in the U.S. as U.S. managers treat them? Must Saudis in the U.S. treat women as U.S. managers treat them?" They continue, "It makes sense to question whether or not the norms of the Nazi society were in fact morally correct" (p. 39). Using rigorous ethical reasoning to solve moral dilemmas is important across cultures.

This does not imply that flexibility, sensitivity, and awareness of individual and cultural moral differences are not necessary; they are. It does mean that upholding principles of rights, justice, and freedom in some situations may conflict with the other person's or culture's belief systems and standards. Depending on the actions taken and decisions made from a person's moral stands, a price may have to be paid for maintaining those moral, and sometimes legal, standards. Often, though, negotiation agreements and understanding can be reached without overt conflict when different ethical principles or cultural standards clash.

ETHICAL RELATIVISM AND STAKEHOLDER ANALYSIS

When considering the principles of relativism in a stakeholder analysis, ask the following questions:

1. What are the major moral beliefs and principles at issue for each stakeholder affected by this decision?

2. What are my moral beliefs and principles in this decision?

3. To what extent will my ethical principles clash if a particular course of action is taken? Why?

4. How can conflicting moral beliefs and principles be avoided or negotiated in seeking a desirable outcome?

3.3 UTILITARIANISM

Jeremy Bentham (1748–1832) and John Stuart Mill (1806–1873) are acknowledged as founders of the concept of **utilitarianism.** Although various interpretations of the concept exist, basically the utilitarian view holds that an action is judged as right, good, or wrong depending on its consequences. The ends of an action justify the means taken to reach those ends. As a *consequentialist principle,* the moral authority that drives utilitarianism is the calculated consequences of an action, regardless of other principles that determine the means or motivations for taking the action. Utilitarianism also includes the following tenets (Carroll 1989; Mill 1957; Velasquez 1988):

1. An action is morally right if it produces the greatest good for the greatest number of people affected by it.

2. An action is morally right if the net benefits over costs are greatest for all affected, as compared to the net benefits of all other possible choices considered.

3. An action is morally right if its immediate and future direct and indirect benefits are greatest for each individual and if these benefits outweigh the costs of the other alternatives.

Utilitarian concepts are widely practiced by government policy makers, economists, and business professionals. Utilitarianism is a useful principle for conducting a stakeholder analysis, since it forces decision makers to (1) consider collective as well as particular interests, (2) formulate alternatives based on the greatest good for all parties involved in a decision, and (3) estimate the costs and benefits of alternatives for the affected groups (Delong 1981).

Ralph Simms of our example would use utilitarian principles in his decision making by identifying each of the stakeholders and groups who would be affected by his decision. He then would calculate the costs and benefits of his decision as it would affect each group. Finally, he would decide a course of action based on the greatest good for the greatest number. For example, after identifying all the stakeholders in his decision, including his own interests, Simms might estimate that rejecting the official's offer would produce the greatest good for the people of the country where the contract would be negotiated, since obtaining bids from the most technically qualified companies would best serve the interests of those receiving the services.

Problems with utilitarianism include the following:

1. No agreement exists about what the "good" to be maximized for all concerned in different situations is. Is it truth, health, peace, profits, pleasure, cost reductions, or national security? (See Hoffman and Moore 1990.) Who decides what is good for whom? Whose interests are primary in the decisions?

2. Utilitarianism does not judge the rightness or wrongness of the actions themselves but, rather, of their consequences. What if some actions are simply wrong? Should decision makers proceed to take those actions based only on their consequences?

3. How are the costs and benefits of nonmonetary stakes such as health, safety, and public welfare measured? Should a monetary value be assigned to nonmarketed benefits and costs such as safety, health, and the environment? (See Kelman 1981.) What if the actual or even potentially harmful effects of an action cannot be measured in the short term but the action is believed to have potentially long-term, say, 20- or 30-year, lagging effects? Should that action be chosen?

4. Utilitarianism as a principle does not consider the individual. It is the collective, the aggregate, for whom the greatest good is estimated. Do instances exist when individuals and their interests should be valued in a decision?

5. The principles of justice and rights are ignored in utilitarianism. The principle of justice is concerned with the distribution of good, not the amount of total good in a decision. The principle of rights is concerned with individual entitlements, regardless of the collective calculated benefits.

Even given these problems, the principle of utilitarianism is still valuable under the following conditions: when resources are fixed, lacking, or scarce; when priorities are in conflict; when no clear choice fulfills everyone's needs and goals; and when large or diverse collectives are involved in a zero-sum decision, that is, when a gain for some corresponds to a loss for others (Delong 1981; Velasquez 1988, 116).

UTILITARIANISM AND STAKEHOLDER ANALYSIS

Because businesses use utilitarian principles when conducting a stakeholder analysis, you as a decision maker should consider the following points:

1. Define how costs and benefits will be measured in selecting one course of action over another. Include social as well as economic and monetary costs and benefits, and include long-term and short-term costs and benefits.

2. Define what information you will need to determine the costs and benefits for comparisons.

3. Identify the procedures and policies you will use to explain and justify your cost/benefit analysis.

4. State your assumptions when defining and justifying your analysis and conclusions.

5. Ask yourself what moral obligations you have toward each of your stakeholders, after the costs and benefits have been estimated for particular strategies.

3.4 UNIVERSALISM

Immanuel Kant (1724–1804) is considered one of the leading founders of the principle of **universalism.** Also referred to as "deontological ethics," universalism holds that the means justify the ends of an action, not the consequences. Universalism, therefore, is also referred to as a **nonconsequentialist** ethic.

Kant's principle of the **categorical imperative,** unlike utilitarianism, places the moral authority for taking an action on an individual's duty toward other individuals and humanity.

The categorical imperative consists of two parts. The first part states that *a person should choose to act if and only if she or he would be willing to have every person on earth, in that same situation, act exactly that way.* This principle is absolute and allows for no qualifications across situations or circumstances. The second part of the categorical imperative states that in an ethical dilemma, *a person should act in a way that respects and treats all others involved as ends as well as means to an end.*

Kant's categorical imperative forces decision makers to take into account their duty to act responsibly and respectfully toward all individuals in a situation. Individual human welfare is a primary stake in any decision. Decision makers also must consider formulating their justifications and reasons as principles to be applied to everyone.

In Ralph Simms's example, if he followed principles of universalism, he might ask, "If I accept the government official's offer, could I justify that anyone anywhere acts the same way?" If he answers no, he should not accept the offer.

The major weaknesses of universalism and of Kant's categorical imperative follow. First, these principles are imprecise and lack practical utility. It is difficult to think of all humanity each time one must make a decision in an ethical dilemma. Second, it is hard to resolve conflicts of interest when using a criterion that states that all individuals must be treated equally. Degrees of differences in stakeholders' interests and relative power exist in certain situations. However, Kant would remind us that the human being and his or her humanity must be considered above the stakes, power bases, or consequences of our actions. Still, it is often impractical not to consider these other elements in an dilemma. Finally, what if a decision maker's duties conflict in an ethical dilemma? The categorical imperative does not allow for prioritizing one's duties. A primary purpose of the stakeholder analysis is to prioritize conflicting duties—duties toward competitors, customers, employees, suppliers, owners, the media, and the public. It is, again, difficult to take absolute positions when limited resources and time and conflicting values are factors in ethical dilemmas.

UNIVERSALISM AND STAKEHOLDER ANALYSIS

The logic underlying universalism and the categorical imperative can be helpful for applying a stakeholder analysis. Even though we may not be able to employ Kant's principles absolutely, we can consider the following as guidelines using his ethics:

1. Identify individuals as well as aggregates and their welfare and risks when considering policy decisions and outcomes.

2. Identify the needs of individuals involved in a decision, the choices they have, and the information they need to protect their own welfare.

3. Identify any manipulation, force, coercion, or deceit that might harm individuals involved in a decision.

4. Recognize the duties of respecting and responding to individuals affected by particular decisions before adopting policies and actions that affect them.

5. Ask if the desired action or policy would be acceptable to the individuals involved if they were informed of the policy intentions. Under what conditions would they accept the decision?

6. Ask if individuals in a similar situation would acceptably repeat the designated action or policy as a principle. If not, why not? And would they continue to employ the designated action?

3.5 RIGHTS

The moral authority that drives the ethics of **rights** is entitlement. Individual rights mean entitlements and unquestionable claims. Every U.S. citizen is guaranteed in the Declaration of Independence the rights of life, liberty, and the pursuit of happiness. The U.S. Constitution also holds that each citizen is guaranteed certain fundamental rights. These rights are given legality through the U.S. system of legislation and justice. The principle of rights is one of the most powerful concepts enabling and protecting individual freedom, dignity, and choice. This principle is the cornerstone of American democracy.

Moral rights are based on legal rights and on the principle of duties. My moral right implies that you have certain duties toward aiding—or at least not obstructing—my rights. Moral rights are also based on and viewed from an *individual* perspective, not a societal or group point of view. Individual freedom, welfare, safety, health, and happiness are the essential core values of moral rights. Chapter 6 deals with the rights of employees and employers in the workplace.

Rights also can override utilitarian principles. Many times, violations of rights are solved by the criterion of "Whose rights have precedence in a given situation?" Lawsuits are won and lost on the principle of individual rights not being upheld or protected.

Ralph Simms, in our earlier example, might ask what his rights are in his situation. If he believes that his constitutional and moral rights would be violated by accepting the offer or by his firm's pressuring him to accept the offer, he would consider refusing to negotiate on the foreign official's terms.

The limitations of the principle of rights include the following:

❏ The entitlement justification of individual rights can be used by certain individuals and groups to disguise and manipulate selfish, unjust political claims and interests (see Steiner and Steiner 1988).

❏ Protection of rights can exaggerate certain entitlements in society at the expense of others. Fairness and equity issues may be raised when rights of certain individuals and groups take precedence over the rights of others in similar situations. Issues of reverse discrimination, for example, have arisen from this reasoning.

❏ Also, the limits of rights come into question. To what extent should industrial and governmental practices that may benefit the entire society but threaten certain individual or group rights be permitted to occur?

RIGHTS AND STAKEHOLDER ANALYSIS

The principle of rights is particularly useful in a stakeholder analysis when conflicting legal or moral rights of individuals occur or when individual and group rights may be violated if certain courses of action are pursued. The following are guidelines for observing this principle (Velasquez 1988):

1. Identify the individuals and their rights that may be violated by a particular policy or course of action.

2. Determine the legal and moral bases of these individuals' rights. Does the decision violate these rights on such bases?

3. Determine to what extent the action to be taken has moral justification from utilitarian principles if individual rights may be violated. National crises and emergencies may warrant overriding certain individual rights for the public good.

3.6 JUSTICE

The principle of **justice** deals with fairness and equality. Here the moral authority that decides what is right and wrong concerns the fair and equitable distribution of opportunities, as well as of hardships, to all. The principle of justice also pertains to punishment for wrong done to the undeserving. John Rawls (1971), a contemporary philosopher, offers two principles of fairness widely recognized as representative of the principle of justice:

1. Each person has an equal right to the most extensive basic liberties compatible with similar liberties for others.

2. Social and economic inequalities are arranged so that they are both (a) reasonably expected to be to everyone's advantage and (b) attached to positions and offices open to all.

The first principle states that all individuals should be treated equally. The second principle states that justice is served when all persons have equal opportunities and advantages through their positions and offices to society's opportunities and burdens. Equal opportunity or access to opportunity does not guarantee equal distribution of wealth. Society's disadvantaged may not be justly treated, some critics claim, whenever only equal opportunity is offered. The principle of justice also addresses the unfair distribution of wealth and the infliction of harm.

Richard DeGeorge (1986, 76) discusses four types of justice. **Compensatory justice** concerns compensating someone for a past harm or injustice. For example, affirmative action programs, discussed in Chapter 6, are justified in part as compensation for decades of injustice and injury that minorities have suffered (Velasquez 1988, 332). **Retributive justice** means serving punishment to someone who has inflicted harm on another. A criterion for applying this justice principle is "Does the punishment fit the crime?" **Distributive justice** refers to the fair distribution of benefits and burdens. Have certain stakeholders received an unfair share of costs associated with a policy or action? Have others unfairly profited from a policy? **Procedural justice** designates fair decision practices, procedures, and agreements among parties. This criterion asks, "Have the rules and processes that govern the distribution of rewards and punishments and benefits and costs been fair?" These four types of justice are part of the larger principle of justice; how they are formulated and applied varies with societies and governmental systems.

Following the principle of justice, Ralph Simms, in our example, might ask whether accepting the government official's offer would provide an equitable distribution of goods and services to the recipients of the new technological system to be implemented in that country. Also, would this decision maintain the self-respect of the individuals involved? If Simms determined that justice would not be served by enabling his company to be awarded the contract without a fair bidding process, he might well recommend that his firm reject the offer.

The obvious practical problems of using the principle of justice include the following: Outside the jurisdiction of the state and its legal judicial systems where ethical dilemmas are solved by procedure and law, who decides who is right and who is wrong? Who has the moral authority to punish whom? Can opportunities and burdens be fairly distributed to all when it is not in the interest of those in power to do so?

Even with these shortcomings, the principle of justice adds an essential and unique contribution to the other ethical principles discussed so far. Beyond the utilitarian's calculation of moral responsibility based on consequences, beyond the universalist's absolute duty to treat everyone as a means and not an end, and beyond the principle of rights, which values unquestionable claims, the principle of justice forces us to ask how fairly benefits and costs are distributed to everyone, regardless of power, position, wealth, and station in life.

JUSTICE AND STAKEHOLDER ANALYSIS

In a stakeholder analysis, the principle of justice can be applied with these questions:

1. How equitable will be the distribution of benefits and costs, pleasure and pain, and reward and punishment among stakeholders if we pursue a particular course of action? Would all stakeholders' self-respect be acknowledged?

2. How clearly have the procedures for distributing the costs and benefits of a course of action or policy been defined and communicated? How fair are these procedures to all affected?

3. What provisions can we make to compensate those who will be unfairly affected by the costs of the decision? What provisions can we

make to redistribute benefits among those who have been unfairly or overly compensated by the decision?

Figure 3.2 summarizes the ethical principles presented here. This figure can be used as a reference for applying these principles individually and in a stakeholder analysis with groups.

3.7 IMMORAL, AMORAL, OR MORAL MANAGEMENT?

It is also possible for owners, managers, and individual stakeholders to relate to their constituencies from at least three broad orientations: immorally, amorally, and morally. *Immoral treatment* of constituencies signifies a minimally ethical or unethical approach: laying off employees without fair notice or compensation; offering upper-level management undeserved salary increases and perks; and giving "golden parachutes" (attractive payments or settlement contracts between a firm and high-ranking executives) when a change in company ownership or control is negotiated (such payments are often done at the expense of shareholders' dividends and often without their knowledge or consent). Managing immorally means intentionally going against ethical principles of justice and of fair and equitable treatment of other stakeholders.

Amoral management happens when owners, supervisors, and managers treat shareholders, outside stakeholders, and employees negligently or unintentionally without concern or care for the consequences of their policies or actions. No willful wrong may be intended, but also no thought is given to moral behavior or outcomes. Minimal actions are taken while setting policies that are solely profit oriented, production centered, or short term. Employees and other stakeholders are viewed as instruments for executing the economic interests of the firm. Strategies, control systems, leadership style, and interactions in such organizations also reflect an amoral, minimalist approach toward stakeholders. Nevertheless, the consequences of unintentional, amoral actions are real for the persons affected. Harm can be done.

Moral management by owners, upper-level executives, and supervisors places value on equitable, fair, and just concern and treatment of shareholders, employees, customers, and other stakeholder interests. Ethics codes are established, communicated, and included in training; employee rights are built into visible policies that are enforced; and employees and other stakeholders are treated with respect and trust. The firm's corporate strategy, control and incentive systems, leadership style, and interactions also will reflect a morally managed organization. Moral management is the preferred mode of acting toward stakeholders, since respect, justice, and fairness are considered in the decisions.

■ FIGURE 3.2

SUMMARY OF FIVE ETHICAL DECISION-MAKING PRINCIPLES AND STAKEHOLDER ANALYSIS

Belief Systems	Source of Moral Activity	Stakeholder Analysis Issues
Ethical Relativism (Self-Interest)	Moral authority is determined by individual or cultural self-interests, customs, and religious principles. An act is morally right if it serves one's self-interests and needs.	1. What are the moral beliefs and principles of the individual(s)? 2. If a particular action or policy is chosen, to what extent will ethical principles clash? 3. While seeking a mutually desirable outcome, how can conflicting moral beliefs and principles be avoided or negotiated.
Utilitarianism (Calculation of Costs and Benefits)	Moral authority is determined by the consequences of an act: An act is morally right if the net benefits over costs are greatest for the majority. Also, the greatest good for the greatest number must result from this act.	1. Consider collective as well as particular interests. 2. Formulate alternatives based on the greatest good for all parties involved. 3. Estimate costs and benefits of alternatives for groups affected.
Universalism (Duty)	Moral authority is determined by the extent the intention of an act treats all persons with respect. Includes the requirement that everyone would act this way in the same circumstances.	1. Identify individuals whose needs and welfare are at risk with a given policy or decision. 2. Identify the use or misuse of manipulation, force, coercion, or deceit that may be harmful to individuals. 3. Indentify duties to individuals affected by the decision. 4. Determine if the desired action or policy would be acceptable to individuals if the decision were implemented.
Rights (Individual Entitlement)	Moral authority is determined by individual rights guaranteed to all in their pursuit of freedom of speech, choice, happiness, and self-respect.	1. Identify individuals and their rights that may be violated by a particular action. 2. Determine the legal and moral basis of≈ these individual rights. 3. Determine the moral justification from utilitarian principles if individuals' rights are violated.
Justice (Fairness and Equity)	Moral authority is determined by the extent opportunities, wealth, and burdens are fairly distributed among all.	1. If a particular action is chosen, how equally will costs and benefits be distributed to stakeholders? 2. How clear and fair are the procedures for distributing the costs and benefits of the decision? 3. How can those who are unfairly affected by the action be compensated?

SOURCE: Copyright © Joseph W. Weiss, Bentley College, Waltham, MA, 1997.

It is helpful to consider these three orientations while observing managers, owners, employees, and coworkers. Have you seen amoral policies, procedures, and decisions in organizations? The next section summarizes four social responsibility modes and roles that business executives historically have characterized and presently view as moral for decision makers. The model presented there complements the five ethical principles offered in this section by providing a more macro-orientation for describing individual ethical orientations toward business decisions. You may want to use the following framework to characterize your own moral and responsibility roles, those of your boss and colleagues, and even those of contemporary international figures in government or business.

3.8 FOUR SOCIAL RESPONSIBILITY ROLES

What social obligations do businesses and their executives have toward their stockholders and society? The traditional view that the responsibility of corporate owners and managers was to serve only or primarily their stockholders' interests has been challenged and modified—but not abandoned—since the turn of this century. The debate continues over whether businesses' and managers' roles include serving social stakeholders as well as economic stockholders. Because of changing demographic and educational characteristics in the workplace and the advent of laws, policies, and procedures that recognize greater awareness of employee and other stakeholders' rights, distinctions have been made about the responsibility of the business to its employees and to the larger society.

Anthony Buono and Lawrence Nichols (1990) offer four ethical interpretations of the social roles of business in society. Figure 3.3 illustrates these roles or modes. The four social responsibility modes reflect the business roles toward stockholders and a wider audience of stakeholders.

Figure 3.3 illustrates two distinct social responsibility orientations of businesses and managers toward society: the *stockholder model* (the responsibility of the corporation is primarily to its economic stockholders) and the *stakeholder model* (the responsibility of the corporation is also to its social stakeholders outside the corporation). The two sets of motives underlying these two orientations are "self-interest" and "moral duty."

The (1) stockholder self-interest (box 1) and (2) stockholder moral-duty (box 3) orientations will be discussed first, followed by the (3) stakeholder self-interest (box 2) and (4) stakeholder moral-duty (box 4) orientations. The two stockholder orientations are *productivism* and *philanthropy*.

Productivists view the corporation's social responsibility in terms of rational self-interest and the direct fulfillment of stockholder interests. Productivists believe the major—and some would say only—mission of business is to obtain profit. The free market is the best guarantee of moral

■ **FIGURE 3.3**

FOUR SOCIAL RESPONSIBILITY MODES AND ROLES

ORIENTATIONS

		Stockholder Model	Stakeholder Model
MOTIVES	Self-Interest	1 Productivism	2 Progressivism
	Moral Duty	3 Philanthropy	4 Ethical Idealism

SOURCE: Anthony F. Buono and Lawrence T. Nichols. 1990. Stockholders and stakeholder interpretations of business' social role. In *Business ethics: Readings and cases in corporate
morality*, 2d ed., edited by W. Michael Hoffman and Jennifer Moore. New York: McGraw-Hill,
172. Reproduced with permission of Anthony F. Buono.

corporate conduct in this view. Supply-side economists as productivists,
for example, argue that the private sector is the vehicle for social improvement. Tax reduction and economic incentives that boost private industry
are policies productivists advocate as socially responsible. Ronald
Reagan's "trickle down" policies of seeking social benefits from private-
sector wealth are a recent example of this view. The economist Milton
Friedman is an example of a productivist.

Philanthropists, who also have a stockholder view of the corporation,
hold that social responsibility is justified in terms of a moral duty toward
helping less-advantaged members of society through organized, tax-
deductible charity and **stewardship.** Proponents of this view believe the
primary social role or mission of the corporation is still to obtain profits.
However, moral duty drives their motives instead of self-interest solely
(the productivist view). Advocates of this view are stewards and believe
that those who have wealth ought to share some of it with the less
advantaged in society. As stockholder stewards, philanthropists share
profits primarily through their tax-deductible activities. Levi Strauss in
the mid-1880s was one such philanthropist. Can you think of other more-
contemporary philanthropists?

Progressivism and *ethical idealism* are the two social-responsibility
modes in the stakeholder model, the other dominant orientation.
Progressivists believe corporate behavior is justified from a motive of
self-interest, but they also hold that corporations should take a broader
view of responsibility toward social change. Enlightened self-interest is a
value that characterizes progressivists. Rheinhold Niebuhr, the famous

Christian theologian, was a modern example of a progressivist who argued for the involvement of the church in politics to bring about reasoned, orderly reform. He also worked with unions and other groups to improve workers' job conditions and wages. Progressivists support policies such as affirmative action programs, environmental protection, employee stock option programs (ESOPs), and energy conservation.

Finally, **ethical idealists** believe social responsibility is justified when corporate behavior directly supports stakeholder interests from moral duty motives. Ethical idealists, such as Ralph Nader, hold that, to be fully responsible, corporate activity should help transform businesses into institutions where workers can realize their full human potential. Employee ownership, cooperatives, and community-based and community-owned service industries are examples of the type of corporate transformation ethical idealists advocate. The boundaries between business and society are fluid for ethical idealists. Corporate profits are to be shared for humanitarian purposes, to help bring about a more humane society.

Of course, a spectrum of beliefs exists for each of these four responsibility modes. For example, a variety of ethical idealists profess different visions and programs regarding the obligations of business to society. Some are more radical than others in orientation. One group of ethical idealists calls for the transformation of society in order to redistribute wealth.

Which orientation best characterizes your current beliefs of business responsibility toward society: productivism, philanthropism, progressivism, or ethical idealism? Why?

3.9 INDIVIDUAL ETHICAL DECISION-MAKING STYLES

In addition to the four social responsibility modes presented here, researchers have defined ethical styles. Stanley Krolick (1987) developed a survey that interprets individual primary and secondary ethical decision-making styles. The four styles he found are (1) individualism, (2) altruism, (3) pragmatism, and (4) idealism. Although these four styles are not exhaustive, they are summarized here to complement the social responsibility modes and the ethical principles discussed earlier. Caution must be taken when considering any of these schemes in order not to label or stereotype oneself or others. These categories are, at best, guides for further reflection, discussion, and study.

Individualists are driven by natural reason, personal survival, and preservation. The self is the source and justification of all actions and decisions. Krolick (1987) states that individualists believe "If I don't take care of my own needs, I will never be able to address the concerns of others."

The moral authority of individualists is their own reasoning process based on self-interests. Individualism is related to the principle of naive ethical relativism and to productivism.

Altruists are concerned primarily with other people. Altruists will relinquish their own personal security for the good of others. They would, as an extreme, like to save the future of the human race. The altruist's moral authority and motivation is to produce the greatest good for the largest number of people. Unlike utilitarians, altruists would not diligently calculate and measure costs and benefits. Providing benefits is their major concern. Altruists justify their actions by upholding the integrity of the community. They enter relationships from a desire to contribute to the common good and to humankind. Altruists are akin to universalists and philanthropists.

Pragmatists are concerned primarily with the situation at hand, not with the self or the other. The pragmatist's bases of moral authority and motivation are the perceived needs of the moment and the potential consequences of a decision in a specific context. The needs of the moment dictate the importance of self-interest, concern for others, rules, and values. Facts and situational information are justifications for the pragmatist's actions. Pragmatists may abandon significant principles and values in order to produce certain results. Pragmatists are closest to utilitarians. Although this style seems the most objective and appealing, Krolick (1987) cautions that the shifting ethics of pragmatism may make this orientation difficult and unpredictable in a business environment.

Idealists are driven by principles, rules, regulations, and values. Reason, relationships, or the desired consequences of an action will not substitute for the idealist's adherence to principles. Duties are absolute for the idealist. Idealism's moral authority and motivation are commitment to principles and consistency. Values and rules of conduct are the justifications idealists use to explain their actions. Seen as people of high morals, idealists also can be rigid and inflexible. Krolick (1987, 18) notes that "This absolute adherence to principles may blind the Idealist to the potential consequences of a decision for oneself, others, or the situation." This style is related to the social responsibility mode of ethical idealism and to the principle of universalism.

Which of the four styles best characterizes your ethical orientation? The orientation of your colleagues? Your boss?

COMMUNICATING AND NEGOTIATING ACROSS ETHICAL STYLES

Krolick (1987) states that when working or communicating with each style, one also must observe *the other person's ethical style*. The first step is to "concede that the other person's values and priorities have their own validity in their own terms and try to keep those values in mind to facilitate the process of reaching an agreement" (20). Toward that end, Krolick proposes these guidelines when communicating, negotiating, or working with one of the four ethical styles:

❏ *Individualist:* Point out the benefits of the other person's self-interest.

❏ *Altruist:* Focus on the benefits for the various constituencies involved.

❏ *Pragmatist:* Emphasize the facts and potential consequences of an action.

❏ *Idealist:* Concentrate on the principles or duties at stake.

Learning to recognize and communicate with other ethical styles and a willingness to be flexible in accommodating your ethical style to others, without sacrificing your own, are important skills for working effectively with others in organizations.

3.10 QUICK ETHICAL TESTS

In addition to knowing the ethical principles, social responsibility modes, and ethical styles presented in this chapter, businesspeople can take short "ethical tests" before making decisions. Many of these quick rules are based on or reflect the principles discussed in this chapter.

These practical, quick guides and "checkpoints," if observed, could change the actions you would automatically take in ethical dilemmas.

The Center for Business Ethics at Bentley College articulated six simple questions for the "practical philosopher." (These questions are duplicated in Bowditch and Buono 1990.) They are used in training programs. Before making a decision or acting, ask the following:

1. Is it right?

2. Is it fair?

3. Who gets hurt?

4. Would you be comfortable if the details of your decision were reported on the front page of your local newspaper?

5. What would you tell your child to do?

6. How does it smell? (How does it feel?)

Other quick ethical tests, some of which are classical, include the following (based on guidelines found in Steiner and Steiner 1988 and rephrased in Carroll 1989):

❏ *The Golden Rule:* "Do unto others as you would have them do unto you." This includes not knowingly doing harm to others.

❏ *The Intuition Ethic:* We know apart from reason what is right. We have a moral sense about what is right and wrong. We should follow our "gut feeling" about what is right.

❏ *The Means-Ends Ethic:* We may choose unscrupulous but efficient means to reach an end if the ends are really worthwhile and significant. Be sure the ends are not the means.

❏ *The Test of Common Sense:* "Does the action I am getting ready to take really make sense?" Think before acting.

❏ *The Test of One's Best Self:* "Is this action or decision I'm getting ready to take compatible with my concept of myself at my best?"

❏ *The Test of Ventilation:* Do not isolate yourself with your dilemma. Get others' feedback before acting or deciding.

❏ *The Test of the Purified Idea:* "Am I thinking this action or decision is right just because someone with appropriate authority or knowledge says it is right?" An action may not be right because someone in a position of power or authority states it is right. You may still be held responsible for taking the action.

Use these principles and guidelines for examining the motivations of stakeholders' strategies, policies, and actions. Why do stakeholders act and talk as they do? What principles drive these actions?

CONCLUDING COMMENTS

Individual stakeholders have a wide range of ethical principles, orientations, and "quick tests" to draw on before taking action or solving an ethical dilemma. Specifically, if in a given business situation decision makers have mapped stakeholders and their stakes (from Chapter 2), this chapter can assist their analysis of the moral dimension of the stakeholder approach by helping them identify what Freeman and Gilbert (1988) call the "ground rules" or "implicit morality" of institutional members:

> Think of the implicit morality of an institution as the internal rules which must be followed if the institution is to be a good one of its kind. The rules are often implicit, because the explicit rules of an institution may well be the reason that the institution functions rather badly. . . . Another way to think of the implicit morality of an institution is as the internal logica of the institution. Once this internal logica is clearly understood, we can evaluate its required behaviors against external standards. (109)

In the following chapter, the conceptual basis of the organization as stakeholder is presented, and the moral dimensions of a corporation's strategy, leadership, culture, and issues of corporate self-regulation are examined.

SUMMARY

Complex ethical dilemmas in business situations involve making tough choices among conflicting and competing interests. This chapter begins with 12 questions and three decision criteria that can assist individuals in determining the most suitable course of action. These also can be applied at the group and corporate levels of analysis.

Individuals can gain a clearer perspective of their own motivations and actions by distinguishing them from those of others. This perspective can be useful for guiding your own decision-making process, and understanding the ethical reasoning and decision criteria from this chapter also can enable you to reason more critically when examining other stakeholders' ethical reasoning.

A primary goal of ethical reasoning is to help individuals act in morally responsible ways. Ignorance and bias are two conditions that blind a person's moral awareness. Five principles of ethical reasoning are presented to expose you to methods of ethical decision making. The five principles are ethical relativism (both naive relativism and cultural relativism), utilitarianism, universalism, rights, and justice. Each principle is discussed in terms of the utility and drawbacks associated with it. Guidelines for thinking through and applying each principle in a stakeholder analysis are provided. These principles are not mechanical recipes for selecting a course of action. They are filters or screens to use for clarifying dilemmas.

Three ethical orientations can also be used to evaluate individuals' and organizations' "ethics." These orientations include (1) moral, (2) amoral, and (3) immoral. Moral and immoral orientations are more discernable. Amoral orentations include lack of concern for others' interests and well being. While no intentional harm or motives may be observed, it is harmful consequences from ignorance or neglect that reflect amoral syles of operating.

Four social responsibility roles or business modes are explained next. Productivism and philanthropy are two roles influenced by stockholder concerns. Progressivism and ethical idealism are driven by stockholder concerns but also are influenced by external stakeholders.

Individuals also have ethical decision-making styles. Four different but not exclusive styles are individualism, altruism, pragmatism, and idealism. It is important to understand another person's ethical decision-making style when engaging in professional or other types of communication and negotiation. These styles are a starting point for reflecting on and identifying our (and others') predominant decision-making characteristics. Styles can change.

The final section of this chapter offers quick "ethical tests" that can be used to provide insight into your decision-making process and actions. The methods and principles of ethical reasoning discussed in this chapter can enable individuals to better understand moral issues as well as their own motivations and intentions.

QUESTIONS

1. What is a first step for addressing ethical dilemmas?
2. What are three criteria that can be used in ethical reasoning to help structure our thinking and arguments?
3. What single focal question is often the most powerful for solving ethical dilemmas?
4. What are two conditions that eliminate a person's moral responsibility for causing injury or harm?
5. Briefly explain five fundamental ethical principles that can be used in ethical reasoning.
6. What are some of the problems associated with cultural relativism? The benefits?
7. Why is utilitarianism useful for conducting a stakeholder analysis? What are some of the problems we may encounter when using this principle?
8. Briefly explain the categorical imperative. What does it force you, as a decision maker, to do when choosing an action in a moral dilemma?
9. Explain the difference between the principles of rights and justice. What are some of the strengths of each principle? What are some of the weaknesses?
10. What are the four social responsibility modes? How can these be used?
11. Briefly explain each of the individual ethical decision-making styles. Which style do you consider most closely characterizes your own?
12. Which of the ethical "quick tests" do you prefer for yourself? Why?

EXERCISES

1. Write an example from your experience of a serious ethical dilemma. Use the 12 questions developed by Laura Nash, presented in the chapter, to offer a resolution to the problem, even if your resolution is different from the first time. Did you use any of the questions in your original experience? Would any of these questions have helped you? How? What would you have done differently? Why?

2. Identify a real-life example of an instance when you thought ignorance absolved a person, group, or organization from moral responsibility. Then identify an example when a person, group, or organization simply failed to become fully informed about a moral situation. Under what conditions do you think individuals are morally responsible for the effects of their actions? Why?

3. Which of the four social responsibility business modes in the chapter do you most identify with? Why? Name a company that reflects this orientation. Explain why. Would you want to work for this company? Would you want to be part of the management team? Explain.

4. Select a company in the news that has acted morally and one that has acted immorally. Using this chapter, characterize the apparent ethics of each company or of its spokespersons or executives.

REFERENCES AND SUGGESTED READINGS

Bowditch, James, and Anthony Buono. 1990. *A primer on organizational behavior.* 2d ed. New York: John Wiley and Sons.

Buono, Anthony F., and Lawrence T. Nichols. 1990. Stockholder and stakeholder interpretations of business' social role. In *Business ethics: Readings and cases in corporate morality,* 2d ed., edited by W. Michael Hoffman and Jennifer Moore. New York: McGraw-Hill.

Carroll, Archie. 1989, 1993. *Business and society: Ethics and stakeholder management.* 1st, 2d eds. Cincinnati: South-Western.

———. 1991. The pyramid of corporate social responsibility: Toward the moral management of organizational stakeholders. *Business Horizons* (July/August): 38–48.

DeGeorge, Richard T. 1986, 1990. *Business ethics.* 2d, 3d eds. New York: Macmillan.

Delong, James V., et al. 1981. Defending cost-benefit analysis: Replies to Steven Kelman. *AEI Journal on Government and Society* (March/April): 39–43.

Freeman, R. Edward, and Daniel Gilbert Jr. 1988. *Corporate strategy and the search for ethics.* Englewood Cliffs: Prentice Hall.

Hoffman, W. Michael, and Jennifer Moore. 1990. *Business ethics: Readings and cases in corporate morality.* 2d ed. New York: McGraw-Hill.

Jackall, Robert. 1988. *Moral mazes: The world of corporate managers.* New York: Oxford University Press.

Kant, Immanuel. 1964. *Groundwork of the metaphysics of morals,* translated by H. J. Paton. New York: Harper & Row.

Keeley, Michael. 1988. *A social-contract theory of organizations.* Notre Dame, IN: University of Notre Dame Press.

Kelman, Steven. 1981. Cost-benefit analysis, an ethical critique. *AEI Journal on Government and Society* (January/February): 33–40.

Krolick, Stanley. 1987. *Ethical decision-making style: Survey and interpretive notes.* Beverly, MA: Addison-Wesley Training Systems.

Mill, John Stuart. 1957. *Utilitarianism.* Indianapolis: Bobbs-Merrill.

Nash, Laura. 1981. Ethics without the sermon. *Harvard Business Review* (November/December): 88.

Rawls, John. 1971. *A theory of justice.* Cambridge: Harvard University Press.

Steiner, George A., and John F. Steiner. 1988, 1991. *Business, government, and society:* A managerial perspective. 5th, 6th eds. New York: Random House.

Toffler, Barbara Ley. 1986. *Tough choices: Managers talk ethics.* New York: John Wiley & Sons.

Velasquez, Manuel G. 1988, 1992. *Business ethics: Concepts and cases.* 2d, 3d eds. Englewood Cliffs: Prentice Hall.

Walton, Clarence. 1988. *The moral manager.* Cambridge, MA: Ballinger.

4

The Corporation as Stakeholder: Moral Dimensions of Strategy, Structure, Leadership, Culture, and Self-Regulation

Asbestosis, mesothelioma, and lung cancer, all life-threatening diseases, share a common cause: microscopically inhaled particles of asbestos over an extended period of time.

The link between these diseases and enough inhaled asbestos particles is a medical fact. Manville Corporation is a multinational mining and forest product manufacturer and has been a leading commercial producer of asbestos. As of March 1977, 271 asbestos-related damage suits were filed against the firm by workers. The victims claimed the company did not warn them of the life-threatening dangers of asbestos. Since 1968, Manville has paid over $50 million in such claims. And since the 1950s, the Manville Corporation has faced hundreds of lawsuits from workers: The estimate is over $1 billion. By 1982, Manville faced over 500 new asbestos lawsuits filed each month. Consequently, in August 1982, Manville filed for Chapter 11 bankruptcy in order to reorganize and remain solvent in the face of the asbestos-related lawsuits; the firm was losing over half the cases that reached trial. The reorganization was approved, and Manville set up a $2.5 billion trust fund to pay asbestos claimants. Shareholders surrendered half their value in stock, and it was also agreed that projected earnings over 25 years would be reduced to support the trust.

The extent of Manville's social responsibility toward its workers, litigants, the communities it serves, and society has, at best, been mixed. Manville, since 1972, has been active and cooperative with the U.S. Department of Labor and the AFL/CIO in developing standards to protect asbestos workers. However, Dr. Kenneth Smith-the medical director of one of the firm's plants in Canada-refused on court record in the 1970s to inform Manville workers that they had asbestosis. Lawsuits ensued.

There is also the complication and confusion of evolving and changing legislation on asbestos. The Supreme Court, as stakeholder, has not taken a stand on who is liable in these situations: Are insurance firms liable when workers are initially exposed to asbestos and later develop cancer, or are they liable 20 years later? Also, right-to-know laws are not definitive in state legislatures. Does that leave Manville and other corporations liable for government's legal indecision?

An update showed that Manville Corp. has devised a settlement that gives Manville Personal Injury Settlement Trust enough cash to continue meeting claims filed by asbestos victims.

Under the settlement, the building-products division stated it will give the trust 20 percent of Manville's stock and will pay a special $772 million dividend in exchange for the trust's releasing its right to receive 20 percent of Manville's profits. After the transaction, the trust will own 80 percent of Manville and have $1.2 billion in cash and marketable securities, plus $2.3 billion in assets. This transaction enables Manville to rectify its balance sheet. Also, it changed its name to Schuller Corp.

The trust was organized in 1988 as a way to pay asbestos claims after Manville spent several years operating under Chapter 11 under the U.S. Bankruptcy Code. Payments stopped in 1991 but under a plan approved in 1994 by a federal court, payments started again. The trust is expected to pay 10 percent of an estimated $18 billion in present and future asbestos claims to 275,000 victims who already have filed claims. The figure could go as high as 400,000 when more symptoms develop in the future. (Tejada 1996)

Was Manville acting responsibly by using bankruptcy as a strategy for not paying for its fair share of damages? Or was bankruptcy a reasonable and responsible corporate response to this situation? Of the 16,500 personal-injury plaintiffs, 2,000 have died since the reorganization in 1982. Manville still faces court battles and the prospect of not remaining solvent. One chairperson and one CEO have resigned, and the company has quit the asbestos business. One estimate is that lawyers stand to gain more than $1 billion in fees from settlements paid by Manville's trust. Who is winning and who is losing? What ethical principles have Manville's executives used to do business? Does Manville deserve to go bankrupt, or have its corporate leaders done the best they could in this situation?

4.1 DOES A CORPORATION HAVE A CONSCIENCE?

The Manville case raises important questions about the nature of and responsibility of corporations as stakeholders in complex legal and moral dilemmas. For example, are corporations such as Manville rational, impersonal institutions? Are corporations collectives of politically and economically driven groups? Does a corporation have a conscience? Is a corporation morally responsible to society? If so, to what extent? These questions are part of an ongoing debate that underscores the following problematic issues:

1. If a corporation does not have a conscience and is primarily an impersonal profit-making institution, what responsibilities does it have for its stakeholders, such as consumers, employees, and government, and to society? What rules, and who, should govern its activities, which have moral implications for its stakeholders, if it cannot or will not do so?

2. If a corporation is more than a profit-making institutional stakeholder, what is the source and basis of its moral responsibility? To whom is it responsible beyond its economic obligations? How should it implement its moral and social responsibilities for its stakeholders?

This discussion begins by presenting and evaluating two contrasting views on the nature of corporations and their social responsibility: (1) The first view holds that the corporation does not have a conscience and is an impersonal institution—a stakeholder committed only to its stockholders; (2) the second view holds that corporations are analogous to individuals—the corporation has a conscience and acts as a moral agent in its stakeholder relationships. Then a third perspective of the corporation as an economic and social stakeholder is explained. This perspective attempts to reconcile the earlier contrasting views. Following this view, the internal organization of corporations as stakeholders and the influence of strategy, structure, and culture on social responsibility are discussed. Finally, the chapter concludes by identifying issues regarding the self-regulation of corporations and shareholders.

FIRST VIEW: CORPORATIONS DO NOT HAVE A CONSCIENCE

No one disputes the fact most corporations like Manville are in business to make profits for owners and shareholders. A key question is whether corporations can and should be morally responsible to stakeholders other than their shareholders. The "corporation as impersonal, profit-making institution" view (the productivist view from Chapter 3) holds that the primary, and some would agree the only, obligation of businesses is to make profits, not to act morally responsible. This view is important to the domain of business ethics, since the definition of corporations as impersonal entities suggests that moral blame and liability cannot be attributed to an institution. This utilitarian-based view assumes corporations provide the greatest (in terms of material wealth) good for the largest number in society.

Adam Smith (1723–1790) was an early proponent of this view. He held that individual "self-interest" motivated and promoted the economic well-being of society and that the "invisible hand" guided and promoted the general welfare of society. Businesses, according to this view, are seen as amoral (not immoral) institutions that promote the self-interests and economic motives of owners. Social responsibility does require rules and rule enforcement. This is considered the responsibility of the state, not of businesses.

Thomas Hobbes's and John Locke's philosophies also reflected this logic. According to their view, the major stakeholders corporations should be concerned about are owners, shareholders, and groups that promote profit-making capabilities. Society benefits when businesses make a profit. The production role of business is emphasized over the distribution and responsibility roles.

Recent advocates of this view include the economist Milton Friedman; Theodore Levitt, a Harvard professor; and John Kenneth Galbraith, a noted economist. Friedman (1970) has been widely quoted as stating that "there is one and only one social responsibility of business—to use its resources and engage in activities designed to increase its profits as long as it stays within the rules of the game, which is to say, engages in open and free competition without deception and fraud." He believes that the free-market system defines the "rules of the game" and that it is adequate for society to help firms meet their primary responsibility of earning profit for owners and shareholders. Friedman advocates that corporations are not in business to help society. He has argued that managers who pursue "social responsibility" activities at work are not using stockholders' money as intended; they are "taxing" shareholders, since they are acting as publicly elected officials instead of private employees (Hoffman and Moore 1990).

Similarly, Theodore Levitt (1958; also quoted in William Shaw 1991) has stated that "business has only two responsibilities—to obey the elementary canons of face-to-face civility (honesty, good faith, and so on) and to seek material gain."

According to this view of corporations, sources of moral responsibility lie outside the firm. The "invisible hand," the "hand of the government," and other means of moral control must monitor and discipline corporate behavior. John Kenneth Galbraith (1956)—also an advocate of viewing the corporation as an impersonal institution—argues for governmental control over corporate moral behavior, rather than increased corporate social responsibility.

Some contemporary philosophers also reflect the view that corporations are not persons and do not have intentions. Persons inside corporations are believed to be socially responsible, however. For example, Manuel Velasquez (1982) argues that corporations should not be seen as persons for two reasons: First, individual wrongdoers cannot be sought and punished if the "corporation" can be held responsible for wrongful acts. Consequently, corporate immoral acts will not be deterred. Second, understanding corporations as intentional persons will cause us to view them as "larger than human" persons "whose ends and well-being are more important than those of its members." Consequently, the corporation's members may "legitimately be sacrificed to the corporation's interests and the good of the individual may be subordinated to the corporation's good" (quoted in Des Jardins and McCall 1990). Therefore, it is the people in the corporation, not the corporation itself, who must be held accountable for illegal and immoral acts. Velasquez argues that although corporations have social and moral obligations, businesses as institutions do not have intentions or act as persons.

In the opening case, Manville was held legally liable as a corporation for its employees who contracted cancer while working with asbestos. What would the advocates of the "corporations as impersonal, profit-making institutions" view argue here? Was Manville as a corporation morally responsible for harm done to the employees who became cancer victims? Who in the corporation over the past several decades should be held legally and morally responsible for the asbestos-related cases?

An important criticism regarding this still-popular view follows. First, understanding organizations as impersonal institutions without intention strengthens the myth discussed in Chapter 1: That is, corporations and their actions are amoral. Arguing that corporations as institutions have no moral basis to be held accountable for suggests that corporate managers have free reign to commit sizable resources to activities that may be harmful to the consuming public. For example, if Manville could not as a corporation be held morally responsible by stakeholders such as the media, interest groups, government, citizens, and employees, then managers might be less restrained in subjecting its workers to dangerous asbestos manufacturing processes. Second, viewing corporations as impersonal institutions without intention could provide protection for powerful owners and top managers at the expense of lower-level employees who could be made scapegoats for illegal activities. Third, corporations are human institutions as well as economic institutions. As such, why should not these legally state-registered institutions be held liable and responsible for the welfare of communities where they do business and for their employees who make their existence possible? Fourth, competitive economic production and profit alone do not necessarily produce the greatest good for the largest number (see Bowie and Duska 1990). Without cooperation from local, state, and federal governments and the public, many businesses could not cover their maintenance or "external costs," that is, the costs incurred by businesses but paid by society (such as the side effects of air and water pollution we must bear). Related to this criticism is the fact not all businesses survive solely under the "survival of the fittest" maxim of the free market. Some businesses are regulated and supported by the government, that is, by the public's tax dollars. Utilities are an example. The "invisible hand" is not so invisible in these and other cases, as the Chrysler Corporation has shown. Without a government loan in 1979, Chrysler probably would not have survived.

Second View: Corporations Have a Conscience

The opposing view holds that corporations are analogous to individuals. As such, corporations have consciences, not literally but as moral agents acting on behalf of the firm's owners and shareholders. Corporate behavior can, therefore, be evaluated according to ethical standards as individual behavior is. Corporations act with intentionality and thus should be held morally accountable for their actions. Also inherent in this view is the notion that firms not only are legally and morally liable for their actions but also should perform socially responsible acts; they should be "good citizens."

Kenneth Goodpaster and John Matthews (1982; see also Hoffman and Moore 1990), for example, argue that because corporations are credited with having goals, economic values, and strategies, they also should have a conscience. These authors do not believe corporations literally should be equated with individuals but that understanding organizations as persons provides a framework superior to the first view presented for analyzing corporate responsibility. If corporations do not have intentionality, these authors argue, how can they be held morally accountable as collectives?

Peter French (1977; see also Hoffman and Moore 1990) also argues that corporations act intentionally and should be held morally accountable for their actions. French contends that corporations act through their "corporate internal decision (CID) structure," which is composed of a corporate flowchart and a corporate policy. Corporate decisions embody the decisional structure of the flowchart and the intentionality of a firm's policy. French links corporate decisions with the notion of individuals through the CID. The CID "incorporates" actions of individuals as a collective.

French (quoted in Hoffman and Moore 1990) wrote, "The CID Structure licenses redescriptions of events as corporate and attributions of corporate intentionality while it does not obscure the private acts of executives, directors, etc." Corporate decisions are not identical to the decisions of individuals within the firm, according to French. Still, decisions passed through the CID represent the firm as a collective of individuals.

Like the first view, this perspective of the corporation also has limitations. It is intuitively difficult to equate collective-command structural and policy decisions only with individuals. Large corporations, in particular, are shifting collectives and coalitions with diverse opinions and decisions—even though presidents and top managers make and enforce decisions that represent the corporation. But is Manville analogous to an individual? Should Manville's decisions regarding asbestos victims' claims for several decades be the liability of the corporation or of the decision makers who authorized the work policies and orders? Or does the liability belong both to individuals in the corporation and to the corporation?

The view of the corporation as an individual and moral agent does place intentionality and social responsibility back inside the corporation; however, as the criticisms here suggest, this view is anthropomorphic and does not take into consideration the political complexity of internal operations and the diverse interests inside contemporary corporations. A third view of the nature and role of corporations regarding social responsibility is presented next. This view, which is supported in this textbook, attempts to reconcile many of the problems with the first two views.

4.2 THE CORPORATION AS SOCIAL AND ECONOMIC STAKEHOLDER

The third view, of the corporation as a social and economic stakeholder in the community, is based on a pragmatic assessment of the nature of the relationships between firms and the constituencies they serve. This section will discuss the moral basis of the relationships between corporations and the groups they interact with.

The stakeholder perspective (see Evan and Freeman 1988) essentially views the for-profit corporation as a legal entity and collective of individuals and groups. The CEO and top-level managers are hired to maximize profits for the owners and shareholders. However, to accomplish this, corporations also must respond to a variety of stakeholders' (employees, customers, suppliers, government agencies) needs, rights, and legitimate demands. From this perspective, the corporation has primary obligations to the economic mandates of its owners; however, to survive and succeed, it must also respond to legal, social, political, and environmental claims from a host of stakeholders inside and outside its boundaries.

Corporations are, then, socially and morally responsible to their constituencies to the extent they maintain responsible relationships with their stakeholders and respond to their legitimate rights and claims according to ethical standards of fairness and justice, as well as to utilitarian costs and benefits analyses. The stakeholder view supports no specific moral principle of right and wrong but enables corporations and their stakeholders to adopt moral principles and guidelines according to the stakes and moral constraints in different situations. The point is that corporations are obligated and constrained to respect the rights and legitimate interests of their constituencies in order to do business well.

In contrast to the second view, corporations are not like individuals, since firms outlive individuals and plan into future generations. Consequently, the interests of corporations are not identical to individual interests. Therefore, attributing consciences to corporations is not an apt metaphor; however, the view that corporations must act socially and morally—as well as legally and economically—toward their stakeholders is an essential part of the stakeholder theory.

THE SOCIAL CONTRACT

The stakeholder view of the corporation is also based on the concept of a **social contract.** Developed by early political philosophers, a social contract is

> a set of rules and assumptions about behavior patterns among the various elements of society. Much of the social contract is embedded in the customs of society. For example, in integrating minorities into the workforce, society has come to expect companies to do more than the law requires. . . . Some of the "contract provisions" result from practices between parties. Like a legal contract, the social contract often involves a quid pro quo (something for something) exchange. (Gordon et al. 1990)

The social contract between a corporation and its stakeholders is often based on implicit as well as explicit agreements. For example, it is argued:

> The success of many businesses is directly related to the public's confidence in those businesses. A loss of public confidence can be detrimental

to the firm and to its investors. One way to retain and to reinforce public confidence is by acting in an ethical manner, a manner that shows a concern for the investing public and the customers of the firm. (Torabzadeh et al. 1989)

Patricia Werhane (1989) illustrated the noneconomic basis that binds corporations to their stakeholders in the following argument against insider trading:

> My contention has been that the principal ethical arguments against insider trading do not, by themselves, suffice to show that the practice is unethical and should be illegal. The strongest arguments are those that turn on the notion of a fiduciary duty to act in the interest of shareholders, or on the idea of inside information as company "property." But in both arguments, the impermissibility of insider trading depends on a contractual understanding among the company, its shareholders and its employees. (177)

Werhane continued by arguing that "fiduciary relationships" are based on "trust and dependence" in which one stakeholder or party acts on behalf of the interest of another. Such relationships, she states, are essential for doing business in a complex society.

Laura Nash's (1990, 101) use of the **covenantal ethic** concept is also related to the social contract (or covenant) concept and lies at the heart of a stakeholder approach. The covenantal ethic focuses on the importance of social as well as economic relationships among businesses, customers, and stakeholders. Relationships and social contracts (or covenants) between corporate managers and customers are oriented toward a "seller must care" attitude, not "buyer or seller beware," Nash states.

> A manager's understanding of problems will not be in terms of concrete products, specific cost reductions, or even balance sheets (though obviously these will be secondary results and scorecards), but in terms of the quality of the relationships that are inevitably created by any business activity. (104)

The covenantal context has the quality of an "enabling relationship," Nash says, that adds value and is based on the mutual benefit of buyer and seller. Without trusting relationships, long-term economic business transactions do not succeed.

The stakeholder perspective as based on social contracts and a covenantal ethic argues that corporations have social and moral—as well as legal, political, economic, and environmental—obligations toward their constituencies to perform so as to maintain and benefit from mutually sustaining relationships. For example, CEOs, upper-level managers, and boards of directors have a primary moral obligation to accurately, honestly, and regularly inform shareholders of the company's economic progress. Acting with social responsibility toward their communities, host countries, and society is an important noneconomic obligation of companies. Corporations have social and moral obligations to provide a safe and healthy work environment for their employees. Firms also must offer fair and equitable wages for work performed. In addition, they have a moral obligation to accurately inform consumers about their services and the contents of their products and to provide safe services and products.

PRAGMATIC PRINCIPLES FOR CORPORATE AND STAKEHOLDER RELATIONSHIPS

Norman Bowie and Ronald Duska (1990, 34–37) argue at a more general level that corporations' obligations—in addition to making a profit—include acting justly; causing no avoidable, unjustifiable harm; and preventing harm where possible and in others' proximity, as well as in situations where no others can intervene. These writers also argue that corporations realistically should be moral according to the criteria of "ought-implies-can" and according to a "moral minimum" standard.

"Ought-implies-can" means that companies are not ethically required to produce the most safe products if the cost will stop consumers from buying them; consumers also weigh price against safety concerns. Why expect or require firms to produce the safest product if it will not sell? Companies *ought* to do what they *can* do.

The "moral minimum" standard holds that firms should not produce products or services or engage in activities that inflict avoidable harm on others. At a minimum, corporations should design, manufacture, distribute, and sell safe products that will sell while following this standard.

THE MORAL BASIS AND SOCIAL POWER OF CORPORATIONS AS STAKEHOLDERS

Keith Davis (1975) reasons that the social responsibility of corporations is based on social power and that "if business has the power, then a just relationship demands that business also bear responsibility for its actions in these areas." He terms this view the "iron law of responsibility." "[I]n the long run, those who do not use power in a manner in which society considers responsible will tend to lose it," he states. Davis discusses five broad guidelines or obligations business professionals should follow to be socially responsible:

1. Businesses have a social role of "trustee for society's resources." Since society entrusts businesses to use their resources, businesses must wisely serve the interests of all their stakeholders, not just those of owners, consumers, or labor.

2. "Business shall operate as a two-way open system with open receipt of inputs from society and open disclosure of its operations to the public."

3. "Social costs as well as benefits of an activity, product, or service shall be thoroughly calculated and considered in order to decide whether to proceed with it." Technical and economic criteria must be supplemented with the social effects of business activities, goods, or services before a company proceeds.

4. "The social costs of each activity, product, or service shall be priced into it so that the consumer (user) pays for the effects of his consumption on society."

5. "Business institutions as citizens have responsibilities for social involvement in areas of their competence where major social needs exist."

These five guidelines provide a foundation for creating and reviewing the moral bases of corporate stakeholder relationships.

LIMITATIONS OF THE STAKEHOLDER VIEW

The stakeholder view of corporations is increasingly becoming a useful perspective for understanding a firm's social and moral responsibilities for its constituencies. But this view also has critics. Some argue that it is mainly economically based and focuses on maximizing profit (Buchholz 1991; Donaldson 1989). It is also argued that this view has no solid theoretical grounding for corporate social responsiveness. For example, Rogene Buchholz (1991) stated that "[T]he stakeholder model is a useful tool to analyze and describe the various relationships a corporation has to its main constituents in society, but it is by no means a serious theoretical attempt to provide a new paradigm that would even begin to replace the economic paradigm."

Although it is true that the stakeholder view of corporations does not dictate an absolute set of ethical standards that firms should follow in doing business, it is realistic and practical and permits researchers and organizational members to apply a range of ethical principles to specific situations. From an ethical point of view, the stakeholder perspective also constrains corporations to act for the benefit of their constituencies, both economically and according to justice, fairness, and utilitarian guidelines. Finally, note that Archie Carroll (1991, 43) includes philanthropic responsibilities (along with economic, legal, and ethical responsibilities) in the stakeholder perspective: "[O]ne would not encounter many business executives today who exclude philanthropic programs from their firms' range of activities. It seems the role of corporate citizenship is one that business has no significant problem embracing." Given the strengths and shortcomings of the stakeholder view of corporate moral responsibility, this text argues that it is the most practical and least absolutist conceptual framework for examining corporate social responsibility in ethical dilemmas. This is because it concentrates on the corporation's relationships and obligations to its constituencies within the marketplace.

The next section focuses attention on inside the corporate stakeholder and discusses how strategy, structure, leadership, and culture influence moral responsibility.

4.3 CORPORATE STRATEGY AND MORAL RESPONSIBILITY

"Structure follows strategy" is an accepted organizational principle in management literature. A corporation's structure, according to managerial contingency theory, should fit its strategy if the organization is to function coherently and competitively. Corporate culture and moral responsibility also follow, and are influenced by, strategy. This and the next section discuss the relationships among corporate strategy, structure, leadership, and moral responsibility. How do strategy and structure influence the moral behavior of employees? Corporate leaders are responsible for directing the formulation and articulation of strategy.

Figure 4.1 illustrates how strategy relates to other organizational dimensions and moral responsibility. For ethical analysis, Figure 4.1 provides a model for discussing the organizational and conceptual relatedness among strategy, structure, culture, professionals, and control

■ FIGURE 4.1

RELATED NATURE OF CORPORATE STRATEGY, ORGANIZATIONAL
DIMENSIONS, AND MORAL RESPONSIBILITIES

systems. Particularly interesting here are the effects of these interactions on the morality of the actions and behavior of corporate employees. This section argues that intended and enacted strategy influences the legality and morality of corporate activities in the following ways:

1. Strategy sets the overall managerial direction of business activities. Enterprise strategy, for example, can emphasize revenue growth over customer satisfaction or product quality. It can emphasize technical concern over professional development. Or corporate-wide strategy can direct a firm's activities toward social issues, employee rights, and other stakeholder obligations.

2. Strategy controls the emphasis of activities top management values and rewards. In this sense, strategy reflects management's statement of what is important ethically.

3. Strategy sets the tone and tenor of business activities and transactions. Strategies that overemphasize profits may set a tone that ignores customer concern and safety or innovative ideas. Furthermore, organizational reward and control systems often reflect the emphasis and tone of the larger strategic direction. Emphasis on profits at the expense of employee development usually is reflected by rigid and unrealistic incentive and revenue quota systems.

Enterprise strategy, then, sets and affects corporate expectations, ways of doing business, rewards, motivations, and performance. Strategy influences the types of control systems that govern business activities and the pressures that lead to moral or immoral behavior.

FOUR LEVELS OF STRATEGY

Chapter 2 explained how a stakeholder analysis is used as a strategic method for mapping a firm's social responsibility toward external stakeholders. Here is a general overview of what strategy is with a focus on how strategy directs and influences a corporation's moral responsibility inside and outside its walls.

Corporations formulate at least four levels of strategies: enterprise, corporate, business, and functional (Hofer and Schendel 1979; quoted in Carroll 1989; see also Thompson and Strictland 1980). The **enterprise strategy** is the broadest level. It identifies the corporation's role in society, defines how the firm will be perceived by stakeholders, represents its principles and values, and shows what the firm stands for (Freeman 1984). The **corporate strategy** identifies the firm's goals, objectives, and business areas its policies and plans are based on. **Business strategy** translates the corporate strategy into more detailed goals and objectives for specific business activities. **Functional strategy** takes business strategy into even more detail in the marketing, research and development, production, sales, and other functional areas.

At the enterprise strategic level, the CEO and upper-level managers state their social responsibility and stakeholder commitments. Corporate strategy also should reflect ethical considerations. For example, Freeman and Gilbert (1988) stated that "[t]o understand why corporations choose to do what they do, we must understand the values at work in the actions of multiple stakeholders. Understanding corporate strategy means understanding the competing value claims of multiple stakeholders." Extending this logic, Freeman and Gilbert stated two axioms for corporate strategy: (1) "Corporate strategy must reflect an understanding of the values of organizational members and stakeholders," and (2) "[c]orporate strategy must reflect an understanding of the ethical nature of strategic choice." The rights of individuals and human goals should be primary in corporate strategy, these writers say.

Johnson & Johnson's now exemplary credo, in Figure 4.2, illustrates a corporation's values statement that underlies its enterprise and corporate strategies.

Here the values of the corporation's members and the firm's responsibilities for its stakeholders are clearly laid out. Another well-recognized values statement that drives both enterprise and corporate strategies is the "Beliefs of Borg-Warner" from the Borg-Warner Corporation, presented in Figure 4.3.

These are broad strategic-value and social-responsibility directives that serve as a basis for elaborating specific business goals, policies, and plans for the functional areas of human resource management, research and development, financial planning, sales, and other managerial tasks. Socially responsive personnel policies serve as a basis and platform for setting and making operational performance and evaluation standards, affirmative-action hiring, layoffs, and outplacement policies. Noneconomic financial objectives that promote customer service can be identified. Sales strategies that seek to inform and protect customers from false information can be established. Product specifications, labels, and warranties that have public interests and safety in mind can be implemented. Without written ethical principles in enterprise strategy statements, companies are less likely to include moral imperatives in their business strategies, plans, operations, and interactions.

The corporate value statements of Johnson & Johnson and Borg-Warner (in Figures 4.2 and 4.3) reflect exceptional companies with executive officers who believe in directing their firms in ethical ways. Experience shows that the enterprise and corporate strategies of companies that emphasize inflexible or unrealistic profit and revenue quotas are more likely to result in illegal and immoral activities, because these companies pursue singularly defined economic mandates. The Heinz Corporation (Goodpaster 1981) illustrated this in the late 1970s. Although Heinz had an ethics code,

JOHNSON & JOHNSON CREDO

Our Credo

We believe our first responsibility is to the doctors, nurses and patients, to mothers and fathers and all others who use our product and services. In meeting their needs everything we do must be of high quality.
We must constantly strive to reduce our costs in order to maintain reasonable prices.
Customers' orders must be serviced promptly and accurately.
Our suppliers and distributors must have an opportunity to make a fair profit.

We are responsible to our employees, the men and women who work with us throughout the world.
Everyone must be considered as an individual. We must respect their dignity and recognize their merit.
They must have a sense of security in their jobs.
Compensation must be fair and adequate, and working conditions clean, orderly and safe.
We must be mindful of ways to help our employees fulfill their family responsibilities.
Employees must feel free to make suggestions and complaints.
There must be equal opportunity for employment, development and advancement for those qualified.
We must provide competent management, and their actions must be just and ethical.

We are responsible to the communitites in which we work and to the world community as well.
We must be good citizens—support good works and charities and bear our fair share of taxes.
We must encourage civic improvements and better health and education.
We must maintain in good order the property we are privileged to use, protecting the environment and natural resources.

Our final responsibility is to our stockholders.
Business must make a sound profit.
We must experiment with new ideas.
Research must be carried on, innovation programs developed and mistakes paid for.
New equipment must be purchased, new facilities provided and new products launched.
Reserves must be created to provide for adverse times.
When we operate according to these principles, the stockholders should realize a fair return.

SOURCE: Johnson & Johnson. Used by permission of Johnson & Johnson, the copyright owner.

it was not reflected in the corporate strategy or in the firm's structure, culture, and operational control systems. Unethical and questionable legal activities followed: lying on employees' and divisions' performance quotas, revising and cheating on quarterly sales figures to meet fixed, unrealistic profit quotas, and expensing prepayments that should have been capitalized. These immoral activities followed the strategic directive of the firm in that period: predictable, sustained earnings.

■ **FIGURE 4.3**

THE BELIEFS OF BORG-WARNER: TO REACH BEYOND THE MINIMAL

Any business is a member of a social system, entitled to the rights and bound by the responsibilities of that membership. Its freedom to pursue economic goals is constrained by law and channeled by the forces of a free market. But these demands are minimal, requiring only that a business provide wanted goods and services, compete fairly, and cause no obvious harm. For some companies, that is enough. It is not enough for Borg-Warner. We impose upon ourselves an obligation to reach beyond the minimal. We do so convinced that by making a larger contribution to the society that sustains us, we best assure not only its future vitality, but our own.

This is what we believe.

We believe in the dignity of the individual.

However large and complex a business may be, its work is still done by dealing with people. Each person involved is a unique human being, with pride, needs, values, and innate personal worth. For Borg-Warner to succeed, we must operate in a climate of openness and trust, in which each of us freely grants others the same respect, cooperation, and decency we seek for ourselves.

We believe in our responsibility to the common good.

Because Borg-Warner is both an economic and social force, our responsibilities to the public are large. The spur of competition and the sanctions of the law give strong guidance to our behavior, but alone do not inspire our best. For that we must heed the voice of our natural concern for others. Our challenge is to supply goods and services that are of superior value to those who use them; to create jobs that provide meaning for those who do them; to honor and enhance human life; and to offer our talents and our wealth to help improve the world we share.

We believe in the endless quest for excellence.

Though we may be better today than we were yesterday, we are not as good as we must become. Borg-Warner chooses to be a leader—in serving our customers, advancing our technologies, and rewarding all who invest in us their time, money and trust. None of us can settle for doing less than our best, and we can never stop trying to surpass what already has been achieved.

We believe in continuous renewal.

A corporation endures and prospers only by moving forward. The past has given us the present to build on. But to follow our visions to the future, we must see the difference between traditions that give us continuity and strength, and conventions that no longer serve us—and have that courage to act on that knowledge. Most can adapt after change has occurred; we must be among the few who anticipate change, shape it to our purpose, and act as its agents.

We believe in the commonwealth of Borg-Warner and its people.

Borg-Warner is both a federation of businesses and a community of people. Our goal is to preserve the freedom each of us needs to find personal satisfaction while building the strength that comes from unity. True unity is more than a melding of self-interests; it results when values and ideals also are shared. Some of ours are spelled out in these statements of belief. Others include faith in our political, economic, and spiritual heritage; pride in our work and our company; the knowledge that loyalty must flow in many directions; and a conviction that power is strongest when shared. We look to the unifying force of these beliefs as a source of energy to brighten the future of our company and all who depend on it.

SOURCE: Borg-Warner Corp. The beliefs of Borg Warner: to reach beyond the minimal. Reprinted with permission of the Borg-Warner Corporation.

Can you identify other firms whose enterprise and corporate strategies omit noneconomic value orientations toward stakeholders and whose business practices proved detrimental to customers, suppliers, employees, and society?

STRATEGY IMPLEMENTATION AND EVALUATION

Implementing and managing strategic social and moral responsibility directives are difficult tasks since these activities are harder to assess and measure than economic ones. This section outlines Hofer and Schendel's (1979) six-step strategic management process and suggests ways moral and social responsibility can be integrated with the strategic implementation of a corporation's objectives.

The strategic management process involves (1) formulating goals, (2) formulating strategies, (3) implementing strategies, (4) controlling strategies, (5) evaluating strategies, and (6) analyzing the environment.

Many of these steps overlap and loop back; implementing and managing strategy is, in practice, not an absolutely linear process. Controlling and evaluating strategies are interactive processes. Analyzing the environment often requires reformulating goals and strategies. The focus here is on how moral and social responsibility, not economic or political, issues can be part of the strategy implementation and evaluation process.

In practice, as noted earlier, economic, political, technological, and environmental goals, strategies, and issues often evolve into social and moral problems and dilemmas for corporations, especially in emergencies and crises—as the Exxon *Valdez* and Manville Corporation cases show.

At the *goal formulation* stage, moral and social responsibility priorities and issues must be identified or sanctioned by the CEO, as stated earlier. The goals reflect the CEO's and the firm's values. Such priorities might include enhancing the physical environment, protecting consumers, and building safe products. Value statements, such as those of Borg-Warner and Johnson & Johnson, illustrate the basis for formulating corporate goals.

The *strategy formulation* stage involves a competitive analysis of the firm's strengths and weaknesses in terms of managerial, financial, and social issues. For social issues, a moral perspective should be articulated at this stage and should reflect a concern for the visibility, vulnerability, and obligations of social issues in a firm's strategies. During this stage, managers not only must estimate the firm's risks and opportunities in pursuing specific goals but also must spell out its obligations to relevant stakeholders (that is, to suppliers, consumers and customers, competitors, the government, communities, and society) vis-à-vis each goal. For example, the Johnson & Johnson credo states that "customers' orders must be serviced promptly and accurately."

During the third stage, *implementing the strategy*, managers and employees from the entire organization are usually involved in different ways. Social and moral responsibilities play a role in strategy implementation by ensuring that the procedures for putting strategy and resources into action are just, fair, and equitable and that the corporation is morally fulfilling its fiduciary responsibilities for its stakeholders. For example, the Johnson & Johnson credo specifically articulates a directive to reduce costs to "maintain reasonable prices."

During the fourth stage, *strategy control,* and the fifth stage, *strategy evaluation,* corporate managers set standards to measure the intended performance against the actual performance of their actions. During these stages, managers also assess the moral and social, as well as the economic, results with their stated performance criteria. During the strategy control stage, corrective action should be taken if results are not in line with stated goals. During both of these stages, the "social audit" (explained next) can be used for checking, evaluating, and correcting unethical activities. The sixth stage then will be discussed.

SOCIAL AUDITS The **social audit** concept (see Baver and Fenn 1973; Carrol and Beiler 1975; Corson and Steiner 1974; and Estes 1976) was developed in the 1970s as a way for corporations to keep track of their social responsibility performance. Measuring a firm's performance against its social goals or issues is the aim. Carroll (1989) listed minority employment, pollution/environment, working conditions, consumerism-concerns, and philanthropic contributions as social issues included in social audits. Internal personnel, consultants, task forces, and board-level committees have been employed to oversee and perform social audits.

The problems with social audit use have been largely in the measurement techniques. Traditional accounting methods have not proved adequate (Sturdivant and Vernon-Wortzel 1990). Currently, companies use several approaches to keep score of their social performance. Still, social audits send a message to the firm's stakeholders: "We take our moral responsibility to our stakeholders seriously."

Finally, during the sixth stage of the strategic implementation process, the *environmental analysis,* managers scan, identify, monitor, and forecast issues and trends in the (1) technological, (2) political, (3) economic, and (4) social environments to determine the effects of targeted issues on the organization—before the issues and trends occur (Fahey 1987; Fleming 1978–85). John Naisbitt's books titled *Megatrends* and Alan Toffler's book *Future Shock* are attempts to scan, monitor, and predict environmental issues and the possible effects they may have on organizations and individuals. Many research think tanks—opinion and survey organizations (such as the Yankelovich Group and the Roper Organization)—exist that perform environmental analyses.

From a stakeholder perspective, a firm would be interested in identifying environmental issues that might affect its stakeholder obligations and relationships. Obtaining accurate information from the environment can help managers estimate the stakes and potential costs associated with an issue's occurrence. Strategies then can be formulated to address the issues. From a social and moral perspective, managers would be concerned about fulfilling their stakeholder obligations through these strategies. Predictions about changes in the workforce in the year 2000, for example, suggest that responsible corporations must be prepared to equitably and justly manage the needs of aging employees and dual-career families and to increase female, foreign, and minority workers. Flextime, health programs, and flexible management styles must be implemented to manage this changing workforce responsibly. Managers must be trained to understand and implement employee programs that address diversity in the workforce. The strategic issues management process is discussed in more detail in Chapter 5.

CORPORATE STRUCTURE AND MORAL RESPONSIBILITY

After strategies are defined, the appropriate organizational structure should be designed and enacted to accommodate their implementation. This section discusses the relationship of structure and moral responsibility.

Most large corporations are hierarchically governed and structured. Figure 4.4 illustrates a typical large corporation's hierarchical governance system.

The hierarchy extends from shareholders to the board of directors, to the CEO, to the upper-level vice presidents, and then to the functional area managers, with the employees reporting to these managers. Although shareholders are not part of the internal corporation, they are included here since their interests should be considered in the structuring and policy-setting decisions of the firm.

Corporations can be structured at levels below the CEO in a number of ways, and large ones usually include several of these levels: functional, product line, geographic, and matrix (that is, functional and by special project or program). Corporations also can be organized by different arrangements: For example, by divisions, by branch offices, or by "strategic business units" (SBUs) that can perform as independent profit centers. Divisional structures can be either centralized or decentralized, depending on the nature of the business, the strategy, and environmental threats and opportunities. Let us turn this discussion to a more general level of analysis, that is, centralized versus decentralized structure, since little is known or has been formally studied regarding ethical behavior and the more specific arrangements.

A survey of 443 industrial salespeople reported in the *Wall Street Journal* found that structure does affect ethical behavior. Specifically, highly supervised employees in bureaucratic firms were more likely to act ethically than employees in entrepreneurial, laissez-faire firms. "There is

■ FIGURE 4.4

HIERARCHICALLY GOVERNED STRUCTURE

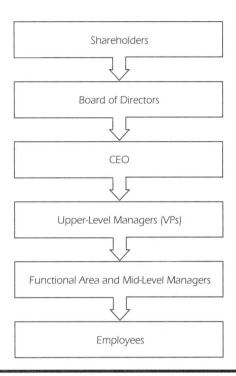

evidence people think through the risk of getting caught" in firms with more supervised structures, the article noted.

Another notable study (Cullen, Victor, and Stephens 1989) reported that a subunit's location in the organizational structure affects its ethical climate:

> At [a] savings and loan association and also at [a] manufacturing plant, the employees at the home offices reported less emphasis on laws, codes, and rules than did the employees at the branch offices. Perhaps control by formal mechanisms becomes more necessary when direct supervision by top management is not feasible.

Decentralization appears to permit, or encourage, more unethical behavior among employees than more supervised, controlled structures.

A recent account of Citicorp bank's credit-card processing division illustrates the relationship among organizational structure, competitive pressures, and immoral and illegal behavior (Lipin 1991). The bank fired the president and 11 senior executives of that division because they had fraudulently overstated revenue by $23 million for two years. The illegal inflating of revenue by division employees may reflect the problem that employee bonuses were tied to unrealistic revenue targets. Citicorp is centralizing its organizational functions. "Some insiders as well as observers believe the decentralized structure left the bank susceptible to potential abuse by employees"(Lippin 1991). A Merrill Lynch banking analyst said about Citicorp: "But as they go through a management centralization and tighten control of independently run businesses, people will look with scrutiny to see whether there are other control problems" (Lipin 1991, A3). Pressures from upper-level managers who overemphasize unrealistic bottom-line quarterly revenue objectives and who give unclear policies and procedures to guide ethical decision making in business transactions may contribute to immoral behavior in more decentralized structures.

Evidence also shows that middle- and lower-level managers, in particular, feel pressured to compromise their personal moral standards to meet corporate expectations (Carroll 1975; Posner and Schmidt 1984). Cases and anecdotal studies suggest that managers in large firms may compromise their personal ethics to corporate expectations for several reasons:

1. Decentralized structures with little or no coordination with central policy and procedures encourage a climate for immoral activities when pressures for profit making increase.

2. Unrealistic, short-term, and bottom-line profit quotas add pressure on employees to commit unethical actions.

3. Overemphasis on numbers-driven financial incentives encourages shortcuts around responsible decisions.

4. Amoral organizational and work-unit cultures can create an environment that condones illegal and immoral actions.

Certainly more studies are needed in this area before definite conclusions can be made. The discussion here is intended to open the topic for debate and elaboration.

PROFESSIONALS, CONTROL SYSTEMS, AND MORAL RESPONSIBILITY

Enterprise and corporate strategies also can influence the professionals and managers hired and retained in corporations, as well as the types of structures and control systems implemented. For this discussion on the moral dimensions of strategy, structure, people, and corporate systems, the earlier argument is repeated here: Corporations that support strategies overemphasizing short-term, numbers-driven profits at the expense of concern for employees, shareholder interest, and customer service generally actively or through negligence protect and even promote those who engage in amoral or immoral behavior. These corporations also tend to have lax accounting and cost-control systems but probably will not have ethics codes—or if such do exist, they will not be properly communicated or enforced.

The Heinz Corporation case cited earlier, which detailed that firm's operations between 1972 and 1980, illustrated many of these questionable legal and immoral practices. Heinz, driven by a strategy that emphasized predictable earnings, had a decentralized divisional structure tied to a fixed-profit quota system that pressured employees to meet divisional revenue projections or face no divisional or individual merit increases. Later audits showed an ineffective financial control system and ethics code. Several managers were illegally and immorally padding their revenues and lying to meet corporate expectations. One such upper-level manager was promoted; no employees involved in the immoral and legally questionable activities were fired. The operations at Heinz during this period raised these questions: What type of corporate culture existed to permit these activities? Where was the board of directors during these happenings? Where was corporate moral and operational leadership during this period? Did the decentralized divisional structure encourage immoral activities? Again, as Figure 4.1 indicates, strategy does drive and influence organizational structure, culture, people, and control systems— in moral, amoral, or immoral ways.

4.4 CORPORATE LEADERSHIP, CULTURE, AND MORAL RESPONSIBILITY

"The glue that holds the high-ethics firm together is not culture, goals, superordinate goals, participating employee stock ownership, or leadership. It is purpose" (from Pastin 1986; quoted in Hoffman and Moore 1990, 627).

Purpose in corporations is *espoused* by the values and principles of the founders and CEOs; purpose is *enacted* through the policies, procedures, examples, and behaviors of the leaders and their followers. Leadership, as argued earlier, influences strategy, culture, control and reward systems, and even the nature and tone of interactions in the corporation. This section discusses the leadership styles of corporate executives and managers that influence the moral, amoral, or immoral culture and direction of the firm. It begins with the following generalizations about the nature of corporate leadership:

1. Without followers, leaders cannot lead. Leadership is, to some extent, a function of followership. In fact, many employees at lower levels embody the conscience of the corporation through their own actions.

2. Related to the first observation is the fact leadership is often dispersed and shared in corporations. This is—and must be—the case for the

firm's moral environment and behavior. One person, even the CEO, cannot be the only moral example in the corporation. Although the top-level leader sets the moral tone and example, the followers must share moral leadership in order for a moral environment to thrive.

3. No single or best style of moral leadership or management exists. In the following discussion, two models of moral leadership are presented. The first is a continuum, and the second is profiled as leadership in three "acts." Both models are intended to show how moral leadership in organizations can be evaluated.

MORAL LEADERSHIP STYLES

For discussing the nature of ethics and leadership, moral leadership in organizations and the ethical systems they are based on can be viewed along a continuum (Hitt 1990, 138–74):

LESS ETHICAL			MORE ETHICAL
Manipulator (end-justifies-means ethic)	Bureaucratic administrator (rule ethic)	Professional manager (social contract ethic)	Transforming leader (personal-istic ethic)

The *manipulator* leadership style is based on a Machiavellian ethic (Machiavelli 1966) that views leadership amorally. That is, the end result justifies the means taken to reach an aim. Power is the driving force behind a manipulator's motives. This is an egotistically and essentially economically motivated moral leadership style. It lacks trust and relationship-building interests and qualities. It is oriented toward the short term. Although the motives underlying this style may be amoral, the consequences could prove immoral for those affected. Have you ever worked under someone who used this style?

The *bureaucratic administrator* is a rule-based moral leadership style. Based on the theories of famed German sociologist Max Weber (Gerth and Mills 1946), the bureaucratic administrator acts on rational principles embodied in an ideal organizational bureaucracy: that is, fixed rules that explain the purpose and functions of the organization; a hierarchy that shows the chain-of-command control structure; well-defined job descriptions; professional managers who communicate and enforce the rules; and technically qualified employees who are promoted by expertise and rewarded by rank and tenure. The driving force behind this style is *effi-*

ciency ("doing things right," functioning in the least wasteful manner) more than effectiveness (producing the intended result or aim, "doing the right things").

Although this leadership style has an admirable aim of basing decisions only on objective, rational criteria, the moral problem with it lies in the "sin of omission." That is, a leader may follow all the rules exactly but hurt someone unintentionally—again, amorally—by not attending to legitimate human needs because the option to do so was not prescribed or included in the rules. A professional bus driver, for example, has orders not to stop between two cities for any reason. During one of the bus trips, a bystander is accidentally shot and appears fatally wounded by a hunter. The driver sees and recognizes the victim but refuses to stop because of the rules. The bystander dies. Is the bus driver's failure to stop morally justified because he or she followed the rules? Rules cannot address all problems and needs in what we know are imperfect and political organizations. The well-intentioned bureaucratic administrator may try to act amorally, but his or her efforts could result in immoral and irresponsible consequences to others. Do you recognize this moral leadership style? Have you ever worked for someone who used it?

The *professional manager* aims at effectiveness, "doing things right." The theory about this style is grounded in Peter Drucker's (1978) principles and view of managers as professionals who have the expertise and tools for accomplishing work effectively through others. Based on a social contract ethic, this management style relies—like the previous two styles—on amoral techniques and assumptions for getting work done. For example, professional career managers use rational objectives and their training to accomplish the organization's work. The organization's corporate culture and the social contract—that is, implicit and explicit agreements—made between managers and organizational executives set the ground rules and ethics that govern the manager's behavior. However, social contracts are not always ethically justifiable.

A major ethical problem with this leadership style lies in the real possibility that the collective corporate culture and dominant governing group may think and act amorally or immorally. Groupthink (consensus-dominated decision making based on uncritical, biased thinking) may occur (Janis 1972). The collective may lead itself astray. Professional managers by training and expertise are still prone to unethical behavior. Do you recognize managers or leaders who act amorally or immorally as "professionals"?

Finally, the *transforming leadership* style, based on James MacGregor Burns's (1978; see also Hitt 1990) theory, is grounded on a personalistic ethic. The transformational leader bases his or her effectiveness on relationships with followers. Also, this style focuses on the charisma, energy, and excitement the leader brings to relationships. The transformational leader is involved in the growth and self-actualization of others and views others according to their potential. This type of leader identifies and elevates the values and motives of others. He or she empowers, coaches, and helps promote other leaders. This leadership style is moral in that "it raises the level of human conduct and aspirations of both leaders and led, and thus has a transforming effect on both" (Hitt 1990).

William Hitt (1990, 170) moved the continuum of moral leadership discussed here one step beyond the transformational leader to what he termed an "encompassing approach to leadership," or "the effective leader-manager." The *encompassing leader* learns from the shortcomings of each of the four leadership styles on the continuum and uses all of their strengths. For example, manipulative leadership does value the effective use of power. However, this style's deception and dysfunctional uses of power should be avoided. The bureaucratic administrator values the effective use of rules, roles, and responsibilities; however, these should not become ends rather than means. The professional manager values results; however, human concerns should be valued more highly than physical and fiscal resources and results. The transformational leader values human empowerment; however, even this characteristic is not the complete job of management.

Note that socially responsible leaders and managers as individual and organizational stakeholders also must critically observe their obligations to all stakeholders, including their own conscience, according to the ethical criteria of rights, justice, and duty—as well as to a utilitarian logic. It is essential for those who must select or hire organizational executives and managers, who also must lead, to know each person's values and moral leadership style.

ACT I, II, AND III MORAL LEADERS

Leaders and leadership styles also can be depicted as Act I, Act II, or Act III profiles. This conceptual discussion is based on Professor Thomas Cronin's (1991, Colorado College) view of leadership. The emphasis here is on the roles and responsibilities leaders assume relative to an issue, policy, or law. The model is also dynamic because leaders can move from one style to another and also because the evolution and relationship between leadership and issues (organizational or societal) can be studied and explained over time and within or outside of institutions.

Act I leaders originate and frame issues. They are usually outside of formal organizations and are on the frontier of change—whether it is organizational or societal. These leaders are the prophets, the grassroots movers and shakers. They are the framers of issues and sometimes the protesters who make previously invisible issues visible. They usually lead by personal example, experience, and charismatic motivation. Martin Luther King Jr. started as an Act I leader in the civil rights movement.

Ralph Nader started as a grassroots consumer advocate. The leaders of the MADD (Mothers Against Drunk Driving) and SADD (Students Against Drunk Driving) movements are Act I leaders.

Act I leaders often act from a moral sense of duty and justice. They have personally experienced or observed a sense of injustice or no justice from the judicial system and move to create awareness of and responsiveness to harm done to themselves, to their relatives, or to a disadvantaged group they represent. It also should be noted that Act I leaders can and do become Act II and even Act III leaders, as did Martin Luther King Jr. and Ralph Nader. Who are other Act I leaders you can identify?

Act II leaders move issues that have been formed by Act I leaders into policy and law. This leadership style requires negotiating, coalition building, politicking, and legislating. These leaders can be either part of formal organizations or adjunct to them. Act II leaders must use formal and informal power effectively to mobilize issues into system policy and laws. Act II leaders are morally motivated from a sense of duty and fairness. They act to consolidate issues into lasting forms of policy and law. They understand their moral obligation to others and other generations. They also have a moral sense of historical mission.

Lyndon Johnson was a preeminent Act II leader. He legislated more bills into law (especially civil rights) than any president has before or since. He attempted to legislate and enact his vision of the "Great Society." Lee Iacocca also can be considered an Act II leader. His presidency at Chrysler helped that firm avoid bankruptcy and return to competitiveness based on quality and service. Can you think of other Act II leaders, nationally, internationally, or locally?

Act III leaders enforce and promote the laws, policies, and issues forged by Act I and Act II leaders. These leaders institutionalize and then symbolize the significance and continuation of issues, policies, and laws. Act III leaders also use charisma and personal example as well as powerful contacts and networks to enforce and perpetuate the viability of these policies and laws. Many times, Act III leaders act from a utilitarian and even egotistical ethic. They weigh the benefits of adopting and promoting policies and laws for others and for their own best self-interests. For example, Ronald Reagan, referred to as "the Great Communicator," could be considered an Act III leader. As a figurehead, he symbolized traditional U.S. values here and abroad. With a significantly increasing national deficit, the loss of industrial competitiveness internationally, and eroding civil rights momentum among minorities, President Reagan continued to successfully symbolize a stable, powerful, proud, and enthusiastic national figure of patriotism and confidence among nations and the American electorate. Jesse Jackson also is an Act III leader. He successfully symbolizes and represents antidrug and crime policies and promotes hope and ideals. Who are other Act III leaders you can name in industry or government or from your work experience?

Act I, II, and III leaders are motivated by a wide range of ethical principles. Act I leaders often are morally motivated by a personal and communal sense of duty and justice. Act II leaders are moved by a sense of
duty and fairness and by a need to affect the future good of generations
to come. Act III leaders are influenced by utilitarian and personal self-
interest ethics.

The relationship between corporate culture and moral leadership needs
to be emphasized. Corporate culture is directly influenced by the examples, strategies, and styles of organizational leaders. Corporate culture, as
discussed in the following section, has become a popular and important
topic in the study of business ethics, since culture embodies and transmits
moral ideals as well as amoral and immoral practices. Still, it is important
to remember that leadership has a significant impact on culture in firms.

CORPORATE CULTURE AND MORAL RESPONSIBILITY

Purpose, as embodied in corporate culture, is the glue that holds organizations together. Corporate culture is the shared values and meanings its
members hold in common and that are articulated and practiced by an
organization's leaders. Organizational and corporate cultures are both
visible and invisible, formal and informal. They can be studied by observation, by listening to and interacting with people in the culture, and by
the following other ways:

❏ Studying the physical setting

❏ Reading what the company says about its own culture

❏ Observing and testing how the company greets strangers

❏ Watching how people spend time

❏ Understanding career path progressions

❏ Noting the length of tenure in jobs, especially for middle managers

❏ Observing anecdotes and stories (Deal and Kennedy 1982)

Corporate culture is related to ethics through the (1) values and leadership styles the leaders espouse and practice; (2) heroes and heroines the
company rewards and holds up as models; (3) rites, rituals, and symbols
organizations value; and (4) way organizational executives and members
communicate among themselves and with their stakeholders.

CORPORATE VALUES

The Johnson & Johnson credo (Figure 4.2) and the beliefs of Borg-Warner
(Figure 4.3) are illustrations of exemplary statements of corporate values.
Both businesses also are successful in the marketplace. In addition, Bill
Hewlett and Dave Packard of the very successful Hewlett-Packard (HP)

company express their corporate values in terms of "the HP Way." Hewlett stated HP's driving values this way:

> I feel that in general terms it is the policies and actions that flow from the belief that men and women want to do a good job, a creative job, and that if they are provided the proper environment, they will do so. But that's only part of it. Closely coupled with this is the HP tradition of treating each individual with consideration and respect, and recognizing personal achievements. (Deal and Kennedy 1982)

Another example of corporate values used to define corporate culture and drive operations is found at the Boeing Corporation of Seattle. Boeing's values were first articulated by its former CEO William Allen (Keogh 1988):

❏ Be considerate of my associates' views.
❏ Don't talk too much . . . let others talk.
❏ Don't be afraid to admit that you don't know.
❏ Don't get immersed in detail.
❏ Make contacts with other people in industry.
❏ Try to improve feeling around Seattle toward the company.
❏ Make a sincere effort to understand labor's viewpoint.
❏ Be definite; don't vacillate.
❏ Act—get things done—move forward.

Strong Corporate Culture Traits

HP, Boeing, Johnson & Johnson, and the Borg-Warner firm (later bought by General Electric) all exemplify what Deal and Kennedy (1982, 9–12) termed "strong cultures": They (1) have a widely shared philosophy; (2) value the importance of people; (3) have heroes (presidents and products) that symbolize the success of the company; and (4) celebrate rituals, which provide opportunities for caring and sharing, for developing a spirit of "oneness" and "we-ness."

What are the values of the company you work for or the institution where you are a student or member? Do the leaders and culture embody these values in their actions and policies? Are the values written down? Do others know the values? Do the values reflect a concern for and obligation toward the organization's stakeholders? Do the values reflect a utilitarian, justice, duty, or egotistical ethic? Are the values taken at face value only, or are they practiced and implemented by other employees?

Cultures in Trouble

Organizations that stress competition, profit, and economic or introverted self-interests over stakeholder obligations and that have no morally active direction often have cultures in trouble. Signs of cultures in trouble or weak cultures include the following (from Keogh 1988):

❑ An inward focus

❑ A short-term focus

❑ Morale and motivational problems

❑ Emotional outbursts

❑ Fragmentation and inconsistency (in dress, speech, physical settings, work habits)

❑ Clashes among subcultures

❑ Ingrown subcultures

❑ Dominance of subculture values over shared company values

❑ No clear values or beliefs about how to succeed in business

❑ Many beliefs with no priorities about which are important

❑ Different beliefs throughout the company

❑ Destructive or disruptive cultural heroes rather than builders of common understanding about what is important

❑ Disorganized or disruptive daily rituals

Heroes and heroines in corporations set the moral tone and direction by their present or even remembered examples. They are the role models; they define what is successful and attainable; they symbolize the company to outsiders and insiders; and they preserve the valued qualities of the firm, set standards of excellence, and motivate people (Keogh 1988). Jack Welch at General Electric, Lee Iacocca at Chrysler, Tom Watson at IBM, Ken Olson at Digital Equipment Corporation, and others have left their mark on corporations as active, concerned, and socially responsive and involved leaders. Jimmy Carter, an unpopular president during his term, now has higher popularity ratings than when he was in office and will probably be remembered as a highly ethical president and person. Carter still works on housing and inner-city projects to assist the poor and economically disadvantaged. Who are the heroes and heroines in your organization? By what qualities and characteristics are they remembered? Are they moral, immoral, or amoral leaders?

Finally, rituals and communication in companies help define corporate culture and its moral nature (Keogh 1988, 64–67). Corporately sanctioned rituals that bring people together, that foster an openness, and that promote cross-functional and integrated hierarchical levels of communication can lower stress and encourage moral behavior. Social gatherings, picnics, recognition ceremonies, and other company outings where corporate leaders are present and where sharing of values, stories, problems, accomplishments, and aspirations occur also can lead to cultures that value people and the company's aims. Companies that reinforce secrecy and hidden agendas and physical settings that isolate executives from managers and employees and that emphasize status over human concern often reflect cultures in trouble. Troubled corporate and organizational cultures can breed and encourage unethical activities. How would you characterize the rituals and communication patterns in your organization or institution? Do these promote moral, immoral, or amoral behavior?

HIGH-ETHICS FIRMS AND CULTURES

This section concludes with a description of Mark Pastin's (1986) characterization of four principles of "high-ethics" firms. High-ethics firms have high-ethics cultures. As Pastin notes, his principles are not meant to foster a Pollyannaish optimism about ethics and businesses; rather, he seeks to "foster a realistic raising of our sights." Pastin studied 25 "high-ethics, high-profit" firms, which include Motorola, 3M, Cadbury Schweppes, Arco, Hilby Wilson, Northern Chemical, and Apple, to name a few. Here are the four principles of high-ethics firms and cultures (Pastin 1986; quoted in Hoffman and Moore 1990):

> *Principle 1:* High-ethics firms are at ease interacting with diverse internal and external stakeholder groups. The ground rules of these firms make the good of these stakeholder groups part of the firm's own good.

> *Principle 2:* High-ethics firms are obsessed with fairness. Their ground rules emphasize that the other person's interests count as much as their own.

> *Principle 3:* In high-ethics firms, responsibility is individual rather than collective, with individuals assuming responsibility for the firm's actions. These firms' ground rules mandate that individuals are responsible to themselves.

> *Principle 4:* The high-ethics firm sees its activities having a purpose, a way of operating that members of the firm value. And purpose ties the firm to its environment.

The last section of this chapter presents the corporation as moral self-regulator. The discussion so far has focused on the internal roles of leadership, strategy, structure, and culture in relation to the ethics of the corporation as stakeholder. Next, it turns to the roles of shareholders, boards of directors, CEOs, and other mechanisms to address who regulates the moral activities of firms.

4.5 THE CORPORATION AS MORAL REGULATOR

Can corporations regulate and govern their own legal and moral behavior? To whom are corporations accountable? Answers to these questions reflect an ongoing debate both in the corporate world and in business ethics circles. Those who argue that corporations can and should regulate themselves, that they are accountable only to their boards of directors (who represent their shareholders), and that they should entrust their governance to their CEOs and other leaders view the corporation as private property. (Representatives of this view include Geneen 1984 and Shapiro 1979. Excerpts from these works are in Hoffman and Moore 1990.) As such, proponents of this position argue that it is the responsibility of corporate boards and upper-level managers to police and govern their own operations.

The major opposing view to this position holds that corporations are more than private property; they are public institutions, since they are part of a democratically governed and constitutionally ruled society (Nader, Green, and Seligman 1976; excerpted in Hoffman and Moore 1990). As such, corporations should have outside members who represent a wider range of stakeholder interests on their boards of directors. Corporations also should be more open to outside review in order to represent the interests of consumers, employees, and the public. Proponents of this view also argue that corporations are unable to govern their operations. Boards of directors often are inept, uninformed, and powerless to govern the corporation. Boards become rubber stamps (Carroll 1989) for CEOs who, in many cases, also chair their own boards. The resulting situation is that CEOs often become their own bosses and the only top-level bosses. Before turning to some mediating recommendations between these two views, this discussion of the debate will examine the consequences of what is happening to poorly governed or misrepresented corporations.

CORPORATE RESTRUCTURING, MERGERS, ACQUISITIONS, AND TAKEOVERS

The debate that surrounds the sweeping activity in the 1980s and into the 1990s of corporate restructuring, mergers, acquisitions, and **takeovers** centers around the two different views of the corporation just outlined: (1) The corporation is private property in a free-market system. As such, it deserves to be bought, dismembered, and sold if it does not earn a profit and remain competitive. (2) The opposing view argues that the corporation is part of the larger public society and economy. Insider trading, greed, and corruption of powerful business interests do not represent the concerns of shareholders or of the economy. Therefore, corporations need representation from society and even protection by it sometimes to be truly competitive.

Those who believe that unlimited takeovers, mergers, and acquisitions are a normal part of a competitive free-market system, and that takeovers usually signal poor management by professionals who did not maximize value, argue that lower-than-expected stock prices reflect failing management practices (Jensen 1984). Carl Icahn, a proponent of this view, states, "Most of the approximately 2,000 takeovers and leveraged buyouts since 1981 have been characterized by a redeployment of assets to create greater competitive and economic gains" (Reich 1989). He continues:

> A most interesting . . . fact about takeovers is that in all bids for control—hostile or friendly—a price much higher than current market value is paid for the company. This is generally referred to as a "premium for control." But generally, what the acquirer is really saying when he or she pays this premium is that the company is actually worth more if the ability to remove top management exists.

This view argues that if corporations cannot govern themselves, they deserve to be sold or restructured. This is a form of effective governance, according to this view.

Robert Reich (1989), a former teacher at Harvard's John F. Kennedy School of Government and Secretary of the Department of Labor under President Clinton, argues the opposing view. "The record of the 1970s and 80s is dismally clear on this point. There is little evidence to suggest that mergers have on the average enhanced the profitability or productivity of merging enterprises," he says. Reich argues further that the American economy has suffered as a result of the massive corporate restructuring, buyouts, and takeovers. He notes that average wages, adjusted for inflation, have stagnated and that corporate profits have not rebounded to 1973 peak levels, as indicated by the Dow Jones industrial average. Reich offers as one major example the 1985 merger of R. J. Reynolds tobacco company with Nabisco, the giant food-processing firm. At the time, that merger was seen as a brilliant strategy. Reynolds would diversify into foods. Three years afterward, the merged enterprise broke up; investment bankers offered billions for the opportunity to dismember the businesses and sell them.

Reich cites four reasons why leveraged buyouts, mergers, and large-scale takeovers done mainly or solely for quick-fix profit motives do not always succeed: (1) myopia, (2) wasted talent, (3) debt, and (4) distrust. First, the myopic, short-term perspective does not enable firms to develop new technologies. Profit pressures inhibit real technological growth. Second, "asset rearranging" by "paper entrepreneurs" wastes the energy of talented scientists and managers. The short-term profit perspective does not encourage business and technological talent. Third, corporate takeovers and buyouts require financial borrowing and leveraging—namely, debt. The average U. S. firm paid 16 cents of every dollar on pre-tax earnings in interest on its debt 15 years ago. This figure was 33 cents in the 1970s. The Brookings Institute predicted that if the level of debt that existed in the 1980s prevails, one in ten U.S. firms will go bankrupt in the coming decades. Finally, Reich argues that an economy based on asset rearranging plays one group's gains against another's losses. "Without trust," he states, "people won't dedicate themselves to common goals. They will turn their energies instead to defending their own interest. In a corporation, this means declining productivity."

Of course not all leveraged buyouts, mergers, and acquisitions are executed from motives of greed or from conspiracies among inside traders, financiers, board members, and upper-level managers. The rampant and uncontrolled growth of these sweeping transactions in the 1980s and the stock market crash in 1987 caused considerable concern among business professionals, economists, and business ethicists over the legitimate use of buying and selling companies as a competitive strategy. These large-scale and numerous transactions not only have national economic repercussions but raise the question of, as discussed earlier, "Who governs the corporation?" While the debate over buying and selling corporations as a competitive strategy continues, concern over increasing the moral power and capability of effective internal governance bodies and systems also remains a vital interest of many business owners, professionals, and ethicists. The remaining parts of this section summarize other governance problems and discuss methods for increasing the effectiveness of corporate governance at the shareholder, board-of-director, and employee levels.

OTHER GOVERNANCE ACTIVITIES IN CORPORATIONS

In publicly held corporations, according to the stakeholder theory (as discussed at the beginning of this chapter), boards of directors and CEOs are obliged to fairly and justly govern the firm by promoting the interests of their shareholders and stakeholders. This has not been the case in many companies, especially in the 1980s. The buying and selling frenzy of corporations for quick profits has increased a host of other questionable legal and moral corporate activities, which raise the question of how to improve responsible corporate governance. (This section is based on Carroll 1989; DeGeorge 1990; Hoffman and Moore 1990; and Prokesch 1988.) For example, **insider trading** (one individual in a firm accessing vital information to use for personal monetary advancement) has led to scenarios such as the one portrayed in the 1987 film *Wall Street*. An individual will use inside professionals to learn if a firm will sell to another company at a certain price per share above current stock price. That person then buys shares at present market value and later sells for profit at a higher price. This type of scandal usually involves cooperation from high-level managers in a firm. Dennis Levine and Ivan Boesky represent the insider trading scandals par excellence in the 1980s. Insider trading is illegal.

Two other questionable legal and moral corporate practices related to hostile takeovers and quick for-profit restructuring are *golden parachutes* and *greenmail*.

Golden parachutes are deals contracted between a firm and its high-level executives to protect and compensate the executives should the corporation be sold, merged, or restructured. Golden parachutes were designed to reward executives for their loyalty, to prevent top officers from leaving before a restructuring was complete, and to inhibit corporate raiders because of the high cost of releasing a firm's executives. More than half the country's largest companies have golden parachutes, up from 35 percent in 1987 (Lublin 1991). Experience has shown that golden parachutes represent deals corporate executives usually make for themselves without shareholder knowledge or approval. Informed and angered stockholders have sued and continue to sue boards of directors for permitting this practice—RCA had allotted golden parachutes to executives for upward of $62 million.

The United Shareholders' Association, an activist group, introduced proxy resolutions at more than a dozen firms in 1990 to kill golden parachutes without shareholder approval. Thirty-two percent of the stockholders voting approved this step (Lublin 1991). The Federal Deposit Insurance Corporation and federal banking regulators also are introducing rules to stop golden parachutes.

Greenmail, the buying back of shares by firms from corporate **raiders** at increased market prices, is another practice spurred by the takeover buying frenzy in the 1980s. As portrayed in the Broadway play and 1991 film *Other People's Money,* a corporate raider buys a percentage of stock in a company. The raider then threatens a hostile takeover of that firm. The firm's executives are leveraged to repurchase the stock from the raider at a higher price. The raider walks away with a quick profit. The company has to use assets or operating funds or has to borrow to buy back the shares. The forced nature of the threatened takeover raises ethical questions about this practice as a legitimate means to correct poor management. Also, the likelihood of insider cooperation by providing information and assistance raises the question of collusion and adequate governance of the firm.

How can governance be improved in corporations to address these and other immoral practices? The remaining parts of this chapter cover recommendations and methods many companies have proposed and used. The following section presents enhanced roles of boards of directors and shareholders. Also, corporate codes of ethics, ombudspersons, and peer review programs are discussed as means to improve moral conduct in corporations.

EXPANDED ROLES OF CORPORATE BOARDS AND SHAREHOLDERS

Harold Geneen (1984), a former ITT CEO, states, "Among the boards of directors of Fortune 500 companies, I estimate that 95% are not fully doing what they are legally, morally, and ethically supposed to do. And they couldn't even if they wanted to" (Hoffman and Moore 1990, 226). Corporate boards of directors are supposed to do the following:

❏ Establish and monitor procedures that assure that operating executives are informed of and obey applicable federal, state, and local laws

❏ Approve or veto all important executive management business proposals, such as corporate bylaws, mergers, or dividend decisions

❏ Hire and dismiss the chief executive officer and be able to disapprove the hiring and firing of the corporation's principal executives

❏ Report to the public and the shareholders how well the corporation has obeyed the law and protected the shareholders' investment (Nader, quoted in Hoffman and Moore 1990, 213)

Reasons why boards of directors do not execute these responsibilities are well known: CEOs often chair the boards, thereby controlling their own agendas. Because board members are not well staffed and do not have the time, money, or interest to monitor companies, they relinquish control to CEOs and high-level managers.

Ralph Nader, the famed consumer advocate, recommends restructuring boards as follows:

1. Hire full-time professional, salaried directors with staffs to carry out a board's functions.

2. Integrate the homogeneity of the board by electing nine corporate directors to limited terms, each with different oversight responsibilities (for example, finances, shareholder rights, employee concerns).

3. Make the shareholder electoral process more democratic. Stockholders who own at least 0.1 percent of common voting stock, or 100 or more individuals—not including a current corporate executive—could nominate three persons as directors to the board.

4. Also, have corporations become "federally chartered" (presently corporations are required to register only in a state) to make them more accountable and to open to public disclosure more of their activities (Nader, quoted in Hoffman and Moore 1990, 214–19).

Nader's proposals, which are viewed as more extreme recommendations than most, move a corporation closer to governance by society than by its privately controlled board. Nevertheless, these suggestions are a starting point for corporate board changes. However, without shareholder interest and commitment and without the necessary corporate leadership to initiate and follow through on these types of recommendations, boards of directors probably will remain rubber stamps of company executives who control the direction, operations, and legal and moral behavior of firms.

ACTIVIST ROLES OF SHAREHOLDERS IN CORPORATE GOVERNANCE

Since the 1970s, shareholders have been taking a more activist role in strategic corporate activities and proposals. Because of corporate abuses involving large-scale restructuring, takeovers, golden parachutes, greenmail, and other legally and morally questionable activities, two groups in particular have formed to exert influence on boards: the Council of Institutional Investors (CII) and the United Shareholders' Association (USA). These groups are exerting their power by influencing corporate agendas on social, economic, and political investing at board meetings; by suing corporations; and by introducing proxy shareholder resolutions on issues such as stopping golden parachutes and *poison-pill* proposals (perks and money guaranteed to be paid to executives if a takeover occurs; the aim is to discourage a takeover by making it too costly). The point here is that shareholders are aligning their interests into visible, powerful groups in order to exert their legitimate and rightful governing influence as a major stakeholder over CEOs and CEO-dominated boards of directors. Because of the political and dispersed nature of power in large corporations, it is often, though not always, necessary for shareholders to use the legal system, as well as organized activist voting roles, to make their voices and votes heard by corporate managers.

CORPORATE SELF-GOVERNANCE

Many corporations do attempt to govern their activities conscientiously by using ethics codes, ombudspersons, and peer review programs and mechanisms. At an operational level, corporate leaders in most large firms establish personnel policies and ethical codes of conduct to instruct and guide employee behavior. Major purposes of **ethics codes** include the following:

- ❏ State corporate leaders' dominant values and beliefs that are the foundation of the corporate culture
- ❏ Define the moral identity of the company inside and outside the firm
- ❏ Set the moral tone of the work environment
- ❏ Provide a more stable, permanent set of guidelines for right and wrong actions
- ❏ Control erratic and autocratic power or whims of employees (Bowie and Duska 1990)
- ❏ Serve business interests (since unethical practices invite outside government, law enforcement, and media intervention)

❑ Provide an instructional and motivational basis for training employees on ethical guidelines and for integrating ethics into operational policies, procedures, and problems

❑ Constitute a legitimate source of support for professionals who face improper demands and intrusions on their skills or well-being

❑ Offer a basis for adjudicating disputes among professionals inside the firm and between those inside and outside the firm

❑ Provide an added means of socializing professionals, not only in specialized knowledge but also in beliefs and practices the company values and rejects (Brooks 1989)

A 1986 survey of U.S. corporate ethics codes found that the most important topics to include were general statements of ethics and philosophy; conflicts of interest; compliance with applicable laws; political contributions; payments to government officials/political parties; inside information; gifts, favors, entertainment; false entries in books and records; and customer/supplier relations (Frankel 1989). Notable firms go further in detailing corporate obligations. For example, as exhibited earlier, Johnson & Johnson's credo and Borg-Warner's codes include and define their obligations to various stakeholders. Also, Boeing, General Mills, GTE, HP, McDonnell Douglas, Xerox, Norton, Chemical Bank, and Champion International, to name a few firms, have exemplary ethics codes and corporate value statements.

The problems with corporate ethics codes in general follow:

1. Most are too vague to be meaningful; that is, the codes do not inform employees about how to prioritize among conflicting interests of distributors, customers, and the company. What does being a "good citizen" really mean in practice?

2. Codes do not set priorities among beliefs, values, and norms. Should profit always supersede concern for customers or employees (Frankel 1989)?

3. Codes are not enforced in firms.

4. Codes are not communicated throughout most firms.

Ethics codes are a necessary but not sufficient means of assisting professionals with managing moral conduct in companies. Often a crisis or scandal that makes national media coverage is required to awaken executives to the need for enforced ethical codes of conduct. Certainly the Clarence Thomas hearings jolted and sensitized organizations in the United States to the problems surrounding sexual harassment in the workplace. Still, as stated in Chapter 1, companies increasingly continue to adopt ethics codes and to include ethics in their training programs without other necessary measures.

OMBUDSPERSON AND PEER REVIEW PROGRAMS   Other processes corporations use to prevent and manage immoral activities in the workplace are ombudsperson and peer review programs. The **ombudsperson** approach provides employees with a means of having their grievances heard, reviewed, and solved. Originating in Sweden, this concept was first tried at Xerox in 1972 and then at General Electric and Boeing (see Carroll 1989). Ombudspersons are third parties inside the corporation to whom employees can take their grievances. At Xerox, employees are encouraged to solve their problems through the chain of command before seeking the ombudsperson. However, if that process fails, the employee can go to the ombudsperson, who acts as an intermediary. The ombudsperson, with the employee's approval, can go to the employee's manager to discuss the grievance. The ombudsperson can continue through each managerial layer, including the president, if the problem is not satisfactorily solved for the employee. Ombudspersons have no power themselves to solve disputes or override managers' decisions.

Complaints usually center on salary disputes, job performance appraisals, layoffs, employee benefits, and job mobility in the firm. At General Electric, ombudspersons report that they handle 150 cases a year.

A problem with the ombudsperson approach is that managers may feel their authority is threatened. Employees who seek out ombudspersons also might worry about their managers retaliating against them from fear or spite. Confidentiality also has to be observed on the part of the ombudspersons.

The program has met with success at Xerox, General Electric, and Boeing. These three companies adopted job-posting procedures as a result of the program; Boeing introduced flexible work hours. The program also reflects the effectiveness of management policies and styles. Moreover, pressures are released and addressed, thus preventing unethical and illegal behavior.

The **peer review panel** is another program more than 100 large companies have used to enable employees to express and solve grievances and complaints, thus relieving stress and pressures that could lead to immoral activities. (This section is based on Carroll 1989 and Rubenstein 1986.) Employees use the chain of command initially whenever a problem exists. If the supervisors or executives do not solve the problem, the employee can request a peer review panel to hear it and help decide a solution. Two randomly selected workers in the same job classification are chosen for the panel along with an executive from another work unit. The selection must be reviewed against company policy. Peer review panels work when top management supports such due-process procedures and when these mechanisms are perceived as long-term, permanent programs.

Privately held and operated corporations must govern their own operations. In reality, governmental agencies, laws, regulations, and to some extent competitive forces in the free-market system act to constrain corporate illegality and immoral activities. The debate over the extent outside professionals and agencies should control private companies' activities will continue. At one end of the spectrum of control is the issue of paternalism; private firms do not want "Big Brother" to dictate their actions. At the other end of the spectrum is the issue of monopoly; without some outside control, corporations will misuse their power and usurp stakeholders' rights and best interests.

ETHICS OFFICES Ethics offices provide another method for handling moral questions and concerns in the workplace. More than 15 percent of the nation's companies that employ 50,000 or more people have established ethics offices over the past five years (Frankel 1989). Several of the largest corporations include Nynex, Pacific Bell, Texas Instruments, General Dynamics, and Dow Corning. Most companies have organized ethics offices to respond to public scandals, potentially harmful misconduct, and competitors' pleas.

Ethics offices serve several purposes. Telephone hot lines are the first step toward opening lines of communication in the organization. Professional staffs in these offices consisting of between 2 and 6 full-time people, with as many as 20 part-time employees, handle personal grievances and complaints, coordinate problems across other functional and staff areas, and create, update, and help enforce ethics codes. At General Dynamics, for example, more than 30,000 contacts with ethics officers since 1985 resulted in 1,419 sanctions, 165 terminations, 58 cases receiving financial reimbursement, 26 demotions, and 10 referrals to lawyers for civil lawsuits or to public prosecutors for criminal proceedings.

Some critics of this program have doubts whether full-time ethics offices are really necessary. They cite examples such as IBM and Johnson & Johnson, companies that have cultivated records of positive ethical conduct by using less-formal alternatives. Despite the skepticism about their effectiveness, ethics offices most likely will continue to increase for two reasons: (1) According to federal sentencing guidelines effective November 1, 1991, judges are asked to look more favorably on firms that can provide evidence of a substantial investment in programs and procedures designed to facilitate ethical behavior; and (2) the demise of several of the large Wall Street investment firms has awakened companies to the fact the unethical conduct of a few employees can have detrimental effects on the entire organization.

Financial concerns factor into the decision of whether or not to set up an ethics office. As stated earlier, many companies, such as Nynex, are investing in these programs in response to a public scandal or known misconduct. Others, such as Texas Instruments (TI), have seen competitors struggling with issues of ethical conduct and have implemented ethics offices to reinforce their previously written company code of ethics.

According to Carl Skoogland, TI's first ethics director, "We have had a written code for over 30 years but we wanted a formal focal point for reinforcing what we felt was an already strong culture." Whatever the motivation, ethics offices appear to be an effective means of handling a variety of personnel issues and moral issues in the workplace.

SUMMARY

This chapter focuses on the issue of whether or not corporations have a "conscience." Two opposing views are presented: The first view defines the corporation as having no conscience and as having responsibilities for its stockholders only. A second view discusses the corporation as a stakeholder with a conscience similar to that of an individual.

A third perspective, supported in this book, attempts to reconcile the two previous views. In this case, the corporation is seen as a social and economic stakeholder. The corporation is obliged to act in morally responsible ways toward its constituencies. Corporations must balance their moral, social, economic, and legal responsibilities for their stakeholders.

The concepts of *social contract* and *covenantal ethic* underlie the stakeholder view of the firm. They argue that corporations do have social and moral obligations to their stakeholders. These concepts also strongly base the success of a corporation on its relationships with its stakeholders.

Leadership, culture, and moral responsibility are influenced by corporate strategy and structure. At least four levels of strategy influence and guide corporate moral responsibility. These are enterprise, corporate, business, and functional strategies.

As a corporation implements and evaluates its strategic plans, social and moral responsibility issues also must be identified and addressed. Social audits are one method corporations have employed to monitor their performance on social responsibility issues.

Corporate structure is influenced by strategy and also affects ethical behavior. Decentralized supervision, lack of explicit policies regarding ethical conduct and leadership expectations, and overemphasis on short-term profits can lead to immoral conduct.

Two models of moral leadership are presented. The first perspective explains leadership across a continuum: manipulator, bureaucratic administrator, professional manager, and transforming leader. The second explains moral leadership in three "acts": from issue originators, Act I, to issue legislators, Act II, to issue institutionalizers, Act III.

Corporate culture is defined, and four principles of "high-ethics" cultures in firms are characterized.

Finally, the roles of shareholders, boards of directors, and CEOs are discussed. Recommendations for enhancing the effectiveness of the governance of these groups are presented. Ethics codes, ombudsperson programs, peer review programs, and ethics offices are explained as self-regulating moral vehicles in corporations.

QUESTIONS

1. Does a corporation have a "conscience"? Explain.

2. What are the problems with discussing corporations as persons? Do you agree? Why or why not?

3. Briefly explain the concept of "corporate internal decision structure." State your opinion of this concept.

4. Explain the *social contract* and *covenantal ethic* concepts. How do they relate to a stakeholder view of the corporation?

5. Identify limitations of the stakeholder perspective as discussed in this chapter. How is this perspective not useful according to critics?

6. In what ways does strategy influence other dimensions of an organization? Explain.

7. What are the differences among Act I, II, and III moral leaders? Identify an example of each type.

8. How is corporate culture related to ethics? Explain.

EXERCISES

1. Keith Davis states that "in the long run, those who do not use power in a manner in which society considers responsible will tend to lose it." Identify a real-life example of such a company and describe the situation. What is the status of the company currently?

2. Choose a corporation you have some experience with or knowledge about. What is the basic corporate strategy? How is that reflected in the corporate structure and culture? Does the firm place an emphasis on social responsibility? How?

3. Identify a moral leadership style you have worked with. Did you work well or poorly with that style? Why? If you could go back and reverse roles with this individual, how would you operate differently? What type of leader would you be? Why?

4. Identify a recent corporate merger, acquisition, or takeover. Do you agree or disagree with the actions taken? Why or why not? Do mergers, acquisitions, and takeovers constitute responsible or immoral business practices? Why or why not?

5. What are the potential advantages and downsides of mergers, acquisitions, and takeovers?

REFERENCES AND SUGGESTED READINGS

Baver, Raymond, and Dan Fenn Jr. 1973. What is a corporate social audit? *Harvard Business Review* (January/February).

Bowie, Norman, and Ronald Duska. 1990. *Business ethics*. 2d ed. Englewood Cliffs: Prentice Hall.

Brooks, Leonard. 1989. Corporate codes of ethics. *Journal of Business Ethics* 8: 117–29.

Buchholz, Rogene. 1991. Corporate responsibility and the good society: From economics to ecology. *Business Horizons* (July/August): 24.

Buchholz, Roger A. 1989. *Fundamental concepts and problems in business ethics*. Englewood Cliffs: Prentice Hall.

Burns, James M. 1978. *Leadership*. New York: Harper & Row.

Carroll, Archie B. 1975. Management ethics: A post-Watergate view. *Business Horizons* (April): 75–80.

———. 1989, 1993. *Business and society: Ethics and stakeholder management*. 1st, 3d eds. Cincinnati: South-Western.

———. 1991. The pyramid of corporate social responsibility. *Business Horizons* 34 (July/August).

Carroll, Archie B., and George Beiler. 1975. Landmarks in the evolution of the social audit. *Academy of Management Journal* (September): 589–99.

Corson, John, and George Steiner. 1974. *Measuring business's performance: The corporate social audit*. New York: Committee for Economic Development.

Cronin, Thomas. 1991. The concept of Acts I, II, III. Lecture at Bentley College.

Cullen, John, Bart Victor, and Carrol Stephens. 1989. An ethical weather report: Assessing the organization's ethical climate. *Organizational Dynamics* 18 (autumn).

Dahl, Jonathan. 1985. Manville offers $2.5 billion to settle claims. *Wall Street Journal*, 5 August, 3.

Davis, Keith. 1975. Five propositions for social responsibility. *Business Horizons* (June): 20–23.

Deal, Terrance, and A. Kennedy. 1982. *Corporate cultures: The rites and rituals of corporate life*. Reading, MA: Addison-Wesley.

DeGeorge, Richard. 1990. *Business ethics*. 3d ed. New York: MacMillan.

Des Jardins, Joseph R., and John McCall, eds. 1990. *Contemporary issues in business ethics*. 2d ed. Belmont, CA: Wadsworth.

Donaldson, Thomas. 1989. *The ethics of international business*. New York: Oxford Press.

Drucker, Peter. 1978. *Management: Tasks—responsibilities—practices*. New York: Harper & Row.

Estes, Ralph. 1976. *Corporate social accounting.* New York: John Wiley & Sons.

Evan, William, and R. Edward Freeman. 1988. A stakeholder theory of the modern corporation: Kantian capitalism. In *Ethical theory and business,* 3d ed., edited by Tom Beauchamp and Norman Bowie. Englewood Cliffs: Prentice Hall.

Fahey, L. 1987. Environmental analysis for strategy formulation. In *Strategic planning and management handbook,* edited by William King and D. Cleland. New York: Van Nostrand Rienhold.

Fleming, John E. 1978–1985. Public issues scanning. In *Research in corporate social performance and policy,* edited by Lee Preston. Greenwich, CT: JAI Press.

Frankel, Mark. 1989. Professional codes: Why, how, and with what impact? *Journal of Business Ethics* 8 : 109–15.

Freeman, R. Edward. 1984. *Strategic management: A stakeholder approach.* Boston: Pitman.

Freeman, R. Edward, and Daniel Gilbert Jr. 1988. *Corporate strategy and the search for ethics.* Englewood Cliffs: Prentice Hall.

French, Peter. 1977. The corporation as a moral person. Paper delivered at the Ethics and Economics Conference, University of Delaware, 11 November.

Friedman, Milton. 1970. The social responsibility of business is to increase its profits. *New York Times Magazine,* 13 September, 126.

Galbraith, John Kenneth. 1956. *American capitalism: The concept of countervailing power.* Rev. ed. Cambridge, MA: Riverside Press.

Geneen, Harold (with Alvin Moscow). 1984. *Managing.* Garden City, NY: Doubleday. Excerpts are found in Hoffman and Moore (1990).

Gerth, H. H., and C. Wright Mills, trans. 1946. *From Max Weber: Essays in sociology.* Cambridge: Oxford University Press.

Goodpaster, Kenneth. 1981. The H. J. Heinz Company: The administration of policy. No. 382-055. Boston: Harvard Business School.

Goodpaster, Kenneth, and John Matthews. 1982. Can a corporation have a conscience? *Harvard Business Review* (January/February).

Gordon, Judith, R. Mondy, A. Sharplin, and S. Premeaux. 1990. *Management and organizational behavior.* Boston: Allyn & Bacon.

Harrington, Susan. 1991. What corporate America is teaching about ethics. *The Executive* 5, no. 1 (February): 21–30.

Hitt, William. 1990. *Ethics and leadership: Putting theory into practice.* Columbus, OH: Battelle Press.

Hofer, Charles, and Dan Schendel. 1979. *Strategic management: A new view of business policy and planning.* Boston: Little, Brown.

Hoffman, W. Michael, and Jennifer Mills Moore, eds. 1990. *Business ethics.* 2d ed. New York: McGraw-Hill.

Hosmer, LaRue. 1987. *The ethics of management.* Homewood, IL: Irwin.

Hyman, Michael, Robert Skipper, and Richard Tansey. 1990. Ethical codes are not enough. *Business Horizons* (March/April): 15–22.

Jackall, Robert. 1988. *Moral mazes: The world of corporate managers.* New York: Oxford Universiy Press.

Janis, Irving. 1972. *Groupthink: Psychological studies of policy decisions and fiascoes.* Boston: Houghton Mifflin.

Jensen, Michael. 1984. Takeovers: Folklore and science. *Harvard Business Review* (November/December).

Keogh, James, ed. 1988. The business roundtable. *Corporate ethics: A prime business asset. A report on policy and practice in company conduct.* New York: The Business Roundtable (February).

Lanza, A. J., et al. 1935. Effects of the inhalation of asbestos on the lungs of asbestos workers. *Public Health Reports* 4 (January): 1–12.

Levitt, Theodore. 1958. The dangers of social responsibility. *Harvard Business Review* 26 (September/October).

Lipin, Steven. 1991. Citicorp unit's top officials are dismissed. *Wall Street Journal,* 11 November, A3.

Lublin, Joann. 1991. Firms rethink lucrative severance pacts for top executives as criticism swells. *Wall Street Journal,* 11 November, B1, B2.

Machiavelli, Niccolò. 1966. *The prince.* New York: Macmillan.

Nader, Ralph, et al. 1990. Who rules the corporation? Quoted in Hoffman and Moore (1990, 213).

Nader, Ralph, Mark Green, and Joel Seligman. 1976. *Taming the giant corporation.* New York: W. W. Norton. Also excerpted in Hoffman and Moore (1990, 210–19).

Naisbitt, John. 1982. *Megatrends: Ten new directions transforming our lives.* New York: Warner Books.

Naisbitt, John, and Patricia Aburdene. 1990. *Megatrends 2000: Ten new directions for the 1990s.* New York: Morrow.

———. 1991. *Megatrends 2000: Ten new directions for the 1990s.* New York: Avon.

Nash, Laura. 1990. *Good intentions aside: A manager's guide to resolving ethical problems.* Boston: Harvard Business School.

Pastin, Mark. 1986. Lessons from high profit, high-ethics companies: An agenda for managerial action. Chapter 11 in *The hard problems of management: Gaining the ethics edge,* 218–28. San Francisco: Jossey-Bass. Also quoted in Hoffman and Moore (1990, 624–28).

Posner, Barry, and W. Schmidt. 1984. Value and the American manager: An update. *California Management Review* (spring): 202–16.

Preston, Lee, ed. 1978–1985. *Research in corporate social performance and policy.* Vols. 1–7. Greenwich, CT: JAI Press.

Prokesch, Steven. 1988. Too much gold in the parachutes? *New York Times,* 26 January, 28f.

Reich, Robert. 1989. Leveraged buyouts: America pays the price. *New York Times*, 14 January, 25.

Rotbart, Dean. 1984. Manville Corp. faces increasing opposition to bankruptcy filing. *Wall Street Journal*, 1 January, 1.

Rubenstein, Larry. 1986. More firms use peer review panel to resolve employee grievances. *Wall Street Journal*, 3 December, 29.

Shapiro, Irving. 1979. Power and accountability: The changing role of the corporate board of directors. Paper presented at Carnegie-Mellon University, 24 October.

Sharplin, Arthur. 1988. Manville lives on as victims continue to die. *Business and Society Review* (spring): 25–29.

Shaw, James B., et al. 1991. From maternalism to accountability: The changing cultures of MA BELL and Mother Russia. *The Executive* 5, no. 1 (February): 7–21.

Shaw, William. 1991. *Business ethics.* Belmont, CA: Wadsworth.

Sturdivant, Frederick, and Heidi Vernon-Wortzel. 1990. *Business and society, a managerial approach.* 4th ed. Homewood, IL: Irwin.

Tejada, Carlos. 1996. Manville settlement gives trust enough cash for asbestos claims. *Wall Street Journal.*

Thompson, Arthur, Jr., and A. J. Strictland III. 1980. *Strategy formulation and implementation.* Plano, TX: Business Publications.

Toffler, Alan. 1970. *Future shock.* New York: Random House.

Torabzadeh, Khalil, et al. 1989. The effect of the recent insider-trading scandal on stock prices of securities firms. *Journal of Business Ethics* 8 : 303.

Velasquez, Manuel. 1982. *Business ethics: Concepts and cases.* Englewood Cliffs: Prentice Hall.

Weiss, Joseph W. 1991. *Act I, II, II leaders: Building a social responsibility model.* Waltham, MA: Bentley College.

Werhane, Patricia. 1989. The ethics of insider trading. *Journal of Business Ethics* 8 : 177.

Where ombudsmen work out. 1976. *Business Week*, 3 May, 114, 116.

5

THE CORPORATION AND EXTERNAL STAKEHOLDERS: MANAGING MORAL RESPONSIBILITY IN THE MARKETPLACE

The Ford Pinto entered the marketplace in September 1970. By 1976, it was Ford's most popular small car—over 2 million were sold. In 1978, in a landmark product liability case $128.5 million was awarded to a 19-year-old who, at age 13, was severely injured while riding with a friend in a Pinto. The car was hit in the rear; the gas tank erupted, killing the friend and burning most of the other boy's body. The fuel tank was located 7 inches from the car's rear bumper. Any significant impact from behind rendered the car a death trap. In June 1978, Ford ordered a complete recall of all 1.5 million Pintos built between 1970 and 1976 due to the growing pressure from the media, the government, pending court cases, and potential loss of future sales.

In an internal memorandum, Ford Motor Co. calculated the benefits and the costs associated with an $11 safety improvement which would have made the Pinto less likely to burn. The benefits would be prevention of death and serious burn injury of Ford Pinto passengers. The cost of a ruined car would have also been a benefit. Ford estimated that there were 180 deaths and an equal number of injuries associated with the Pinto. Ford, furthermore, estimated that each life was valued at $200,000 and that each serious burn injury was valued at $67,000. Ford also estimated that there were 2,100 burned vehicles, each with an associated cost of $700. The total value of the benefit would have been $49.5 million. The costs associated with an $11 safety improvement was installation of that device on 11 million cars and 1.5 million light trucks. Therefore, the total cost would have been $137 million (*Business and Society Review* 1977; Ford's $128.5 Million Headache 1978; Weinberger and Romeo 1989).

In July 1989, Ford Motor Company reported that it recalled 518,000 subcompact cars to repair defects that caused engine fires. The 1984 Escort, the Mercury Lynx, and the EXP had defects that could cause oil to leak onto the hot engine manifolds. Ford stated it did not tally the actual number of fires reported (Templin 1989).

Managing legal and moral responsibility in the marketplace is a major business of corporations. At stake are sizable lawsuits from consumers, boycotts of products, loss of image, reputation, name brand loyalty, competitiveness, and even survival. As the now classic Ford Pinto example shows, judges and juries can and do hold liable manufacturers who do not prevent and adequately manage dangerous products.

Other classic cases of corporations having to manage moral and legal obligations in the marketplace exist (see, for example, Barett 1985; Buchholz 1989; Geyelin 1991; Matthews et al. 1991; Weinberger and Romeo 1989), including the following cases:

❑ Between 1971 and 1974, more than 5,000 product liability lawsuits were issued by women who suffered severe gynecological damage from A. H. Robins Company's Dalkon Shield, an intrauterine contraceptive device. Although the company never recalled its product, it paid more than $314 million to settle 8,300 suits. It also established a $1.75 billion trust to settle ongoing claims.

❏ Procter & Gamble's Rely tampon was pulled from the market in 1980 after 25 deaths were allegedly associated with toxic shock syndrome from tampon use.

❏ In 1982, someone inserted cyanide into Johnson & Johnson's Extra-Strength Tylenol tablets, killing seven people. The company acted swiftly to remove the product until safety procedures were ensured.

❏ In 1978, the Center for Auto Safety said it had reports that Firestone's steel-belted radial TPC 500 tire was responsible for 15 deaths and 12 injuries. In October 1978, after attacking the publicity this product received, Firestone executives recalled 10 million of the 500-series tires.

❏ More recently, the Dow Corning Corporation faces liability suits against its silicone-gel breast-implant products. A number of women have reported illnesses due to the implants. A jury already awarded $7.3 million to one woman whose implant burst, causing her illness. More than 600,000 implants have been performed over the past 30 years. The company is alleged to have rushed the product to market in 1975 without proper safety tests and to have misled plastic surgeons about the potential for silicone to leak out of the surgically implanted devices. Dow spokespersons have stated the breast implants are "safe and effective." A Food and Drug Administration (FDA) moratorium on breast implants has been set, and Dow has stopped manufacturing the product, even though it is not recalling any products as of this writing (*Wall Street Journal*, 14 January 1992, A3).

These are only a few of numerous examples of corporations that have produced questionably safe or poor products that have had damaging effects in the marketplace and of firms that have had to manage sabotage or misuse of products—as in the Tylenol case.

Managing corporate responsibility in the marketplace is a negotiated process, usually involving numerous stakeholders. The media, industry and consumer groups, government agencies, community watchdog groups, scientific organizations, and PACs debate and negotiate the reasonableness and acceptability of controversial ads and of questionable product safety in the marketplace. Even the standards that affect the public's health and the uses of the environment are negotiated among a variety of stakeholders. Although many unsolved disputes between corporations and stakeholders go to courts for decisions, the competing claims also are settled through negotiated logic and the ethics of judges and juries.

This chapter raises the question What ethical principles and standards are appropriate for corporations and their stakeholders who negotiate differing moral claims about controversial advertisements, unsafe products, and questionable uses of the environment? As discussed in Chapter 3, is utilitarianism always a sufficient principle in these types of stakeholder debates and settlements? How relevant and applicable are the principles of justice, duty, and rights to corporations' and their stakeholders' activities when dealing with these kinds of issues and their settlement?

This chapter also provides an overview of the ethical obligations and problems corporations across industries manage in their pursuit of or flight from moral and legal responsibility to their stockholders and stakeholders. It begins by extending the discussion started in Chapter 4: the corporation's moral responsibility to the public and consumer stakeholders, in particular. What specific and realistic moral obligations do corporations have to consumers, other than to produce a reliable, salable product? Next, the chapter presents an overview of businesses' ethical responsibilities in advertising. This is an important topic, since public consumption begins when a firm persuades customers to buy products or services. What is the relationship between ethics and advertising? The discussion includes product safety and liability. Who is liable for unsafe products? What is the price to be paid and by whom for the use of questionable products that may be unsafe or that may be safe but used improperly? Then, Chapter 5 turns to the topic of a corporation's ethical responsibility to the environment. To what extent are corporations responsible for their industrial use of the environment? Who does the environment belong to? What is the relationship between ethics and ecology? The moral challenges corporations face and the methods several use to manage strategic issues are then discussed. An overview explains how corporations can understand and manage crises—which can have profound moral effects on the firm and its stakeholders. Finally, the chapter closes by discussing another powerful marketplace stakeholder of corporations: the government. Chapter 4 discussed methods firms use to regulate themselves; here the business/governmental regulatory process is discussed. How does the stakeholder approach enhance our understanding of the business/governmental regulatory process? Is government regulation of business activities really necessary?

5.1 CORPORATE RESPONSIBILITY FOR CONSUMER STAKEHOLDERS

Consumers are the most important business stakeholders. If consumers do not buy, commercial businesses cease to exist. "Consumer confidence" and spending also are important indicators of economic activity as well as of business prosperity. Because of this, businesses should theoretically put consumer interests foremost when designing, delivering, and servicing products. Unfortunately, this often is not the case. As the examples at the beginning of this chapter illustrate, many companies continue to manufacture or distribute unreliable products, placing consumers at risk; many advertisers continue to make false and misleading claims about products; and many food labels continue to have unclear and untrue statements about nutritional content. What, then, is the nature of corporate responsibility for consumers as stakeholders?

FREE-MARKET THEORY

The free-market theory holds that the primary aim of business is to make a profit. As far as business obligations toward consumers, this view assumes that an equal balance of power, knowledge, and sophistication of choice in the buying and selling of products and services exists between companies and customers. If businesses deliver what customers want, customers buy. Customers have the freedom and wisdom to select what they want and to reject what they do not want. Faulty or undesirable products are not supposed to sell. If businesses do not sell their products or services well, it is their own fault. The marketplace is an arena of arbitration. Consumers and corporations are protected and regulated, according to this view, by the "invisible hand."

PROBLEMS WITH THE FREE-MARKET THEORY   Although this theory has some validity, controversy also exists regarding its assumptions about consumer/business relationships. For example, consider these arguments:

1. Most businesses are not on equal footing with consumers at large. Large firms spend sizable amounts on research aimed at analyzing, creating, and—some argue—manipulating the demand of targeted buyers. Children, for example, are not aware of the effects of advertising on their buying choices.

2. Whether many firms' advertising activities truthfully inform consumers about product reliability, possible product dangers, and proper product use is questioned. As discussed in the next section, a thin line exists between deceit and artistic exaggeration in advertising.

3. The "invisible hand" is often nonexistent regarding consumer protection against questionable advertising and poorly manufactured products released to market. One reason a stakeholder view has become a useful approach for determining moral, legal, and economic responsibility is because the issues surrounding product safety, for example, are complex and controversial. Who is right and who is wrong and who is innocent and who is liable are problems that must be examined before informed judgments are made. The question then arises, what are realistic company obligations toward consumers in marketplace relationships and exchanges?

SOCIAL CONTRACT VIEW: CORPORATE DUTIES AND CONSUMER RIGHTS

Chapter 4 discussed the stakeholder view as based on a social contract between a corporation and its stakeholders. The social contract concept is grounded on certain obligations a firm has toward its constituencies, in this case consumers, and to society. Some of the more obvious but substantial duties of firms follow (Velasquez 1988):

❑ The duty to inform consumers truthfully and fully of a product and service's content, purpose, and uses

❑ The duty not to misrepresent or withhold information about a product or service that would hinder consumers' free choice

❑ The duty not to force or take undue advantage of consumers through fear or stress, or by other means that constrain rational choice

❑ The duty to take "due care" to prevent any foreseen injuries or mishaps a product (in its design and production) or its use may inflict on consumers

Additional and related rights consumers have in their social contract with corporations include the following:

❑ *The right to safety:* to be protected from harmful commodities that injure

❑ The right to free and rational choice: to be able to select among alternative products

❑ The right to know: to have easy access to truthful information that can help in product selection

❑ The right to be heard: to have available a party who will acknowledge and act on reliable complaints about injustices regarding products and business transactions

❑ The right to be compensated: to have a means to receive compensation for harm done to a person because of faulty products or for damage done in the business transaction (Buchholz 1992; Holloway and Hancock 1973)

These ethical guidelines can be applied to everyday individual business transactions as well as to more complicated exchanges between corporations and consumer groups. The guidelines also serve as the legal and moral foundations of corporate and consumer stakeholder relationships regarding advertising and issues surrounding product safety and liability.

5.2 CORPORATE RESPONSIBILITY IN ADVERTISING, PRODUCT SAFETY, AND LIABILITY

Advertising is big business in itself. In 1991, $126.7 billion was spent on this activity (*Wall Street Journal*, 13 January 1992, B1). Advertising is also a changing and innovative field. Recently, for example, **infomercials** have been introduced on television. These are program-length, soft-sell, pseudodocumentary ads that air late at night and imitate *Donahue* and *Nightline* in selling products. Sears, MCI, Volvo, GM, and a number of brand-name products are sold in infomercials. The Home Shopping Network is considered an all-infomercial channel. At issue is whether consumers can distinguish infomercials from factual news documentaries. The FDA has filed a dozen lawsuits since 1988 and has collected several million dollars in fines, judgments, and settlements from firms and ad agencies—including a baldness remedy company—that aired infomercials (*Wall Street Journal*, 14 January 1992, B6).

The purposes of advertising are to inform customers about products and services and to persuade them to purchase them. A corporation's ethical responsibility in advertising is to inform and persuade consumer stakeholders in ways that do not lie, deceive, conceal, or withhold the truth. This does not always happen.

PATERNALISM OR MANIPULATION?

Moral responsibility for consumers in advertising can be viewed as a continuum. At one end or extreme of the spectrum is paternalism; that is, "Big Brother" (or government) regulates the free market to ban and control what consumers can or should be allowed to hear and see. Too much protection could lead to too much control and enforcement over free choice. This is not desirable in a democratic market economy. At the other extreme of the continuum is corporate manipulation and control over consumers' free choice through cleverly researched ads aimed at deception. This is also undesirable, since it limits consumer choice and knowledge. Ideally, corporations should seek to inform consumers truthfully while using nonmanipulative persuasive techniques to sell their products.

Enforcement of advertising also can be viewed along this continuum. Outright bans on ads can result in court decisions that rule that consumer free choice has been violated and that a party was or could be harmed. On the other end, companies and industry groups can police themselves, as has been the case in the alcohol industry with the U.S. Brewers Association issuing guidelines against beer ads that promote overindulgence. Where moral and legal disputes over specific ads actually occur on the continuum is a matter of perception and judgment. Therefore, the general debate over the pros and cons of what constitutes ethical advertising continues—whether the topic centers on claims that women are discriminated against in beer ads; on claims that the general public is being deceived by food labels that show half-truths about fat and cholesterol content; on claims that tobacco ads target unsophisticated buyers by promoting smokers who live enviable, successful lifestyles; or on claims that jeans and lingerie ads may be too sexually explicit. The following discussion summarizes the major arguments for and against advertising.

ARGUMENTS FOR ADVERTISING

Arguments that justify advertising and the tactics of puffery and exaggeration include the following:

1. Advertising introduces people to and influences them to buy goods and services. Without advertising, consumers would be uninformed about products.

2. Advertising enables companies to be competitive with other firms in domestic and international markets. Firms across the globe use advertisements as competitive weapons.

3. Advertising helps a nation maintain a prosperous economy. Advertising increases consumption and spending, which in turn creates economic growth and jobs, which benefit all. "A rising tide lifts all ships." The tobacco industry alone adds 350,000 jobs to the economy. It indirectly affects the employment of another 1.5 million in related industries, and it contributed $10 billion in taxes in 1988. The alcohol industry earned revenues of more than $40 billion in 1988 (Steiner and Steiner 1991, 582, 591)

4. Advertising helps a nation's balance of trade and debt payments, especially in large industries, such as the food, automobile, alcoholic beverage, and computer technology industries, whose exports help the country's economy.

5. Proponents of advertising also argue that customers' lives are enriched by the images and metaphors advertising creates. Customers pay for the illusions as well as the products advertisements promote (Moore 1990).

6. Those who defend the general practice of advertising claim consumers are not ignorant. Buyers know the differences among lying, manipulation, and colorful hyperbole aimed at attracting attention. Consumers have freedom of choice. Ads do not coerce anyone to buy anything. Ads try to influence desires already present in people's minds. Companies have a constitutional right to advertise in free and democratic societies. Moreover, studies tend to show that advertising does not effectively cause people to buy products or services. In fact, the effectiveness of advertising in general is questionable (Velasquez 1988, 292–94).

ARGUMENTS AGAINST QUESTIONABLE ADVERTISING

Critics of questionable advertising practices argue that advertising can be harmful for the following reasons. First, a thin line exists between puffery and deception that advertisements often cross. For example, unsophisticated buyers, especially children and youth, are targeted by companies. The American Academy of Pediatrics, a consumer-oriented group, recently called for a ban on all televised food ads aimed at children. The charge is against sugary cereals, candy, and cookies. It is reported that

96 percent of Saturday morning food ads are for such products that lead to obesity. The Academy charged that "young children are unable to distinguish between programs and commercials and do not understand that commercials are designed to sell products" (Lipman 1991a).

Another argument against questionable advertising is that advertisements tell half-truths, conceal facts, and intentionally deceive with a profit goal in mind, not consumer welfare. For example, the $300 billion to $400 billion food industry is increasingly being watched by the FDA for printing misleading labels that undermine nutritional information. Misleading labels using terms such as "cholesterol free," "lite," and "all natural" are under attack with an added push from the Nutritional Education and Labeling Act of 1990. Consumers need to know quickly how much fat (a significant factor in heart disease) is in food, understandable standard serving sizes, and the exact nutritional contents of foods (Noble 1991). At stake in the short term for food companies is an outlay of between $100 million and $600 million for relabeling. In the long term, product sales could be at risk.

Critics of advertisements also argue that advertising stereotypes women—and men—and uses sex in manipulative ways to sell products. Stroh's Brewery recently spent millions on a TV ad for Old Milwaukee beer featuring a "Swedish Bikini Team." The brewer was charged with sexual harassment by five female employees. Stroh's ad agency, Hal Riney and Partners, also was sued by a female employee for sexual harassment. Further compounding the issue for Stroh's was the bikini team's nude appearance in the January 1991 issue of *Playboy.* It was discovered that members of the team also had a $3/minute call-in 900-number for sexually explicit conversations (Lipman 1991b).

Other industries also use sex to sell products. Calvin Klein's TV perfume ads (for Escape and Obsession products) feature models in sexually explicit poses. Calvin Klein's jeans ads present fully nude models. Coors beer TV ads highlight seminude adults. Davidoff's Cool Water fragrance ad features water-drenched male nudes in the sun. Jockey's underwear ads show baseball star Jim Palmer scantily clad. Sony uses seminudes to advertise photo printing paper. A Teledyne TV ad has angled shots of a nude man demonstrating the Water Pik massage showerhead (Elliot 1991). The debate on the increasing use of nudity in ads centers on (1) whether the United States is becoming more European in its tastes, helped along by European company owners with more liberal attitudes, or (2) whether consumers are being exploited without their consent or approval.

Critics also argue that tobacco and alcohol advertising, in particular, continue to unjustifiably promote ads for products that are dangerously unhealthy and whose effects endanger others. The tobacco industry spent $6.54 billion in magazine advertising in 1991. Cigarette companies reportedly are targeting ads at low-income women and minorities and focusing less on college-educated consumers. The December 1991 issue of the *Journal of the American Medical Association* reported that Old Joe Camel, the cartoon ad campaign for Camel cigarettes, lures youth to smoking. About seven years ago, surveys of 1,055 students ages 12 to 19 years showed that 97.7 percent had seen the ad, 97.5 percent knew the product, 58 percent thought the ads "look cool," 35 percent said they "like Joe as friend," and 33 percent reported Camel as their favorite brand. R. J. Reynolds contested these reports, noting that the average Camel smoker is 35 years of age (*Business Week* 1991, 34). The FDA recently asked R. J. Reynolds to remove the ad voluntarily. At stake for consumers who have a history of smoking, and for passive consumers (those indirectly affected by smokers), is the likelihood of getting lung cancer, heart disease, and other physical ailments. (Almost 400,000 people die each year from diseases related to smoking.) Also, smoking-related diseases reportedly cost the United States $52 billion annually in increased insurance premiums, health care charges, and lost productivity (Smoking 1990).

Alcohol ads also raise problems for consumers. Critics against alcohol ads argue that targeted youth, in particular, are enticed by suggestive messages linking drinking to contemporary lifestyles, popularity, and success. Consumer and public lobbying groups such as Mothers Against Drunk Driving (MADD) attest to the problems alcohol use and abuse cause in society.

ETHICS AND ADVERTISING

The debate on these issues in advertising will continue. Given the pros and cons presented so far, answers to the controversial questions cannot be absolutely determined. These issues are matters of judgment, values, and changing societal standards. As stated earlier, corporate moral responsibility for advertising to consumers must be reasoned on a case-by-case basis.

Ethically, corporations can use the following questions to address the moral responsibility of their advertising activities:

1. Is the consumer being treated as a means to an end or as an end? What and whose end?

2. Whose rights are being protected or violated intentionally and inadvertently? At what and whose costs?

3. Are consumers being justly and fairly treated?

4. Are the public welfare and good taken into consideration for the effects as well as the intention of advertisements?

At the same time, companies have a right to promote their products through advertising. The ethical questions, again, concern issues of who is unfairly harmed by information in certain ads.

ADVERTISING AND FREE SPEECH

Should certain ads be banned or restricted by courts? The Supreme Court has differentiated commercial speech from pure speech in the context of the First Amendment. (See *Central Hudson Gas and Electric Corporation v. Public Service Commission,* 1980, and *Posadas de Puerto Rico Associates v. Tourism Company of Puerto Rico,* 54 LW 4960; see also Steiner and Steiner 1991, 596, 597, for a discussion of this topic.) "Commercial speech" in ads and business transactions has not been as protected in courts as "pure speech." Pure speech is more generalized to ideas relating to political, scientific, and artistic expression in marketplace dealings. Commercial speech refers to language in ads and business dealings. The Court balances both these concepts of speech against the general principle that freedom of speech must be weighed against the public's general welfare. The four-step test developed by Justice Lewis F. Powell Jr. and used to determine whether commercial speech in advertisement could be banned or restricted (see Steiner and Steiner 1991) follows:

1. Is the ad accurate, and does it promote a lawful product?

2. Is the government's interest in banning or restricting the commercial speech important, nontrivial, and substantial?

3. Does the proposed restriction of commercial speech assist the government in obtaining a public policy goal?

4. Is the proposed restriction of commercial speech limited only to achieving the government's purpose?

The following section explores corporations' responsibility for consumer stakeholders regarding the manufacture, distribution, and sale of products.

PRODUCT SAFETY AND LIABILITY

Managing product safety is one of the most important tasks of corporations. Ethical responsibilities and economic issues go hand in hand in this area. A sign in one engineering facility reads, "Get it right the first time or everyone pays!" Product quality, safety, and liability are interrelated topics that increase in importance as product technology advances, adding to the risks for end users.

Product quality, competitiveness, safety, and liability are also sides of the same issue, whether the industry sells drugs, toys, household items, automotive products, asbestos, or silicone-gel implants. Manufacturers and businesses must be innovative to be competitive and profitable, but products also must be safe in order to protect individuals and to prevent damaging liability suits that cost companies millions of dollars and sometimes their survival. This section discusses the ethics of product safety and the nature of product liability.

HOW SAFE IS SAFE? THE ETHICS OF PRODUCT SAFETY

Thousands of people die and millions are injured each year using consumer products such as toys, lawn mowers, appliances, power tools, and household chemicals (U.S. Consumer Product Safety Commission 1994). But how safe is safe? Few, if any, products are 100 percent safe. Adding the manufacturing costs to bolster safety features to the sales price would, in many instances, discourage price-sensitive consumers. Just as companies use utilitarian principles when developing products for markets, consumers also use this logic when shopping and purchasing. Risks are calculated by both manufacturer and consumer. However, enough serious instances of questionable product quality and of lack of manufacturing precautions taken (for example, the Ford Pinto and the Firestone 500 tire cases mentioned earlier) occur to warrant more than a simple utilitarian ethic for preventing and determining product safety for the consuming public. This is especially the case for commercial products such as air-, sea-, and spacecraft that consumers have little, if any, control over.

The ValuJet crisis in 1996 sent a message to airline users: How much are you willing to pay, or not pay, for a safe flight? The fatal ValuJet crash awakened the Federal Aviation Administration (FAA) and resulted in the temporary grounding of that airline until safety requirements were met. The FAA rejected a recommendation, made three years before, that airlines install smoke detectors and fire suppression systems in cargo holds because the installation was too expensive. It is believed that lack of such safety systems may have cost the lives of 110 passengers on ValuJet Flight 592. Investigators believe a fire that raged in the plane's forward cargo hold was fueled by 144 oxygen generators—these generators should not have been on board. Burning generators also could have caused the crash of the aging DC-9 on May 11, 1996.

The cost of designing and installing such safety devices is estimated as less than $1 each per flight. The FAA calculated it would have cost $100,000 (other industrial estimates could have been as low as $50,000) to upgrade each plane. With 3,500 planes in the United States requiring upgrades, the total bill would be $350 million. For each of the 548 million passengers who flew on U. S. carriers in 1995, it is estimated the cost would have been 64 cents per passenger. Bill Wadlock at the Aviation Resource Safety Center at Embry-Riddle University in Prescott, Arizona, states: "There's a phrase in the airline business, and it's kind of depressing. 'If it's cheaper to fix something, they'll fix it. If it's cheaper to kill you, they'll kill you.'"

Product Safety Criteria The National Commission on Product Safety (NCPS) notes that product risks should be reasonable (see Hoffman and Moore 1990). Unreasonable risks are those that could be prevented or that consumers would pay to prevent if they had the knowledge and choice, according to the NCPS. Three steps firms can use to assess product safety from an ethical perspective follow (DeGeorge 1990, 182, 183):

1. How much safety is technically attainable, and how can it be specifically obtained for this product or service?

2. What is the acceptable risk level for society, the consumer, and the government regarding this product?

3. Does the product meet societal and consumer standards?

These steps, of course, will not be the same for commercial aircraft as for tennis shoes.

Estimates regarding the monetary value of human life vary. As Figure 5.1 illustrates, these "expert" estimates range from $3 million to $5 million.

Regulating Product Safety   Because of the number of product-related casualties and injuries each year and because of the growth of the consumer movement in the 1960s and 1970s, Congress passed the 1972 Consumer Product Safety Act, which created the Consumer Product Safety Commission (CPSC). This is the federal agency empowered to protect the public from unreasonable risks of injury and death related to consumer product use. The five-member commission is appointed by the president. The commission has regional offices across the country. The agency develops uniform safety standards for consumer products; assists industries in developing safety standards; researches possible product hazards; educates consumers about comparative product safety standards; and works to recall, repair, and ban dangerous products. Each year the commission targets potentially hazardous products and publishes a list of them with consumer warnings.

The commission has been somewhat successful in its efforts. It sent 1,200 recalls that affected 7 million products between 1972 and 1978. Another estimate showed the commission issuing more than 1,500 recalls and correcting 200 million products since its inception in 1972. The commission's effectiveness is related to the politics in Washington, DC. Its budget went from $42.1 million with a staff of 978 in 1981 to $34.5 million with 519 people in 1989 (see Steiner and Steiner 1991). The Bush administration also scaled back business safety regulations in many areas.

Consumer Affairs Departments   It also should be noted that many companies monitor their customers' satisfaction and safety concerns. Consumer Affairs Departments (CADs) are set up and coordinated in companies to ensure customer confidence and corporate responsiveness. Procter & Gamble, Digital Equipment Corporation, Federal Express, and Pepsi-Cola, to name only a few, have initiated such departments (see Steiner and Steiner 1991, 577, 578). Paying attention to customer suggestions and complaints is also good business.

■ FIGURE 5.1

How Much for a Life? $3 Million to $5 Million

Assume it would cost $500 per car to put antiskid brakes in each of 10 million cars sold this year—a total of $5 billion. Then assume that installing gadgets on this year's fleet ultimately would save 5,000 lives, or $1 million per life. Next assume that, on average, individuals value their lives at $5 million. Since the $1 million cost of saving a life is less than the $5 million value of life, the safety feature might be worth buying.

If seat belts cost, say, $50 per car and equipping 1 million cars with seat belts will save 1,000 lives, then regulators must assume lives are worth at least $50,000 a piece. Take another example. If smoke detectors cost $20 each and are widely seen as reducing the risk of a death by 1 chance in 10,000, then buyers surely would value their lives for at least 20 times $10,000, or $200,000. Again, if it takes an extra $100,000 in lifetime earnings to persuade miners to cope with 1 extra chance in 100 of premature death underground, then miners implicitly must value their lives at no more than 100 items $100,000, or $10 million.

The following table has estimates of the minimum value of a human life found in a sampling of governmental regulations. The figures take into account the medical and hospital costs avoided if calculated lives are saved, but these figures ignore other benefits of regulations, such as prevention of property damage and injuries that do not result in death. The estimates are based on risk experts' calculations of what a human life is worth considering all costs of installing various lifesaving gadgets. For example, if the government spent $110 million annually on a B-58 bomber ejection system and 5 lives would be saved, then each life is esitmated at $22 million ($110 million divided by 5).

Automobiles	Child restraint in cars	$ 1.3	million
	Dual master cylinders for car brakes	7.8	million
Ejection System	For the B-58 bomber	22.0	million
Flashing Lights	For railroad crossings	.73	million
Sea Walls	For protection against 100-year storm surges	96.0	million
Asbestos	Banned in brake linings	.23	million
	Banned in automatic transmission parts	1,200.0	million
Radiation	Safety standards for X-ray equipment	.4	million
	Safety standards for uranium mine tailings	190.0	million

SOURCE: Harvard Center for Risk Analysis.

Who is to say a life is worth $5 million rather than $500 million? Numerous studies calculate the value of life. But these studies do not produce uniform answers, nor do risk analysts claim this. People have very different estimates for risk. But researchers are still willing to generalize. Most middle-income U.S. citizens usually act as if their lives were worth $3 million to $5 million, based on what individuals demand in extra pay for dangerous jobs and what they spend for safety devices.

SOURCE: Peter Passell. 1995. How much for a life? Try $3 million to $5 million. *New York Times*, 29 January, F3. Reprinted by permission.

PRODUCT LIABILITY DOCTRINES   Who should pay for the effects of unsafe products, and how much should they pay? Who determines who is liable? What are the punitive and compensatory limits of product liability? The doctrine of product liability has evolved in the court system since 1916, when the dominant principle of *privity* was used. Until the *MacPherson v. Buick Motor Company* case, consumers injured by faulty products could sue and receive damages from a manufacturer if the manufacturer was judged to be negligent regarding a product defect. Manufacturers were not held responsible if consumers purchased a hazardous product from a retailer or wholesaler (Des Jardins and McCall 1990, 255). In the *MacPherson* case, Buick, the defendant, was ruled liable for harm done to Mr. MacPherson. A wheel on the car had cracked. Although MacPherson had bought the car from a retailer and although Buick had bought the wheel from a different manufacturer, Buick was charged with negligence. Even though Buick did not intend to deceive the client, the court ruled the company responsible for the finished product (the car), which—the jury claimed—should have tested its component parts (see Posch 1988, 3, and Sturdivant and Vernon-Wortzel 1991, 305). The doctrine of *negligence* in the area of product liability thus was initiated.

The negligence doctrine meant that all parties, including the manufacturer, wholesaler, distributor, and sales professionals, could be held liable if reasonable care in producing and selling a product that injured a person was not observed.

The doctrine of *strict liability* is an extension of the negligence standard. Strict liability holds that the manufacturer is liable for a person's injury or death if a product goes to market that is dangerous because of a known or knowable defect. A consumer has to prove three things to win the suit: (1) an injury happened, (2) the injury resulted from a product defect, and (3) the defective product was delivered by the manufacturer being sued (Carroll 1989, 258; Des Jardins and McCall 1990, 255).

Absolute liability is a further extension of the strict-liability doctrine. Absolute liability was used in 1982 in the *Beshada v. Johns Manville Corporation* case. Employees sued Manville for diseases later found related to exposure to asbestos. The court ruled the manufacturer liable for not warning of product dangers, even though the danger was scientifically unknown at the time of the production and sale of the product (Carroll 1989, 259). Medical and chemical companies, in particular, whose products could produce harmful, but unknowable, side effects years later would be held liable under this doctrine.

Legal and Moral Limits of Product Liability   The legal and moral limits of product liability suits evolve historically and are, to a large degree, determined by political as well as legal stakeholder negotiations and settlements. Consumer advocates and stakeholders (for example, the Consumer Federation of America, the National Conference of State Legislators, the Conference of State Supreme Court Justices, and activist groups) argue for and lobby for strong liability doctrines and laws to protect consumers against powerful firms that, these stakeholders contend, seek profits over consumer safety. In contrast, advocates of product liability law reform (for example, those led by former vice president Dan Quayle, corporate stockholders, Washington lobbyists for businesses and manufacturers, and the President's Council on Competitiveness) argue that liability laws in the United States have become too costly, excessive, routine, and arbitrary. Liability laws inhibit companies' competitiveness and willingness to innovate, they claim. Also, insurance companies claim that all insurance-paying citizens are hurt by excessive liability laws that allow juries to award hundreds of millions in punitive cases; as a result, insurance rates rise.

However, a recent two-year study of product liability cases concluded that punitive damages are rarely awarded, more rarely paid, and often reduced after the trial (*Wall Street Journal*, 6 January 1992, B1). The study, partly funded by the Roscoe Pound Foundation in Washington, DC, is the most comprehensive effort to date to show the patterns of punitive damage awards in product liability cases over the past 25 years.

The results of the study follow:

1. Only 355 punitive-damage verdicts were given by state and federal court juries during this period. One fourth of those awards involved a single product—asbestos.

2. In the majority of the 276 cases with complete posttrial information available, punitive damage awards were abandoned or reduced by the judge or the appeals court.

3. The median punitive damage returned to all product liability cases paid since 1965 was $625,000—a little above the median compensatory damage award of $500,100. Punitive damages were significantly larger than compensatory awards in only 25 percent of the cases.

4. The factors that led to significant awards—that lawyers most frequently cited when interviewed or surveyed—were "failure to reduce risk of a known danger and failure to warn consumers of those risks.

Other studies confirm these findings. A 1990 federal study of product liability suits in five states showed that plaintiffs won less than 50 percent of the cases; a Rand Corporation study that surveyed 26,000 households nationwide found that only 1 in 10 of an estimated 23 million people injured each year thinks about suing; and the National Center for State Courts surveyed 13 state court systems from 1984 to 1989 and found that the 1991 increase in civil caseloads was for real-property rights cases, not suits involving accidents and injuries (*Wall Street Journal*, 6 January 1992, B1).

Presently, 33 states have laws in the making to limit liability and reduce damage awards. Seven states already have limited the amount of punitive damages that can be awarded (*Wall Street Journal*, 6 January 1992, B1). The different stakeholders have drawn battle lines on the issue of limiting product liability laws. We must continue to observe changes in tort reform, industrial competitiveness, general economic conditions, and public opinion to understand how product liability laws will evolve. The next section discusses corporations' obligations to the environment.

5.3 CORPORATE RESPONSIBILITY FOR THE ENVIRONMENT

General Motor Corporation will spend approximately $45 million to settle federal government charges which allege the company has installed illegal pollution devices inside nearly a half million Cadillacs since 1991. These installations have resulted in carbon monoxide emissions of up to three times the legal limit. The case, which is the largest brought under the Clean Air Act, ruled on behalf of the Environmental Protection Agency and imposed an auto recall aimed at curbing damage to the environment. GM will pay an $11 million fine, as well as spend approximately $25 million to recall and retrofit the polluting vehicles. The company will also spend an additional $8.75 million on projects to offset emissions from these vehicles, including buying back older vehicles or purchasing new school buses that burn cleaner fuels. (Environmental Laboratory Washington Report 1995)

A time existed when corporations used the environment as a free and unlimited resource. That time is ending, in terms of international public awareness and increasing legislative control. The magnitude of environmental abuse, not only by industries but also by human activities and nature's processes, has awakened an international awareness to protect and save the environment. At risk is the most valuable stakeholder, the earth itself. Depletion and destruction of air, water, and land are at stake in terms of natural resources. Consider the destruction of the rain forests in Brazil; the thinning of the ozone layer above the earth's atmosphere; climatic warming changes from carbon dioxide accumulations; the smog in Mexico City, Los Angeles, and New York City; and the pollution of the seas, lakes, rivers, and groundwater supplies contaminated from toxic dumping. At the human level, environmental pollution and damage cause heart and respiratory diseases and lung and skin cancer.

MOST SIGNIFICANT ENVIRONMENTAL PROBLEMS

The U. S. public and experts at the Environmental Protection Agency (EPA) differ in their identification of the nation's top-four environmental problems. A national random survey of 1,413 people by the Roper Organization, Inc., found the following ranking: (1) water pollution from manufacturing plants, (2) oil spills, (3) hazardous-wastes releases, and (4) industrial air pollution. Destruction of the ozone layer was ranked 5th, and global warming was ranked 15th. In contrast, EPA environmental experts offered the following ranking: (1) global climate change, (2) habitat destruction, (3) species extinction, and (4) ozone-layer depletion. The EPA ranking was based on the "huge scale of the problems, their irreversible aspects and the length of time needed to solve them" (Stipp 1990).

A subcommittee of EPA experts also noted the following risks to human health: air pollution, worker exposure to toxic chemicals, and drinking contaminants. These findings, based on a recent EPA report, "Reducing Risks: Setting Priorities and Strategies for Environmental Protection," are significant since EPA advisers state that the agency will begin to set priorities based not only on public concerns but also on rigorous risk assessment aimed at policies that give importance to "overall ecological destruction" as well as to lowering human health risks from specific pollutants (Stipp 1990).

The scope and seriousness of environmental abuse consumers and corporations, in particular, are contributing to are illustrated here:

❏ "The United States produces an estimated 212 million tons of hazardous waste each year—about a ton for every man, woman, and child in this nation. . . . [T]he vast bulk of this is refinery or chemical waste. . . . [O]utput of hazardous waste is estimated to be growing at the rate of about 3 percent per year. The great danger is that at some point an underground aquifer will be contaminated, which could threaten the health of thousands" (Bloom and Morton 1991, 80).

❏ More than 2,500 excess cancers are linked to daily exposure to toxic air pollution. In the United States, 135 million people live in areas threatened by air pollution (Shabecoff 1989). Five U.S. manufacturing companies alone released approximately 1.3 billion pounds of toxic chemicals into the air, water, and earth in 1988.

❏ A study by the American Society of Zoologists announced that the Florida Keys could be destroyed at the beginning of the twenty-first century. Pollution from human sewage and agricultural runoff is a major cause of the harm (Keating 1991).

❏ Increased amounts of carbon dioxide from automobile exhaust and of chlorofluorocarbons (CFCs) from coolants, aerosols, solvents, and other products are depleting the ozone layer in the stratosphere. This is causing global warming, a condition that could lead to melting polar glaciers, rising sea levels, and destroyed agricultural lands. Moreover, each 1 percent decrease in ozone is estimated to result in a 4 percent to 6 percent increase in skin cancer (Shea 1989; cited in Buchholz 1992). Scientists also report that by the turn of the century, depletion of the ozone layer will cause 1.6 million additional cataracts a year and 300,000 new skin cancers worldwide. Ultraviolet radiation, also a cause of ozone layer decay, depresses the human immune system—which increases the risk of infectious diseases (Ozone depletion 1991).

Representatives of more than 100 governments agreed in 1995 to phase out developed countries' production of methyl bromide, an agricultural pesticide that is the only industrial chemical responsible for weakening the earth's protective ozone shield that had not been previously designated for elimination.

Scientists say that if the production of methyl bromide were to continue, it would account for 15 percent of ozone depletion in the year 2000. CFCs were phased out by the developed countries by the end of 1992. Developing countries are to phase them out by 2010 (Stevens 1995).

❏ In the United States, individuals and industries throw out 400,000 tons of solid waste—trash—each day. Landfills are overflowing, while communities are fighting the addition of dump and incineration sites to their areas. NIMBY ("Not in My Back Yard") groups are protesting site proposals due to the side effects of air and underground water pollution from trash dumping (Environmental Protection Agency 1988; cited in Buchholz 1992).

The list goes on. Cancer-related diseases are caused by asbestos fibers found in building insulation, automobile brakes, and scores of other products; acid rain carrying nitrogen and sulfur oxide particles in the form of water vapor is killing fish and damaging forests; a major cause of air pollution is the burning of fossil fuels—smog has rendered Mexico City's air quality one of the worst in the world; indoor air pollution results from formaldehyde and other chemical fumes as well as from cigarette smoke; and surface water and groundwater pollution results from runoffs that transport chemicals from agricultural sites, oil-coated roads, and construction sites. Large bodies of water have been severely damaged: the Boston Harbor, Lake Erie, the Hudson River, the Love Canal near Niagara Falls, and the Mississippi River, to name only a few. The cumulative effect of these pollutants adds up to significant air, water, and earth damage.

CAUSES OF ENVIRONMENTAL POLLUTION

Some of the most pervasive factors that have contributed to the depletion of resources and damage to the environment follow:

1. *A growing consumer affluence.* Increased wealth—as measured by real personal per capita income—has led to increased spending, consumption, and waste.

2. *Increasing materialistic cultural values.* Values have evolved to emphasize consumption over conservation—a mentality that believes "bigger is better," "me first," and a throwaway ethic.

3. *Increasing urbanization.* Concentrations of people in cities increase pollution.

4. *Population explosion.* From 1900 to 1990, the global population grew from 1.2 billion to 5.5 billion. Population growth means more industrialization, product use, waste, and pollution.

5. *New and uncontrolled technologies.* Technologies are produced by firms that prioritize profits, convenience, and consumption over environmental protection.

6. *Industrial activities.* The magnitude of industrial activities that, as stated earlier, have emphasized depletion of natural resources and destructive uses of the environment for economic reasons has significantly caused environmental decay (Steiner and Steiner 1991). This book is most concerned with industrial activities that abuse the environment.

ENFORCEMENT OF ENVIRONMENTAL LAWS

A number of governmental regulatory agencies have been created to develop and enforce policies and laws to protect the general and workplace environments. The Occupational Safety and Health Administration (OSHA), the Consumer Product Safety Commission, the Environmental Protection Agency , and the Council on Environmental Quality (CEQ) are among the more active agencies that regulate environmental standards. The EPA, in particular, has been a leading organization in regulating environmental abuses by industrial firms.

In 1970, the Nixon administration concentrated EPA's mission and activities on controlling and decreasing the following pollution areas: toxic substances, radiation, air, water, solid waste (trash), and pesticides. The EPA has used its regulatory powers to enforce several important environmental laws:

❏ *The Clean Air Act of 1970, 1977, 1989, and 1991.* The latest revision of this law includes provisions for regulating acid rain, ozone reduction, and the capability of companies to sell or transfer their right to pollute within same-state boundaries—before, pollution rights could be bought, sold, managed, and brokered like securities.

❏ *The Federal Water Pollution Control Act of 1972.* Revised in 1977, this law controls the discharge of toxic pollutants into the water.

❏ *The Resource Conservation and Recovery Act (RCRA) of 1980.* This legislation provides guidelines for the identification, control, and regulation of hazardous wastes by companies and state governments. The $1.6 billion Superfund also was created by Congress in 1980. It provides for the cleanup of chemical spills and toxic-waste dumps. Chemical, petroleum, and oil firms' taxes help keep the Superfund going, along with U.S. Treasury funds and fees collected from pollution control. By 1989, the EPA had $8.5 billion in the program (see Sturdivant and Vernon-Wortzel 1991, 324). During 1991, the EPA's enforcement of the Superfund experienced legal setbacks because the courts were less willing to view federal environmental concerns as superseding states' statutory and constitutional language (Moses 1991).

The overall effect of enforcing and controlling environmental pollution and resource depletion is incrementally improving. An expert reports:

> Since 1975, when most of the consistent environmental measurements began, overall improvement amounts to only 15 percent. In a few scattered instances, pollution levels have been significantly reduced, by 70 percent or more: lead in the air; DDT and PCBs in wildlife and people; mercury pollution in the Great Lakes; strontium 90 in the food chain; and in some local rivers, phosphate pollution. Each of these pollutants has been effectively controlled not by high-tech devices, but by simply stopping its production or use. Still, the EPA continues to enforce environmental pollution laws. (Commoner 1990)

The EPA's annual enforcement scorecard for 1991 showed 125 indictments, 72 convictions, 550 months of prison sentences served by convicted defendants (a 121 percent increase over 1990), and $14.1 million in fines collected. Critics argue that few larger firms receive jail terms for polluting. Sixty percent of firms that were caught and convicted had sales under $1 million and fewer than 50 employees (Allen 1991). Although enforcement of corporate violations is ongoing, the effectiveness of enforcement is debatable.

THE ETHICS OF ECOLOGY

The role of corporations as economic institutions based primarily on a utilitarian ethic is under attack (Buchholz 1991; Sagoff 1990). Advocates of a new environmentalism argue that when the stakes approach the damage of the earth itself and human health and survival, the utilitarian ethic alone is an insufficient logic to justify continuing negligence and abuse of the earth. For example, Sagoff (1990) argues that cost/benefit analysis can measure only desires, not beliefs. In support of corporate environmental policies, he asks:

> Why should we think economic efficiency is an important goal? Why should we take wants and preferences more seriously than beliefs and opinions? Why should we base public policy on the model of a market transaction rather than the model of a political debate? . . . [E]conomists as a rule do not recognize one other value, namely, justice or equality, and they speak, therefore, of a "trade-off" between efficiency and our aesthetic and moral values. What about the trade-off between efficiency and dignity, efficiency and self-respect, efficiency and the magnificence of our natural heritage, efficiency and the quality of life? (363)

This line of reasoning raises questions such as What is human life worth? What is a "fair market" price or replacement value for Lake Erie? The Atlantic Ocean? The Brazilian rain forests? The stratosphere?

Buchholz (1991, 19) gives five arguments for corporate social responsibility in advocating for an ecology-based organizational ethic:

1. Organizations' responsibilities go beyond the production of goods and services at a profit.

2. These responsibilities involve helping to solve important social problems, especially those they have helped create.

3. Corporations have a broader constituency than stockholders alone.

4. Corporations have impacts that go beyond simple marketplace transactions.

5. Corporations serve a wider range of human values than a sole focus on economic values can capture.

Although these guidelines serve as an ethical basis for understanding corporate responsibility for the environment, utilitarian logic and cost/benefit methods still will continue to play key roles in corporate decisions regarding their uses of the environment. Also, judges, courts, and juries will use cost/benefit analysis in trying to decide who should pay and how much when settling case-by-case environmental disputes. Costs will be estimated. For example, it has been estimated it could cost $300 billion to clean up existing hazardous waste sites (Bloom and Morton 1991). The EPA estimates additional spending to enforce the Clean Air Act of between $2 billion to $8 billion a year to control acid rain, between $8 billion to $20 billion for smog control, and between $1 billion and $6 billion to control toxic air pollution (Shabecoff 1989; also see Statistical Abstract of the United States 1996, 116th ed., p. 329). Some experts and industry spokespersons argue that costs for further controlling pollutants such as smog outweigh the benefits. Nevertheless, an administrator of the Clean Air Working Group—the major industry lobbying organization—states, "At stake is our hides" (Shabecoff 1989).

RIGHTS OF FUTURE GENERATIONS AND RIGHT TO A LIVABLE ENVIRONMENT

The evolution of laws, regulations, and corporate practices and restrictions regarding the use and abuse of the natural environment continues. Different stakeholders will protect their turf and promote their competing interests. However, as global warming, depletion of the ozone layer, and pollution of air, land, and water continue at an accelerated pace into the twenty-first century, the following ethical principles will gain importance in legal and moral ecological controversies: (1) rights of future generations and (2) right to a livable environment.

The debate about the rights of future generations centers around the extent present generations should bear disproportionate burdens for the sake of future generations. In other words, how much of the environment can a present generation use or destroy to advance its own economic welfare? According to the ethicist John Rawls (as paraphrased by Velasquez

1988, 254), "Justice requires that we hand over to our immediate successors a world that is not in worse condition than the one we received from our ancestors."

The right to a livable environment is an issue William Blackstone (1974) advanced (see also Velasquez 1988). The logic is that each human being has a moral and legal right to a decent, livable environment. This "environmental right" supersedes individuals' legal property rights and is based on the belief that human life is not possible without a livable environment. Therefore, laws must enforce the protection of the environment based on human survival. It has been noted (again, see Velasquez 1988, 239) that several landmark laws in the late 1960s and 1970s (Water Pollution Control Act, 1972, 1977; Clean Water Act, 1977; Air Quality Act, 1967; Clean Air Amendments, 1970, 1991) were not based on utilitarian cost/benefit analysis but more on the logic related to Blackstone's "environmental right." Although cost/benefit analysis will remain a central method for determining fault and liability in environmental court cases, principles of rights, justice, and duty as discussed here and in Chapter 3 also will serve as important criteria for determining benefits and costs, as well as for ecological legislation.

RECOMMENDATIONS TO MANAGERS

This section on the environment concludes with four questions Bloom and Morton (1991, 83) suggest as advice to managers. Although the questions are aimed at assessing corporate responsibility regarding hazardous waste, they apply to managing environmental problems as well:

1. How much is your company really worth? (This question refers to the contingent liability a firm may have to assume depending on its practices.)

2. Have you made hazardous-waste risk analysis an integral part of your strategic planning process?

3. Does your information system look out for environmental problems?

4. Have you made it clear to your officers and employees that strict adherence to hazardous-waste requirements is a fundamental tenet of company policy?

These are practical questions that reflect the relatedness of economic and ethical concerns.

5.4 THE GOVERNMENT AS CORPORATE REGULATOR AND STAKEHOLDER

Governmental regulation is an integral part of the economic affairs of business in America. The U.S. Constitution (Article 1, Section 8) and system of national governance define the roles of federal government as lawmaker, regulator, and enforcer over interstate and foreign commerce, taxes, duties, imports, tariffs, excises, the military, foreign affairs, bankruptcy, copyrights, and patents. Still, the nature of the changing business/government relationship in the United States is dynamic. As discussed next, the dynamic character of this relationship is based on (1) adversity , (2) their clashing value systems , and (3) the politics of the regulation process.

The nature of the government/business relationship is adversarial; that is, business and government professionals often have contrary missions, goals, and roles. Government officials see their roles as "probers, inspectors, taxers, regulators, and punishers of business transgressions" (Jacoby 1975). Business professionals, in contrast, tend to see their roles as entrepreneurs, investors, and risk takers who do not need or desire unnecessary bureaucratic controls.

This adversity is based on an underlying set of clashing values. Governmental goals and operations are grounded in collectivistic values aimed at serving the public interest and good. Business goals and practices are based on individualistic values that serve private, economic self-interests (Jacoby 1975). Governmental values emphasize group self-interests; business values stress economic return on investment for individual stockholders and stakeholders. These opposing values account for much of the ongoing conflicts of interest among businesses, government, and the public.

The business/government relationship in the United States is also political in nature. At the national level, Democratic and Republican presidents, Congresses, and judicial officials and judges with different political ideologies determine or influence to a large degree the direction, nature, and extent of legislation; regulations and enforcement; and expenditures that empower regulations. President Lyndon Johnson, for example, created the "Great Society" concept in the 1960s and passed more social legislation than any other president. President Ronald Reagan campaigned for less governmental control and regulation in the 1980s and succeeded in building on President Ford's and President Carter's deregulation of railroads, airlines, trucking, financial firms, natural-gas companies, and other industries.

The making, enforcement, and dispute settlement of laws and regulations also reflect the political process of coalition building, which helps shape and determine regulatory outcomes. Senators and congresspersons are generally influenced by paid lobbyists and political action committees that promote special interests and legislation to support or inhibit the passage of specific laws affecting labor, unions, realtors, educators, home builders, medical doctors, and other professional and private groups.

THE ETHICS OF POLITICS AND REGULATION

Critics of the politics of the regulatory process as it has evolved ask two major questions: Who represents the interests of the public, and who regulates whom? This has been a retort to the first question: Which public? Whose particular interests? Without paid lobbyists or representation from PACs, critics of the regulatory "game" argue, it is difficult, if not impossible, to implement legislation and regulations regarding particular interests. The ethical problem raised in the politics of paid lobbyists and of PACs is whether and to what extent the public's freedoms embodied in the First Amendment are being exercised, violated, and even bought. Who regulates whom seems to depend on the "golden rule": "Who has the gold, rules" (Sabato 1984). The U.S. pluralistic capitalism ideal is a balance between a free, open political process and a "marketplace of political ideas" (Steiner and Steiner 1991). From an ethical perspective, these questions arise: To what extent is the government responsibile for promoting and protecting the rights of individual citizens? To what extent should the government ensure the just distribution of resources within its society? What is the government's duty regarding the public's freedom of choice in the marketplace?

THE GOVERNMENT'S ROLES IN REGULATING AND INFLUENCING BUSINESS

The U.S. government plays several regulatory and nonregulatory, even contradictory, roles with business. The government is a major purchaser of business goods and services (such as military hardware) as well as a regulator and controller of business activities. The government competes with some businesses (such as in postal services) while financing and subsidizing other businesses (for example, agriculture). The government not only breaks up business monopolies (for example, AT&T) but also bails them out (for example, the 1979 $1.2 billion loan to Chrysler and the ongoing savings and loan multimillion-dollar bailout). Depending on the climate of national and global economics, on industrial competitiveness, and on geopolitics, the roles of government with business change. During the Reagan years, less government was seen as better. Deregulation was emphasized, as was a hands-off approach. In the 1990s, with the rise of Japanese superior industrial and economic competitiveness, the automotive, computer, and auto parts industries, in particular, are calling for more governmental protection and intervention.

In general, the national government influences business by doing the following (see Steiner and Steiner 1991, 285–90):

1. Defining the rules of the competitive game (for example, labor/management relations, advertising, safety regulations, antitrust laws)

2. Promoting and subsidizing business (such as loan guarantees, tariff protections, tax incentives, purchase of business goods and services—$1.1 trillion by federal, state, and local governments)

3. Using business as an instrument of governmental aims (for example, enforcing companies to pay minimum wages, to use minority hiring policies, to subcontract to minority businesses)

4. Setting national economic goals

5. Protecting society's social, physical, and workplace interests (such as environmental laws, safety laws, consumer laws)

6. Redistributing resources to meet moral and social goals (for example, transfer payments, research and development expenditures, tax incentives)

7. Promoting and conserving quality-of-life needs (such as environmental laws)

8. Setting standards to promote public interests and to resolve potential business conflicts (for example, businesses sometimes seek regulation that is good for the environment but that cannot be implemented unless all competitors comply; otherwise, some businesses would profit at others' expense)

9. Controlling unfair business practices (such as monopolies)

Most of these functions cannot be accomplished by individual businesses.

TYPES OF GOVERNMENTAL REGULATION IN BUSINESS

Governmental regulation of business activities involves designated agencies, boards, and commissions created by, empowered by, and funded by Congress to set and enforce standards for particular industries and, as is the case more recently, for particular business areas and their policies across industries (that is, marketing, manufacturing, purchasing, international operations, legal, personnel, planning, finance, and so on). (See Weidenbaum 1989 for a more complete listing of federal regulatory agencies and business functional areas.) For example, the Federal Trade Commission (FTC); the Food and Drug Administration; the Consumer Products Safety Commission; the United States Department of Agriculture (USDA); the Department of Health, Education, and Welfare (HEW); and others work to regulate and monitor marketing and advertising activities. The Department of Energy, the Treasury Department, the Drug Enforcement Administration (DEA), the Nuclear Regulatory Agency, the Environmental Protection Agency, and the Occupational Safety and Health Administration monitor manufacturing standards and activities. The Equal Employment Opportunity Commission (EEOC), the National Labor

Relations Board (NLRB), and others set guidelines and enforce personnel standards and laws. In finance, the Internal Revenue Service, the Securities and Exchange Commission (SEC), and the Federal Reserve, among others, regulate laws and guidelines. The FTC and the SEC regulate legal functions in companies. International operations of firms are regulated by the International Trade Commission (ITC), the Commerce Department, and the Treasury Department, to name some of the more prominent agencies.

COSTS AND BENEFITS OF GOVERNMENTAL REGULATION

Is governmental regulation worth the costs to consumer stakeholders? To business stakeholders? To society? To future generations? What are the benefits of governmental regulation? Who benefits and who loses? What would U. S. society be like without governmental regulation? Who would suffer most? Although these questions have no simple answers, they do raise the major issues behind trying to determine the costs and benefits of regulation. Although no consensus exists on the value or price of human health and life, air, water, and earth, the costs and benefits of regulating the environment, safety, equality, and free-market competitiveness will be estimated and debated continuously by those who must pay the costs and by those who must bear the consequences of nonregulation.

An Arthur Andersen (1979) study showed that the incremental costs (that is, costs the firms would not have spent without regulations) of 48 firms in meeting six federal agency program standards was $2.6 billion (see also Steiner and Steiner 1991). Realistically, it is impossible to estimate all the costs to firms that conform to governmental regulations. Some of the more pronounced types of compliance costs entail (1) hiring and maintaining lawyers and other professionals to meet human resource standards such as affirmative action and to settle legal disputes, (2) submitting paperwork required to meet compliance standards (approximately $25 billion to $32 billion each year; U. S. Commission on Federal Paperwork 1977), and (3) purchasing equipment and manufacturing costs for implementing and maintaining safety standards. Also included are the indirect costs of regulation, such as losses in productivity from having to comply with confusing, contradictory, and time-consuming standards; losses from unbuilt facilities because of noncompliance problems and losses from plant closings due to unmet standards; losses in hiring and employment because of minimum-wage restrictions (Buchholz 1989); and losses in innovation from pretesting requirements and overcompliance measures (Buchholz 1989; Schnee 1979).

The benefits of governmental regulation are as difficult to estimate as the costs. One such study estimated air-pollution-control benefits at $5 billion to $58 billion annually, water pollution cleanup benefits at $9 billion, and a reduction in costs by avoidance of workday accidents and fatalities during a two-year span at $15 billion (Carroll 1989, 181; *Congressional Quarterly's Federal Regulatory Directory* 1985–1986).

These benefits must be weighed against the many intangible and often inestimable benefits of governmental regulation. What would U.S. society be like without any governmental regulations? Would the environment benefit without the Clean Air Act or the Federal Water Pollution Control Act? Would consumers be as protected without product liability and safety regulatory legislation? Would minorities have equal opportunities in the marketplace without civil rights legislation? Would consumers be better off without antimonopoly legislation? Without governmental regulation, society's social aims could not be implemented and its direction could not be guided. The issue of costs and benefits should, perhaps, center more on the specific methods, volume, and costs of regulation than on whether regulation is needed to set social goals and to monitor industries' moral and economic obligations toward stakeholders and the public (see Steiner and Steiner 1991).

Again, it is difficult to evaluate all the benefits of the Clean Air Act, the Toxic Substances Control Act, the Clean Water Act, and OSHA and EPA regulatory standards for the workplace and the environment. A key issue concerning the controversial topic of the costs versus the benefits of environmental protection and of other regulations remains: What would be the effects on the environment, on the workplace, and on employee safety and equality without laws and regulations addressing and enforcing such issues? Cost/benefit analyses and the principles of justice, duty, rights, and obligations will continue to be weighed by managers, judges, and juries in decisions and disputes regarding administrative, judicial, legal, and business stakeholder concerns.

Although corporate self-regulation is certainly necessary, this text argues that it is not sufficient in a complex society where public health and safety and the environment must be protected against changing technologies and industrial activities aimed primarily at profit making.

SUMMARY

Businesses have legal and moral obligations to provide their consumers with safe products without false advertising and without doing harm to the environment. The complexities and controversies with respect to this obligation stem from attempts to define "safety," "truth in advertising," and levels of "harm" caused to the environment.

Corporations need to balance their social responsibilities for the consuming public with the return-on-investment demands of their stockholders. Increasing concern over the destruction of the ozone layer, destruction of the rain forests, and other environmental issues has presented firms with another area where economic and social responsibilities must be balanced.

The very survival of many corporations can depend on how quickly and responsively they deal with a crisis of public confidence brought on by sabotage or faulty products. Crisis and issues management models, presented in Chapter 2, complement the stakeholder approach by adding the dynamic dimension of tracing and evaluating changing issues in the environment. These models are especially useful for the issues covered in this chapter; they help corporate stakeholders understand how crises happened, who the external stakeholders were, and what issues emerged, as well as how to prevent damaging events.

Crisis management is a process of minimizing the risks and uncertainty and of restoring as much control as possible to the corporation's future management. The four stages of one crisis model, the prodromal, acute, chronic, and resolution stages, require accurate observation and informed judgment.

Issues management deals with anticipating and addressing issues that may harm the firm or its stakeholders. Issues develop through a "life cycle." The issues management process adds to the stakeholder analysis not only by identifying issues but also by prioritizing them and by detecting and resolving potential or existing business-related crises.

The government also has a stake in helping to manage the social obligations of business toward its stakeholders. The relationship of business and government tends to be adversarial because of business's pursuit of individualistic values that conflict with the government's collectivist public-value goals. Despite the difficulty in measuring the specific costs or values associated with human health, quality of life, and environmental damage, some governmental regulation is necessary in order to help balance U.S. corporations' goal of profit maximization with their social and moral obligations. Arguments for and arguments critical of governmental regulation of business were discussed.

QUESTIONS

1. What is the free-market theory of corporate responsibility for consumers, and what are some of the problems associated with this view? Compare this view with the social-contract and stakeholder perspective of corporate social responsibility.

2. Identify arguments for and against questionable ethical advertising. Which do you not agree with? Explain.

3. Describe an advertisement in the media that you believe is unethical. Explain your argument.

4. What is the four-step process developed by Justice Powell to determine whether commercial speech in advertising can be restricted or banned?

5. What constitutes "unreasonable risk" concerning the safety of a product? Identify considerations that define the safety of a product from an ethical perspective.

6. Explain the differences among the doctrines of negligence, strict liability, and absolute liability. What do you believe should be the "limits" to the product liability doctrine? Explain.

7. Identify moral arguments for corporate responsibility toward the environment. Do you believe trees, lakes, oceans, and animals should have rights? Explain.

8. What are some of the ways the federal government acts to influence business behavior? Do you agree or disagree that the government should regulate businesses? Explain your reasoning.

9. What are some business areas federal or state governments should not be involved or intervene in? Explain.

EXERCISES

1. Identify a recent example of a corporation accused of false or deceitful advertising. How did it justify the claims made in its ad? Do you agree or disagree with the claims? Explain.

2. In a few paragraphs, explain your opinion of whether advertising is a valid or legitimate industry.

3. Can you think of an instance when you or someone you know was affected by corporate negligence in product safety standards? If so, did you communicate the problem to the company? Did it respond to the complaint? Characterize the response. How could or should the company have responded differently?

4. Find an article discussing environmental damage caused by a corporation's activities. Recommend methods the firm in the article should employ to reduce harmful effects on the environment.

REFERENCES AND SUGGESTED READINGS

Alexander, George. 1967. *Honesty and competition.* Syracuse, NY: Syracuse University Press.

Allen, Frank. 1991. Few big firms get jail time for polluting. *Wall Street Journal,* 9 December, B1.

Arthur Andersen and Co. 1979. *Cost of government regulation study for the business roundtable.* New York: Arthur Andersen.

Barett, William. 1985. Dalkon Shield maker concedes possible user injuries. *Dallas Times Herald,* 3 April, A8. Cited in Buchholz 1989, 202.

Beauchamp, Tom, and Norman Bowie. 1988. *Ethical theory and business.* 3d ed. Englewood Cliffs: Prentice Hall.

Blackstone, William. 1974. Ethics and ecology. In *Philosophy and environmental crisis,* edited by W. Blackstone. Athens: University of Georgia Press.

Bloom, Gordon F., and Michael Morton. 1991. Hazardous waste is every manager's problem. *Sloan Management Review* (summer): 80.

Boston Sunday Globe. 1996. 9 June, 25.

Buchholz, Rogene. 1982. Education for public issues management: Key insights from a survey of top practitioners. *Public Affairs Review* 3: 65–76.

———. 1989. *Fundamental concepts and problems in business ethics.* Englewood Cliffs: Prentice Hall.

———. 1991. Corporate responsibility and the good society: From economics to ecology. *Business Horizons* (July/August): 19–31.

———. 1992. *Business environment and public policy: Implications for management and strategy.* 4th ed. Englewood Cliffs: Prentice Hall.

Business Week. 1991. 23 December, 34.

Carroll, Archie B. 1989, 1993. *Business and society: Ethics and stakeholder management.* 1st, 3d eds. Cincinnati: South-Western.

Commoner, Barry. 1990. Failure of the environmental effort. In *Contemporary issues in business ethics,* edited by Joseph Des Jardins and John McCall. Belmont, CA: Wadsworth.

Congressional Quarterly's Federal Regulatory Directory. 1985–1986, 30. Also cited in Carroll 1989, 181.

DeGeorge, Richard. 1990. *Business ethics.* 3d ed. New York: Macmillan.

Des Jardins, Joseph, and John McCall, eds. 1990. *Contemporary issues in business ethics.* Belmont, CA: Wadsworth.

Elliott, Stuart. 1991. Has Madison Avenue gone too far? *New York Times,* 15 December, Business sec., 1, 6.

Environmental Laboratory Washington report. 1995. 14 December, Federal Notes, vol. 6; no. 22.

Environmental Protection Agency. 1988. *Environmental progress and challenges: Update.* Washington, DC: Government Printing Office, 87. Also cited in Buchholz 1992, 441.

Ford's $128.5 million headache. 1978. *Time,* 10 February, 65.

Galbraith, John Kenneth. 1958. *The affluent society.* Boston: Houghton Mifflin.

———. 1967. *The new industrial state.* New York: New American Library.

Geyelin, Milo. 1991. Dalkon Shield trust lawyers draw fire. *Wall Street Journal,* 12 November, B5.

Gray, Irwin. 1975. *Product liability: A management response.* New York: AMACOM.

Hoffman, Michael, and Jennifer Moore. 1990. *Business ethics: Readings and cases in corporate morality.* 2d ed. New York: McGraw-Hill.

Holloway, Robert, and Robert Hancock. 1973. *Marketing in a changing environment.* 2d ed. New York: John Wiley and Sons.

Iannone, A. Pablo, ed. 1989. *Contemporary moral controversies in business.* New York: Oxford University Press.

Jacoby, Neil, ed. 1975. *The business government relationship: A reassessment.* Pacific Palisades, CA: Goodyear.

Keating, Dan. 1991. Florida Keys may be dying by the year 2000, study finds. *Boston Sunday Globe,* 29 December, 9.

Levitt, Theodore. 1970. The morality (?) of advertising. *Harvard Business Review* (July/August), as cited in Hoffman and Moore 1990, 422.

Lipman, Joanne. 1991a. Pediatric academy prescribes ban on food ads aimed at children. *Wall Street Journal,* 24 July, B8.

————. 1991b. Stroh's ad campaign spins out of control. *Wall Street Journal,* 12 December, B6.

Matthews, John B., Kenneth Goodpaster, and Laura Nash. 1985. *Policies and persons: A casebook in business ethics.* New York: McGraw-Hill.

————. 1991. *Policies and persons: A casebook in business ethics.* 2d ed. New York: McGraw-Hill.

Moses, Jonathan. 1991. Court sets back EPA on enforcement for Superfund. *Wall Street Journal,* 6 November, B5.

Naisbitt, John, and Patricia Aburdene. 1990. *Megatrends 2000: Ten new directions for the 1990s.* New York: William Morrow and Company.

Noble, Barbara P. 1991. After years of deregulation, a new push to inform the public. *New York Times,* 27 October, F5.

Ozone depletion is said to harm immune system. 1991. *The Boston Globe,* 16 November, 3.

Passell, Peter. 1995. How much for a life? Try $3 million to $5 million. *New York Times,* 29 January, F3.

Posch, Robert. 1988. *The complete guide to marketing and the law.* Englewood Cliffs: Prentice Hall.

Sabato, Larry. 1984. PAC-man goes to Washington. *Across the Board* (October): 16.

Sagoff, Mark. 1990. Economic theory and environmental law. In *Contemporary issues in business ethics,* edited by Joseph Des Jardins and John McCall. Belmont, CA: Wadsworth, 360–64.

Schnee, Jerome. 1979. Regulation and innovation: U.S. pharmaceutical industry. *California Management Review* 22, no. 1 (fall): 23–32. Also cited in Buchholz 1989, 129.

Shabecoff, Phil. 1989. In search of a better law to clear the air. *New York Times,* 14 May, sec. 4, p. 1.

Shea, Cynthia P. 1989. Protecting the ozone layer. *State of the world 1989.* New York: Norton, 82. Cited in Buchholz 1992, 581.

Smoking: All clear (cough, cough). 1990. *Los Angeles Times,* 25 February. Also cited in Steiner and Steiner 1991, 591.

Statistical Abstract of the United States 1996. U.S. Department of Commerce, Michael Kantor, Secretary. Issued October 1996.

Steiner, George, and John Steiner. 1991. *Business, government, and society: A managerial perspective, text and cases.* 6th ed. New York: McGraw-Hill.

Stern, Louis. 1967. Consumer protection via increased information. *Journal of Marketing* 31, no. 2 (April): 48–52.

Stevens, K. William. 1995. 100 nations move to save ozone shield. *New York Times,* 10 December, 20.

Stipp, David. 1990. EPA, public differ over major risks. *Wall Street Journal,* 1 October, B1, Col. 6.

Sturdivant, Frederick, and Heidi Vernon-Wortzel. 1991. *Business and society: A managerial approach.* 4th ed. Homewood, IL: Irwin.

Templin, Neal. 1989. Ford is recalling 581,000 cars tied to engine fires. *Wall Street Journal,* 18 July, C25.

U.S. Commission on Federal Paperwork. 1977 *Final report summary.* Washington, DC: Government Printing Office.

U.S. Constitution. Art. 1, Sec. 8.

U.S. Consumer Product Safety Commission. 1985. Washington, DC: Government Printing Office, September, 1.

Velasquez, Manuel. 1988, 1992. *Business ethics concepts and cases.* 2d, 3d eds. Englewood Cliffs: Prentice Hall.

Wall Street Journal. 1992. 6 January, B1.

———. 1992. 13 January, B1.

———. 1992. 14 January, A3, B6.

Weidenbaum, Murray. 1979. *The future of business regulation.* New York: AMACOM.

———. 1981. *Business, government, and the public.* 2d ed. Englewood Cliffs: Prentice Hall.

Weinberger, Marc, and Jean Romeo. 1989. The impact of negative product news. *Business Horizons* (January/February): 44–50.

6

EMPLOYEE STAKEHOLDERS AND THE CORPORATION

When Richard Rathemacer, a systems engineering manager, left IBM in August 1987, he wasn't really fired, the company said. And the 30-year veteran agreed. Instead, he said IBM threatened him with an "unsatisfactory" job rating and then "suggested" he sign up for a 1986 early retirement plan. He initially signed up under duress but then wavered. IBM, meantime, stripped him of his title and duties and reassigned him to an abandoned office, with no supplies, no switchboard, and no secretary. Weeks later, Rathemacer, then 55, arrived at work to find that his office had been cleared out the night before. (Galen 1991, 33)

The employee in this case sued IBM for lost pay of $75,000 a year, along with punitive and other damages. Rathemacer had been an excellent performer at IBM for most of his tenure. He won numerous sales and achievement awards. IBM denied Rathemacer was mistreated and claimed he left "voluntarily" with a "very generous severance and retirement package" (Galen 1991). Furthermore, IBM denied this is a case of age discrimination and claimed Rathemacer had serious performance problems. Rathemacer countered that IBM used negative job appraisals to force early retirement. Moreover, Charles Quinn, a new IBM manager in 1985, denied Rathemacer a promotion, opting instead—according to Rathemacer—for "new young blood in that job." Court records in 1986 stated that Quinn reorganized the unit and put Rathemacer in charge of mainframe computers. All Rathemacer's experience had been in small systems. His performance was subsequently downgraded. Rathemacer stated that he protested to superiors about age discrimination and that he formally filed an open-door complaint with the office of IBM's CEO in March 1987. In June, Rathemacer sought a rehearing. IBM claims Rathemacer's performance showed "persistent negativism, insensitivity, rudeness, verbal abuse, and poor interpersonal relations with his co-workers" (Galen 1991).

IBM had a lot at stake in this particular case. First, this case challenged the firm's capability to downsize using early-retirement incentives as a strategy during a severe industry downturn—accompanied by increasing international competition. IBM, at the time of this incident, announced plans to cut 17,000 more workers, mainly through retirement incentives. IBM also faced the charge that it used early-retirement plans to cover age discrimination. This charge questioned the firm's image and integrity with its workforce, particularly its aging workforce. IBM also could be forced to change its performance standards as well as the practices and principles that underlie these standards.

The question of age discrimination is only one of the personnel and moral problems corporations face in the United States in this and the next decade. Workforce problems discussed in this chapter involve one of a corporation's most important stakeholders: its employees. The chapter begins by addressing significant changing characteristics of the workforce in the United States. What is different about the workforce, and how does this affect the corporation's ethical responsibilities? It then discusses the following questions: What binds employees to their companies? What is the nature of the employer/employee social contract? How has this contract changed historically? Then, the rights and obligations of employers and employees are briefly presented to offer a perspective on what they expect from each other. Problems of discrimination in the workplace and affirmative action legislation are examined next. The text addresses the question What is illegal and immoral regarding workplace discrimination? Then it defines sexual harassment and the law and offers recommendations for organizations and individuals for preventing and dealing with this problem. Finally, Chapter 6 looks at issues surrounding whistle-blowing versus loyalty to the firm. What are the boundaries of employee loyalty? When do employees have the right or obligation to "blow the whistle" on the company?

6.1 EMPLOYEE STAKEHOLDERS: THE WORKFORCE IN THE TWENTY-FIRST CENTURY

The workforce and the workplace in America are significantly changing in ways that affect management practices and moral issues. David Jamieson and Julie O'Mara in their book *Managing Workforce 2000: Gaining the Diversity Advantage* (1991) described the following major trends affecting the workplace: The workforce is aging; women entrants are increasing in number; cultures are mixing, as are values; the education gap is increasing; and the number of workers with disabilities is expanding. These trends are based on statistical projections as well as ongoing occurrences. The ethical implications of these changes for corporations will be discussed after the major trends are summarized.

THE AGING WORKFORCE

The workforce is aging. By A.D. 2000, half of the workforce—the baby boomers (those born between 1946 and 1964)—will be middle-aged. At the same time, those ages 16 to 24—the "baby busters" (those born after the boomers)—will make up 16 percent of the workforce and will continue to decline. The seniors—those over age 55—will represent about 13 percent of the workforce.

WOMEN IN THE WORKFORCE

By 2000, women will represent 50 percent of the workforce, or six out of seven working-age women. Two-thirds of the new entrants between 1985 and 2000 will be female. Three-fourths of all working women will be in their childbearing years; women with children under six years old represent the most rapidly increasing segment of the workforce. Female managers, administrators, and executives are also increasing—up 35 percent in 1987. Moreover, dual-career families also will increase by 75 percent.

THE INCREASING CULTURAL MIX

By 2080, more than 27 percent of the U.S. population will be nonwhite; nonwhite people will consist of 15 percent of the U.S. workforce. By 2000, U.S.-born people of color and immigrants are projected to make up 43 percent of newcomers to the workplace. The large increase of immigrants and people of color to the workforce will consist of Hispanics, Asians, Latin Americans, and black people. Presently, California is projected to have a workforce of minorities exceeding 50 percent by 2005.

THE GROWING EDUCATION GAP

A growing dichotomy in the education levels of those in and those entering the workforce is occurring. Although the United States has the most educated workforce in its history, the number of less-educated entrants is also increasing. For example, in the mid-1980s, 86 percent of 25- to 29-year-olds had graduated from high school; but in 1988, 20 million functionally illiterate people were living in the United States. Of the 18- to 21-year-old population, 13.6 percent did not complete high school. A *Business Week* (19 September 1988) article reported that "most 17-year-olds in school cannot summarize a newspaper article, write a good letter requesting a job, solve real-life math problems, or follow a bus schedule."

MAINSTREAMING DISABLED WORKERS

Hiring and mainstreaming qualified disabled workers is increasing in importance because of the combined effects of the shrinking and aging workforce. A survey by the International Center for the Disabled found that two-thirds of the working-age disabled were not in the workforce, while a "large majority" said they preferred to work. Disabilities affect a large number of the workforce. Disabilities are categorized as permanent (for example, physical disabilities), temporary (such as those resulting from injury or stress), and progressive (for example, AIDS, alcohol and drug addiction, cancer; 26). According to these definitions, disabled workers can and will number into the millions. One alarming 1991 statistic, for example, was that 10,000 to 15,000 heterosexuals were getting AIDS every year (Bunzel 1991, A20). AIDS is no longer identified by a particular group or category.

ETHICAL IMPLICATIONS AND THE CHANGING WORKFORCE

The aging workforce will necessitate changes in the management of employees' motivations, rewards, and career opportunities. Moral and legal conflict likely will increase in workplace situations with regard to the following:

1. *Age discrimination* (as illustrated in the opening case): When are experienced workers not able to work? According to whose and what standards? Should companies, such as IBM in the opening case, treat aging employees differently during economic downturns or when technologies require new or different skills?

2. *Clashes of values and expectations between managers and employees:* Will the experience of aging workers be devalued? How well will aging, experienced workers and younger, better-educated workers integrate with different compensation and reward systems?

3. *Health care cost increases:* How will companies deal with the increasing health care costs of aging employees, especially during economic recessions and in industries losing their international competitiveness?

The existence of increasing numbers of women in the workforce is already signaling changes in the tensions and moral problems of what has been a white, male-dominated workforce. These tensions translate into the following moral and managerial problems:

1. *Sexual harassment and discrimination in the workplace.* More women are speaking out under the protection of Title VII of the amended Civil Rights Act, which will be discussed in section 6.5 of this chapter.

2. *Miscommunication and conflict between genders in the workplace, especially between male bosses and female employees.* The book *You Just Don't Understand* by Deborah Tannen (1990) illustrates the different communication styles of men and women. Many consulting companies a offer "gender training" to ease the tensions and miscommunications between men and women in the workplace.

3. *Policy demands that strain corporate relationships and finances and cause conflict between management and workers.* Requests for childbirth and child-care leave programs will increase. Requests for flextime, part-time, and work-at-home jobs also will increase. Less willingness to relocate will strain corporate decisions.

The incoming mix of cross-cultural backgrounds is introducing values, norms, ways of communicating, motivations, expectations, work styles, and work ethics into the workplace. What is right and wrong for members of one cultural group may be different or unacceptable to others. Again, the potential for conflict will be enhanced.

The growing educational gap will increase workplace problems. Highly educated workers demand more involvement and autonomy, less control, more information, more career opportunities, and rewards commensurate with performance. The less-educated workers often require more training, more educational opportunities, more supervision, and structured opportunities to increase mobility. The mix of the two educational levels will strain work, personal, moral, and managerial/employee relationships.

Finally, mainstreaming workers with disabilities challenges corporations to accommodate legislation and to collaborate with social, medical, and educational institutions in society, which thus are becoming corporation stakeholders. Management already is confronting a range of moral issues in this area, such as (1) discrimination issues over drug and AIDS testing and the violation of privacy rights and (2) health care and other organizational costs from workers suffering from addictions and diseases such as AIDS.

Although many of these problems lead to costly economic and moral dilemmas for managers, the fact remains that society and the workforce are changing. Corporations must change with the people they manage in order to succeed.

CHANGING WORKFORCE VALUES

From surveying 350 managers and human-service professionals, Jamieson and O'Mara identified the following work-related values that are now considered most important and that would continue to be valued in the near future:

❏ Recognition for competence and accomplishment
❏ Respect and dignity
❏ Personal choice and freedom
❏ Involvement at work
❏ Pride in work
❏ Quality of lifestyle
❏ Financial security
❏ Self-development
❏ Health and wellness

As workforce demographics and values change, this question is central to ethics in the workplace: What are the social doctrines that have defined and presently define the legal and moral basis of the employer/employee relationship? This is an important subject, since the social contract between employer and employee influences managerial decisions and conflict resolution. The changing employer/employee social contract is discussed in the next main section.

ADVANCEMENT OF WOMEN IN THE WORKFORCE

Businesses owned by women currently employ 15.5 million people, 35 percent more than *Fortune* 500 companies. Catalyst, a New York–based working women's organization, surveyed 461 top female executives with the title of vice president or higher at the 1,000 largest U.S. companies to determine the three highest-ranking barriers to advancement for women. This study was noted as the first large-scale study of women in senior management (Dobrzynski 1996; Sullivan 1996). The findings follow:

❏ Fifty-two percent believed male stereotyping and preconceptions of women was a primary factor in holding women back.

❏ Forty-nine percent believed exclusion from informal networks of communication was a primary reason.

❏ Forty-seven percent chose lack of general-management or line experience as a primary barrier to advancement.

In a parallel study of *Fortune* 500/Service 500 chief executives, of whom 99 percent were men, only 25 percent of male chief executives cited male stereotyping and preconceptions of women as a top factor for holding women back. Fifteen percent believed that exclusion from informal networks was a primary barrier to women's advancement. Eighty-two percent said the most serious deterrent to women's advancement was lack of general management or line experience. The conclusion to the study pointed out the gender gaps in the male corporate culture and what female executives and companies must do in order to bridge this gap.

With the assistance of affirmative action, women have made significant strides over the past 30 years. The number of women getting "in the door" has increased. In 1972 women comprised 38 percent of all U.S. civilian workers, by 1980 this number had risen to 42.4 percent, and by 1994 it had increased to 46 percent. In 1983 women held 40.9 percent of all managerial and professional jobs, and a decade later this had climbed to 47.8 percent (Shoa 1995).

6.2 THE SOCIAL CONTRACT BETWEEN CORPORATIONS AND EMPLOYEES

The social contract that has historically defined the employee/employer relationship is known as the **employment-at-will (EAW) doctrine.** This implied legal agreement has been in effect since 1884, when the *Payne* v. *Western A.R.R. Co.* judgment ruled that "all may dismiss their employees at will, be they many or few, for good cause, for no cause, or even for cause morally wrong without being thereby guilty of legal wrong."

Essentially, the EAW doctrine can be defined as "the right of an employer to fire an employee without giving a reason and the right of an employee to quit when he or she chooses" (Fulmer and Casey 1990, 102). If employees are unprotected by unions or other written contracts, they can be fired, according to this doctrine.

The EAW doctrine evolved as part of the laissez-faire philosophy of the Industrial Revolution. Between the 1930s and 1960s, however, exceptions to the doctrine appeared. Federal legislation since the 1960s has been enacted to protect employees against racial discrimination and to provide rights to a minimum wage, to equal hiring and employment opportunities, and to participate in labor unions.

Moreover, since the 1970s, state court decisions also have limited the EAW doctrine. Specifically, state courts have upheld employees' rights to use legal action against their employers if an employee termination violated "public policy" principles: for example, if employees were pressured to commit perjury or fix prices; if employees were not permitted to perform jury duty or file for workers' compensation; if employees were terminated because they refused to support a merger; or if employees reported alleged employer violations of statutory policy (whistleblowing).

An important 1981 California Appeals Court decision, *Pugh* v. *See's Candies, Inc.*, ruled that in a noncontractual employment arrangement, an implied promise from the employer existed. The employer could not act arbitrarily with its employees regarding termination decisions when considering the following factors: (1) duration of employment, (2) recommendations and promotions received, (3) lack of direct criticism of work, (4) assurances given, and (5) the employer's acknowledged policies (Fulmer and Casey 1990, 103, 104).

Although the EAW doctrine has undergone change, it is not dead, as is illustrated in Figure 6.1. Figure 6.1 is an actual contract an employee must sign before beginning work at this reputable company in Massachusetts. Large numbers of people still are fired at will. For example, upper-level and midlevel white-collar management positions are vulnerable during economic recessions and due to streamlining and downsizing operations; nonunionized beginners are threatened; workers without union contracts and temporary workers can be terminated at will; and sports coaches and professional athletes are frequently fired (DeGeorge 1990, 334).

Currently, the courts have demonstrated that when employers make a promise of job security, whether it is implied verbally or in writing (as in a personnel handbook, contract, or other document), employers are bound by that promise. However, the courts have not ruled that employers must state how employees will be terminated and under what conditions they may be fired. Employers can eliminate references to or promises of job security in their documents. Some employers, such as Sears, have asked employees to sign disclaimers when hired stating that

EMPLOYEE CONTRACT UNDER THE **EAW** DOCTRINE

READ CAREFULLY BEFORE SIGNING:

I understand that refusal to submit to the testing noted [elsewhere] or a positive drug screen result will eliminate any consideration for employment.

I also certify that the statements and information furnished by me in this application are true and correct. I understand that falsification of such statements and information is grounds for dismissal at any time the company becomes aware of the falsified notification. In consideration of my employment, I agree to conform to the rules and regulations of the company and acknowledge that my employment and compensation can be terminated, with or without cause, and with or without notice, at any time, at the option of either the company or myself. I further understand that no policy, benefit or procedure contained in any employee handbook creates an employment contract for any period of time and no terms or conditions of employment contrary to the foregoing should be relied upon, except for those made in writing by a designated officer of the Company.

I agree and hereby authorize XYZ, Inc. to conduct a background inquiry to verify the information on this application, other documentation that I have provided and other areas that may include prior employment, consumer credit, criminal convictions, motor vehicle and other reports. These reports may include information as to my character, work habits, performance, education and experience along with reasons for termination of employment from previous employers. Further, I understand that you may be requesting information from various Federal, State and other agencies which maintain records concerning my past activities relating to my driving, credit, criminal, civil and other experiences as well as claims involving me in the files of insurance companies. I authorize all previous employers or other persons who have knowledge of me, or my records, to release such information to XYZ, Inc. I hereby release any party or agency and XYZ, Inc. from all claims or liabilities whatever that may arise by such disclosures or such investigation.

_____   _____

Date of Application   Signature of Applicant

no binding contract exists between the employer and employee. Sears has won employee termination judgments based on its disclaimer statements (Fulmer and Casey 1990, 105). Employers have no hard and fast rule to protect themselves against repercussions from employee terminations.

Courts to date generally have ruled to reverse decisions based on EAW principles (Beauchamp and Bowie 1988, 259).

The next section presents specific employee rights and employer obligations and offers recommendations to managers for avoiding arbitrary and immoral termination decisions.

6.3 EMPLOYEE AND CORPORATION RIGHTS AND OBLIGATIONS

The relationship between employer and employee in the United States has evolved from the employment-at-will doctrine just described to include expanded federal and state legislation aimed at protecting workers and promoting minority employees' rights and opportunities. This was a transition from a feudal European governance context to a contemporary U.S. pluralistic setting. Employee rights in the workplace are still evolving. Changing social, political, legal, technological, scientific, and competitive forces present new issues, opportunities, and controversies between employee rights and corporate duties.

Moreover, in a market economy, employer/employee rights and obligations are based on contrasting, sometimes conflicting, assumptions and values. Employers control private property and proprietary rights over their intellectual property. Employees claim their constitutional rights to individual freedom, liberty, and control over their private lives. Employers try to maximize productivity and profits, to sustain financial growth and stability, to minimize costs, to improve quality, to increase marketshare, and to stabilize wages. Employees seek to increase their wages and benefits, to improve working conditions, to enhance mobility, and to ensure job security. These differences can collide in policy decisions, especially during economic downturns and increased competition. Although no perfect boundary intersects employer/employee rights in a capitalist market economy, specific moral principles can guide people and help resolve some of the differences and conflicts among employer/employee stakeholder interests.

Before discussing specific rights and obligations between employers and employees, this section begins by presenting three organizing concepts that underlie employee rights: balance, governmental rights, and moral entitlement. The concept of balance is based on utilitarian ethical reasoning; that of governmental rights is based on reasoning related to inalienable individual rights; and that of moral entitlement is based on Kantian nonconsequentialist reasoning. Although these concepts are not mutually exclusive, it is helpful to understand their distinctive logic in order to argue their merits and shortcomings as they apply to specific workplace controversies.

THE BALANCE CONCEPT AND THE SOCIAL CONTRACT

As common law and custom have evolved from the EAW doctrine to implied employee rights, employers now must consider more than stockholder and financial interests when dealing with employee stakeholders. The new social contract between employers and employees is based on a more symmetrical contractual relationship justified by a principle of *balance* and mutual fairness: the employer's interest in operating the business as she or he determines balanced against the employee's welfare and interest (Steiner and Steiner 1991, 1996). Employers generally have more power than employees in the contractual relationship. Nevertheless, employees have implied as well as explicit rights in the relationship, as discussed so far. Accordingly, employees can negotiate and dispute employers' arbitrary uses of their power over employees.

The balance concept expands rights beyond the historically narrow limits of the EAW doctrine. Regarding adversarial termination decisions, courts weigh employer rights against the interests of the "economic system" and "public good" (*Monge* v. *Beebe Rubber Co.*, 1974).

RIGHTS FROM GOVERNMENTAL LEGISLATION

Employee rights also are based on principles determined by law, as will be discussed in the next main section. Certain employee *governmental rights* are not negotiable in written or implied contracts: for example, rights related to the minimum wage; sexual harassment; discrimination based on race, creed, age, national origin, sex, or disability; and the right to assemble. Although employee rights based on certain legislation are not normally negotiated according to employer/employee self-interests, these rights can be disputed, depending on circumstances. Reverse discrimination, to be discussed later, is one such example.

RIGHTS OF MORAL ENTITLEMENT

Joseph Des Jardins and John McCall (1985) argue that employees also have "rights possessed independently of any contractual agreement or legislation." Due process is one such principle based on **moral entitlement.** Moral entitlements differ from rights established by either contracts or legislation, since the latter can be negotiated in regard to business and employee interests. Rights based on moral entitlement are nonnegotiable. They represent "a general and presumptive moral entitlement of any employee to receive certain goods and to be protected from certain harms in the workplace." Moral entitlement rights such as due process are different from rights based on contracts or legislation also because "the basic moral rights of human persons can place constraints on the treatment those persons receive when operating within their institutional or social roles."

Des Jardins and McCall (1985) also argue that employee rights based on moral entitlements "function to prevent employees from being placed in the fundamentally coercive position of having to choose between their job and other basic human goods or treatments" (369). Again, these rights are not open to normal negotiating processes (such as increasing profit margins or wage levels), although instances may occur when such rights can be overruled (for example, economic conditions requiring justifiable downsizing).

Obligations between Employers and Employees

Employers and employees have rights and duties each should honor with respect to the other. This section discusses these mutual obligations that stem from each party's rights.

EMPLOYER OBLIGATIONS TO EMPLOYEES Employers are obliged to pay employees fair wages, to provide safe working conditions, and to provide meaningful work.

Obligation to Pay Fair Wages. Fair wages are determined by factors such as what the public and society support and expect, conditions of the labor market, competitive industry wages in the specific location, the firm's profitability, the nature of the job and work, laws governing minimum wages, comparable salaries, and the fairness of the salary or wage negotiations (Velasquez 1988, 364, 365). As will be discussed in section 6.4, fair wages for comparable jobs held by men and women are not always paid.

Obligation to Provide Safe Working Environments. Employers also are obliged to provide workers with a safe working environment and working conditions. OSHA and federal laws and regulations provide safety standards and enforce employer institution of its own safety standards. The problems of employers providing—and of employees accepting— safe working environments stem from (1) lack of knowledge and of available, reliable information about levels of health risks; (2) lack of appropriate compensation proportional to the level of occupational risk; and (3) employees accepting known risks in the absence of comparable options or mobility (Velasquez 1988, 367). When the option is employment versus no employment, workers—especially in low-income, noncompetitive employment regions—often choose jobs with hazardous risks to their health or life.

Employers, then, are obliged to pay competitive wages commensurate with the occupational risks associated with a profession, job, or work setting. For example, race car drivers would not be expected to receive the same pay as college professors. Employers also are expected to provide full information on the risks and health hazards related to the work, products, and working environments to all employees exposed to those risks. Finally, employers also should offer health insurance programs and benefits to employees exposed to workplace hazards (Velasquez 1988, 368). We know that in actuality not all employers meet these obligations.

Obligation to Provide Meaningful Work. Employers are obliged to offer employees working conditions that provide meaningful tasks and job satisfaction. This argument is based on the view that employees as human beings work most productively when they can participate in the control of their tasks, when they are given responsibility for and autonomy over their assignments, and when they are treated with respect. Although some people debate this topic, studies generally support the connection between worker productivity and **quality-of-work-life (QWL)** programs that provide employees with more autonomy, participation, satisfaction, and control in their work tasks (Bjork 1975; Simmons and Mares 1983). Many companies are organizing self-designing work teams and quality circles in order to use employee creativity and abilities. Workers and managers both gain from such programs and new organizational forms.

EMPLOYEE OBLIGATIONS TO EMPLOYERS Employees are obliged to fulfill their contracted responsibilities to the corporation; to follow the goals, procedural rules, and work plans of the organization; to offer competence commensurate with the work and job assignments; and to perform productively according to the required tasks. Other obligations include timeliness and avoiding absenteeism; acting legally and morally in the workplace and while on job assignments; and respecting the intellectual and private property rights of the employer.

Conflicts of Interest. Employee obligations to employers become complicated when conflicts of interest appear, that is, when an employee's private interests compete or are not aligned with the company's interests. More obvious conflicts of interest arise in a number of situations, such as taking or offering commercial and personal bribes, kickbacks, gifts, and insider information for personal gain.

The so-called gray areas are more problematic for determining whose interests are violated at the expense of the other's: for example, when an employee quits a firm, joins a competitor, and then is accused by the former employer of stealing proprietary property (that is, passing on intellectual property, sharing trade secrets, or offering a competitive advantage by divulging confidential information). Whose interests are violated? Beauchamp and Bowie (1988) note that some courts have used a "balancing model" based on utilitarian logic to resolve trade-secret-protection cases; that is, an employee's interest in mobility and opportunity is weighed against the employer's right to decide the extent of protection given to confidential information. For example, the following three criteria have been used to decide whether trade secrets have been divulged by employees (264):

1. True trade secrecy and established ownership must be shown.

2. A trade secret must have been disclosed by an employee, thus breaching a duty of confidentiality.

3. The employer's interest in keeping the secret must outweigh the employee's interest in using the secret to earn a living and the public's interest in having the secret transmitted.

Courts also use other considerations in these types of rulings (for example, contract obligations, promises made, truthfulness, confidentiality, and loyalty). The point here is that as technology and expertise become more sophisticated and as employee mobility—as well as downsizing—increase, workplace and courtroom criteria regarding the proof of conflict of interest also grow more complicated. Although a utilitarian model is used to help determine conflict-of-interest court cases, such as for trade secrecy, ethical principles such as rights, duty, and justice also remain essential considerations for determining right and wrong; violations of loyalty, confidentiality, or truthfulness; and harm done to either employers or employees.

EMPLOYEE RIGHTS IN THE WORKPLACE

Labor, along with money and materials, is considered capital in a free-market system. However, labor is not the same as materials and money; labor also means human beings who have general constitutional rights that should not be relinquished between 8 A.M. and 5:30 P.M. (DeGeorge 1990; Ewing 1977). However, clashes of interests and of stakes between employee rights and management demands frequently occur. The boundary between an employer's private property and an employee's individual rights is often blurred in everyday experience. Employee rights more often than not are violated; this is especially true for nonunion workers. Still, understanding employee rights is an important part of business ethics education. Implementing and protecting those rights is another matter. When employees and employers cannot agree on whose rights are seriously violated, third-party negotiation, arbitration, and even settlement may be required. This section presents major types of employee rights in the workplace: the right to a job and the right not to be terminated without just cause; the right to due process; the right to privacy; the right to know and workplace health and safety; the right to organize and strike; and rights regarding plant closings. These rights become even more important in a society that rapidly transforms technological and scientific inventions into the human workplace environment.

The employee stakeholder has constitutional rights as a citizen in society, and these translate into workplace rights. Although many employee rights must be balanced against those of the employer, it is also true that certain employee rights are nonnegotiable moral entitlements. This discussion begins with the moral reasoning for an employee's right to a job and the right not to be arbitrarily fired.

RIGHT TO A JOB AND THE RIGHT NOT TO BE TERMINATED WITHOUT JUST CAUSE   Employees probably have more of a right not to be terminated arbitrarily or without just cause than they do to a job in a free-market economy. The right or moral entitlement to have a job is still a debated issue. This right is based on the argument that holding a job means having social status and self-esteem. Without work, one has no self-respect as a member of society (Beauchamp and Bowie 1988, 260, 261).

It also has been argued that workers should have three rights regarding work to maintain self-respect: the right to employment, the right to equal opportunity, and the right to participate in job-related decisions (Meyers 1988). This chapter already has discussed an employee's right not to be terminated arbitrarily. The right to equal opportunity has been legislated for minorities, as discussed later in this chapter. The right to participate in job-related decisions has strong backing from those who argue that productivity, job satisfaction, and motivation are related to participation.

RIGHT TO DUE PROCESS   Due process is one of the most important underlying rights employees have in the workplace, since it affects most of their other rights. **Due process** refers to the right to have an impartial and fair hearing regarding employers' decisions, procedures, and rules that affect employees. As applied in the workplace, due process essentially refers to grievance procedures.

At a more general level, due-process rights protect employees from arbitrary and illegitimate uses of power. These rights are based on the Fifth and Fourteenth Amendments of the Constitution, which state that no person shall be deprived of "life, liberty, or property, without the due process of law" (Des Jardins and McCall 1990, 131).

Werhane (1985) states that the following corporate procedural mechanisms are needed to ensure employees' right to due process:

❑ Right to a public hearing

❑ Ability to have peer evaluations

❑ Ability to obtain external arbitration

❑ An open, mutually agreed on grievance procedure

The right to due process applies to other employee rights such as those involving privacy, safety and health, working environment conditions, assembling, hiring, firing, and other human resource decisions.

RIGHT TO PRIVACY Employees' right to privacy remains one of the most debated and controversial rights. It raises these questions: Where does the employer's control over employee behavior, space, time, and property begin and end? What freedoms and liberties do employees have with employer property rights? What rights do employers have to protect their private property, earnings, and costs from employees? The U.S. Constitution does not actually refer to a person's right to "privacy." The working definition of employees' right to privacy has come to mean "to be left alone." Privacy in the workplace also can refer to employees' right to autonomy and to determine "when, how, and to what extent information about them is communicated to others" (Werhane 1985, 118).

The extent of an employee's privacy in the workplace remains an unsettled area of controversy. The definition of what constitutes an employee's privacy is still somewhat problematic. Included is the notion of psychological privacy (involving one's inner life) and the notion of physical privacy (involving one's space and time; Velasquez 1988, 376). In the 1965 *Griswold* v. *Connecticut* case, the Supreme Court ruled that the Constitution guarantees individuals a "zone of privacy" around them the government cannot intrude on. Proponents of this definition argue that this zone includes personnel records and files and protection against polygraph and psychological testing and surveillance in the workplace. It also is intended to protect employees in their after-work activities; their need for peace and quiet in the workplace; their dress, manners, and grooming; and their personal property in the workplace. Identifying this "zone of privacy" has proved complicated, especially in the technological world of changing inventions and applications in the workplace.

Polygraph and Psychological Testing. Employers are particularly concerned about employee privacy rights, since these protect against polygraph and psychological testing and other techniques that many managers would like to use to prevent and detect crime in the workplace. Workplace theft has been estimated to cost between $30 billion and $40 billion a year in the United States (Carroll, 1989). Here are some of the issues surrounding the use of polygraphs and psychological testing:

1. These tests are not reliable or valid; they are only indicators.

2. The tests, to some extent, can be manipulated and influenced by the operators.

3. The tests may include irrelevant questions (pertaining to gender, life, religion, after-work life and activities) that invade a person's private life.

4. Employees do not have control over the test results or how the information will be used.

Workplace Surveillance. Surveillance of employees at work (that is, employers using technology to spy on and invade workers' privacy) is also a subject of concern. Software programs are used to monitor an estimated 4 million workers who use computer terminals (Carroll 1989, 371, 372). Employers can detect the speed of employees' work, number and length of phone calls made and received, breaks taken, when machines are in use, and so on. Although some form of work-related monitoring is certainly legal and even necessary, the ethical issues the American Civil Liberties Union (ACLU) raises are the possible invasion of employee privacy and fair treatment. What type of information does an employer have a right to, and what effects do stress and anxiety from monitoring have on employee welfare? The Electronic Communications Privacy Act, signed during the Reagan administration, renders electronic eavesdropping through computer-to-computer transmissions, private videoconferences, and cellular phones illegal.

A study released by the Society for Human Resource Management, a trade association in Alexandria, Virginia, showed that 80 percent of the organizations in the study used E-mail. Only 36 percent of those groups had policies concerning E-mail use, and only 32 percent had written privacy policies. The issue of individual employee privacy remains somewhat undefined in the workplace (Samuels 1996).

Drug Testing. Privacy is also an issue in drug testing. Advocates for employee drug testing argue that employers' health costs and costs associated with sick and lost (nonproductive) days are affected when employees contract serious diseases, such as AIDS, as well as suffer from drug and alcohol addiction. Also, in industries (such as the airline industry or nuclear plant operations) where drug abuse can cost the lives of innocent people, screening drug abusers is viewed as in the public's interest. Those who oppose forced employee drug testing argue that the practice violates employees' rights to due process and privacy. Also, questions remain about the reliability of drug tests.

These guidelines can be used for drug-testing programs (Des Jardins and McCall 1990, 204–6):

1. Tests should be administered only for jobs that have a clear and present potential to cause harm to others.

2. Procedural testing limitations should include prior notice to those being tested.

3. Employees tested should be notified of the results.

4. Employees tested should be informed that they are entitled to appeal the results.

5. The employer should demonstrate how the information will be kept confidential (or destroyed).

Privacy and Computer-Stored Data Systems. The increasing use of sophisticated computerized personal data systems also has threatened the privacy of employees and other citizens. At stake for employees and others whose personal information is stored in computer data systems is access without consent to confidential information from any number of commercial and governmental sources.

At stake for executives of practically every business that relies on client credit and mailing information is the cost of the impact of regulations that govern these systems. Goldstein and Nolan (1975) note that computer privacy regulation affects virtually every organization that collects and uses personal information about its own employees. Several states and foreign governments already have enacted privacy laws.

Four steps managers can take to develop corporate policy guidelines to prepare for privacy regulation follow (Goldstein and Nolan 1975):

1. *Prepare a "privacy impact statement."* This analysis of the potential privacy implications should be taken as part of all proposals for new and expanded systems.

2. *Construct a comprehensive privacy plan.* The privacy impact statement provides the input for planning; the plan specifies all that has to be achieved.

3. *Train employees who handle personal information.* Make employees aware of protecting privacy and of the particular policies and procedures that should be followed to do so.

4. *Make privacy part of social responsibility programs.* Keep organizational members informed about company plans regarding privacy issues, with or without regulatory pressures.

THE RIGHT TO KNOW AND WORKPLACE HEALTH AND SAFETY Every employee is entitled to a safe, healthy workplace environment. Because one of ten employees in private industry suffers from an industrial accident or disease while working, information about unsafe, hazardous workplace conditions and some form of protection from these hazards are needed (Des Jardins and McCall 1990, 213). Employees have a right to know the nature and extent of hazardous risks they are exposed to as well as rights to information and training about and protection from those risks. Right-to-know laws have been passed in 20 states since the mid-1980s.

The Occupational Safety and Health Administration is the federal agency responsible for researching, identifying, and determining workplace health hazards; setting safety and health standards; and enforcing the standards. These remain major tasks. Critics of OSHA claim they are too overwhelming for one agency to monitor and execute effectively. As discussed in Chapter 5, the missions and budgets of government regulatory agencies—including OSHA—are also a function of the governing administration's and congressional politics. For example, President Reagan's administration emphasized business and free-enterprise activities over regulation in the 1980s. Consequently, OSHA's clout and effectiveness in the area of workplace health and safety decreased. Although workplace safety and health issues and standards cover an extensive range of industries and potential illnesses, this section will discuss two of the more notable contemporary health problems in the workplace: AIDS and smoking.

AIDS in the Workplace.   Americans first began to hear about AIDS and the human immunodeficiency virus (HIV) in the 1970s. HIV is the virus that causes AIDS. If an individual is infected with HIV, he or she does not necessarily have AIDS. HIV is an infection that can weaken the body's natural ability to fight diseases. This infection progresses in stages. While there has been a reported slight decline in the number of people infected with the HIV virus, AIDS remains a serious illness.

According to a recent Wyatt survey of 536 midsized and large U.S. employers, only 36 percent have developed company-wide policies for dealing with AIDS. Employees with HIV or AIDS qualify as "disabled" under the Rehabilitation Act of 1973 and the Americans with Disabilities Act of 1990. Both of these acts "confront discrimination in all stages of the employment process against people with disabilities" (Franklin 1992). The Americans with Disabilities Act (ADA) of 1990 is potentially the most significant piece of civil rights legislation enacted in the past three decades. It is designed to protect more than 43 million people. Organizations covered by ADA—private entities and public agencies that employ at least 15 full-time workers—are prohibited from discriminating against otherwise qualified disabled Americans in selection, retention, retirement, and termination policies and practices.

Nearly 500,000 Americans have contracted AIDS since the late 1970s; of these, approximately 97 percent are of working age, and 75 percent are in the prime working cohort of 25 to 44 years old. Although estimates vary, it also is quite probable that more than 1 million Americans are unknowingly HIV positive (Slack 1995).

The number of persons infected with AIDS in the United States has grown at an alarming rate. The U.S. Centers for Disease Control reported in January 1992 that the number of reported AIDS cases stood at 206,392, and 133,232 persons had died from the illness. The same source reported that of the 206,392 cases, the first 100,000 differed from the latest 100,000 in that (1) 7 percent of the newest 100,000 AIDS cases were traced to heterosexual transmission, up 44 percent from the first 100,000 cases; (2) 12 percent of the second 100,000 cases were women, compared with 9 percent of the first 100,000; and (3) 31 percent of the second 100,000 cases were black people, compared with 27 percent earlier (U.S. AIDS cases 1992).

Here are other facts (Rochell 1994):

❑ One million Americans are infected with HIV.

❑ These people are between the ages 25 and 44.

❑ The majority of the nations workforce is in this age group.

❑ AIDS is the leading cause of death among men in this age group.

❑ Ninety percent of HIV-infected people are employed.

HIV/AIDS is an expensive illness. According to C. Everett Koop, the former U.S. Surgeon General, in 1992 the expected five-year health and support costs to a company for an employee with AIDS was $40,000. In addition, businesses are accountable for the indirect costs of HIV, including decreases in productivity of HIV-infected employees. Companies also can incur hefty legal fees and litigation costs if they fail to ignore laws regarding AIDS-infected employees (Ayers 1994).

Some self-insured companies have tried to eliminate or limit coverage for HIV/AIDS. The Americans with Disability Act of 1990 states that limitations on coverage for certain illnesses are lawful as long as they are uniformly applied to all insured individuals, regardless of disability (Bordwin 1995).

Along with the social, ethical, and financial decisions about AIDS/HIV that must be addressed in the workplace, as many, if not more, legal issues must be observed when dealing with infected employees. In 1988 alone, 92,458 discrimination cases were filed based on HIV status; 37 percent were related to employment issues.

In the workplace, AIDS spells trouble for both employees and employers. Beyond the human and emotional toil are the fear and uncertainty of how the disease is transmitted and of who is at risk, the privacy and due-process issues of testing, and the liability concerns of who should pay what for the costs incurred by those who transmit as well as receive the disease. Health care workers in clinics run a greater risk of being infected by patients with HIV than do any other occupational or public group, including patients and doctors. Each year 12,000 health care workers are infected with hepatitis B virus, and others contract hepatitis C, which, like the AIDS virus, is transmitted by contact with blood. Each year 250 health care workers die of these viruses, which they receive from patient contact—usually from accidental needle sticks (Curfman 1991; Leary 1991). Statistics also show that doctors are a low-risk group for contracting HIV. Forty-seven doctors have been reported to have contracted the disease as of December 1991. Patients are at minimal risk of contracting AIDS from doctors. Federal authorities estimate that "an infected physician would have to perform 41,667 to 416,667 invasive procedures to infect one patient" (Leary 1991). The only known case of a health worker's transmitting AIDS to a patient involved a Florida dentist who died of the disease. Five of his patients, including Kimberly Bergalis (who died of AIDS December 8, 1991) were infected with HIV, but it is not conclusively known if they were infected by the dentist.

Presently, AIDS testing of private-sector employees is not a common practice. Limited screening procedures for jobs and industries that place professionals and workers at risk with the public are under review. Although the American Medical Association does not currently approve of an AIDS risk list of procedures doctors and health workers should perform if they are infected by AIDS, new protective gloves, surgery face masks, and other products are in place in many hospitals to protect against HIV transmission.

Employees who have been infected by HIV are protected in their employment if they are performing work responsibilities satisfactorily. Employers need to provide and sponsor more proactive education and training in the workplace to dispel misconceptions that AIDS is transmitted by casual means and to relieve stress about the disease itself. In the meantime, employees have a right to their privacy and to due process regarding AIDS testing and other related issues.

Smoking in the Workplace: Whose Rights? Should smoking be completely banned in all workplaces in the United States? Because it has been proved that smoking causes cancer, should nonsmokers have a right to their health and life from nonexposure to smoke? Whether and to what extent smoking should be restricted and banned in the workplace remains a controversial topic among major stakeholders. Among stakeholders who argue and lobby against smoking in the workplace are the EPA, OSHA, and ASH (Action on Smoking and Health—the powerful national antismoking group). Prosmoking advocates include the tobacco industry and its lobbying group, the Tobacco Institute, and the Bakery, Confectionery and Tobacco Workers union. OSHA has not been able to place an absolute ban on smoking in all workplaces to date. The issue reflects societal habits and attitudes as well as the politics and economics of the industry.

Consider these facts. It is estimated that 28 percent of Americans age 18 and over are smokers. Approximately 400 city and county ordinances restrict smoking at work; only 10 ban it. Thirty-seven states have adopted laws restricting smoking at work. Almost 75 percent of 1,794 facility managers in a survey claim they ban or segregate smoking in their workplaces (Karr and Guthfield 1992). One of OSHA's recent strategies has been to link smoking in the workplace to indoor air-quality problems and pollution and to legislate against it. The Clean Air Act is one such move to further restrict indoor smoking in public facilities. Employers need to keep track of laws and regulations that affect employee rights regarding smoking in the workplace.

RIGHT TO ORGANIZE AND STRIKE Workers have a right to organize, just as owners and managers do. Individuals, as workers and citizens, have the right of free association to seek common ends. This also means employees have a right to form unions. Although unions have a right to exist, they have no special rights beyond those due organizations with legal status (DeGeorge 1990, 322–24).

Unions first emerged as a countervailing force against corporations that exerted undue pressure on employees to accept immoral working conditions and practices. Unions also provided a means for employees to strike against management. Strikes are a form of pressure and protest against an action(s) of management that organized workers disagree with. Strikes usually are a last resort after negotiations have failed. Unions have the right to call strikes, since each employee has the right to quit the job, with the conditions that (1) no prior negotiated agreements not to strike are broken and (2) no legitimate moral, safety, or security rights of others are violated (Velasquez 1988, 389–90).

PLANT CLOSINGS AND EMPLOYEE RIGHTS Companies have the right to relocate and transfer operations to any place they choose. If firms can find cheaper labor, raw materials, and transportation costs, lower taxes, no unions, and other business advantages for making a profit, they often will close plants and move. Companies also close plants because of loss of competitiveness, financial losses, and other legitimate economic reasons. The ethical questions posed to corporate managers regarding plant closings are What rights do the employees have who are affected by the closing? What responsibilities does the company have toward the affected communities, and even toward the national economy?

As of August 1988, companies with more than 100 employees must by law give 60 days' notice to workers before closing. Employees also have the following moral rights when companies decide to relocate or close: to be treated fairly, equally, and with justice. That is, employees have the right to be compensated for the costs of retraining, transferring, and relocating; they have the rights to severance pay and to outplacement and support programs that assist them in finding alternative employment; and they have the right to have their pension, health, and retirement plans honored (Velasquez 1988, 388).

Employees also should be given the rights to find a new owner of the plant and to explore the possibility of employee ownership of the plant before it is closed (see Carroll 1989, 1993). These rights extend beyond workers and include the welfare of the communities where the plant operated. Plant closings affect jobs, careers, families, and the local tax base and can even negatively affect the regional and national economies when sizable operations are shut down or moved abroad.

Whatever the motivations for corporations' closing or transferring facilities out of local geographies, the rights of employees and local community groups stand, even though these rights are often negotiated against the utilitarian interests of corporations in specific economic contexts.

THE FAMILY AND MEDICAL LEAVE ACT OF 1993

The Family and Medical Leave Act (FMLA) was enacted into law in 1993, eight years after it was introduced in Congress by Christopher Dodd, William Clay, and Patricia Schroeder. The FMLA entitles eligible employees to a maximum of 12 weeks of unpaid leave per year for the birth or adoption of a child, to care for a spouse or immediate family member with a serious health condition, or when an employee is unable to work due to personal illness. The 12 weeks need not be used consecutively since intermittent leave or reduced work schedules are allowed under the act. To be considered eligible, an employee must have been employed for a continuous 12-month period for at least 1,250 hours during the year preceding the leave.

Companies that employ at last 50 people within a 75-mile radius are mandated to offer such leave. The employer is required to maintain any preexisting health coverage during the leave. Once the leave is concluded, the employee must be reinstated to the same position or an equivalent job. An equivalent position must have the same pay, benefits, working conditions, authority, and responsibilities.

Employers have the right to request a 30-day advance notice for foreseeable absences and may require employees to present evidence to support medically necessitated leave. Employers may request employees to obtain a second medical opinion at the employers' expense. Employers may deny reinstatement of employment to "key employees." Such employees must be among the highest-paid 10 percent of all employees, and their absence must have a serious economic impact on their organization. It is the duty of employers to inform employees of their status as "key employees" when they request a leave.

6.4 DISCRIMINATION, EQUAL EMPLOYMENT OPPORTUNITY, AND AFFIRMATIVE ACTION

It is difficult to imagine that throughout most of the nineteenth century, women in America could not vote, serve on juries, issue lawsuits in their own name, or initiate legal contracts if they lost their property to their husbands. In an 1873 Supreme Court decision, *Bradwell* v. *Illinois*, a woman had "no legal existence, separate from her husband, who was regarded as her head and representative in the social state" (Kanowitz 1969, 36; also quoted in Velasquez 1988, 324).

It is also difficult to imagine the legal status of black people in the United States in 1857. In the Dred Scott case, one of the opinions of the Supreme Court considered blacks as "beings of an inferior order . . . and so far inferior that they had no rights that the white man was bound to respect" (Fehrenbacher 1978). It is against this background that the doctrines, laws, and policies of discrimination, equal opportunity, and affirmative action must be considered.

DISCRIMINATION

Discriminatory practices in employer/employee potential or actual relationships include unequal or disparate treatment of individuals and groups (Des Jardins and McCall 1990, 377–82). Unequal or preferential treatment is based on irrelevant criteria such as gender, race, color, religion, national origin, and disability. Systematic and systemic discrimination is based on historical and institutionally ingrained unequal and disparate treatment against minorities, the disadvantaged, and women.

Examples of contemporary and systemic discrimination in employer/employee relationships are found in practices such as recruitment, screening, promotion, termination, and conditions of employment (Velasquez 1988, 328–29). Recruiting procedures that are biased toward certain groups and that do not openly advertise to minority groups are discriminatory. Screening practices that exclude certain groups and that use biased tests or qualifications are discriminatory. Promotion procedures that have "glass ceilings" (that is, invisible discriminatory barriers to advancement) for women and minority groups are discriminatory. Seniority tracks that favor white males or other groups over minorities or women are discriminatory. Terminating employees on the basis of sex, age, race, or national origin is discriminatory. This chapter's opening case questions whether IBM terminated Richard Rathemacer because of his age. Paying some people lower salaries, wages, and bonuses than others who do the same work is discriminatory.

EQUAL EMPLOYMENT OPPORTUNITY AND THE CIVIL RIGHTS ACT

Title VII of the Civil Rights Act of 1964 makes discrimination on the basis of gender, race, color, religion, or national origin in any term, condition, or privilege of employment illegal. The law prohibits discrimination in the practices just discussed: hiring, classifying, referring, assigning, promoting, training, retraining, conducting apprenticeships, firing, and dispensing wages and fringe benefits. The Civil Rights Act also created the Equal Employment Opportunity Commission as the administrative and implementation agency to investigate complaints individuals submit. The EEOC negotiates and works with the Justice Department regarding complaints; however, the EEOC cannot enforce the law except through grievances.

The Civil Rights Act of 1991 extends for the first time punitive damages to victims of employment discrimination. This law states that job bias based on gender, disability, religion, or national origin will be punished as severely as job discrimination based on race. It also makes it easier for job-bias plaintiffs to win lawsuits. This legislation shifts the legal burden to the employer, who must defend any intentional or unintentional employment bias, especially if the practice in question has a "disparate impact" on minorities or women. Under this law, the employer must demonstrate that the alleged discriminatory act is "job-related for the position in question and consistent with business necessity" (Noah and Karr 1991, 31). "Job-related" and "business necessity" are undefined and will be determined by the courts. The act specifies that employers with more than 500 employees could be liable for up to $300,000 in compensatory and punitive damages. Smaller companies are liable for less, depending on the number of workers.

The Equal Employment Opportunity Act of 1972 amended the 1964 act to empower the EEOC to enforce the law by filing grievances from individuals, job applicants, and employees in the courts. Under the revised act, all private employers with 15 or more persons fall within its jurisdiction, with the exception of bona fide tax-exempt private clubs. All private and public educational institutions and employment agencies are covered by the law. Labor unions (local, national, and international) with 15 or more members are included. Joint labor/management committees that administer apprenticeship, training, and retraining programs are also under this law's jurisdiction.

AGE AND DISCRIMINATION IN THE WORKPLACE The Age Discrimination in Employment Act of 1967 (ADEA), revised in 1978, prohibits employers from discriminating against individuals based on their age (between 40 and 70) in hiring, promotions, terminations, and other employment practices. In 1987, ADEA again was amended when Congress banned any fixed retirement age.

COMPARABLE WORTH AND EQUAL PAY The Equal Pay Act of 1963, amended in 1972, prohibits discriminatory payment of wages and overtime pay based on gender. The law, in large part, is based on the doctrine of "comparable worth." This doctrine and the Equal Pay Act hold that women should be paid wages comparable to men who hold jobs that require equal skill, effort, and responsibility and that have the same working conditions. Women generally are paid 60 cents for each dollar men earn in the marketplace. This law addresses this inequity and also applies to executive, professional, sales, and administrative positions (Buchholz 1990, 318).

AIDS AND DISCRIMINATION AIDS victims are increasingly being discriminated against in the United States. In 1983 the number of complaints based on reports of discrimination and referrals received by legal services and HIV/AIDS organizations was zero. By 1988, that number was more than 2,500. Under the Americans with Disabilities Act of 1992, it is illegal for most companies to fire or reassign an employee only because the person is HIV positive. Although many states have had such laws, this act made employment discrimination illegal at any company with at least 25 employees (Lambert 1991). In 1996, the law began to apply to companies with at least 15 employees.

This law also makes it easier for employees with HIV to sue for punitive damages from discriminatory practices. It extends coverage to address discriminatory practices against HIV-positive people in the areas of housing, health care, and insurance.

This law is only the beginning of what will become more refined and detailed legislation in this area. Presently, it does not apply if an HIV-positive employee's illness presents a threat to others and if the worker cannot find a reasonable way to eliminate that risk.

The laws discussed so far certainly are not inclusive of all the equal-opportunity legislation or federal policy directives passed and amended in the 1960s and 1970s, but these represent some of the more basic, prominent ones.

Laws alone cannot guarantee or equalize employment opportunities, fairness, and justice to members of groups that have been discriminated against historically and that experience bias currently. Stereotypes and biases can be manipulated through subtle, legal means, such as in the ways job descriptions and evaluations are written and carried out, by the types of qualifications included in job descriptions, in advertising methods for jobs, and by other exclusionary conditions and practices of employing and terminating people. Still, equal-opportunity laws and their enforcement are important—even if many do not go far enough in their implementation—in a free-market system governed by law. These laws set social goals and send messages to all involved in employment that minority and disadvantaged groups have equal protection.

AFFIRMATIVE ACTION

Affirmative action programs are a proactive attempt to recruit applicants from minority groups in order to create opportunities for those who, otherwise, because of past and present discriminatory employment practices, would be excluded from the job market. Affirmative action programs attempt to make employment practices blind to color, gender, national origin, disability, and age. Although the doctrine of equal opportunity states that everyone should have an equal chance at obtaining a job and promotion, affirmative action goes further. "Affirmative action implies a set of specific result-oriented procedures designed to achieve equal employment opportunity at a pace beyond that which would occur normally" (Buchholz 1990, 325). As such, affirmative action programs set goals, quotas, and time frames for companies to hire and promote women and minorities in proportion to their numbers in the labor force and in the same or similar occupational categories within the company (Buchholz 1990).

Courts have come to regard affirmative action approaches as integral to the Civil Rights Act, summarized earlier. Federal contractors, for example, are required to analyze their labor force and to file affirmative action plans with goals and time frames to demonstrate how minority hiring will be carried out and reflected in company statistical profiles. When company labor force statistics by job classification show that minority hiring, recruitment, and promotions do not meet affirmative action goals and quotas the company set, or when such statistics show minority "underutilization," discrimination may exist.

DeGeorge (1990) presents four arguments that explain and summarize affirmative action as it applies to hiring, promotions, and terminations:

1. Affirmative action does not justify hiring unqualified minority group members over qualified white males. All individuals must be qualified for the positions in question.

2. Qualified women and minority members can be given preference morally, on the basis of gender or race, over equally qualified white males to achieve affirmative action goals.

3. Qualified women and minority members can be given preference morally over better-qualified white males, also, to achieve affirmative action goals.

4. Companies must make adequate progress toward achieving affirmative action goals even though preferential hiring is not mandatory.

CORPORATE GUIDELINES FOR MANAGING DIVERSITY

Women and minorities quit companies 2.5 times as often as white males. This fact costs employers millions of dollars in lost training and productivity. Companies can retain female and minority employees by doing the following:

❏ Focus on hiring the best talent, not on meeting numerical goals.

❏ Develop career plans for employees as part of performance reviews.

❏ Set up mentoring programs among employees of same and different races.

❏ Promote minorities to decision-making positions, not just staff jobs.

❏ Hold managers accountable for meeting diversity goals.

❏ Diversify the board of directors.

AFFIRMATIVE ACTION AND COMPENSATORY JUSTICE

Affirmative action as a doctrine and the programs and laws derived from the doctrine are defended on the principle of compensatory justice. The argument is that because white males have historically dominated and continue to dominate the highest-paying, most-prestigious employment positions in society, members of groups who have been excluded from comparable employment opportunities because of past and present discriminatory practices deserve to be compensated through affirmative action programs embodied in equal-opportunity laws.

REVERSE DISCRIMINATION: ARGUMENTS AGAINST AFFIRMATIVE ACTION

Arguments against affirmative action are directed toward the doctrine itself and against its implementation of quotas. The doctrine has been criticized on the grounds that nondiscrimination requires discrimination (that is, reverse discrimination). Reverse discrimination is alleged to occur when an equally qualified woman or member of a minority group is given preference over a white male for a job or when less-qualified minorities are given hiring preference over white males through a quota system (Buchholz 1990, 325). Affirmative action, opponents argue, discriminates against gender and race: white males. Some even say affirmative action discriminates against age: white, middle-aged males.

Another major argument against affirmative action observes that individuals are held responsible for injustices they were and are not responsible for. Why should all contemporary and future white males as a group have to compensate for discriminatory practices others in this demographic category committed in another historical time or currently commit?

Although these claims have some validity, proponents of affirmative action argue that injustices from discrimination have been institutionalized against minority groups. It happens that white males continue to benefit from the competitive disadvantages that past and present discriminatory practices have created for others. To compensate and correct for these systemic disadvantages based on color, gender, and other irrelevant (nonemployment related) characteristics, social affirmative action goals and programs must be implemented. Still, the law is not a perfect means to correct past or present injustices. Victims of all colors will continue to be hurt by discrimination and reverse discrimination practices. In the meantime, the court system will continue to use civil rights laws, affirmative action guidelines, and moral reasoning to decide on a case-by-case basis the justice and fairness of employment-related practices. The following discussion is a summary of four notable Supreme Court cases and one U.S. circuit course case that illustrate how affirmative action and discrimination issues have been addressed.

SUPREME COURT RULINGS AND REVERSE DISCRIMINATION

The Bakke Case. Allan Bakke, a white male, sued the Regents of the University of California at Davis because he was denied admission to the medical school in 1973. He sued on the basis of reverse discrimination. Bakke charged that the university gave preferential treatment to less-qualified minorities. Of 100 places in the entering class of 1973, 84 were open for competitive admission; 16 places were given preference for minority candidates. In 1978, the Supreme Court ruled in a five-to-four vote in favor of Bakke. The decision argued against strict quotas but upheld the criterion of race as a consideration in admissions policies. The ruling sent the message that quotas based on race were illegal when no previous discrimination had been proved. However, quotas could be used to offset inequalities as part of settlements when previous discrimination was shown (*Bakke* v. *Regents of the University of California;* Buchholz 1990, 326; Bakke wins, quotas lose 1978).

The Weber Case. Brian Weber, a white male, sued his employer, Kaiser Aluminum and Chemical Corporation, and the Steelworkers Union on the basis he had been discriminated against by his exclusion from a quota-regulated training program. Weber won the case at the lower District Court and at the Court of Appeals. However, in 1979, the Supreme Court, in a five-to-two vote, overturned these decisions (*Weber* v. *Kaiser Aluminum and Chemical Corporation*). The Court ruled that African Americans can be given special consideration for what have been white-dominated jobs and that affirmative action programs are legal in order to rectify "manifest racial imbalances." The message the Supreme Court sent to employers was that reverse-discrimination charges should not prevent them from implementing affirmative action programs. In this case, white citizens were not displaced or hurt because of the quota-based training program.

The Stotts Case. Carl Stotts, a black district fire chief in Memphis, sued the Memphis Fire Department in a class-action suit in 1977, charging that the department discriminated against him and other black citizens in its policy of "last hired, first fired" (or LIFO, "last in, first out"). The city announced layoffs in 1981 because of a budget deficit. It implemented the layoffs with a union-negotiated seniority policy. Stotts won at the District Court level but lost in an appeal by the city of Memphis and the labor union in the Supreme Court in 1984. The majority vote in the Supreme Court ruled that bona fide seniority systems are protected under the 1964 Civil Rights Act and could not be disrupted, especially during layoff periods. The ruling, in effect, sent a message to employers that bona fide seniority systems are blind to color.

The Adarand Constructors v. *Pena Case.* The Court's attitude on minority preference programs has begun to change. In 1995, its ruling in *Adarand*

Constructors v. *Pena* effectively eliminated mandatory contract-set-aside programs for minorities. The case questioned the legality of a federal mandate that required at least 10 percent of federally funded highway projects go to businesses owned by minorities or women. The majority opinion, written by Justice Sandra Day O'Conner, states that all racial classifications must be held to rigorous judicial standards, whether passed by Congress or the states, and must be narrowly tailored to advance governmental interests. This overrules the previous 1990 decision that allowed Congress to mandate a program specifically designed to increase the number of minority broadcasters. In *Missouri* v. *Jenkins,* the Supreme Court reviewed a federally directed racial-integration program that required the State of Missouri to spend more than $200 million a year to improve inner-city schools. The Court ruling did not dismantle the program but questioned the methods used to measure its progress (The end of affirmative action 1995).

The Hopwood v. Texas Case. A U.S. circuit court ruled that the University of Texas could not use race as a determining factor for admissions. In this case, several white students sued the school when they were not admitted because of the school's policy to admit a certain number of non-white students. This ruling opened the door for other educational systems to reevaluate their admission quotas. It also may have the potential to limit admission policies that consider the racial diversity of students. If this case affects other educational institutions, affirmative action policies could be questioned in business as well. Presently, it is not easy to predict. The issue remains: Is the playing field level in the U.S. society or not regarding race (Mollins 1995; Gwynne 1996)?

These cases show that the Supreme Court can change directions in its decisions on and guidelines for affirmative action and the protection of minority and women stakeholders in their business environments. Nevertheless, the Court continues to interpret affirmative action on a case-by-case basis. The messages the Court has sent to employers indicate that (1) it is in the best interests of businesses to take a proactive approach in addressing affirmative action and Equal Employment Opportunity goals, timetables, and guidelines in their recruitment, hiring, promotion, and termination policies; and (2) bona fide seniority systems are still generally protected under civil rights laws. For employer and employee stakeholders, moral reasoning and legal guidelines regarding affirmative action go hand in hand with making employment-related decisions.

6.5 SEXUAL HARASSMENT IN THE WORKPLACE

A former marketing representative for International Business Machines Corp. was awarded $65,000 by a state court jury in Santa Monica, Calif., in a sexual harassment case. In her unusual lawsuit, Veronica Gunther had alleged that she was pressured to resume a sexual relationship with a senior Defense Department official in order to secure federal funding for the company. The jury, in a 9-3 vote, found that IBM had harassed Ms. Gunther and awarded her damages for emotional distress. (Holden 1995)

Sexual harassment was not a specific violation of federal law before 1981. It now may be difficult to imagine flagrant acts of sexual violation against women, as recent as 20 years ago, such as when women entered mines and, like their male counterparts, were stripped and soaked in axle grease in a primitive hazing ritual, and then, unlike the male employees, the women were tied to wooden supports in spread-eagle positions (Strom 1991, 22). More recently, the Senate hearings on sexual harassment charges against Supreme Court nominee Clarence Thomas awakened public and corporate concern about sexual harassment in society and the workplace. In addition, the overt sexual harassment of female naval professionals also has brought attention to this issue. Although sexual harassment can be and is committed by both men and women, it is more often women who are the unwilling victims.

Is sexual harassment in the workplace widespread or isolated? In a *National Law Journal* survey, 60 percent of 900 women in 250 top law firms indicated they had experienced sexual harassment (DeWitt 1991, 29). Moreover, sexual harassment was ruled in 6,342 job-discrimination cases filed in 1984, an increase over the 5,110 claims filed in 1983. By 1985, the number of complaints climbed to 7,273. Between 1979 and 1984, federal courts had dealt with 300 sexual harassment cases (Sexual harassment 1986). An AT&T spokesperson states that 19 out of every 20 complaints about sexual harassment are valid.

Sexual harassment in the military has been exposed and has come under scrutiny. Widespread incidents in the Navy and Army show that women, in particular, have been harassed by superior ranking officers who have threatened women's job status and security.

WHAT IS SEXUAL HARASSMENT?

The Supreme Court ruled in 1986 that sexual harassment is illegal under Title VII of the 1964 Civil Rights Act and that when a "hostile environment" is created through sexual harassment in the workplace, thereby interfering with an employee's performance, the law is violated—regardless of economic harm done or of demands for sexual favors in exchange for raises, promotions, bonuses, and other employment-related opportunities (Machlowitz and Machlowitz 1986, 20; Wermiel and Trost 1986, 2).

Under Title VII, the EEOC guidelines (1980) define sexual harassment as follows:

Unwelcome sexual advances, requests for sexual favors, and other verbal or physical conduct of a sexual nature constitute sexual harassment when (1) submission to such conduct is made either explicitly or implicitly a term or condition of an individual's employment, (2) submission to or rejection of such conduct by an individual is used as the basis for employment decisions affecting such individual, or (3) such conduct has the purpose or effect of unreasonably interfering with an individual's work performance or creating an intimidating, hostile, or offensive working environment.

The courts have defined sexual harassment as conduct ranging from blatant grabbing and touching to more subtle hints and suggestions about sex. Forms of sexual harassment include the following (Hayes 1991, B1; Lublin 1991, B1):

- ❑ Unwelcome sexual advances
- ❑ Coercion
- ❑ Favoritism
- ❑ Indirect harassment
- ❑ Physical conduct
- ❑ Visual harassment (for example, courts have ruled that sexual harassment was committed when graffiti were written on men's bathroom walls about a female employee and when pornographic pictures were displayed in the workplace)

WHO IS LIABLE?

The EEOC guidelines place absolute liability on employers for actions and violations of the law by their managers and supervisors, whether or not the conduct was known, authorized, or forbidden by the employer. Employers also are liable for coworkers' conduct if the employer knew, or should have known, of the actions in question, unless the employer shows—after learning of the problem—that it took immediate and appropriate action to correct the situation. Employers may be liable for non-employees under the same conditions as those stated for coworkers (Mastalli 1991, 157, 158).

Moreover, under EEOC guidelines employers are responsible for establishing programs (as well as standards) that develop, train, and inform employees about sanctions and procedures for dealing with sexual harassment complaints (see Figure 6.2). It is in the employer's economic as well as moral interest to institute such programs, since courts mitigate damages against companies that have harassment prevention and training programs.

Some of the leaders in establishing sexual harassment policies and programs are AT&T, Du Pont, Digital Equipment Corporation, Corning Inc., and Honeywell, to mention only a few.

■ **FIGURE 6.2**

GENERAL MOTORS' SEXUAL HARASSMENT POLICY

Sexual Harassment Policy

1. Sexual harassment is a violation of the corporation's EEO policy. Abuse of anyone through sexist slurs or other objectionable conduct is offensive behavior.

2. Management must ensure that a credible program exists for handling sexual harassment problems. If complaints are filed, they should receive prompt consideration without fear of negative consequences.

3. When a supervisor is made aware of an allegation of sexual harassment, the following guidelines should be considered.

   a. Obtain information about the allegation through discussion with the complainant. Ask for and document facts about what was said, what was done, when and where it occurred, and what the complainant believes was the inappropriate behavior. In addition, find out if any other individuals observed the incident, or similar incidents, to the complainant's knowledge. This is an *initial* step. In no case will the supervisor handle the complaint process alone.

   b. If the complaint is from an hourly employee, a request for union representation at any point must be handled as described in the labor agreement.

   c. The immediate supervisor or the department head and the personnel department must be notified *immediately*. When a complaint is raised by, or concerns, an hourly employee, the local labor relations representative is to be advised. When a complaint is raised by or concerns a salaried employee, the personnel director is to be advised.

4. The personnel department will conduct a complete investigation of the complaint for hourly and salaried employees. The investigation is to be handled in a professional and confidential manner.

*Policy example is based on General Motors' Corporate policy on sexual harassment.

SEXUAL-HARASSMENT AND FOREIGN FIRMS IN THE UNITED STATES

Two foreign companies operating in the United States have recently reacted differently to sexual harassment charges—a perilous area where the law and societal norms are rapidly changing. These companies' reactions have exposed them to increased liability. One of the firms, Astra— a Swedish pharmaceutical firm—fired its CEO of the U.S. subsidiary and two other top managers. The other company, Mitsubishi, has denied all charges, has maintained that EEOC is wrong, and has mounted a full-scale public-relations campaign to discredit complainers. Both the companies lack one of the most basic requirements consultants recommend: a clear and strong written policy on sexual harassment (Johannes 1996).

INDIVIDUAL GUIDELINES

Although sexual harassment often occurs as part of a power issue—that is, people in more-powerful positions exert pressure over people in less-powerful posts—a frequent observation is that men and women tend to see sexual harassment differently. This certainly does not justify legally or morally unwelcome sexual advances. It does suggest, however, that employers need to provide adequate education, training, and role-playing between the sexes so that gender differences in perceptions and feelings on what constitutes sexual harassment can be understood. Some practical guidelines employees (men in this instance) can use to check their motives and behavior regarding sexual harassment include the following (Foreman and Lehman, 1991):

- ❏ If you are unsure whether you have offended a woman, ask her. If you did offend, apologize, and don't do it again.
- ❏ Talk over your behavior with noninvolved women and with men you can trust not to make a mockery of your concerns.
- ❏ Ask yourself how you would feel if a man behaved toward your daughter the way you feel you may be behaving toward women.
- ❏ Ask yourself also if you would act this way if the shoe were on the other foot—if the woman were your boss or if she were physically stronger or more powerful than you.
- ❏ Most of all, don't interpret a woman's silence as consent. Silence is, at least, "a red light." Through silence, a woman may be trying to send you a signal of discomfort.
- ❏ Be very certain your comments or behaviors are welcome, and if they are not, stop them.

6.6 WHISTLE-BLOWING VERSUS ORGANIZATIONAL LOYALTY

Among all of the rights discussed in this chapter, one of the most valued of a U.S. citizen is the freedom of speech. But how far does this right extend into the corporation, especially if an employee observes an employer committing an illegal or immoral activity that could harm others? What are the obligations and limits of employee loyalty to the employer? Under what, if any, circumstances should employees blow the whistle on their supervisors, managers, or firms?

Whistle-blowing is "the attempt of an employee or former employee of an organization to disclose what he or she believes to be wrongdoing in or by the organization" (James 1990, 332). Whistle-blowing can be internal (reported to an executive in the organization), external (reported to external public interest groups, the media, or enforcement agencies), personal (harm reportedly done only to the whistle-blower), and impersonal (harm observed as done to another; James 1990, 333). Whistle-blowing goes against strong U.S. cultural norms of showing loyalty toward one's employer and compatriots and of avoiding the snitch label. However, strong cultural norms regarding fairness, justice, a sense of duty, and obedience to the law and to one's conscience also exist. A moral dilemma occurs when a loyal employee observes the employer committing or assisting in an illegal or immoral act and must decide what to do.

For example, Roland LeBlanc of Natick, Massachusetts, and a former inspector for the Defense Department's contract administration service, has charged Raytheon with knowingly shipping defective missile and radar parts to the army and navy and fraudulently fabricating data to hide the problems. LeBlanc sued Raytheon under the Federal False Claims Act, which was intended to encourage citizens to report fraud by awarding whistle-blowers 25 percent of any damages paid to the government. The issue perplexing the courts in this case is whether government employees can bring a case under this statute given their knowledge of alleged wrongdoing acquired in the course of their work. The First U.S. Circuit Court of Appeals ruled in 1990 that LeBlanc, as an employee, could not sue his employer, Raytheon. The U.S. Supreme Court in 1991 declined to hear an appeal by LeBlanc of that decision. Since then, the Eleventh and Ninth Courts of Appeals have contradicted the First Court's decision and ruled that a federal employee is not barred from issuing a lawsuit under the act. LeBlanc is suing Raytheon in the U.S. District Court in Orlando, Florida. He had been fighting the case for more than seven years (Hemp 1992).

Under what conditions, then, is whistle-blowing morally justified? DeGeorge (1990, 208–14) discusses five conditions:

1. When the firm through a product or policy will commit serious and considerable harm to the public (as consumers or bystanders), the employee should report the firm.

2. When the employee identifies a serious threat of harm, he or she should report it and state his or her moral concern.

3. When the employee's immediate supervisor does not act, the employee should exhaust the internal procedures and chain of command to the board of directors.

4. The employee must have documented evidence that is convincing to a reasonable, impartial observer that his or her view of the situation is

accurate and evidence that the firm's practice, product, or policy seriously threatens and puts in danger the public or product user.

5. The employee must have valid reasons to believe that revealing the wrongdoing to the pubic will result in the necessary changes to remedy the situation. The chance of succeeding must be equal to the risk and danger the employee takes to blow the whistle.

The risks to whistle-blowers can range from outright termination to more subtle pressures, such as strong and hidden criticisms, undesirable and burdensome work assignments, lost perks, and exclusion from communication loops and social invitations (Near, Miceli, and Jensen 1983; cited in Carroll 1989). Although 21 states have laws protecting corporate and governmental whistle-blowers from reprisal, experience shows that the government's actual protection to whistle-blowers, even if after resigning or being fired they are reinstated with back pay and compensation for physical suffering, is weak because of the many subtle forms of retaliation, such as those just listed (Carroll 1989, 356).

WHEN WHISTLE-BLOWERS SHOULD NOT BE PROTECTED

The most obvious conditions when whistle-blowers should not be protected are when their accusations are false and when their motives are not justifiable or accurate.

David Ewing (1977) states the following instances when whistle-blowers should not have freedom of speech against their employers:

❏ When divulging information about legal and ethical plans, practices, operations, inventions, and other matters that should remain confidential and that are necessary for the organization to perform its work efficiently

❏ When an employee's personal accusations or slurs are irrelevant to questions about policies and practices that appear illegal or irresponsible

❏ When an employee's accusations do not show a conviction that a wrongdoing is being committed and when such accusations disrupt or damage the organization's morale

❏ When employees complain against a manager's competence to make daily work decisions that are irrelevant to the legality, morality, or responsibility of management actions

❏ When employees object to their discharge, transfer, or demotion if management can show that unsatisfactory performance or violation of a code of conduct was the reason for the decision

FACTORS TO CONSIDER BEFORE
BLOWING THE WHISTLE

Whistle-blowing is a serious action with real consequences. It often involves a decision to be made among conflicting moral, legal, economic, personal, family, and career demands and choices. No single answer may appear. A stakeholder analysis and questions can help the potential whistle-blower identify the groups and individuals, stakes, priorities, and trade-offs when selecting among different strategies and courses of action.

The following 12 guidelines offer factors (James 1990) a person should consider when deciding whether to blow the whistle on an employer:

1. Make sure the situation warrants whistle-blowing. If serious trade secrets or confidential company property will be exposed, know the harm and calculated risks.

2. Examine your motives.

3. Verify and document your information. Can your information stand up in a hearing and in court?

4. Determine the type of wrongdoing and to whom it should be reported. Knowing this will assist in gathering the type of evidence to obtain.

5. State your allegations specifically and appropriately. Obtain and state the type of data that will substantiate your claim.

6. Stay with the facts. This minimizes retaliation and avoids irrelevant mudslinging, name-calling, and stereotyping.

7. Decide whether to report to internal contacts or external contacts. Select the internal channel first if that route has proved effective and less damaging to whistle-blowers. Otherwise, select the appropriate external contacts.

8. Decide whether to be open or anonymous. Should you choose to remain anonymous, document the wrongdoing and anticipate what you will do if your identity is revealed.

9. Decide whether current or alumni whistle-blowing is the best alternative. Should you blow the whistle while you are an employee or resign first? Resigning should not be an automatic option. If the wrongdoing affects others, your decision is not only a personal one, but also you are fulfilling moral obligations beyond your own welfare.

10. Follow proper guidelines in reporting the wrongdoing. Check forms, meeting deadlines, and other technicalities.

11. Consult a lawyer at every step of the way.

12. Anticipate and document retaliation. This assists your effectiveness with courts and regulatory agencies.

MANAGERIAL STEPS TO PREVENT EXTERNAL WHISTLE-BLOWING

Managers have a responsibility to listen to and respond to their employees, especially regarding the observations of and reporting of illegal and immoral acts. Chapter 4 discussed mechanisms such as "ethics offices," ombudsperson programs, and peer review programs. These are part of a corporation's responsibility to provide due process for employees to report personal grievances, to obtain effective and just resolution of them, and to report wrongdoings of others, including the employers. Four straightforward and simple steps management can take to prevent external whistle-blowing follow (James 1990; see also Ezorsky 1987; Grosman 1989; Walters 1975):

1. Develop effective internal grievance procedures and processes that employees can use to report wrongdoings.

2. Reward people for using these channels.

3. Appoint senior executives and others whose primary responsibilities are to investigate and report wrongdoing.

4. Assess large fines for illegal actions. Include executives and professionals who file false or illegal reports, who knowingly market dangerous products, or who offer bribes or take kickbacks.

Preventing, reporting, and effectively and fairly correcting illegal and immoral actions, policies, and procedures are the responsibilities of employers and employees. Management cannot expect employees to be loyal to a company that promotes or allows wrongdoing to its stakeholders. Whistle-blowing should be a last resort. A more active goal is to hire, train, and promote morally and legally sensitive and responsive managers who communicate with and work for the welfare of all stakeholders.

SUMMARY

The demographics of workforce 2000 are changing and will continue to change. These changes include the aging of employees and thus the "shrinking" of the workforce, an increasing number of women and minority entrants, the growing gap in educational levels, and a greater demand for the skills of disabled workers. These changes in the composition of the workforce signal changes in work-related values and motivations. Corporations and managers can expect moral tensions to rise regarding issues such as age discrimination, health care demands, conflicting communication, and requests for flexible as well as more structured work schedules. "One size fits all" management techniques will not work.

The social contract between corporations and employees has changed and will continue to do so. The original employment-at-will doctrine has been replaced by the doctrine of implied employee rights; still, the EAW policy is not dead. Many firms, large and small, use this policy—some explicitly, others less visibly. The three underlying concepts of employee rights are balance, governmental rights, and moral entitlement.

The nature of legal and moral relationships between employers and employees is also changing. Recent court decisions have backed down in supporting racial affirmative action practices. Although EEOC policies and affirmative action practices remain a part of federal law, some states are showing less acceptance of these laws and procedures. Current and future issues related to sexual harassment and reverse discrimination will continue to shape legal and moral guidelines for corporations. Conflicts regarding due process, privacy, and other employee rights issues will continue to be resolved through court cases and legislation; their resolution will influence corporate policies in the future.

Sexual harassment laws and guidelines for employers and employees were presented and discussed. The moral dilemma of organizational loyalty versus personal ethics was analyzed. The justification of whistle-blowing was evaluated and alternatives to it were provided. Guidelines were offered for employees to consider before blowing the whistle and for corporations to prevent external whistle-blowing.

QUESTIONS

1. Identify five major trends in the changing demographics of the workforce. Can you think of other changes now occurring in the workforce?

2. Identify moral tensions and conflicts associated with these changes in question 1.

3. What are major factors an employer should consider to avoid arbitrarily terminating an employee?

4. What does the term *moral entitlement* mean as it relates to employee rights? Give an example. Do you agree that employees have moral entitlement to some rights in the workplace? Explain.

5. According to Patricia Werhane, what are some procedural mechanisms that ensure an employee's right to due process?

6. What are the changes in the Civil Rights Act of 1991?

7. Do you believe members of groups in the United States who have been historically discriminated against should be protected and compensated under affirmative action now? Explain.

8. What are some arguments for and against "reverse discrimination"? Is the "playing field" in U.S. corporations more level now? What is your view on this topic?

9. Describe criteria used to determine whether verbal or physical actions constitute sexual harassment. What are some specific types of sexual harassment? Have you been sexually harassed in a work setting? Can you describe what happened and the outcome?

10. Are employees more or less loyal to employers and their companies now? Explain. Should employees be more loyal to their employers? Why or why not?

11. Do you believe whistle-blowing is justifiable in corporations? Why or why not?

12. How can corporate managers prevent whistle-blowing? Explain.

EXERCISES

1. Identify an example in the recent news of a court decision relating to discrimination or reverse discrimination. Briefly describe the case and the outcome. What are the implications of this decision for employers and other stakeholders? Do you agree with the outcome? Explain.

2. Select an employee right in the workplace from the chapter. Give an example, based on your own outside reading or experience, of a case involving this right. Was it violated? How? What was the outcome? What should the outcome have been? Why?

3. Identify an example from your own experience of discrimination or sexual harassment. Did this experience influence your view of affirmative action or employee protection programs? If so, how?

4. Write a paragraph or two describing a situation from your experience in which you felt justified in blowing the whistle. Did you? Why or why not? Under what circumstances do you feel whistle-blowing is justified? Use this justification to support your opinion of the case of Roland LeBlanc.

REFERENCES AND SUGGESTED READINGS

Atlanta Journal, 26 January 1996.

Ayres, Marilyn B. 1994. When AIDS hits home. *Small Business Reports* (July): 14–19.

Bakke v. *Regents of the University of California*, 553 p. 2d 1152 (1976).

Bakke wins, quotas lose. 1978. *Time*, 10 July, 8–20.

Beauchamp, Tom L., and Norman E. Bowie. 1988. *Ethical theory and business*. 3d ed. Englewood Cliffs: Prentice Hall.

Bjork, Lars. 1975. An experiment in work satisfaction. *Scientific American* (March): 17–23.

Bordwin, Milton. 1995. AIDS: The disease for which you call your lawyer. *Management Review* (January): 42–44.

Buchholz, Rogene A. 1990. *Essentials of public policy for management.* 2d ed. Englewood Cliffs: Prentice Hall.

Bunzel, John H. 1991. AIDS risks in black and white. *Wall Street Journal,* 17 December.

Carroll, Archie B. 1989, 1993. *Business and society: Ethics and stakeholder management.* 1st, 3d eds. Cincinnati: South-Western.

Curfman, Gregory. 1991. Patients vs. physicians. *Boston Globe,* 1 October, 17.

DeGeorge, Richard T. 1990. *Business ethics.* 3d ed. New York: Macmillan Publishing.

Des Jardins, Joseph R., and John J. McCall. 1985. A defense of employee rights. *Journal of Business Ethics* 4: 367–76.

———. 1990. *Contemporary issues in business ethics.* 2d ed. Belmont, CA: Wadsworth.

DeWitt, Karen. 1991. As harassment drama plays, many U.S. employees live it. *New York Times,* October, 29.

Diversity: Beyond the numbers game. *Business Week,* 14 August, 60.

Dobrzynski, Judith H. 1996. The glass ceiling for corporate women made crystal clear, once again. *International Herald Tribune,* 4 March.

The end of affirmative action. 1995. *New Republic,* 3 July, v213, p. 7.

Equal Employment Opportunity Commission. 10 November 1980. *Guidelines on discrimination on the basis of sex.* Washington DC: Government Printing Office.

Ewing, David. 1977. *Freedom inside the organization: Bringing civil liberties to the workplace.* New York: McGraw-Hill.

Ezorsky, Gertrude, ed. 1987. *Moral rights in the workplace.* New York: State University of New York Press.

The Family and Medical Leave Act of 1993. Department of Labor. Federal Register, 31794, 31798, 31798, 31804, 31805.

Fehrenbacher, Don. 1978. *The Dred Scott case.* New York: Oxford University Press.

Foreman, Judy, and Betsy Lehman. 1991. What to do if you think you may be guilty of sex harassment. *Boston Globe,* 21 October.

Franklin, Geralyn M., Alice B. Gresham, and Gwen F. Fontennot. 1992. AIDS in the workplace: Current practices and critical issues. *Journal of Small Business Management* 30 (April): 61.

Fulmer, William, and Ann Casey. 1990. Employment at will: Options for managers. *Academy of Management Review* 4, no. 2: 102.

Galen, Michele. 1991. Is Big Blue hostile to gray hairs? *Business Week,* 21 October, 33.

Goldstein, Robert, and Richard Nolan. 1975. Personal privacy versus the corporate computer. *Harvard Business Review* (March/April): 62–70.

Griswold et al. v. *Connecticut*, No. 496, 85 Sup. Ct. 1678 (1965).

Grosman, Brian. 1989. Corporate loyalty: Does it have a future? *Journal of Business Ethics* 8: 565–68.

Gwynne, S. C. 1996. Undoing diversity; a bombshell court ruling curtails affirmative action. *Time*, 1 April, v147, p. 54.

Hayes, Arthur. 1991. How the courts define harassment. *Wall Street Journal*, 11 October, B1.

Hemp, Paul. 1992. Whistle-blower suing Raytheon. *Boston Globe*, 21 February, 59, 65.

Holden, A. Benjamin. 1995. IBM set back in sexual harassment case. *Wall Street Journal*, 18 July, B7.

Human capital: The decline of America's work force. 1988. *Business Week*, 19 September, 129.

James, Gene. 1990. Whistle blowing: Its moral justification. In *Business ethics: Readings and cases in corporate morality*. 2d ed. Edited by Michael Hoffman and Jennifer Moore. New York: McGraw-Hill, 332.

Jamieson, David, and Julie O'Mara. 1991. *Managing workforce 2000: Gaining the diversity advantage*. San Francisco: Jossey-Bass.

Johannes, Laura, and Joann S. Lublin. 1996. Sexual-harassment cases trip up foreign companies. *Wall Street Journal*, 9 May, B4.

Kanowitz, Leo. 1969. *Women and the law*. Albuquerque: University of New Mexico Press.

Karr, Albert, and Rose Guthfield. 1992. OSHA inches toward limiting smoking. *Wall Street Journal*, 16 January, B1.

Lambert, Wade. 1991. Discrimination afflicts people with HIV. *Wall Street Journal*, 19 November, B1, B6.

Leary, Warren. 1991. A.M.A. backs off of an AIDS risk list. *New York Times*, 15 December, 38.

Lublin, Joann. 1991. Companies try a variety of approaches to halt sexual harassment on the job. *Wall Street Journal*, 11 October, B1.

Machlowitz, Marilyn, and David Machlowitz. 1986. Hug by the boss could lead to a slap from the judge. *Wall Street Journal*, 25 September, 20.

Mastalli, Grace. 1991. Appendix: The legal context. In *Policies and reasons: A casebook in business ethics*. 2d ed. Edited by John Matthews, Kenneth Goodpaster, and Laura Nash. New York: McGraw-Hill, 157, 158.

Meyers, Diana. 1988. Work and self-respect. In *Ethical theory and business*. 3d ed. Edited by Tom L. Beauchamp and Norman E. Bowie. Englewood Cliffs: Prentice Hall, 275–79.

Mollins, Carl. 1995. Shaky freedoms: The U.S. Supreme Court challenges liberalism. *Maclean's*, 17 July, v108, p. 22.

Monge v. *Beebe Rubber Co.*, 114 N. H. 130, 316 A. 2nd 549 (1974).

Near, Janet, Marcia Miceli, and Ramila Jensen. 1983. Variables associated with the whistle-blowing process. Working Paper Series 83-111 (March), Ohio State University, College of Administrative Science, Columbus, 5. Cited in Carroll 1989, 354, 355.

Noah, Timothy, and Albert Karr. 1991. What new civil rights law will mean: Charges of sex, disability bias will multiply. *Wall Street Journal*, 4 November, 31.

Payne v. *Western A.R.R. Co.*, 81. Tenn 507 (1884). Also cited in Steiner and Steiner 1991, 625.

Pugh v. *See's Candies, Inc.*, 161 Cal. App. 3rd 311, 171 Cal. Rqtr. 917 (1981).

Rochell, Anne. 1994. World AIDS day. *Atlanta Journal and Constitution*, 4 December.

Samuels, Patrice Duggan. 1996. Who's reading your E-mail? Maybe the boss. *New York Times*, 12 May, 11.

Sexual harassment: Companies could be liable. 1986. *Business Week*, 31 March, 35.

Shoa, Maria. 1995. Working and coexisting affirmative action hasn't yet altered the balance of power in corporate America, but it has changed the working environment. *Boston Globe*, 24 May, 1.

Simmons, John, and William Mares. 1983. *Working together*. New York: Knopf.

Sitomer, Curtis J. 1986. Privacy and personal freedoms: The impact of technology. *Christian Science Monitor*, 5 December, 1.

Slack, D. James. 1995. The Americans with Disabilities Act and the workplace: Management's responsibilities in AIDS-related situations. *Public Administration Review* (July/August): 365–70.

Steiner, George A., and John F. Steiner. 1991. *Business, government and society: A managerial perspective*. 6th ed. New York: McGraw-Hill.

Strom, Stephanie. 1991. Harassment rules often not posted. *New York Times*, 20 October, 1, 22.

Sullivan, Barbara. 1996. Breaking the glass ceiling slowly. *Chicago Tribune*, 28 February, 3.

Tannen, Deborah. 1990. *You just don't understand*. New York: Morrow.

U.S. AIDS cases hit 206,392; quicker spread is feared. 1992. *Boston Globe*, 17 January, 10.

Velasquez, Manuel G. 1988, 1992. *Business ethics: Concepts and cases*. 2d, 3d eds. Englewood Cliffs: Prentice Hall.

Walters, Kenneth. 1975. Your employees' right to blow the whistle. *Harvard Business Review* (July/August): 160–62.

Weber v. *Kaiser Aluminum and Chemical Corporation*, 563 F. 2nd 216 (5th Cir. 1977).

Werhane, Patricia. 1985. *Persons, rights and corporations*. Englewood Cliffs: Prentice Hall.

Wermiel, Stephen, and Cathy Trost. 1986. Justices say hostile job environment due to sex harassment violates rights. *Wall Street Journal*, 20 June, 2.

7

NATIONS AND MULTINATIONAL STAKEHOLDERS

At 23, Naren is on the fast track. A recent computer science graduate from one of the best schools in India, Naren is a hotshot programmer at Bangalore-based Infosys Technologies Ltd., one of the most respected contract programming firms in the country. Programmers like Naren, "twenty-something" and ambitious, are hotter than Indian curry in a market that can't seem to churn them out fast enough. Starting salaries average $4,500 a year, high by Indian standards, but about one-tenth of what comparable U.S. programmers earn. With a relatively small market, at around $500 million a year, India's software business is mushrooming. It grew by 115% in 1993 and 61% in 1994, according to the National Association of Software and Service companies (Nasscom). And in a survey of Indian information technology companies, 42% expect India's worldwide market share to grow to six times its current size in the next three to five years. It is no longer only the low-end legacy system jobs that are migrating to such countries as India. Work involving relational databases, C++, computer-aided software engineering tools, object-oriented programming, multimedia, networking and some niche market applications are starting to go over the satellite to India. In some cases, U.S. companies are shipping all their development work overseas. (Moshavi 1994)

The global environment is changing. The "five economic tectonic plates" (Thurow 1996, 8) or forces driving these unprecedented changes include (1) the end of communism and the opening of closed economies; (2) a technological shift to an era dominated by human brainpower industries; (3) shifting demographics; (4) a global economy; and (5) an era with no dominant economic, political, or military power. In addition, entrepreneurship, as the opening paragraph suggests, is no longer only an American or Western ideal. Entrepreneurs are younger and more mobile than before, skilled, intelligent, and thriving worldwide. As a result of these changes, nation-states are moving toward capitalism as the preferred economic system. This chapter discusses the characteristics of the global business environment and nations as stakeholders.

7.1 THE COMPETITIVE GLOBAL BUSINESS ENVIRONMENT

The twenty-first century global environment started evolving after World War II and began to change rapidly in the late 1970s when global firms were organizing (Porter 1986). In addition to the forces mentioned earlier, the following factors also contributed to the emergence of global firms and the present competitive business environment:

❑ The rise of Japan's and Germany's dominant economies, which supported many of the non-U.S. multinational corporations now responsible for ending North American dominance in several world markets

❑ The entrance of newly industrialized countries (NICs), such as Spain, Taiwan, Korea, China, and Indonesia, that produce and push low-cost, high-quality commercial products into markets faster than U.S. firms

❑ The convergence of consumer needs and preferences in what Kinichi Ohmae (1985) termed the "Triad," which includes the economies of Japan, Europe, and North America—a combined market of 640 million people with purchasing power. The firms that penetrate and control these markets dominate their global competition. Since 50 percent of free-world trade is concentrated in the Triad, global firms that can mass-produce consumer products ahead of the competition will win market share (Ohmae 1985).

❑ The emergence of other new market economies and blocs in addition to the Triad, such as eastern Europe, the C.I.S. (or former U.S.S.R.), and Canada/United States/Mexico, that also are dropping trade barriers, expanding the competitive playing field, and providing new opportunities, rules, and success criteria for competing (Daft 1992).

❑ The open access to information across geographies through the Internet and within companies through intranet technologies.

EIGHT MEGATRENDS FOR ASIA

The rising Asian market also must be included as a significant force in the emerging global economy. Nasbitt's (1996) eight trends for Asia illustrate the importance of this region as a major economic player.

1. FROM NATION-STATES TO NETWORKS   Japan as a powerful nation-state is transitioning into a dynamic collaboration with the Chinese network. Considerations about China and the overseas Chinese now drive decision making in Asia as China becomes central to the Pacific region. The overseas Chinese network will dominate the region—not China. According to estimates, Chinese around the world hold between $2 trillion and $3 trillion in assets.

2. FROM TRADITIONS TO OPTIONS   Predestination beliefs are being replaced by ideas of diversity and a new individualism. In economic competition the West is handicapped by the heavy burden of the welfare state, which the East will not adopt. A new Asian assertiveness has emerged. The top Asian values for individuals include hard work, respect for learning, and honesty. The top Asian values for society include orderliness, harmony, and accountability of public officials.

3. FROM EXPORT LED TO CONSUMER DRIVEN   By A.D. 2000, Asia will have almost half a billion middle-class people. Built on exports, Asian economies will increasingly be fueled by consumer spending and an emerging middle class. The middle class, not counting Japan, is spending $8 trillion to $10 trillion, 50 percent more than today's U.S. economy.

4. FROM GOVERNMENT CONTROLLED TO MARKET DRIVEN   Central governmental control and the direction of the region's economies have shifted to a market system. Asian politics and ideology are becoming increasingly irrelevant to citizens. With a 7 percent annual economic growth rate, no one wants a revolution. Tales of the success of Asia's "Four Tigers" are legendary. Hong Kong, Singapore, South Korea, and Taiwan leapfrogged over the industrial revolution and pushed full force into the information age.

5. FROM FARMS TO SUPERCITIES   The migration from farms to cities in Asia is extraordinary. By 2010, 30 cities will have a population of more than 5 million, compared to only 2 U.S. cities and 6 European cities with these numbers. Asian cities also are racing to put up symbols of success. Of the world's top-ten tallest buildings scheduled for completion in the 1990s, nine are in Asia.

6. FROM LABOR INTENSIVE TO HIGH TECHNOLOGY   A massive shift from labor-intensive agriculture and manufacturing to state-of-the-art technology in manufacturing and services is occurring in Asia, especially in the computer and telecommunications fields. India is Asia's answer to Silicon Valley. Since 1989, India's software exports have averaged a stunning 40 percent increase. Hong Kong has the world's most-sophisticated phone system (Singapore might disagree). In 1991, Taiwan embarked on a $300 billion six-year, national infrastructure development plan.

7. FROM MALE DOMINANCE TO THE EMERGENCE OF WOMEN   In China, women make up 25 percent of all entrepreneurs. Women as voters, consumers, and members of the workforce now are participating in all aspects of Asian life in unprecedented ways. In Korea, women hold 60.6 percent of all the jobs. Of the 9.9 million women in Taiwan, 4.4 million have full-time careers.

8. FROM WEST TO EAST   An "Asianization" of the world is occurring. The global axis of influence is shifting from West to East. Only 35 years ago East Asian economies, including Japan's, contributed 4 percent of the world's output. Now Asia contributes 24 percent, the same amount as the United States, Canada, and Mexico. By the end of this century, the number will rise to 33 percent.

Some of the major competition success factors for global firms in this emerging global economy follow:

1. The capability to design, manufacture, and deliver high-quality innovative products to world markets at low costs

2. The ability to deliver products that compete in service and price

3. Just-in-time manufacturing capability to transform innovative ideas into commodities backed up by service

4. The ability to flexibly organize around customers and end users in order to close the gap between product idea and delivery

5. The rise of entrepreneurship across countries and cultures

6. Mergers and acquisitions—as well as strategic alliances between multinational and national firms

The key to global competitiveness is organizing integrated companies that (1) operate on the imperatives of continuous quality improvement, responsiveness, speed, and loose-knit and entrepreneurial structures and (2) collaborate with and link to suppliers, competitors, venture capitalists, and other resources to focus on targeted markets. These success factors are different from the assembly-line, top-down control and manufacturing processes that U.S. firms used right after World War II to dominate markets.

Underlying and driving the emergence of a changing global economy is the force of capitalism. The next section discusses capitalism as a global system with regional variations.

7.2 CAPITALISM: ONE SYSTEM WITH DIFFERENT FACES

Capitalism is a worldwide system (Shaw and Barry 1995). Multinationals, for example, operate without regard for traditional political, economic, or social boundaries. The economies of capitalist nations are intricately interconnected even though their systems of capitalism vary, as will be discussed.

Capitalism can be defined as an economic system whose major portion of production and distribution is in private hands, operating under what is termed a *profit* or *market system*. Key components and features of capitalism follow:

1. *Companies.* Capitalism permits the creation of companies or business organizations that exist separately from the people associated with them. Large companies such as Exxon, AT&T, Ford, and IBM are, in fact, incorporated businesses, or corporations.

2. *Profit motive.* A second characteristic of capitalism lies in the primary motive of companies and other capitalists: to make a profit. The profit motive implies and reflects a critical assumption about human nature: Human beings are basically economic creatures who recognize and are motivated by their financial self-interests.

3. *Competition.* Capitalism and competition are interchangeable concepts. Competition keeps the prices of desired goods from escalating and discourages individual greed. Although capitalism generally has been regarded as a monolithic system, evidence shows that with the end of communism, several forms of capitalism are emerging (Farrell 1994).

THE FACES OF GLOBAL CAPITALISM

From the 1760s to the 1830s, steam engines, textile mills, and the Enlightenment drove the Industrial Revolution. The years between 1880 and 1930 were shaped by the spread of electric power, mass production, and democracy. The approaching twenty-first century signals simultaneous upheavals in politics, technology, and economics and the development of different forms of international capitalism. Underlying these unprecedented changes lies one powerful idea: openness. Governments everywhere are pursuing liberal economic policies. Multinational corporations are accelerating the exchange of innovations across open borders. Global investors are pressuring companies to open their books. Populations are demanding stronger political and civil rights.

On a global scale, freer trade encourages growth by providing entrepreneurs from major economies access to larger markets. Open trade also spurs the growth of new technologies and manufacturing techniques. General Electric, for example, is sinking tens of millions of dollars into building factories and power plants in Mexico and India. Microsoft, along with many other high-tech and software firms, receives more than 50 percent of its revenue from international sales. Toyota Motors is powering its way into Southeast Asia. Volkswagen has opened businesses in China. Emergent systems of international capitalism are developing, and some are experimental. These systems are presently not well documented or studied. They will evolve as trade, global economies, politics, technologies, and strategic business alliances change. Figure 7.1 illustrates four emerging international types of capitalism.

The four "faces of capitalism" discussed next are consumer, frontier, producer, and family capitalism. These forms of capitalism require more research and validation; they are presented here to stimulate further discussion and investigation. Following this section, the corporate U.S. and Japanese capitalist systems are discussed in more detail.

CONSUMER CAPITALISM Consumer capitalism is represented by the United States, Britain, Canada, and Australia and can be characterized

■ **FIGURE 7.1**

THE GLOBAL FACES OF CAPITALISM

Consumer Capitalism
U.S., Britain, Canada, Australia
Traits: Laissez-faire, open borders, small
government, profit mentality
Potential problems: income inequality, low
savings rate, weak central governments

Producer Capitalism
Germany, France, Japan, Mexico
Traits: Emphasizes production, employment,
statist policies
Potential problems: Fraying of social safety
net, slowing innovation, consumer
dissatisfaction

The Faces of Capitalism

Family Capitalism
Taiwan, Malaysia, Thailand, Indonesia
Traits: Created by Chinese diaspora,
extended clans dominate business and
capital flows
Potential problems: Creating modern
corporate organizations and money markets

Frontier Capitalism
China, Russia
Traits: Government pursues for-profit
business activities, entrepreneurial class
sprouts
Potential problems: Must establish rule of
law and open borders, curb criminality

SOURCE: Christopher Farrell. 1994. The triple revolution. *Business Week*, Special McGraw-Hill companies Bonus Issue, 16.

as having a laissez-faire, profit-oriented ideology. Competition is also a
central driving element of this form of capitalism. Governments generally
take a hands-off approach to regulating business, although their involvement depends on the political party in power and economic conditions.
For example, the governmental role in Canada's economic system differs
from that of the United States. The U.S. system currently appears more
seamless with regard to its trade boundaries.

The downsides of consumer capitalism include institutionalized income inequality, typically low savings rates, and a weak central government, although this characteristic depends on the country. It is interesting
to note that consumer capitalism in the United States recently has included the characteristic of "IPO (Initial Public Offering) capitalism." The
IPO markets in the early to mid-1990s have helped fuel innovations that
are transforming the U.S. economy into one of the world's productivity
powerhouses. Forces behind the technologically driven IPO capitalism
are risk-taking entrepreneurs and attractive Internet, software, and

wireless technologies. Backing these entrepreneurs are some of the most sophisticated capital markets in the world.

Innovators also are reshaping old-line industries, such as the airlines, steel, telecommunications, and retailing industries, while driving young industries, such as those just mentioned—software, biotechnology, and on-line information services such as the Internet.

IPO capitalism is propelled by a series of simultaneous, self-reinforcing trends: successful first-generation, high-tech entrepreneurs; technology that creates new opportunities for entrepreneurs; and pension and mutual funds managers who are increasingly investing in emerging companies. Taken together, money and ideas are combining at a faster rate than before, creating new markets and new products that, in turn, replenish and shape IPO capitalism.

A downside of the IPO aspect of consumer capitalism is "boom and bust" economic cycles that create jobs and economic opportunities quickly and then result in a disappearance (or transformation) of growth into layoffs and dips—or even crashes—in financial markets.

FRONTIER CAPITALISM   Frontier capitalism is a new, experimental, and entrepreneurial system of economic activity. China and Russia are evolving these systems of capitalism from former socialist communism ideologies. Rules, infrastructures, and discipline are at first absent but develop with experience. Frontier capitalism has emerged in stretches of the former Soviet Union, China, parts of Latin America, and Vietnam. Corruption and criminal activity are often rampant; violence erupts regularly; legal systems are weak; and scams abound. The risks to life and limb are present. The winnings can be great for those willing to take these risks.

Sustained growth in these systems requires more than reckless risk taking. Eventually, frontier economies need large capital infusions from outsiders—individual investors, corporations, and banks. To make the leap to the next stage of growth, these economies have to begin "civilizing." That is, they will have to put in place an array of laws and institutions ranging from effective judiciaries to functioning financial markets. In the twenty-first century, economies such as Russia's and China's may be well on their way toward making those changes.

Frontier capitalism evolves in the following stages:

Stage one: Statist economies collapse or fade away. Black marketers profit enormously, while some become gangsters. Government corruption spreads.

Stage two: Small-scale entrepreneurs, often financed by family loans, flourish. Rule of law remains weak but businesspeople start creating their own rules of commerce.

Stage three: Economic growth is brisk but hard to measure. Financial markets begin to evolve, tapping savings and attracting foreign institutional investors. Clearer legal codes appear.

PRODUCER CAPITALISM Producer capitalism is based on controlled production, employment, and statist policies governed and controlled by top-down central bureaucracies. Countries such as France and Japan (discussed later in the chapter) symbolize producer capitalism. In France, the Ecole Nationale d'Administration is an institution of more than 100 students. It is the training ground for the brightest technocrats who run ministries, manage companies, and in general run the centralized economy. Many of France's leaders of producer capitalism were educated in this institution.

France's "hypereducated" technocrats realize that the statist system has become a serious economic handicap. Paris has wasted resources on ill-conceived ventures in computers and high-definition television. The state's overbearing role is a constraint for potential foreign partners. For example, Renault's planned merger with Sweden's Volvo was a casualty of France's rigid system of doing business.

The French practice of blurring the line between public and private is under intense attack. A series of investigations is probing corruption at the highest level of French public life. Nonetheless, economic efficiency is gradually replacing political goals in France's economy. Socialist leaders began the change in the 1980s by introducing the profit motive at state companies, a revolutionary notion at places such as Renault, whose *raison d'etre* has been to provide jobs.

Producer capitalism, unlike consumer capitalism, can be a rigid system. "Customer focus" is not at the center of supply and demand. Producers and corporations determine price, quantity, availability, and access to consumer markets and products.

FAMILY CAPITALISM Family capitalism is represented in Taiwan, Malaysia, Thailand, Indonesia, and to some extent Japan. Japan's *keiretsu* (corporate structure) system is actually an outgrowth of family capitalism, a system in which extended families and clans bond together into corporate interlocking cross-company and industry networks to provide capital, investment, and resource and risk sharing to grow wealth and business opportunities.

In family capitalism, the family and clan elders traditionally set the interwoven business, cultural, social, and infrastructural rules that govern the structure and functioning of businesses. Trust, loyalty, blood relationship, and dedication are the glues that bind the business together in this system. A hindrance to this system is the creation of modern companies that need to grow to the next level of globally sophisticated competitors, where blood ties may not be the most advantageous factors in moving ahead. Also, family-based and traditional rules and customs dictate decisions. Lack of openness to innovation and to new alliances can present obstacles to expansion of this form of capitalism.

In the following section, a more detailed comparison of the Japanese and U.S. systems of capitalism are discussed with reference to trade, competitiveness, and ethics.

7.3 MULTINATIONAL COMPETITION: JAPAN AND THE UNITED STATES

Successful multinational competition in world markets has demonstrated several important lessons: First, corporate competitiveness, as the Japanese have shown, is based on focused, coordinated, and government-supported long-term capitalized blueprint strategies. Second, global competitors focus less on piecemeal, random market approaches and more on domination of targeted critical industries and technologies to capture mass markets. Third, the emphasis has been on low-cost, high-quality products backed by a workforce committed to continuous improvement. This section on Japan and the United States focuses the discussion on how corporate competitiveness relates to national culture, the government system, and human resources as part of two very different uses of capital. (This is, intentionally, an abbreviated overview of this topic. Sources in the References section provide more in-depth analyses.) Some Japanese scholars also agree that their system of capitalism is unique and different from that of the West (Matsumoto 1991; Sakakibara 1990). Figure 7.2 illustrates dimensions for comparing countries' systems of governance, trade strategies, and business practices.

Components of the U.S. and Japanese systems are compared and explained next.

JAPAN, INC.

Interest and debate continue to surround Japan's industrial strategies for winning markets and overtaking U.S. competitors. Since World War II, Japanese companies have leveled, and in some cases dominated, the current playing field in industries producing the following: consumer electronics, automobiles, semiconductors, machine tools, steel, textiles, and flat-screen computer panels (Dertouros et al. 1989; Steiner and Steiner 1991, 435). However, the United States presently maintains its competitive edge in university education, supercomputers, software engineering, artificial intelligence, computer-aided design and engineering, telecommunications, genetic engineering, laser and fiber optics, and high-performance materials (see Sethi, Namiki, and Swanson 1984, Chapter 2, on which this

DIMENSIONS FOR COMPARING COUNTRIES

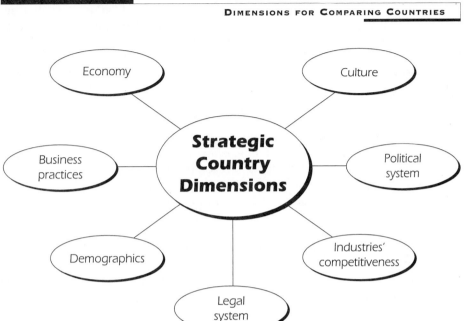

SOURCE: Copyright © Joseph W. Weiss, 1996.

discussion is based). The question that has gained the attention of the media, the White House, Congress, U.S. corporate presidents, and business schools is Why are the Japanese so successful? Less attention has been given to the question At what and at whose costs? Let us look at the success factors first.

The success factors behind "Japan, Inc.," as it has been called, are a mix among national cultural values and practices, business/government/ political institutional relationships, corporate structures **(keiretsu),** and human resource strategies, uses of capital, and management. The nature of and results of these combined relationships make up Japan's unique system of capitalism.

CULTURAL CHARACTERISTICS   Japan is a homogeneous culture. Maintaining the purity of its race is a valued cultural priority. This entails keeping foreign elements out (Sethi, Namiki, and Swanson 1984). The principal values of the Japanese society include *amae* (dependence), *on* (duty), *giri* (social obligation), and *ninjo* (human feeling). *Amae* begins early in human development and continues throughout adulthood. It is this feeling that underlies adults' emotional attachment to each other, the group, the corporation, and even the state. *On* involves obligations the recipient is indebted to repay. Giri relates to moral obligations that are mutual within a collectivity. *Ninjo* refers to what people prefer to do as well as what they believe they must avoid doing because of status or group membership. Maintaining harmony in the family, the group, the work organization, and the state is the theme these values revolve around.

The family, household, and group form the center of the Japanese social structure. Individualism and standing out from the group are not valued. Instead veneration for authority and interpersonal relationships are highly valued. All of these values and characteristics are shared by the society and are reflected in all major Japanese institutions, including corporations. Teamwork, consensus decision making, and a holistic concern for employees are based on and supported by these cultural values.

The respect for authority in vertical relationships is also a central part of the Japanese culture. This relationship with authority begins at home, is absolute, and is found in informal groups and work groups. Leaders are expected to show leadership characteristics, such as wisdom, vision, sympathy, and unselfishness. This tradition is based on the Confucian system of ethical conduct and was passed on in the ideologies and practices of the Samurai.

SOCIOPOLITICAL CONTEXT The sociopolitical context of Japanese institutions can be summarized as an interdependent network of shared values, strategies, and traditions. Economic power historically has been—and continues to be—shared by government and business. This relationship was further cemented after World War II when the government actively sought to rebuild its economy and support business growth. The Japanese government, unlike in the United States, coordinates business activities through long-term planning and industrial policy and manages businesses in trouble. Also, top-level government officials generally are well educated and respected and thus exercise powerful decisions in business activities. One of the most powerful agencies of Japan's six "economic bureaucracies" is MITI, the Ministry of International Trade and Industry. This agency shares significant power with private enterprises, especially since, like the other ministries, it provides financial assistance and guidance to corporations. It is a working partnership.

Even though Japan's political system is a democracy, it is best characterized as semifeudal in nature. Because Japan never experienced a "people's revolution," the political system has shared few traditions with the public. Political parties compete for power and privileges, status, and positions within the ministries. Consequently, "Wheeling and dealing, bribery, coercion, collusion, threats and violence (including assassination) are as much a part of Japanese politics as they are of Japanese life" (Sethi, Namiki, and Swanson 1984; Yanaga 1965). In effect, the power and authority of the political system are ineffective in controlling business activity to protect the public. Scandals are discovered after the fact, and attempts are made to quickly resolve business and political crises.

It also should be noted that Japan's social system focuses on the commercialization of knowledge. Japan's industries and companies are interweaved with government to the extent that it rewards business activities, as these bring returns on investment to the society—more so than to any individuals.

INDUSTRIAL GROUPS: *KEIRETSU*   Against this cultural and political background are imbedded the powerful *keiretsu*, oligopolistic firms networked together in industrial cartels (Peck 1988). To understand the success of the Japanese competitive enterprise is to understand the *keiretsu* and their strategies and use of capital. The *keiretsu* are the inheritors of the post–World War II **zaibatsus,** economic monopolies started by powerful families and broken up by the U.S. occupation. *Zaibatsus* were holding companies with large stock ownership in core companies. Each *zaibatsu* was controlled by a family trust. The core companies included manufacturing enterprises, a bank, a trust company, an insurance firm, and several smaller companies. *Keiretsu* are organized around the former *zaibatsu*.

The six dominant *keiretsu* include Mitsubishi (101 companies), Sumitomo (87 companies), Mitsui (65 companies), Fuji (87 companies), Sanwa (61 companies), and DKB (43 companies; Klein 1987). As of 1980, these six groups accounted for 18 percent sales, 14 percent corporate profits, and 6 percent employment in Japan. By 1992, the *keiretsu* accounted for almost a quarter of Japan's total business assets and revenues (Kelly et al. 1992). The *keiretsu* share stock ownership with the large core firms holding equity, the firms' suppliers, and the suppliers holding equity in the *keiretsu*. They are interlocking partnerships and allies.

At the center of each *keiretsu* is a bank or cash-rich company that offers low-cost capital. Stocks are held mostly by other companies, therefore allowing managers to plan and operate on long-term market-domination goals.

The largest manufacturer in the *keiretsu* dictates everything from prices to terms of delivery to the hundreds of suppliers bound to it. These cartels, then, have readily available capital from their member companies, from the bank in their group, and from government funds to target and exploit any market or technology on the globe.

JAPANESE CAPITALISM   The *keiretsu* make up the industrial or business segment of Japan's unique system of communal capitalism, as depicted in Figure 7.3. This system is summarized as follows:

1. Close alliances exist between government and business. These intimate relationships allow prices to be controlled, strategic industries to be targeted for growth, and the regulation of industry through fuzzy

■ FIGURE 7.3

CAPITALISM JAPANESE STYLE

Government/Industry Ties

Benefits: Protects failing industries, nurtures growth industries
Drawbacks: Distorts market prices, hinders newcomers' entry

Keiretsu

Benefits: Relationships between companies allow high-risk sharing, access to capital and technology.
Drawbacks: Excluded companies have trouble competing.

Corporate Loyalty

Benefits: High productivity and quality, stable workforce and top management team
Drawbacks: Excessive employee obedience and dependence limit time for socializing and leisure.

Few Outside Shareholders

Benefits: Managers don't need to focus on short-term results.
Drawbacks: Managers don't feel shareholder accountability

SOURCE: Robert Neff. 1992. Japan takes a good hard look at itself. *Business Week*, 17 February, 33.

guidelines instead of rules, which also serve to keep outsiders out. If you do not understand the rules, you cannot play in the game.

2. The *keiretsu* control Japan's business interests. Cartels enable business groups to coordinate and focus capital from banks, the government, and other sources to obtain strategic global market share.

3. In the *keiretsu* system, the role of independent shareholder is, as stated earlier, weakened, since three quarters of Japanese companies' stocks are held by other firms. Consequently, Japanese managers concentrate on investing in long-term R&D projects and in competing for long-term market share instead of meeting short-term quarterly profits.

4. The relationship between Japanese workers and their firms is also different in this capitalist system (Neff 1992). Lifetime employment, consensual decision making, collective implementation of responsibilities, a slow evaluation and promotion system, informal and implicit control by peer groups and cultural norms, nonspecialized career paths, and a holistic concern for employees all mark different human resource practices than those found in the West (Ouchi and Jaeger 1978).

Taken together, these four components of the Japanese capitalistic system present a formidable force for competing against countries and companies that are less organized and that have less infrastructural support.

ETHICAL ISSUES WITH JAPANESE MANAGEMENT AND CAPITALISM   The Japanese management system (based on the characteristics just given in number 4) has demonstrated superior performance in global markets. As with other countries, the management system is embedded in the culture and in the capitalist system. At a closer view, it does have problems. Workers lack individual freedom in the militaristic, rigid systems of control. Substandard wages, unsafe working conditions, and discrimination against women and temporary workers are also some of the more prominent moral issues in the Japanese management system (Sethi, Namiki, and Swanson 1984, 48–52). Lack of incentives for creativity and innovation are also a result of the consensus-oriented, conformist work group structure.

Lifetime employment is not a benefit shared equally by all; it is, in practice, more a function of the prosperity of the industry and firm. Most employees retire at age 55; in the more-successful firms, 58 is the retirement age. Moreover, retirement benefits are minimal. When forced into retirement, as is more often the case in large firms, many retirees have financial difficulties.

Lifetime employment is believed to be given to 35 percent to 40 percent of the workforce; that number is 40 percent to 60 percent in large manufacturing firms and trading houses. Recession and other economic downturns also affect lifetime employment practices. Layoffs have occurred and are occurring in Japanese firms. It is also important to note that women are excluded from the lifetime employment benefit. Moreover, women often take more menial jobs than do men.

Long and exhausting working hours with little leisure or time off is another problem in the Japanese management system. Quality of work life has been a foreign concept to Japanese workers. Government agencies now are studying how to maintain high performance while building more leisure attitudes and time into the workforce.

PROBLEMS WITH JAPANESE CAPITALISM   As recent stock market upheavals have shown, Japanese capitalism is not immune from the risky investments of the 1980s or from economic downturns. Institutional ownership of stocks does not protect falling values of investments.

At a system level, problems have evolved with Japanese capitalism from an international perspective. Japan's $1 trillion current-account surplus has caused critics to question Japan's trade policies and practices. Japanese companies, for example, have been caught and fined for price-fixing and for dumping products in the computer and electronic consumer-products industries in the United States.

Critics also claim the *keiretsu* oligopolies do not go after market share only; they strategically target U.S. industries to dominate them and ultimately to put them out of business. Critics have accused Japan of practicing "predatory capitalism" in a militaristic, warlike fashion. Japanese automobile and computer firms, for example, surround designated U.S. companies and deliberately seek to dominate and control these industries and firms by moving in the *keiretsu* manufacturing, financial, technological, and component suppliers with the aim of lowering prices until other firms cannot compete on price or quality. The U.S. auto parts industry is one example. Although U.S. auto parts are world-class leaders in price and quality, the industry has failed in selling parts to Japanese automakers in Japan and in the United States. Why? One response follows:

> A number of academic studies have demonstrated that Japanese multi-national companies don't act like other multinational companies when they go overseas. They are far less likely to buy local parts and equipment and to hire local people for high management positions than are European and American multinationals, and they are far more likely to give most of their business to other Japanese companies. (Murray 1992, A1)

Former President Bush's now-memorable trip to Japan was an attempt to convince Japanese automakers in the United States to double their purchases from U.S. suppliers from $7 billion in 1990 to $15 billion by 1994 (Holbrook 1991–1992). Some have argued that this agreement represents "managed trade" and shows that Japan must be pressured to act more fairly. It also is argued that Japan's markets for critical technologies and products remain closed.

Some of the criticisms of Japan's industrial and trade practices may be unfounded. Defenders of Japanese capitalism and competitiveness claim that U.S. industries and companies are not accustomed to being second best or less successful than the Japanese. Holbrooke states, "[A]ccepting a more assertive and independent Japan will prove difficult for many Americans, who have come to regard Japan as a junior partner on most important foreign policy issues." It also is argued that U.S. industries that are conservative and unwilling to change management practices are to blame for lack of competitiveness, not Japan. It also is pointed out that without Japanese investment and manufacturing operations in the United States, Americans would suffer even more, since competitors from other countries would pose similar threats to our standard of living and industrial weaknesses.

The debate continues over whether and to what extent Japan is competing fairly in international markets. Is Japan combining protectionist trade practices, price-fixing, and predatory tactics with legitimate *keiretsu* strategies to dominate U.S. and global prize industries such as the auto, electronics, and semiconductor industries? Is Japan simply playing by the rules of the countries where it does business and capitalizing on industry and corporate weaknesses and trade loopholes? The moral and industrial challenge for Japan will be its ability to maintain its productivity while competing with other countries in ways that are politically and legally compatible with other capitalist systems.

U.S. CAPITALISM AND MANAGEMENT

The U.S. capitalist and management systems differ significantly from those in Japan. This section summarizes some of the major themes already alluded to in other parts of the book, namely, dominant characteristics of the U.S. national culture, government, and corporate management system. The aim is to compare the United States' uses of capitalism with Japan's and to discuss the problems of U.S. capitalism in the global arena.

CULTURAL CONTEXT The United States is a country of countries. Garreau (1981) argues that historically and culturally North America is made up of nine nations (see also Kahle 1988). As such, the United States is an ethnically diverse society where distinctive traditions and customs coexist and share the following common values: individualism, self-reliance, self-discipline, a Protestant-influenced work ethic, the value of private property, and the belief in fairness and individual rights. Some argue that the Protestant work ethic has undergone significant change. Preoccupation with the self has developed into narcissism, and justice is being defined as fairness (Sethi, Namiki, and Swanson 1984, 104).

Individual rights and ownership of private property are at the center of the U.S. value system. The Declaration of Independence focuses on rights as *inalienable*. Ownership of private property reinforces individualism in the social fabric. Americans also value family and collective membership. Group membership, however, is based more on voluntarism than on cultural norms. (This section draws on Sethi, Namiki, and Swanson 1984, Chapters 5 and 6.) The distinction between U.S. and Japanese values is apparent. Japan is essentially a group-oriented culture, whereas American values center on self and individualism. These value differences are reflected in the way U.S. businesses reward and recognize entrepreneurs and inventors. Knowledge as it is patented and protected legally is the private property of the individual, not of the society, as is the case with Japan. In Japan the individual is not considered the focal point of industrial innovation or success.

SOCIOPOLITICAL AND GOVERNMENTAL CONTEXT The United States is a pluralistic political and government system. The Constitution grounds ultimate authority in the people and separates power among the executive, legislative, and judicial branches of government. Within this pluralistic system, the government, businesses, and unions share power and solve problems through adversarial relationships. Cooperation continually must be negotiated through advocacy, argument, and special-interest and political-action-group lobbying.

Competition and fragmentation are built into the system, the very infrastructure of government and politics. Federal and state governments compete over the power of budgets, policies, and resources. For example, the national government lacks an industrial policy for the country, so the states develop their own and compete with each other for domestic and foreign investment. Iowa has used handsome tax incentives to convince Japanese auto manufacturers to build and operate along Interstate 75. At the same time, Detroit automakers have unsuccessfully lobbied the president to adopt some form of a broad national industrial policy to limit Japanese auto imports and manufacturing in the United States. While Japan operates in global markets as a united front through combined governmental, union, and *keiretsu* cooperation and strategies, the United States operates in a piecemeal, state-by-state, and corporation-by-corporation manner. As one U.S. auto parts manufacturer commented on the comparison of American and Japanese business practices, "Japan is a blueprint; the United States is an event."

U.S. CAPITALISM   U.S. capitalism is based on the ideology of "free-market enterprise." Large corporations in the past have embodied U.S. business wealth and success and therefore have defined the rules of the capitalist system. Such corporations obtain equity capital from private investors and capital markets. These institutions compete among themselves and with the government for funds. Unlike the Japanese example, U.S. banks are not permitted to buy stock in corporations; this helps to prevent conflicts of interest. Also unlike Japanese *keiretsu*, the government is more often than not the watchdog and regulator of business growth and activity—not the strategic partner. The U.S. corporation, then, must depend on the attractiveness of its stock on the open market to survive and succeed (Meyer and Gustafson 1988; Sethi, Namiki, and Swanson 1984).

Because most of the largest corporations sell shares to the public, the stock market defines the health of a firm. The trading price of a company's shares also determines the firm's ability to obtain capital and resources to grow and innovate. Corporations, then, walk a tightrope between their debt and equity in their capital structure. "A highly leveraged company is more risk prone and must pay a higher cost for funds unless its growth prospects are phenomenal and investors are willing to assume above-average risks," researchers Sethi, Namiki, and Swanson (1984, 115–16) note.

Consequently, U.S. corporations are continuously monitored by the public and shareholders. Reliance on companies' stock trading prices, quarterly earnings reports, and profit-and-loss statements and on financial markets' perceptions of firms characterize U.S. capitalism as short-term oriented and price sensitive. For American managers, unlike their Japanese counterparts, this means short-term planning, investing, and strategies are the rules and boundaries managers must operate under.

Global competition and the changing nature of international markets are pressuring this system to change.

U.S. MANAGEMENT PRACTICES   In practice, the U.S. management system is not a single system. American entrepreneurs have not followed—and probably will not follow—any single set of rules for borrowing, inventing, investing, or doing business. However, a historical background of management systems and thought exists that, again, large and traditional corporations have embodied.

Although entrepreneurial firms differ from larger, older ones and although a variety of management systems and changing styles exist in the United States, certain generalizations still can be made about American management practices, because these practices have been historically grounded in the country's dominant value system, sociocultural context, business/government relationships, and form of capitalism. These generalizations include the following emphases:

1. Short-term time, profit, planning, and strategy horizons based on some of the cultural and sociosystem background factors explained so far

2. Individual decision making, responsibilities, performance, and rewards

3. Managers who are understood, trained, and treated as professionals separate from any specific knowledge base

4. Outcomes over processes, measured and monitored by short-term financial tools

5. Specialized and vertical career paths

6. Individual career development

These characteristics are familiar, since they have been addressed in management literature and journals (see Ouchi and Jaeger 1978).

U.S. management practices also have been greatly influenced by the school of scientific management, proposed by Frederick Taylor (1947) at the turn of the century. Taylor separated managers from workers and viewed managers as professionals; he articulated a logic for making and maintaining a division of labor and chain of command; he laid the basis of building organizational structures on carrying out separate tasks; and he defined work and management so that both could be measured and executed "scientifically," in a cost/benefit, compartmentalized, individualistic, and piecemeal way.

The legacy of scientific management is the "stovepipe" organization with isolated, specialized management functions. The artificial division of worker from manager, top-down decision making, and the eventual need for unions to advocate benefits for workers alienated from management and economically disadvantaged also were set in motion. Productivity was defined apart from the enterprise's mission and more on an individual piece-rate basis. Attention to process was lost. These components of U.S. management are being ripped apart by global competition and by the changing rules of knowledge technology as it replaces the assembly line.

PROBLEMS WITH U.S. CAPITALISM AND MANAGEMENT

The U.S. capitalist system's short-term overemphasis on financially measured corporate growth and returns has not been successful when compared with the Japanese *keiretsu* system. Not only have the Japanese mastered process technology, total quality, continuous improvement, and just-in-time inventory and management techniques for getting product ideas to market in one-third less time than U.S. competitors, but also they have a head start of several decades in doing so. Moreover, the U.S. adversarial system of pluralistic competition and governance is still intact. The relationships among governments, businesses, and unions are still politically divisive.

Among the most prominent problems with the United States' lagging competitiveness have been the blindspots—the inability of American managers to recognize the importance and prowess of international competition. The results of the 1989 Korn/Ferry/Columbia study, "Reinventing the CEO," stated,

> [I]t is troubling that the executives of most U.S. corporations, perhaps by virtue of minimal international exposure, discount the importance of an international outlook. What is most disturbing is that they do not acknowledge this liability, and so risk selecting a successor with the same narrow vision.

The U.S. legal system also may be part of the U.S. competition problem. Although antitrust and other regulatory laws effectively controlled monopolies in this country at the turn of the century, these same laws are impeding the ability of American firms to form *keiretsu*-like coalitions to compete with the Japanese. Like professional managers, lawyers have mushroomed. The United States has 307.4 lawyers per 100,000 people, compared with Britain's 102.7, Germany's 82, and Japan's 12.1. In 1971, the United States had 355,242 lawyers, compared with 750,000 in 1990 and a projected 1 million by 2000. In 1984, 14.1 million state court filings (lawsuits) occurred; by 1990, that number reached 18.4 million. Moreover, the legal costs U.S. companies pay could have been spent in R&D and other competitive pursuits. For example, Dow Chemical spends more than $100 million a year on legal services and liability insurance (Guilty: Too many lawyers 1992). This question arises: How much law and how many lawyers are necessary in the United States to do what, for whom, at what, and at whose costs? Presently, many companies are hiring dispute settlement professionals to lower legal costs.

Given these observations, it is important to note that the global competition game is just beginning. The European Union market is just beginning to take off. U.S.-based multinationals also are competing with German, French, Italian, Swiss, and other European multinational competitors in the new global marketplace.

Because many large corporations and traditional industries are losing their competitiveness in the emerging global market, traditional and questionable U.S. management governance and leadership practices also have come under scrutiny. The U.S. public is morally as well as economically concerned because citizens are losing jobs, community tax bases are eroding, the effectiveness of school systems is challenged, the roles of the government and politicians are questioned, the standard of living is deteriorating, and it is uncertain whether America will be a technological and manufacturing leader in the future or an assembler and distributor of other nations' innovative products. The effectiveness of the entire U.S. system of business, government, education, research and development, and production has been challenged. Immoral conduct and practices in this system and other American institutions are likely to be less tolerated by the public in such a deteriorating economic and competitive environment.

REGAINING COMPETITIVENESS   Despite these trends, many U.S. companies have regained much of the global competitiveness lost in the 1980s. Some of the more entrepreneurial flagship American firms that have in the 1990s helped drive U.S. productivity and competitiveness include Sun Microsystems, Intel, Angen, Wal-Mart, Federal Express, Microsoft, and Internet companies, to name a few. Although no magical formulas reinvent U.S. competitiveness, many guidelines have been suggested and many changes already are occurring. This section summarizes some of the suggested directions U.S. corporations and governments should take.

Changes in Corporate Governance.   As was discussed in Chapter 5, the unusually high CEO salaries, benefits, and perks and the roles of corporate boards of directors, shareholders, and top-level managers are being questioned, especially in companies that are not performing. Businesses are making changes. The General Motors board of directors startled the corporate world by cutting former CEO Stempel's salary by one-third (down to $1 million) and by closing plants and shedding thousands of workers. This move may shake up other corporate boards and move them to take action against waste and corruption and toward more entrepreneurial policies and practices.

American **Keiretsu.**   U.S. firms in industries that have been competing head-on with Japanese *keiretsu* have realized that the competition is too great to go it alone. As a result, U.S. companies have been forming their own kind of *keiretsu*. Ford has been focusing on its automotive and financial-services businesses through the strategies of acquisitions, equity holdings, international linkages, and research consortiums. In its vehicle assembly business, for example, Ford has a 25 percent equity stake in Mazda, 10 percent in KIA Motors in Korea, 75 percent in Aston Martin Lagonda and 48 percent in Iveco Ford Truck in Britain, and 49 percent in Autolatina in Brazil and Argentina. Ford also is a member of eight R&D consortiums that investigate environmental issues and other innovative projects. In addition, Ford has partners in its parts, production, financial services, and marketing businesses (Kelly et al. 1992, 52–60). IBM also is becoming a kind of American *keiretsu*.

In the 1980s U.S. industries created more than 250 R&D consortiums. The federal government funded $120 million to Detroit's automakers to work jointly on a new battery technology for electric cars (Kelly et al. 1992, 53). Finally, U.S. firms are following the strategy "If you can't beat them, join them." Detroit's auto manufacturers and U.S. computer firms have several strategic alliances and joint ventures with their Japanese counterparts. Ford has aligned with Mazda and Mitsubishi in Japan. Chrysler also is aligned with Mitsubishi. GM is in an alliance with Suzuki. Honeywell and Nippon Electric of Japan share business dealings, and IBM and Matsushita are partners.

Reinventing American Management Practices.   In addition to the new rules required for competing in the global marketplace discussed earlier, a number of books and studies have offered suggestions for improving U.S. productivity and competitiveness. Among the most notable is Dertouros, Lester, and Solow's *Made in America: Regaining the Productive Edge* (1989). Steiner and Steiner (1991) use this source, among others, to summarize the following points offered to U.S. firms: (1) Think globally; (2) balance short-term and long-term thinking; (3) implement global strategy; (4) give high priority to the improvement of production processes; and (5) improve human resource management (451–54). Also, the U.S. government should focus on public policies that strengthen scientific and technological advantages and should increase the tax credit for R&D projects.

W. Edwards Deming, the American management guru who was shunned by the U.S. corporate establishment after World War II, had turned to Japan to impart total quality management, continuous productivity improvement, and statistical system control methods. Now, after the past four decades, Deming has been welcomed back by U.S. firms. His 14 points for improving management's productivity are summarized in Figure 7.4.

U.S. entrepreneurship is also a driving force that industrial leaders are striving to reward and maintain in the midst of changing corporate structures and manufacturing techniques. The challenge is not how to become

■ FIGURE 7.4

DEMING'S 14 POINTS FOR IMPROVING MANAGEMENT'S PRODUCTIVITY

W. Edwards Deming: If Japan Can . . . Why Can't We?

1. *Create constancy of purpose.* Strive for long-term improvement more than short-term profits.
2. *Adopt the new philosophy.* Accept as gospel the need for total quality with no tolerance for delays and mistakes.
3. *Cease dependence on mass inspection.* Build quality into the process and identify and correct problems early rather than late.
4. *End the practice of awarding business on price tag alone.* Don't purchase from the cheapest supplier. Build long-term relationships based on loyalty and trust.
5. *Improve constantly and forever the system of production and service.* At every stage of the process, strive to continually improve and satisfy internal as well as external customers.
6. *Institute training and retraining.* This includes continual updating and training in statistical methods and thinking.
7. *Institute leadership.* Remove barriers that prevent employees from performing effectively, and continually provide the resources needed for effectiveness.
8. *Drive out fear.* People must believe it is safe to report problems or mistakes or to ask for help.
9. *Break down barriers among departments.* Promote teamwork and communications across departments, and provide common organizational vision.
10. *Eliminate slogans, exhortations, and arbitrary targets.* Supply methods, not just buzzwords.
11. *Eliminate numerical quotas.* Quotas place a limit on improvement and are contrary to the idea of continuous improvement.
12. *Remove barriers to pride in workmanship.* Allow autonomy and spontaneity. Abandon regular performance reviews.
13. *Institute a vigorous program of education and retraining.* This is similar to point 6 but is meant to highlight a philosophy that people are assets not commodities.
14. *Take action to accomplish the transformation.* Provide access to top management, an organization structure, and information that allows the other 13 points to be adhered to on a daily basis.

SOURCE: Reprinted from *Out of the Crisis* by W. Edwards Deming by permission of MIT and the W. Edwards Deming Institute. Published by MIT, Center for Advanced Educational Services, Cambridge, MA 02139. Copyright © 1986 by The W. Edwards Deming Institute.

like the Japanese or any other management system. We cannot. The challenge is how to adopt successful elements from world-class management systems to U.S. entrepreneurial business practices. Figure 7.5 illustrates a modified American management system (Type Z) based on the integration of successful Japanese practices (Type J) into the existing dominant U.S. practices (Type A).

Again, no quick fixes will turn the U.S. economy and corporations back to global competitiveness. Some argue the United States will never again command the scope of global control of manufacturing and production power it had after World War II; the world's economies and politics are too complex and competitive. The United States should, therefore, assume its competitive and cooperative place within this new economic

■ FIGURE 7.5

MODIFIED U.S. MANAGEMENT SYSTEM BASED ON
INTEGRATION OF U.S. AND JAPANESE PRACTICES

	Type A (American)	Type J (Japanese)	Type Z (Modified American)
Employment	Short term	Lifetime	Long term
Decision Making	Individual	Consensual	Consensual
Responsibility	Individual	Collective	Individual
Evaluation	Rapid evaluation and promotion	Slow evaluation and promotion	Slow evaluation and promotion
Control	Explicit, formulized	Implicit, informal	Implicit, informal with explicit, formalized measures
Career Path	Specialized	Nonspecialized	Moderately specialized
Concern for Employees	Segmented	Holistic	Holistic

SOURCE: William G. Ouchi and Alfred M. Jaeger. 1978. Type Z organizations: Stability in the midst of mobility. *Academy of Management Review* 3: 308.

environment. Still, to do so requires momentous changes, including many occurring now, and a major question remains: Can the United States afford to maintain its democratic and constitutional principles in the face of less-principled international business practices?

7.4 MULTINATIONAL ENTERPRISES AS STAKEHOLDERS

Multinational enterprises (MNEs) are corporations that "own or control production or service facilities outside the country in which they are based" (United Nations 1973, 23). MNEs also are referred to as global, transnational, and international companies (Czinkota and Ronkainen 1989, 338).

Although MNEs often reflect and extend their home nation's culture and resources, many act as independent nations. This section focuses on MNEs as independent, powerful stakeholders, using their power across national boundaries to gain comparative advantages, with or without home-country support. Common characteristics MNEs share include (1) operating a sales organization, manufacturing plant, distribution center, licensed business, or subsidiary in at least two countries; (2) earning an estimated 25 percent to 45 percent of revenue from foreign markets;

and (3) having common ownership, resources, and global strategies (Sturdivant and Vernon-Wortzel 1990, 189–90). Since MNEs often span nations, governments, and different types of businesses and markets, their operations are based on a shared network of strategies, information and data, expertise, capital, and resources (Vernon and Wells 1986, 2). MNEs have become the most strategically powerful stakeholders in the race to compete and dominate global industry market shares.

Many MNEs are more economically powerful than the nations where they do business. For example, IBM operates in more than 126 countries, communicates in 30 languages, runs 23 foreign plants, and obtains more than one-half its total net income from its foreign business (Donaldson 1989, 31, 32). The ten largest U.S.-based MNEs in terms of export sales dollars are shown in Figure 7.6. Figure 7.7 lists the ten largest MNEs headquartered outside the United States. Of these foreign-based multinationals, seven are located in western Europe and three are located in Japan. America's largest international exporters, comprising some not shown in Figure 7.6, include Boeing, GM, GE, Ford, Chrysler, Philip Morris, and others. The foreign-sales share of total sales for the world's largest MNEs, once estimated at one-fourth, is now closer to 40 percent.

The dominant goal of MNEs is to make a profit. Corporations expand and do business across national boundaries to take comparative advantage of marketing, trade, cost, investment, labor, and other factors. At the same time, MNEs assist local economies in many ways, as will be explained later. The ethical questions critics of MNEs have raised are reflected in the following statement by the noted Harvard professor Raymond Vernon (1971): "Is the multinational enterprise undermining

■ **FIGURE 7.6**

TEN LARGEST U.S. EXPORTERS

1994 Rank	Company	Export Sales ($mil.)	% Change from 1993	% of Total Revenues	Revenue Rank
1	General Motors	16,127.10	8.10	10.40	1
2	Ford Motor	11,892.00	25.40	9.30	2
3	Boeing	11,844.00	(19.00)	54.00	29
4.	Chrysler	9,400.00	11.90	18.00	11
5	General Electric	8,110.00	(4.60)	12.50	6
6	Motorola	7,370.00	47.70	33.10	28
7	International Business Machines	6,336.00	(13.20)	9.90	7
8	Philip Morris	4,942.00	20.40	9.20	10
9	ArcherDaniels Midland	4,675.00	61.20	41.10	92
10	Hewlett-Packard	4,653.00	(1.80)	18.60	22

SOURCE: Excerpted from *Fortune*, 13 November 1995. Copyright © *Time*, Inc.

■ **FIGURE 7.7**

TEN LARGEST NON-U.S. MULTINATIONAL COMPANIES

1994 Rank	Company	Revenue ($mil)	% Change from 1993	Profits ($mil)	% Change from 1993
1	Mitsubishi	175,835.60	9.80	218.70	28.40
2	Mitsui	171,490.50	4.90	263.80	85.80
3	Itochu	167,824.70	8.20	81.60	—
4	Sumitomo	162,475.90	3.10	73.20	8.20
5	Marubeni	150,187.40	3.90	104.40	105.00
6	Nisho/wai	100,875.50	5.70	52.70	(47.00)
7	Royal Dutch/Shell	94,881.30	(0.30)	6235.60	38.40
8	Toyota Motor	88,158.60	3.40	1184.60	(19.60)
9	Hitachi	76,430.90	11.40	1146.70	89.60
10	Nipon Life Insurance	70,843.60	6.20	2682.10	(4.50)

SOURCE: Excerpted from *Fortune*, 5 August 1995. Copyright © *Time*, Inc.

the capacity of nations to work for the welfare of their people? Is the multinational enterprise being used by a dominant power as a means of penetrating and controlling the economies of other countries?" The next subsection addresses these questions in a discussion of the mutual responsibilities and expectations of MNEs and their host countries.

Recent crises since the birth of the multinational corporation after World War II have raised international concern over the ethical conduct of MNEs in host and other countries. For example, Union Carbide's chemical spill in Bhopal, India, which resulted in thousands of deaths and injuries, alarmed other nations over questionable safety standards and controls of MNE foreign operations. Nestlé's marketing of its powdered infant milk formula that resulted in the illness and death of a large number of infants in less-developed countries raised questions about the lack of proper product instructions issued to indigent, less-educated consumers. (Nestlé's practice resulted in a boycott of the company from 1976 to 1984.) Also, the presence of MNEs in South Africa has raised criticisms over the role of large corporations in actively supporting apartheid or government-supported racism. Because MNEs have to pay taxes to the South African government, and because apartheid is a government-supported policy, MNEs—it is argued—support racism. Several U.S.-based MNEs that operated in South Africa witnessed boycotts and disinvestments by many shareholders. Many MNEs, including IBM and Polaroid, later withdrew. The post apartheid environment in South Africa has opened reentry to companies from all countries. Another long-standing moral issue is the practice of MNEs not paying their fair share of taxes in countries where they do business and in their home countries.

Through transfer pricing and other creative accounting techniques, many MNEs have shown paper losses, thereby enabling them to avoid paying any taxes. The ethical concerns that surround MNEs regarding their presence in host countries are discussed in the following overview of two perspectives (of the MNE and of the host country).

MNE PERSPECTIVE

The MNE enters a foreign country primarily to make a profit. For example, they seek to benefit from currency fluctuations, more available and cheaper labor costs, tax and trade incentives, and the use of natural resources. They also hope to gain access to more foreign markets and to create or maintain competitiveness.

MNEs benefit their host countries through foreign direct investment. MNEs can assist their host countries in these ways:

❏ Attract local capital to projects

❏ Provide for and enhance technology transfer

❏ Develop particular industry sectors

❏ Intensify competition in the country by introducing new products, services, and ideas

❏ Help decrease the country's debt and improve its balance of payments and standard of living

Moreover, MNEs open less-developed countries (LDCs) to international markets, thereby helping the local economy attract greatly desired hard currencies. Also, new technical and managerial skills are brought in, and local workers receive training and knowledge. Job and social-class mobility is provided to inhabitants (Czinkota and Ronkainen 1989, 346–47). Some MNEs also introduce schools, colleges, and hospitals to their host countries.

The MNE must manage overlapping and often conflicting multiple constituencies in its home and host-country operations. Figure 7.8 illustrates some of the major environments and stakeholder issues the MNE must technically and ethically balance and manage in its foreign location. From the MNE's perspective, managing these stakeholder issues is difficult and challenging, especially as the global economy presents new problems.

MNE executives and other managers also complain of what they consider unethical practices and arbitrary control by host-country governments. For example, local governments can and sometimes do the following:

❏ Limit repatriation of MNE assets and earnings

■ FIGURE 7.8

MNE STAKEHOLDER ENVIRONMENTAL ISSUES AND ETHICAL CONCERNS

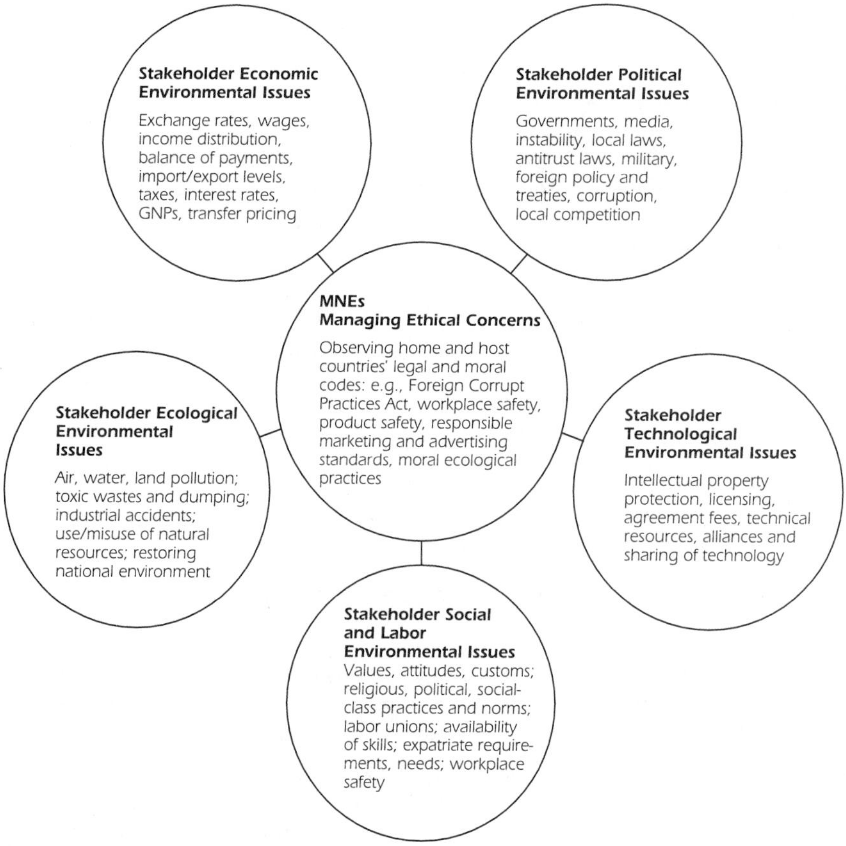

Stakeholder Economic Environmental Issues

Exchange rates, wages, income distribution, balance of payments, import/export levels, taxes, interest rates, GNPs, transfer pricing

Stakeholder Political Environmental Issues

Governments, media, instability, local laws, antitrust laws, military, foreign policy and treaties, corruption, local competition

MNEs Managing Ethical Concerns

Observing home and host countries' legal and moral codes: e.g., Foreign Corrupt Practices Act, workplace safety, product safety, responsible marketing and advertising standards, moral ecological practices

Stakeholder Ecological Environmental Issues

Air, water, land pollution; toxic wastes and dumping; industrial accidents; use/misuse of natural resources; restoring national environment

Stakeholder Technological Environmental Issues

Intellectual property protection, licensing, agreement fees, technical resources, alliances and sharing of technology

Stakeholder Social and Labor Environmental Issues

Values, attitudes, customs; religious, political, social-class practices and norms; labor unions; availability of skills; expatriate require-ments, needs; workplace safety

SOURCE: Copyright © Joseph W. Weiss, Bentley College, Waltham, MA, 1997.

❑ Pressure and require MNEs to buy component parts and other materials from local suppliers

❑ Require MNEs to use local nationals in upper-level management positions

❑ Require MNEs to produce and sell selected products in order to enter the country

❑ Limit imports and pressure exports

❑ Require a certain amount or percentage of profit to remain in or be invested in the country

Finally, MNEs always face the threat of expropriation or nationalization of their operations by the host government (Steiner and Steiner 1991, 397–99).

HOST-COUNTRY PERSPECTIVE

Six arguments critical of the presence and practices of MNEs in host and other foreign locations will be discussed here.

First, MNEs dominate and protect their core technology and research and development, thus keeping the host country a consumer, not a partner or producer. For example, the Brazilian government counteracts this by having entry barriers and laws that protect against the complete control of its own electronics industries from foreign manufacturers since the 1970s. It is also argued (or feared) that Japan's MNEs could in the long term dominate certain critical industries (such as electronics and perhaps automobile) in the United States and use American labor more as assemblers rather than technology R&D partners

Second, MNEs destabilize national sovereignty by limiting a country's access to critical capital and resources, thereby creating a host-country dependency on the MNE's governments and politics.

Third, MNEs create a "brain drain" by attracting scientists, expertise, and talent from the host country.

Fourth, MNEs create an imbalance of capital outflows over inflows. They produce but emphasize exports over imports in the host country, thereby leaving local economies dependent on foreign control.

Fifth, MNEs disturb local government economic planning and business practices by exerting control over the development and capitalization of a country's infrastructure. Also, by providing higher wages and better working conditions, MNEs influence and change a country's traditions, values, and customs. "Cultural imperialism" is imported through business practices.

Finally, MNEs sometimes destroy, pollute, and endanger host-country and LDC environments and the health of local populations. For example, the mining of and dangerous exposure to asbestos continues in some LDCs and in Canada.

Obviously, these criticisms do not apply to all MNEs. These criticisms represent the concerns of host-country and less-developed-country governments that have suffered abuses from multinationals over the decades. Tensions in the relationships between MNEs and host countries and other foreign governments, especially in the least-developed settings, endure. Whenever the stakes for both parties are high, so will be the pressures to negotiate the most profitable and equitable benefits for each stakeholder. Often, it is the less-educated, indigent inhabitants of LDCs who suffer the most from the operations of MNEs.

7.5 MNE GUIDELINES FOR MANAGING MORALITY

Guidelines for managing international ethical conduct have received detailed attention and exertion over the past four decades in the areas of consumer protection, employment, environmental pollution, human rights, and political conduct. (This section is based on Frederick 1991, 165–77.) The driving forces behind the development of these published guidelines, or universal rights, include the United Nations, the International Labor Office, and the Organization for Economic Cooperation and Development.

The underlying normative sources of the guidelines these global organizations developed include the beliefs in (1) national sovereignty, (2) social equity, (3) market integrity, and (4) human rights and fundamental freedoms (168–69).

The following MNE guidelines are summarized under the categories of employment practices and policies, consumer protection, environmental protection, political payments and involvement, and basic human rights and fundamental freedoms (166–67).

Employment Practices and Policies

❑ MNEs should not contravene the workforce policies of host nations.

❑ MNEs should respect the right of employees to join trade unions and to bargain collectively.

❑ MNEs should develop nondiscriminatory employment policies and promote equal job opportunities.

❑ MNEs should provide equal pay for equal work.

❑ MNEs should give advance notice of changes in operations, especially plant closings, and mitigate the adverse effects of these changes.

❑ MNEs should provide favorable work conditions, limited working hours, holidays with pay, and protection against unemployment.

❑ MNEs should promote job stability and job security, avoiding arbitrary dismissals and providing severance pay for those unemployed.

❑ MNEs should respect local host-country job standards and upgrade the local labor force through training.

❑ MNEs should adopt adequate health and safety standards for employees and grant them the right to know about job-related health hazards.

❑ MNEs should, minimally, pay basic living wages to employees.

❑ MNEs' operations should benefit the low-income groups of the host nation.

❏ MNEs should balance job opportunities, work conditions, job training, and living conditions among migrant workers and host-country nationals.

Consumer Protection

❏ MNEs should respect host-country laws and policies regarding the protection of consumers.

❏ MNEs should safeguard the health and safety of consumers by various disclosures, safe packaging, proper labeling, and accurate advertising.

Environmental Protection

❏ MNEs should respect host-country laws, goals, and priorities concerning protection of the environment.

❏ MNEs should preserve ecological balance, protect the environment, adopt preventive measures to avoid environmental harm, and rehabilitate environments damaged by operations.

❏ MNEs should disclose likely environmental harms and minimize the risks of accidents that could cause environmental damage.

❏ MNEs should promote the development of international environmental standards.

❏ MNEs should control specific operations that contribute to pollution of air, water, and soils.

❏ MNEs should develop and use technology that can monitor, protect, and enhance the environment.

Political Payments and Involvement

❏ MNEs should not pay bribes nor make improper payments to public officials.

❏ MNEs should avoid improper or illegal involvement or interference in the internal politics of host countries.

Basic Human Rights and Fundamental Freedoms

❏ MNEs should respect the rights of all persons to life, liberty, security of person, and privacy.

❏ MNEs should respect the rights of all persons to equal protection of the law, to work, to choice of job, to just and favorable work conditions, and to protection against unemployment and discrimination.

❏ MNEs should respect all persons' freedoms of thought, conscience, religion, opinion and expression, communication, peaceful assembly and association, and movement and residence within each state.

❏ MNEs should promote a standard of living to support the health and well-being of workers and their families.

❏ MNEs should promote special care and assistance to motherhood and childhood.

Frederick (167) states that these guidelines should be viewed as a "collective phenomenon," since all do not appear in each of the five international pacts they originated from: the 1948 United Nations Universal Declaration of Human Rights, 1975 Helsinki Final Act, 1976 OECD Guidelines for Multinational Enterprises, 1977 International Labor Organization Tripartite Declaration of Principles Concerning Multinational Enterprises and Social Policy, and 1972 UN Code of Conduct on Transnational Corporations.

The guidelines serve as broad bases for all international organizations to design specific corporate policies and procedures and apply them to areas such as these:

> child care, minimum wages, hours of work, employee training and education, adequate housing and health care, pollution control efforts, advertising and marketing activities, severance pay, privacy of employees and consumers, information concerning on-the-job hazards and . . . for those companies with operations in South Africa . . . as the place of residence and free movement of employees *(167)*

The problem remains: Who enforces these types of principles across geographic boundaries when complex situations involve competing interests and power demands?

7.6 ETHICS AND GLOBAL STAKEHOLDER DISPUTES

In the real world of trade, MNEs and host governments will continue to quarrel and litigate over the control of high-stakes technologies and intellectual patents and over controversial issues relating to industrial abuses of health, physical environments, and cultural traditions. Governments will claim they have a right, for example, to their apartheid laws, while other countries will boycott companies who do business in such nations. Countries such as Brazil may attempt to continue protecting their small-to-midsized computer firms by imposing laws and regulations over foreign companies that attempt to overwhelm these nations' R&D ability in the computer industry, while Western high-technology producers may threaten to leave Brazil and other nations if their control is jeopardized. The Fujitsus of Japan and other countries and the IBMs of the United

States and Europe continue to debate over what constitutes "intellectual property," over whose definition should be used, and over what moral and legal criteria should be applied to settle alleged violations.

These examples, again, take us back to Chapters 1 and 3 of this book: Who is right and who is wrong in ethical dilemmas when the stakes are high for both parties and when both could be considered right? Whose morals and solutions should be followed?

These questions become even more difficult in international disputes when both sides have valid, legitimate claims, according to their historical traditions, customs, and legal history and practices.

The summary of universally recognized rights of international firms and countries listed as guidelines in section 7.4 is a starting point for identifying conflicts of interest. After that, advocating a specific ethic usually does not satisfy a solution when cultural, religious, economic, and legal "rights" of two disputing parties historically differ. The conflicting claims must be negotiated.

Thomas Donaldson (1989) offered an "ethical algorithm" to help resolve difficult conflicts of interest between international parties. However, this logic appears somewhat cumbersome and even mechanical in real-time experience.

This textbook advocates a more practical exercise that business and legal professionals are accustomed to using, namely a stakeholder analysis (see Chapter 2). Once the issues, stakes, and priority ranking of stakes are identified, then the two parties should begin to discuss the differing legal, cultural, historical, and social value systems that underlie each party's claims and motivations. The different ethical value systems in Chapter 3 can be applied as a "first pass" to understand the moral nature of the claims, even though other moral traditions also may be relevant to the situation. Specifically, the guidelines, or universal rights, in section 7.4 provide a starting point for reviewing issues of justice and duty and the parties' moral obligations, but, beyond this exercise, negotiation techniques are required to thrash out assumptions and specific issues to settle disputes (see Chapter 8).

Once more, no quick fixes can resolve high-stakes ethical and economic dilemmas between international players when both sides are right. Sensitivity to communication and diligence with negotiation techniques that help everyone understand and consider the differences in cultural traditions, language, and assumptions are required in order to reach what Roger Fischer, in his influential book on negotiations (1983, 1996), termed "getting to yes."

SUMMARY

The global business and economic environment has dramatically changed since the 1970s. The rise of Japan's and Germany's strong economies, the entrance of newly industrialized countries, and the convergence of consumer needs and preferences in these developing industrial countries as well as in the "Triad" (Europe, North America, and Asia) have created new global markets and competitive opportunities. In this context, industrial competitiveness is no longer dominated by U.S. firms. International forces that have supported and reflect the emergence of successful Japanese and European multinational firms were presented in this chapter. Also, the new industrial rules of global competition were identified and used to compare U.S. corporations' competitiveness.

Three new "faces of capitalism" are emerging in the global economy: In addition to consumer capitalism, they are producer, family and frontier capitalism. These were discussed in the chapter.

Arguments regarding the "ethics" of U.S. versus Japanese uses of capital in the global environment were presented. Japanese *keiretsu* (corporate alliances) were discussed as a cultural and sociopolitical extension of Japan's society. Elements of the dominant U.S. management system were compared to those of the Japanese management system. Steps for regaining U.S. competitiveness in the global economy were outlined.

Moral issues and practices that historically and currently pertain to multinational conduct also were identified. Guidelines drawn from over four decades of international agreements and charters were summarized to illustrate a consensus of host-country rights that have been used to help multinationals design equity into their policies and procedures.

Finally, because of the complexity and differences of national stakeholders' cultural, legal, economic, and value systems, no single moral or ethical code will be sufficient for resolving business disputes over issues when both parties are right, such as the issues of infringement of intellectual property and technological transfer. Global negotiating skills with knowledge of and sensitivities to language and to national sociopolitical and legally different systems and assumptions are required. The stakeholder approach becomes an important method in this new global business arena for identifying the different ethical assumptions of issues and for establishing compatible bases to morally resolve disputes between parties who are both right.

QUESTIONS

1. Describe the emerging competitive global business environment and the forces that define it. What is different about the changing global environment?

2. Define "competitiveness" as discussed in the chapter. How have U.S. corporations become more competitive? Give some examples.

3. Identify and characterize the four forms of capitalism. What are

some competitive and moral advantages and disadvantages of each in the global marketplace? Why?

4. Characterize Japan's system of capitalism.

5. Characterize the U.S. system of capitalism.

6. What are the advantages and disadvantages of Japan's and of the U.S.'s system of capitalism for doing business internationally?

7. Explain the differences in perception and experience of moral issues of (a) a host country toward an MNE and (b) an MNE toward a host country. Which perspective are you more inclined to support or sympathize with? Why?

8. Evaluate the practicality and use of the guidelines in section 7.4 from an MNE's perspective.

EXERCISES

1. Argue and defend your positions on the following statements:
   (a) "Only one system of world capitalism really exists, even though it may be practiced differently regionally."
   (b) "Japan is more globally competitive and has a large trade surplus because of unfair trade practices, not because of its system of capitalism and corporate practices."
   (c) "The U.S. management system cannot become more competitive than the Japanese system because of the two capitalist systems' differences."
   (d) "MNEs cannot financially afford to follow the guidelines in section 7.4; it would be too costly for them."
   (e) "When two national MNEs are both right over a controversial issue—for example, violation of patent or intellectual property rights—ethics should be avoided and other, more-concrete issues should be used to resolve the dispute."

2. Identify from the news or current press a dispute between (a) two multinational corporations and (b) a multinational corporation and a nation.

3. Answer these questions for 2a and 2b: Who is right and who is wrong? Why? How would you propose to resolve the dispute? Include a moral perspective in your answer.

REFERENCES AND SUGGESTED READINGS

Competitiveness survey: *HBR* readers respond. 1987. *Harvard Business Review* (September/October): 8–11.

Council on Competitiveness. 1988. *Competitive index,* May.

Czinkota, Michael, and Ilkka Ronkainen. 1989. *International business.* Chicago: The Dryden Press.

Daft, Richard. 1992. Contemporary designs for global competition. In *Organization theory and design.* 4th ed.. St. Paul, MN: West, 218–41.

Dertouros, Michael, Richard Lester, Robert Solow, and the MIT Commission on Industrial Productivity. 1989. *Made in America: Regaining the productive edge.* Cambridge: Massachusetts Institute of Technology Press.

Donaldson, Thomas. 1989. *The ethics of international business.* New York: Oxford University Press.

Dunning, John, and R. D. Pearce. 1981. *The world's largest industrial enterprises.* Farnborough, Eng.: Gower.

Farrell, Christopher. 1994. The triple revolution. *Business Week,* special bonus issue, 16.

———. 1995. The boom in IPOs. *Business Week,* 18 December, 64.

Fischer, Roger. 1983, 1996. *Getting to yes: Negotiating agreement without giving in.* New York: Penguin.

Frederick, William. 1991. The moral authority of transnational corporate codes. *Journal of Business Ethics* 10: 165–77.

Garreau, Joel. 1981. *The nine nations of North America.* New York: Avon.

Greenhouse, Steven. 1992. Attention America! Snap out of it! *New York Times,* 9 February, Sec. 3, pp. 1, 2, 8.

Guilty: Too many lawyers, too much litigation. 1992. *Business Week,* 13 April, 61.

Holbrook, Richard. 1991–1992 Japan and the United States: Ending the unequal partnership. *Foreign Affairs* (winter): 52.

Industrial policy: Call it what you will, the nation needs a plan to nurture growth. 1992. *Business Week,* 6 April, 72.

Kahle, Lynn R. 1988. The nine nations of North America and the value basis of geographic segmentation. In *Regional cultures, managerial behaviors, and entrepreneurship: An international perspective,* edited by Joseph Weiss. New York: Quorum Books, 43–60.

Kelly, Kevin, Otis Port, James Treece, Gail DeGeorge, and Zachary Schiller. 1992. Learning from Japan. *Business Week,* 27 January, 52–60.

Klein, Lisa. 1987. The impact of group structure on the strategy of the Japanese firm. Yale College Senior Essay, Yale University, New Haven, CT.

———. Kigyo keiretsu soran, the impact of group structure. *Oriental Economist,* 2.

Kochan, Thomas, Robert McKerie, and Henry Katz. 1986. *The transformation of American industrial relations.* New York: Basic Books.

Korn/Ferry International and Columbia University Graduate School of Business. 1989. *21st century report: A journal on critical issues affecting senior executives and the board of directors, reinventing the CEO.* A Global Study by Korn/Ferry International and Columbia University Graduate School of Management, New York.

Matsumoto, Koji. 1991. *The rise of the Japanese corporate system.* New York: Routledge Chapman and Hall.

Meyer John, and J. Gustafson. 1988. *The U.S. business corporation: An institution in transition.* Cambridge, MA: Ballinger.

Morton, Michael S. Scott. 1991. *Corporations of the 1990s: Information technology and organizational transformation.* New York: Oxford University Press.

Moshavi, Sharon. 1994. Selling shares in India Inc. *Business Week,* special issue, 60.

Murray, Alan. 1992. Managed trade may serve a purpose. *Wall Street Journal,* 20 January, A1.

Nagayasu, Yukimasa. 1992. Japanese economic system and business ethics. Paper presented at the Ninth Bentley Conference on Business Ethics, 31 March, Bentley College, Waltham, MA.

Naisbitt, John. 1996. *Megatrends Asia.* New York: Simon & Schuster.

Neff, Robert. 1992. Japan takes a good, hard look at itself. Is its brand of capitalism simply better? *Business Week,* 17 February, 32–34.

Ohmae, Kinichi. 1985. *Triad power: The coming shape of global competition.* New York: Free Press.

Ouchi, William, and Alfred Jaeger. 1978. Type Z organizations: Stability in the midst of mobility. *Academy of Management Review* 3: 305–14.

Peck, Merton. 1988. The large Japanese corporation. In *The U.S. business corporation: An institution in transition,* edited by John Meyer and J. Gustafson. Cambridge, MA: Ballinger, 21–42.

Pennar, Karen, Peter Galuszka, Lowry Miller. 1994. Frontier economies : Enter if you dare. *Business Week,* special bonus issue, 26–28.

Piore, Michael, and Charles Sabel. 1984. *The second industrial divide.* New York: Basic Books.

Porter, Michael, ed. 1986. *Competition in global industries.* Boston: Harvard Business School Press.

Rubner, Alex. 1990. *The might of the multinationals: The rise and fall of the corporate legend.* New York: Praeger.

Sakakibara, Eisuke. 1993. *Beyond capitalism: The Japanese model of market economics.* Lanham, MD: University Press of America.

Sethi, S., Nobuaki Namiki, and Carl Swanson. 1984. *The false promise of the Japanese miradi: Illusions and realities of the Japanese management system.* Boston: Pitman.

Shaw, H. William, and Vincent Barry. 1995. *Moral issues in business.* 6th ed. Belmont, CA Wadsworth.

Steiner, George A., and John F. Steiner. 1991. *Business, government & society: A managerial perspective.* 6th ed. New York: McGraw-Hill.

Sturdivant, Frederick, and Heidi Vernon-Wortzel. 1990. *Business and society: A managerial approach.* Homewood, IL: Irwin.

Taylor, Frederick W. 1947. *Scientific management.* New York: Harper & Row.

Thurow, Lester. 1996. *The future of capitalism.* New York: William Morrow, 326.

Toy, Stewart. 1994. Non-Dirigisme : Dragging France's bureaucrats out of industry. *Business Week,* special bonus issue, 30–32.

United Nations. 1973. *Multinational corporations in world development.*

Vernon, Raymond. 1971. *Sovereignty at bay.* New York: Basic Books.

———. 1977. *Storm over the multinationals.* Cambridge: Harvard University Press.

Vernon, Raymond, and Louis Wells Jr. 1986. *Manager in the international economy.* 5th ed. Englewood Cliffs: Prentice Hall.

Vijayan, Jaikumar. 1996. Look out, here comes India. *Computerworld,* 26 February.

Webber, Alan, and William Taylor. 1992. Is what's bad for General Motors bad for the U.S.A.? *Boston Globe,* 1 March, 73, 76.

Wilkins, Mora. 1970. *The emergence of multinational enterprise: American business abroad from the Colonial Era to 1914.* Cambridge: Harvard University Press.

Yanaga, Chitoshi. 1965. *Japanese people and politics.* New York: Wiley.

8

BUSINESS ETHICS INTO THE TWENTY-FIRST CENTURY

8.1 A PERSPECTIVE ON THE FUTURE OF BUSINESS AND ETHICS

The legitimacy of U.S. business institutions was founded on the notion that the free-market system operated to provide value to society and to serve the public good. The historical role of business initially was to maximize profits in order to effect greater economic welfare for the general public. It was believed business fulfilled its social and economic responsibilities through the "invisible hand" working in the market system (Weaver 1988). The underlying public support for business as a legitimate institution stems from that perception.

In recent decades, perceptions about the contributions of business to society have changed. Abuse of human rights (child labor) by multinational corporations, destruction of the physical environment, oil spills, toxic dumping, and other business-related crises discussed earlier in this book have decreased public confidence in the legitimacy of business as an institution. The single goal of maximizing profits no longer will be sufficient to legitimatize the idea that business activities promote a good society. Increased public perceptions and experience that the free-market system alone does not adequately contribute to the public's general welfare has eroded the notion that corporate management's sole responsibility should be to its shareholders.

The stakeholder perspective taken in this book argues that businesses have both moral and economic obligations to their constituencies. Although a time existed when the moral obligations of corporations were taken for granted and were assumed to be fulfilled when economic functions were achieved, that time is past. A stakeholder perspective holds that the legitimacy, power, and long-term success of a company depends on the extent it serves the public through its economic competitiveness and innovativeness while meeting moral obligations to its stakeholders. These are not mutually exclusive goals. A firm, for example, should not destroy the environment while using it to produce short-term profits. A firm should not market dangerous products to its customers. The stakeholder view acknowledges the economic and competitive nature of the corporation while arguing that the moral imperative of serving the public good through the responsible design, manufacture, and distribution of products and services is essential to the firm's long-term survival and relationship to its buying public. The government as a consumer and business partner also acts as a regulator when corporations overstep their legal and moral boundaries with consumers and stakeholders.

Issues that businesses must prioritize in the twenty-first century include their economic, political, and moral obligations toward a wide range of stakeholders. For example, some of the more predominant issues follow:

❏ Resolving national rivalries over trade wars and over competing cross-cultural stereotyping

❑ Prioritizing consumer protection and product safety

❑ Preventing environmental pollution and depletion of the ozone layer and natural resources

❑ Actively using economic influence and investments to alleviate domestic and international social injustices

❑ Providing safe and healthy working environments

❑ Providing policies and procedures that prevent discrimination within the organization

These issues are now global in scope.

Stakeholders that must be given increased importance in this decade include national trading partners and competitors, consumers (particularly those in less-developed nations who are unprotected by institutions and laws), public interest groups, employees, suppliers, end users, and the media. As business alliances across national boundaries increase, nations and international alliances (e.g., trading blocs) become stakeholders of international businesses. Business leaders will continue to confront the task of balancing national and international interests. Serving consumers in developed and less-developed nations through fair competitive practices must be a high moral priority for corporations that seek to uphold their reputations. Relationships between corporations and stakeholders are also changing, since end users and suppliers are becoming strategic partners with businesses. Therefore, the value and intensity of these relationships will increase as economic and social exchanges become more frequent and strategic. For businesses, becoming more moral means valuing and attending to both inside and outside stakeholder relationships.

The following sections summarize and extend what have been major themes throughout this textbook. Here, the emphasis is on the argument that business economic and moral responsibilities to the global environment, employee welfare, and the general public are increasing in urgency given the accelerated pace technological changes, industrial activity, and destruction to the environment are occurring.

Before turning to an overview of these social issues, this discussion begins with some of the broader fundamental changes that affect the importance of ethics for business institutions.

8.2 FUNDAMENTAL CHANGES FOR THE FUTURE OF BUSINESS ETHICS

Changes in society's values and the resultant demands on business reflect the growing need for ethical standards as an integral part of corporate policy. Leonard Brooks (1989) discussed six reasons why corporations are increasing their present and future focus on business ethics:

1. The growing public crises of public confidence in corporate activities

2. An increasing emphasis on quality of life (that is, on health, leisure time, attention to family needs)

3. Growing corporate expectations of paying high penalties for unethical behavior

4. Increased ethical awareness through the growing power of special-interest groups

5. The degree of publicity the first four factors have generated

6. Changes in corporate objectives that influence the control of business activities

Each of these themes is briefly summarized next.

PUBLIC CRISES OF CONFIDENCE

Many corporations currently face the public's lack of confidence in their credibility and contribution to society. One poll showed that 69 percent of those surveyed thought business has too much power over U.S. lives; 47 percent believed firms would damage the environment for profit (The public is willing 1989). More recently, widespread sexual harassment and rape in the U.S. Army, U.S. Navy, and private-sector corporations reveal a lack of respect for employees in power structures.

An increasing number of corporate executives now wish to formalize corporate ethical standards into their operations in order to control illegal behavior and to improve corporate competitiveness. Johnson & Johnson, Nynex, and Procter & Gamble are three firms that have effectively incorporated ethics into their operating procedures.

EMPHASIS ON QUALITY OF WORK LIFE

The second driving force that has awakened executives' interest in business ethics is the increasing value the U.S. society has placed on the **quality of work life (QWL).** General Motors, GTE, Digital Equipment Corporation, Xerox, and Packard Electric are a small sample of U.S. firms that have implemented QWL programs. Because of the growth in dual-career working couples, an expanded national awareness of personal and family health, and an increasing concern for balanced lifestyles, employees and employers are seeking to enhance their quality of life at work. Flex-time, emphasis on health and fitness, compressed workweeks, work-at-home programs, child-care centers in companies, and other programs are being implemented by employers who wish to attract and keep a productive workforce.

Implementation of QWL programs along with quality circles, that is, increased worker involvement and participation in decision making, has been effective in improving employee morale, job interest, commitment, and satisfaction (Pearce and Ravlin 1987). Trends point to a greater use of QWL types of programs to effectively meet employees' social and employment needs.

PENALTIES FOR UNETHICAL BEHAVIOR

Employment discrimination and violations of pollution standards, safe working conditions, and on-the-job health and right-to-know information requirements have all contributed to sizable legal and other economic penalties and costs for companies that have not prevented or curbed illegal activities in these areas. Federal and state governments have demonstrated their willingness in courts to enforce laws to protect the environment and employees from arbitrary and unjust management practices.

The increased expectations of stiffer penalties for companies engaging in unethical behavior also represents a fundamental change in society's views about the role of business. Corporations are expected to act responsibly not only to their shareholders but also to all stakeholder groups and society in general. As a result, large corporations, in particular, are implementing "ethics offices," discussed in Chapter 4, and other employee-related programs that encourage open discussion of complaints and observed wrongdoings before such actions lead to illegal activities.

POWER OF SPECIAL-INTEREST GROUPS

Special-interest groups continue to target and showcase in the media corporations that threaten the public welfare. Ralph Nader, for example, pioneered the consumer interest-group movement, which has increased and diversified since the first organization, Public Citizen, in 1971. Other consumer interest groups include the Health Resources Group, the Citizen Action Group, the Litigation Group, and Congress Watch, to name a few (Frederick, Davis, and Post, 1988, 271).

Brooks (1989) also cites three broader groups in particular whose influence has been felt strongly in the capital markets, which also have drawn attention to corporate ethical performance. These groups are minority interests, institutional investors, and ethical investors (31–38).

ROLE OF MEDIA AND PUBLICITY

Publicity through increased media attention also has become a major concern of companies today. The media as major stakeholders will continue to significantly affect and shape public perceptions about businesses in the future. The Exxon *Valdez* incident, the Three Mile Island disaster, the ValuJet catastrophe, and other publicized events and crises have brought instant and sometimes prolonged media coverage into the public living room. Corporations also need to "police" the media to ensure fair practices. For example, the National Broadcasting Company (NBC) overstepped its boundaries by fabricating stories of how dangerous GM vehicles were.

Corporations must continue to learn how to relate responsibly to the media as a public stakeholder. Crisis management techniques, discussed in Chapter 5, will increase in importance as commercial accidents and incidents continue to involve the public's welfare and interests.

CHANGING CORPORATE FORMS AND ETHICS

As corporations outsource their operations and evolve into geographically dispersed networks, alliances, partnerships, strategic business units, and independent profit centers, the following ethical questions arise:

1. How are individual and organizational control and accountability to be defined and maintained?

2. Who has the focus of responsibility in final decisions removed from any center of operations?

3. Who decides conflicts, and what are the rules for resolving them in dispersed, changing business relationships?

4. Who will balance competing and contradictory moral interests between governments and firms? between manufacturers and customers? between purchasing agents and suppliers?

5. As individual and operational-unit discretionary power increases and becomes independent from single government, legal system, and "headquarters" authority, who will intervene and resolve complaints involving consumers, the public interest, and corporate actors? (See Badaracco 1988, 67–91.)

Although no easy answers to these dilemmas exist, some clues do. First, previous conceptions of business structure, efficiency, and social responsibility relationships must be revised. Hierarchically based theories of corporations are inadequate to explain how to manage moral responsibility in networked organizations. Working on and solving problems in networks and other dispersed, decentralized structures are current research themes that require more fieldwork, especially regarding the ethical questions just posed.

Second, business ethics also must focus concepts, applications, and guidelines on individuals and teams working in these changing architectural organizational structures. For example, the following topics will need to be explored:

❏ Articulating independent responsible *choices* compatible with the corporation's and other stakeholders' values and missions

❏ Understanding the uses and limits of responsible corporate power in autonomous business relationships

❏ Maintaining responsibility in flexible business relationships while balancing profit with different ethical imperatives

❏ Negotiating among cross-cultural values, interests, and expectations while maintaining one's core values and business commitments

❏ Listening to and assertively communicating under conflicting moral demands to reach a consensus without sacrificing one's ethical position

These are not new skills for managing morality in business transactions, but they increase in scale, importance, and risk as employees gain independence, autonomy, authority, and control in dispersed organizations. Although the ethical principles discussed in Chapter 3 remain important moral guidelines for employees in networks and other independent organizational units, an added emphasis is being placed on identifying ethical values that balance an individual's sense of professional integrity and worth with the corporation's. This means understanding one's own ethical values, as well as the corporation's ethical imperatives, guidelines, and boundaries, to ensure a psychological contract between the two interests. This is and always has been a complex undertaking. International managers have experienced these challenges. Now, domestic managers and employees must learn these lessons.

The new ethical challenge is not choosing the "right" course of action; it is negotiating between two or more "right" alternatives, especially when dealing with other stakeholders' values and business priorities. Communicating and negotiating a moral business consensus with external stakeholders without sacrificing 'personal moral integrity is a major corporate task of this era.

CHANGING CORPORATE OBJECTIVES

The final factor, the nature of corporate objectives, has come under scrutiny as an important indication of a business's ethical directions and intentions. For example, as noted throughout this text, short-term profit objectives, in particular, are under criticism as a primary goal of many large corporations. A new emphasis is being placed on achieving long-term value and success by producing quality products and services that increase a firm's global and domestic competitiveness and add to a society's public welfare.

U.S. corporations also are pooling and sharing resources through strategic alliances and consortia to compete with Japanese *keiretsu*, discussed in Chapter 7. A number of American firms are pooling capital and resources to protect their industries against more-focused, government-supported foreign competition. This collectivist type of corporate objective represents a significant change from individual and singularly pursued company objectives in the United States since the 1960s and 1970s.

Some of "America's Most Admired Corporations"—Merck, Rubbermaid, Wal-Mart, Liz Claiborne, Levi Strauss, Johnson & Johnson, Coca-Cola, 3M, PepsiCo, and Procter & Gamble—share eight key attributes that lead to successful company reputations. These attributes, which reflect the changing nature of corporate objectives, are(1) quality of management; (2) financial soundness; (3) quality of products or services; (4) ability to attract, develop, and keep talented people; (5) use of corporate assets; (6) value as a long-term investment; (7) innovativeness; and (8) community and environmental responsibility (Ballou 1992). Such attributes reflect a balance between marketplace competitiveness and public responsibility that corporations must strive to achieve to meet their stockholder and stakeholder responsibilities.

CONCEPT OF "TOTAL ETHICS"

A central concept evident in many successful and moral companies is termed **total ethics** (Evans 1991). This concept is similar to the "zero defects" theory of organizational behavior. The basic premise of the concept is that businesses must understand their ethical responsibilities not as responses to external pressures or threats but as integral components of their ongoing activities.

Evans (1991) questions the long-standing perception that businesses should *coexist* with society, rather than intentionally seek to be active, concerned *participants* in society. If business organizations view themselves and are viewed as integral members of the society, then ethical concerns regarding the effects of 'their actions on others will become priorities of corporate executives.

Since an increasing number of companies are becoming international, business decisions have far-reaching consequences on different populations and cultures. The "total ethics" concept calls for business decision makers to think beyond the maximization of profits and containment of damage to make decisions that will eliminate human and environmental damage. This proactive view advocates the stakeholder model for examining whether the company is meeting its ethical responsibilities for a wider-than-before range of groups, such as creditors, employees, investors, consumers, and suppliers, and for the public at large.

Evans (1991) illustrates the "total ethics" concept by offering the practical example of Traidcraft Plc. Traidcraft was founded in Bangladesh in 1979. The company began by selling craft items from Bangladesh. The underlying mission of the founders was to reform existing trading policies in order to help redistribute some of the wealth between impoverished less-developed countries and wealthy industrialized nations.

In 1986, Traidcraft established a "Statement of Objectives," which was developed primarily by employees. This document illustrates an effort to consider and involve all groups affected by Traidcraft's operations. The company also published its purchasing policy and made it available to suppliers and the public. The policy attempts to protect the aims of all parties involved and provides the basis for solid business relationships. The role of ethics in business practices has been questioned in terms of whether ethical behavior helps to yield financial success. As an example, Traidcraft offers a way for future corporations to act with a "total ethics" objective.

When Traidcraft's first prospectus came out, the English newspaper *Guardian* stated:

> A Gateshead company called Traidcraft urgently needs a £300,000 cash injection from new shareholders, but it is offering them in return only "love, justice and equity." And equity to Traidcraft means putting a higher value on sharing the world's resources fairly than on its own share certificates. Investors must prefer goodness to greed, and should never expect "personal gain or profit" the prospectus warns. (Evans 1991)

The reaction in England was extremely favorable and demonstrated that consumers often are willing to pay higher prices in order to benefit from moral as well as economic business objectives.

This textbook argues that successful corporations must include a "total ethics" perspective in their corporate and operating objectives in order to meet stakeholder obligations. Integrating ethical standards from the top executive down, through all levels, formally and informally, in corporations ensures a total ethics perspective. Corporations that depend only on ethics codes or formal statements of ethical intent and do not implement, reward, and discipline the use of ethical standards in daily operations will not realize a total ethics perspective.

8.3 GLOBAL ETHICS: INTERNATIONAL INTERDEPENDENCIES

The number of multinational firms operating in the global marketplace today has set the stage for increasing interdependencies. Although further globalization of multinational corporations provides new business and economic opportunities, it also provides a background for conflicts between cultures with differing values and moral codes of conduct. This is especially true given the opening of territorial and cultural boundaries in Europe and the Commonwealth of Independent States (formerly the

U.S.S.R.). Corporate objectives, policies, and skills must effectively deal with cross-cultural and moral differences in doing business.

Buller, Kohls, and Anderson (1991) define ethics to include "both the moral codes and values used in the reasoning process as well as the decisions and the behaviors that result from them." Their goal is to determine and achieve a global *level of consensus* among international parties regarding the rightness or wrongness of particular acts, policies, and decisions. The authors suggest that four interrelated levels (individual, corporate, societal, and global) strongly influence each other. The ethics of an individual, for example, is greatly influenced by ethical standards common to his or her society and corporate environment. Likewise, although corporate ethics largely reflect the society where the organization is operating, individuals within the organization also bring their own perspectives and ethical beliefs into the firm.

The concept of global ethics is even more complex because people and institutions reflecting different individual, corporate, and societal ethical standards interact. The higher the degree nations and multinational enterprises share values, beliefs, and opinion consensus on ethical conduct for specific issues, the greater is everyone's ability to establish global ethical guidelines. The challenges are learning (1) to become aware of value and perceptual differences across cultures at all levels and (2) to become competent in negotiating differences into consensual agreements.

The strongest argument in support of the development of global ethics is that such ethics can clarify common moral goals that underlie cultural and national differences. For example, a global ethic that possibly could gain consensus across individual, corporate, and societal levels is an ecology policy designed to protect natural forests and bodies of water. Such an ethic could help reduce conflicts in the increasingly diverse realm of environmentally harmful industrial activities. However, a danger in adopting global ethics lies in consolidating a consensus of opinions that could later impede the search for improved methods in that particular policy area. Also, once a certain practice has attained a global ethical standard, it may be difficult to change behavior, even if that practice is later viewed as undesirable.

Nevertheless, multinational corporations are in a unique position to promote global ethics. As more firms develop international ties, they will increase their interdependencies, and the need for cooperation among nations will become more important. This process may give rise to uniform ethical guidelines for conducting business on a global scale in the near future. The most realistic promise for the emergence of a global ethic lies in the mutual perception and negotiation of individuals and nations as members of an international community that shares joint goals and concerns. The resurgence of democratic principles in what were once Communist bloc and less-developed countries, along with joint environmental concerns, is pressuring nations to adopt an environmental global ethic. However, until global ethics are defined for environmental and other critical areas, corporations and governments must continue to negotiate their competing economic, political, and moral interests.

CROSS-CULTURAL CONFLICT NEGOTIATION

Negotiating cross-cultural value and business differences will be imperative in this and the next decade as corporations seek new alliances, partners, mergers, and acquisitions across geographies. This section will not deal with this topic in depth but will introduce some central concepts to illustrate the importance of negotiating for business in the global arena.

Nancy Adler (1991, 182) states that "negotiation is one of the single most important international business skills." Since negotiation is the process whereby one party attempts to persuade another to accept its ideas, plans, or behavior, it is obvious a range of factors and options can influence this goal. The following six factors influence how a corporation or party interprets a situation to determine whether to negotiate:

1. *Value of the Exchange:* The more beneficial a corporation views the exchange of resources with a foreign firm, the harder the corporation will pursue negotiations.

2. *Commitment:* The higher the level of commitment a company holds toward a particular issue, the greater the extent it is willing to negotiate. If an issue is important to the firm, it will invest the time in negotiations.

3. *Relationship:* The more valuable a successful relationship with a foreign firm is regarded, the more a corporation is willing to negotiate.

4. *Time:* Since negotiation is a time-consuming process, the firm will pursue it as a strategy only if sufficient time exists to allow completion of the process. The more urgent the situation, the less viable negotiation is as a strategy.

5. *Trust Level:* The higher the trust level between the two parties, the greater the possibility for successful negotiations. Serious good-faith negotiation also will help to increase the trust level.

6. *Power Distribution:* If a firm's power position is low relative to the other party, it will be more apt to negotiate because it is at a relative disadvantage in terms of ability to implement its own objectives. A firm in a greater relative power position would be more likely to possess a take-it-or-leave-it attitude. (See Adler 1991, 185–215, for a detailed discussion of these factors.)

The more successful negotiators tend to consider a greater number of possible outcomes and alternatives, to talk more about mutually beneficial areas of interest, to concentrate more on long-term issues, to concentrate on discussing issues versus a set sequence of topics, and to set a range of possible outcomes instead of rigid expectations (Adler 1991).

Buller, Kohls, and Anderson (1991) present seven approaches for dealing with cross-cultural conflicts. These are summarized as techniques for managing ethical issues across cultures. Although these approaches are not new, they illustrate starting points for discussing several choices a corporation or party has for persuading another to accept a goal, idea, or behavior. The seven approaches are avoidance, forcing, education/ persuasion, infiltration, negotiation/compromise, accommodation, and collaboration. It is important to note that the success of these techniques depends on individual characteristics, situational contingencies, and their strategic process. Although a win-win outcome is always desirable, it is not always feasible. These approaches suggest ways to minimize further conflict as well as to solve all conflicting demands:

1. *Avoidance:* In this technique, the conflict is relegated to a background position and is not dealt with directly. If one party is in a significantly stronger bargaining position, avoidance as a negotiation and conflict-resolution strategy may be used to prevent further or escalating ethical conflicts.

2. *Forcing:* This technique is used when one party imposes its will over another. Many multinational corporations have been accused of disrespecting and intruding on host-country cultures. Host-country governments, such as Brazil and Spain, have responded in the past by forcing restrictions on MNEs' profits, such as requiring profits stay in the country, and by limiting technological manufacturing. Forcing is a high-risk strategy in the international arena and should be considered only when the situation, people, and interests require it. Some critics argue the U.S. government should use this tactic more with Japan regarding trade policies. The United States, it is argued, has negotiated with Japan from a position of weakness and has not identified what long-term stakes the U.S. government really needs in order to bargain.

3. *Education/Persuasion:* This technique employs a specific means of relating the values of one party's perspectives in order to persuade the other to adopt its position. Multinationals have educated host-country employees on the value and uses of new technologies, and MNEs have learned from host governments how to share resources and help develop local economies.

4. *Infiltration:* This technique is an often slow process of introducing others to one party's ethic. Infiltration can result in wide acceptance of particular ideas if they hold some appeal for these individuals. Infiltration is often used unintentionally rather than strategically. For example, many former Eastern bloc countries are pursuing market economies based on their interaction with and evolving desires for Western societal structures

and values. As Western market-oriented nations penetrate these economies, infiltration of marketing concepts and methods occurs.

5. *Negotiation/Compromise:* This technique is used when the ethical conflict presents a severe obstacle to productivity. Resolution through negotiation often will lead to compromise on both sides. Although negotiation/compromise may allow the business transaction to occur, it often can leave both sides feeling the underlying issue was never resolved.

6. *Accommodation:* For this technique, either party may find it beneficial to adopt the ethic of the other and may do so with little, if any, resistance. Accommodation requires patience, "give-and-take," and listening.

7. *Collaboration:* When implementing this technique, both parties would discuss the conflict and attempt to reach a mutually beneficial solution. Willingness to learn, to change attitudes, and to renegotiate interests are vital for collaboration. This is the most desired form of conflict resolution because it deals directly with the source (767–75).

It should be noted that negotiation is an art and a skill. Professor John Graham at the University of Southern California lists key characteristics of American, Japanese, Taiwanese, and Brazilian managers who negotiate well (see Adler 1991, 187). Some of the skills that overlap cultures and countries include sufficient preparation and planning, listening well, exercising judgment and intelligence, integrity, thinking clearly under pressure, thorough product knowledge, and the ability to win and respect the other party's confidence. Some general suggestions for negotiating follow: Know your strengths and start the process with these; avoid time pressures to complete the process; remain vague at first until all stakes of all parties are on the table; and be confident in your ability to win concessions.

Learning to read and understand cross-cultural cues, historical contexts, systems of law, customs, and expectations based on political, historical, and religious traditions will increase in importance as more businesses globalize. Cross-cultural negotiation skills are essential for business professionals in the next decade, especially when meeting moral obligations involves conflicting cultural values.

8.4 CHANGES IN THE WORKFORCE

The composition of the workforce has been changing and will continue to change into the next century, as Chapter 6 indicated. The U.S. labor pool that will be available in the twenty-first century and beyond will require employers and managers to review their values about and expectations of work and workers. The twenty-first century workforce changes discussed in Chapter 6 are briefly summarized here with ethical implications for the future of business.

THE AGING WORKFORCE

The aging of the "baby-boom" generation combined with the relatively low supply of younger entrants to the labor market will have definite implications for the value systems of many corporations. For example, health and wellness programs, retirement planning, and reward systems that provide more leisure time in place of financial benefits are likely to become more prevalent. Also, an increase in the demand for young workers will lead to an increase in the demand for those available, including women, immigrants, and disabled workers. Companies will need to institute adequate training programs to develop necessary skills in a labor pool that most likely will lack many specific skills. This change in demand also will lead to increasing competition for entry-level workers. Restructured compensation packages will be required to respond to the needs and values of young and other "nontraditional" workers.

The clustering of employees at the middle and upper levels of organizations also will lead to a decline in the percentage of available promotions. This can cause employee frustration and dissatisfaction with their careers. Many companies will need to face the challenge of providing a stimulating and rewarding work environment for those who find promotions in scarce supply. Dependent care and family responsibilities also will appear as dominant concerns for a growing majority of the workforce. All of these changes will put pressure on established values and stakeholder's rights.

WOMEN IN THE WORKFORCE

It is estimated that women will account for more than 50 percent of the active workforce by 2000. As a result, corporations hoping to attract and retain qualified female employees will need to address issues relevant to women in particular. Some of these will include changes in the measurements of success, as more females reach the executive level; changes in leave policies to accommodate family responsibilities; the varying benefit requirements of single mothers, women in dual-career families, and women without children; emphasis on child care; and offering flexible or home-based positions. The quantity of "fairness" issues will increase.

ETHNIC AND CULTURAL DIVERSITY IN THE WORKFORCE

The decline in the availability of young entrants to the workforce also will increase the demand for immigrants, thus creating greater cultural diversity within the labor pool. The challenge here will be to integrate varieties of values, norms, and ethical principles. Corporations will need to adopt many new policies and procedures in order to meet this challenge. Some of these may include providing cultural awareness training; redesigning jobs and establishing training to compensate for language barriers; establishing reward systems and promotion possibilities that correspond to different value systems; developing new and improved methods for dealing with cultural diversity; and perhaps formally recognizing managers who are successful at integrating a diverse workforce.

DISABLED WORKERS

Once again, a diminishing traditional labor pool will precipitate the need to tap into currently dormant resources. The disabled worker population has remained largely underused, but an increasing future demand is predicted for skills this group offers. Disabled workers typically have had problems finding and maintaining jobs even though legislation has been enacted to protect their rights. This is due in large measure to distorted perceptions of the skills of the disabled and a lack of support for those who attempt to fit into rigid corporate cultures. Corporations will need to implement policies to assist and support both disabled workers and nondisabled workers unaccustomed to such coworkers. Programs to provide education to nondisabled coworkers, career development programs for the disabled, and other effective employee assistance programs; flexible hours and working conditions; and interaction with legislators and health care providers are but a few of the necessary steps for companies to deal effectively with this unique human resource.

THE EDUCATION GAP IN THE WORKFORCE

The concern here is with the growing segment of the population known as the functionally illiterate. A smaller percentage of the U.S. population is obtaining quality higher education than in the past, and more people are graduating from high school without the basic skills necessary to function in a business environment. This disparity will divide the workforce into two segments: (1) the highly educated middle-aged employees who will demand a challenging, semiautonomous, and performance-based environment, and (2) the less-educated employees who will require structured special training. The company may need to sponsor programs within the community to facilitate this training. Firms also will need to research appropriate motivators for success within this population.

The task of managing the wide range of employee needs, values, and ethical standards will be indeed a primary challenge for corporations in the future. Managers need to be increasingly aware of the mix of values they are dealing with. Accurate understanding of the diverse cultures and underlying value systems inherent in a particular workforce can lead to the establishment of effective motivational and reward systems and can mean the difference between business success and failure.

8.5 INTERNET AND ONLINE CENSORSHIP IN CYBERSPACE

The Internet (Net) and the World Wide Web are among the largest and fastest-growing industries in the world. The stakes are high. A study by Morgan Stanley estimates that revenues for the global Internet industry in 1996 were $15.9 billion. The forecast predicts revenues of $79.1 billion by 2000. Estimates of worldwide Internet users top 30 million. The U.S. accounts for almost half of all host computers capable of dishing out information over the Internet. Six of the remaining top ten countries are in Europe. Germany is second with nearly 453,000 host computers. The United Kingdom ranks third; after Canada, the top users are Australia, Japan, Finland, the Netherlands, Sweden, and France.

A major problem that has surfaced in "cyberspace," a term for all that encompasses the Internet network, is the issue of censorship versus free speech. The Telecommunications Competition and Deregulation Act, signed into law by President Clinton in February 1996, has an "indecency" provision that makes graphic displays of sex and nudity on the Internet illegal. *Penthouse* magazine already has removed most nude photos from its site and replaced them with black squares advising users to contact congressional members. Many companies participated in a protest by turning Internet pages black with white lettering for 48 hours. Supporters of the legislation claim it is necessary to protect children, while civil libertarians say the Internet should have no more restrictions on free speech than books have. Several groups, including the American Civil Liberties Union and the Electronic Frontier Foundation, are challenging the "'indecency'" law in court.

Another censorship problem has emerged: "Who sets the limits for the context of information?" Especially of concern are pornography and gambling. States such as Nevada, in which gambling is legal, are introducing online gambling services. Censoring cyberspace is a difficult endeavor, especially on a global scale. Although governments' efforts to legally impede the spread of "indecent" content on the Internet have begun, the issues have yet to be settled among stakeholders.

In the United States, an amendment to the telecom-reform legislation would make it a crime to knowingly transmit "indecent" materials over the Net. The punishment: $100,000 and two years in jail. As the Internet industry is embroiled with regulation and censorship, children are being targeted in a very different way. In fact, children's advocacy groups have called on the federal government to regulate the growing volume of cyberspace marketing aimed at children. The Center for Media Education, a public-interest organization leading the fight, targeted 32 snack-food, toy, entertainment, and online computer service companies that sell products or services for children. The report contends the companies are using the Internet's World Wide Web and other interactive computer sites to communicate with unsuspecting youngsters—as young as four years old. The companies also are obtaining personal information about children and making aggressive pitches to children for their products. Children's advocacy groups have called for strong governmental and industry actions to set standards governing online marketing aimed at children. The idea is not to ban ads for children on the Internet but to make it a safer place for child viewers.

ONLINE INTERNATIONAL RESPONSES TO CENSORSHIP

In China, the government is planning to introduce new regulations to restrict the flow of "pornographic and detrimental" information into the country via the Internet. In Germany, lawmakers are clamping down on online service providers that allow access to child pornography, which violates German criminal law. The country also has a task force to sort out online jurisdictional issues as well as issues such as liability, licensing, and the government's role in delivering new services. Sweden may soon unveil a liability standard for online service providers. France is considering legislating the industry along the lines of the maritime business. Conservative countries such as Saudi Arabia also are preparing guidelines to address online censorship.

8.6 ENVIRONMENTAL ISSUES

One estimate states that the developed world must provide the less-developed world with an additional $70 billion of new aid, in addition to the current $50 billion annually provided, to protect and sustain the physical global environment (Gutfeld 1992, A2). Global warming, acid rain, air and water pollution, and toxic waste are all environmental concerns discussed in Chapter 5. Businesses both cause and are affected by these concerns. Industries that participate in polluting the environment also must help pay for the effects of this damage. Environmental destruction will have a growing impact on future social, political, and business policies. The environment is a concern that affects all people of all nations. Ethical decision making by businesses can play an important role in preserving and protecting the environment now and for future generations. Conferences such as the Earth Summit meeting in Rio de Janeiro in 1992 and another meeting in 1996 were a step toward defining international commitments to the environment.

Global warming was termed "the greatest crisis ever faced collectively by humans" (Stevensen 1991) at the Conference on Global Warming and Climate Change in 1989. A crisis of this magnitude demonstrates the need for an international business code of conduct aimed at protecting the environment and at searching for alternative energy sources. A transnational global ethic is needed in this area.

The stakeholder approach to decision making can be implemented in this instance to address the variety of values and interests a global energy policy would affect. Developing countries have resisted suggestions for regulating carbon dioxide emissions. Many feel they cannot restrict their emissions while they are in an economically industrial growth stage and that they are being unjustly penalized for pollution caused primarily by developed industrialized countries. Future generations also share a stake in current energy policies. More education, resource sharing, and economic cooperation between wealthy and impoverished nations must occur to relieve environmental damage of the rain forests, the ozone layer, and bodies of water.

Alternatives to fossil fuels are beginning to be seriously researched around the world. Special-interest groups and individual stakeholders likely will take strong positions on these issues and will press for viable solutions. For example, in 1989, Canada's environment minister indicated he supported research into nuclear energy sources. This met with widespread opposition and concern. For such decisions, it is important for business and political leaders to monitor their stakeholders' concerns and to negotiate with the claims of all groups involved. The environment's condition affects everyone.

Lucien Bouchard, Canadian environment minister in 1989, stated at the Symposium on the Arctic and Global Change: "We must change to development processes that are environmentally sustainable." This suggestion provides a basis for research and development, as well as an ethical guideline for future business operations that affect the global environment.

A recent United Nations study found that the most efficient way to combat global warming is to use private financial markets for bartering pollution activities. The study suggests creating a global Environmental Protection Agency. The agency would be responsible for distributing pollution allowances that could, in turn, be exchanged between polluters and with others. The study also proposes creating an exchange-based over-the-counter futures and options market for pollution rights.

The proposal would have to be reviewed by the governments of the Conference on Trade and Development and the United Nations. However, according to Frank Joshua, economic affairs officer for the U. N.

Conference on Trade and Development, this plan could establish a global precedent for using financial markets to clean up the environment.

8.7 IMPLEMENTING CODES OF CONDUCT INTO PRACTICE

Ethical principles and practices in business start with top leaders' expressed, shared, and implemented values. The corporate culture then embodies these values and practices. The development of and implementation of these ethical values into codes, ethics training courses, ethics offices, sexual harassment programs, and ombudsperson and peer review programs so they become operating initiatives allows corporations to remain competitive and responsible and to build and sustain trusting relationships with stakeholders. The implementation of these ethical values into operating programs requires the leaders' commitment, time, and effort 'in order to structure the company to best serve all the relevant stakeholders. L. J. Brooks (1989) offers seven recommendations for realistically implementing ethical codes of conduct and practices into corporate strategies, culture, and values:

1. Confidentiality should not be so restrictive that it prohibits employees from consulting with internal personnel regarding ethical questions.

2. A fair and objective hearing process should follow any report of an ethical problem or conflict.

3. Assurance should be given to all employees that their rights with respect to discrimination and to adequate notice and compensation in the event of a layoff will be protected.

4. A section in the code on employer rights or terms of employment should follow the employee rights section, in order to facilitate open communication and clarify expectations.

5. Executive support of the code of conduct should be demonstrated in the form of clear sanctions against those who violate it.

6. Conflicts of interest revolving around ownership interest in related concerns need to be addressed, as these conflicts can cloud judgments.

7. Consider any external ethical codes of conduct that influence employees in the corporation, and design the corporate code so it does not conflict with these.

Ethical conduct in corporations must be a shared vision and shared practices that are actively communicated and modeled by executives, managers, and employees on an ongoing, daily basis. As shareholders become more informed about and involved in the moral management of

companies, CEOs and boards of directors also must work more coopera-
tively and responsively as partners with the firm's stakeholders to ensure
that justice is exemplified by the firm's leadership and integrated into
everyday operations of the organization.

SUMMARY

A business is a vital partner with its employees, its stockholders, the government, consumers, suppliers, and the general public. This network of
relationships is based on trust as well as performance. As the twenty-first
century approaches, the adversarial and segmented bases underlying
these relationships must give way to cooperative alliances grounded on
responsibility as well as profit motives for all stakeholders. This must
happen because global competitiveness requires it. Short-term objectives
based on the greed or self-interests of a few groups often prove costly to
overall society and consumers. Total quality management processes introduced by Dr. Edward Deming have worked in Japan and now are
being mastered, after 40 years, by U.S. firms. Without a total-quality,
continuous-improvement, and team-oriented approach to doing business,
companies will continue to fall behind.

Underlying this holistic method of competition are the moral imperatives of a stakeholder approach: Stakeholders should be respected and
treated fairly; stakeholder and stockholder relationships should be based
on trust as well as performance criteria; society as a whole and consumers
are strategic stakeholders and must be included in business strategies;
and ethics is an integral part of doing business.

REFERENCES AND SUGGESTED READINGS

Adler, Nancy J. 1991. *International dimensions of organizational behavior.* Boston: PWS-Kent.

Ambah, S. Fazia. 1995. An intruder in the kingdom. *Business Week,* 21 August, 40.

Badaracco, Joseph. 1988. Changing forms of the corporation. In *The U.S. business corporation: An industry in transition,* edited by John Meyer and James Gustafson. Cambridge,
MA: Ballinger, 67–91.

Ballou, Kate. 1992. America's most admired corporations. *Fortune,* 10 February, 40–46.

Brooks, L. J. 1989. Corporate ethical performance: Trends, forecasts, and outlooks. *Journal of
Business Ethics* 8: 31–38.

Buller, Paul, John Kohls, and Kenneth Anderson. 1991. The challenge of global ethics.
Journal of Business Ethics 10: 767–75.

Cortese, Amy, John Carey, and David Woodruff. 1996. ALT.SEX.BONDAGE is closed. Should we be scared? *Business Week,* 15 January, 39.

Evans, Richard. 1991. Business ethics and changes in society. *Journal of Business Ethics* 10: 871–76.

Fillion, Roger. 1996. FCC vows quick action on new telecom law. *Boston Globe,* 13 February, 43.

Frederick, William, Keith Davis, and James Post. 1988. *Business and society corporate strategy, public policy, ethics.* 6th ed. New York: McGraw-Hill.

Gutfeld, Rose. 1992. Earth summit has put Bush on the spot. *Wall Street Journal,* 7 April, A2.

Hoffman, W. Michael, and Jennifer Mills Moore. 1990. The future corporate ethos. In *Business ethics: Readings and cases in corporate morality.* 2d ed. New York: McGraw-Hill, 607–34.

Jamieson, David, and Julie O'Mara. 1991. *Managing workforce 2000: Gaining the diversity advantage.* San Francisco: Jossey-Bass.

Karr, R. Albert. 1996. Groups propose regulating ads for kids on the Net. *Wall Street Journal,* 29 March, A7B.

Murray, Shailagh, and L. Richard Hudson. 1996. Europe seeks to regulate the Internet, as industry fears support for controls. *Wall Street Journal,* 18 March, A7A.

Naik, Gautam. 1996. Landmark telecom bill becomes law. *Wall Street Journal,* 9 February, B3.

Pearce, J. A., II, and E. C. Ravlin. 1987. The design and activation of self-regulatory work groups. *Personnel Psychology* 40: 97–111.

The public is willing to take business on. 1989. *Business Week,* 20 May, 29. Results from a 1989 Harris Poll.

Sandberg, Jared. 1995. Regulators try to tame the untamable on-line world. *Wall Street Journal,* 5 July, B1.

Stevensen, Mark, and Victor S. Godden, eds. 1991. Ethics and energy supplement. *Journal of Business Ethics* 10: 641–48.

Taylor, Jeffrey. 1991. Global market in pollution rights proposed by U. N. *Wall Street Journal,* 31 January, C1.

Wagner, Mitch. 1996. Tempers flare over Web censorship; telecom deregulation law blocks indecency on-line. *Computerworld,* 12 February, vol. 30, no. 7, 6(1).

Weaver, Paul H. 1988. After social responsibility. In *The U.S. business corporation: An institution in transition,* edited by John Meyer and James Gustafson. Cambridge, MA: Ballinger Publishing Co.

CASES

CASE 1

DOW CORNING CORPORATION AND SILICONE BREAST IMPLANTS

On May 15, 1995, after years of controversy surrounding silicone breast implants, Dow Corning Corp. (DCC)—a joint venture of Dow Chemical and Corning Inc.—filed for Chapter 11 bankruptcy protection. Richard Hazelton, the CEO of DCC, explained the decision: "It became clear to Dow Corning that to continue our current course ultimately would make it impossible to either resolve this controversy responsibly or remain a healthy company. A Chapter 11 reorganization will bring closure and preserve underlying business, which is healthy and continues to grow."[1]

Background

The first silicone gel implant took place in 1964. Since that time, "about two million women nationwide have received breast implants, most of them for cosmetic reasons."[2] Although the majority of these women were satisfied with the implants, "a small minority of recipients in both Canada and the United States have complained that the implants have ruptured, allowing gel to leak into the breast cavity and migrate to other parts of the body. Some women maintain that implant problems cause pain in the chest, arms and back, as well as debilitating autoimmune diseases such as rheumatoid arthritis. Some also complain that scar tissue formed around the implants, causing a hardening of the breasts."[3] The lawsuits filed by these women have caused DCC's severe financial problems.

One of the first lawsuits filed was by a woman who "claimed that a silicone breast implant manufactured by DCC caused her to contract a disabling immune-system disorder. The case, brought in 1989 by Mariann Hopkins, was among the first breast-implant lawsuits. In 1991, a federal jury in San Francisco had ordered Dow Corning to pay Hopkins $840,000 in compensatory damages and $6.5 million in punitive damages. The award at the time was the largest ever in a breast-implant case."[4] Dow Corning claimed that this award "triggered the explosion of breast-implant litigation. . . . State and federal courts have been inundated with cases . . . against all manufacturers of mammary prostheses in which plaintiffs claim whatever injury, disease or illness from which they suffer is causally related to their implants."[5]

In response to the litigation, Dow Corning, Bristol-Myers Squibb Co., and Baxter Health Care Corp. attempted to handle the individual suits together in a class action suit. These companies agreed to pay $4.25 billion to women who contended that implants caused illness. The settlement was designed to provide women with net payments ranging from $105,000 to $1.4 million, depending on their physical condition and age. These amounts could be reduced if an unexpected number of women registered to participate and if companies refused to pay more. Women would have an opportunity to leave the settlement if payments were reduced. Such conditions possibly could jeopardize the entire settlement plan.[6] "The settlement contributions would be based on each manufacturer's market share, litigation exposure, and ability to defend the claims, with Dow Corning paying $2 billion, Bristol-Meyers $1.5 billion, and Baxter $556 million."[7] The manufacturers also had the ability "to drop out if a certain number of victims chose not to participate. Each manufacturer would be left to their own discretion to determine if the number of participants was significant."[8] The manufacturers were trying to push this class action settlement knowing that "if the cases are all tried together . . . every recipient in a successful suit would probably get a small settlement, much less than the multimillion dollar awards that a handful have gotten."[9]

Many people feel DCC threatened bankruptcy early on to scare women into opting to join the class action suit. The various methods manufacturers used to get women to join the suit were not completely successful, however, as "more than 11,300 women rejected the $4.25 billion settlement. Those women have reserved their right to sue implant manufacturers individually."[10] These individual lawsuits, coupled with the difficulties Dow Corning experienced in coming to agreement with so many other women, led to DCC's filing for Chapter 11. "The bankruptcy filing signaled the breakdown in an attempt by Dow Corning and three other corporate defendants to funnel claims through a no-fault facility somewhat similar to the still-unresolved problem of asbestos cases in the 1980's."[11]

As DCC and the other manufacturers learned, when a crisis arises due to product liability, it is not easily resolved. "The difficulties were legion. Among the women involved, there was a wide range of consequences and varying degrees of certainty about the link between implants and subsequent medical difficulties. The intensity of the pursuit varied from lawyer to lawyer, and the willingness of parties to settle changed with time, making patterns of settlement difficult to establish."[12]

DCC provided a compelling modern-day example of the close relationship that has developed between product liability suits and Chapter 11 filings, an issue Congress must finally address. "If bankruptcy is now the ultimate limit on liability, what figure short of that can Congress agree on to avoid the danger implicit in Dow Corning's case: that an otherwise viable business, and the jobs that go with it, might go down the drain of tort practice?"[13]

The Financial Picture

In order to fully explain the financial implications silicone has had on DCC, it is essential to note the sales and reported earnings of DCC and its parent companies, Corning Inc. and Corning Chemical.

In 1967, just after the first silicone implant surgery, DCC reported sales of $102 million. By 1970, sales had climbed to $140.3 million on earnings of $13.8 million. By 1980 DCC's reported sales soared to $681.5, while earnings rose to $73.9 million. An estimated 130,000 individuals annually sought implants for augmentation or reconstruction.[14] In Boston the surgical fees for an implant can run from $2,000 to $5,000, according to Dr. Sharon Webb, a plastic surgeon at the Faulkner Breast Center. Anesthesia and hospitalization could add another $2,000 to the tab.[15]

Dow Corning's sales growth significantly enhanced its two parent companies, Corning Inc. and Dow Chemical. In 1970, Corning Inc. reported sales of $593 million on earnings of $39.5 million. This figure rose to $1,529.7 million in 1980 on earnings, of $114.7 million. A similar impact was seen on overall sales for Dow Chemical with reported sales of $1,911 million in 1970 on earnings of $103 million. These figures rose to $10,626 million in sales on earnings of $805 million in 1980.

The 1980s saw continued growth in the breast implant market. This growth led to DCC's reported sales of $901.1 million on earnings of $95.2 million in 1985. "By the middle of the decade, surgeons were performing more than 130,000 breast implant operations every year. The average patient was a college educated woman in her early thirties, who was married and had two children."[16] By 1990, DCC had reached sales of $1,718.3 million on earnings of $171.1 million. Corning Inc.'s sales were $2,940.5 million on earnings of $292 million, and Dow Chemical reported sales of $19,773 million on earnings of $1,378 million.

Unfortunately for Dow Corning, as illustrated earlier, it soon found itself at the center of one of the largest product liability suits in U.S. history. The suits caused DCC's litigation expenses to rise sharply. In 1993, DCC reported sales of $2,043.7 million while actually losing $287 million dollars. Reported litigation expenses were $25 million in 1991. This figure rose to $69 million in 1992, and by 1993 DCC reported spending more than $640 million in litigation. DCC had 1994 sales of $2.2 billion but reported a $6.8 million loss, which it attributed to the expense of the breast implant claims.[17]

Dow Corning's financial outlook appeared grim. Merrill Lynch estimated that DCC would earn $8.20 per share in 1995 (down from the earlier estimate of $9.00 per share) and $9.15 per share in 1996 (down from the earlier estimate of $9.50 per share).[18] Merrill Lynch also reduced the five-year earnings-per-share growth rate for DCC to 0 percent.[19]

A Historical Perspective

In 1976, the federal government passed an amendment to the Federal Food, Drug, and Cosmetic Act, which provided stricter reporting and inspection standards on all new medical devices. At this time 1,700 types of devices were on the market, many of them containing silicone. Through a grandfather clause, these devices were allowed to remain on the market with minimal FDA review. A manufacturer simply filed a "510 (k)" form informing the FDA of the new product and its similarity to an existing product already on the market. In 1996, the FDA acknowledged that 58,000 medical devices, many containing solid silicone, had entered the market through this 510(k) process.[20]

Almost 12 years had passed before further government attention was given to the breast implant controversy. "A Public Citizen, physician Dr. Sydney Wolfe, said in a petition, '. . . an increasingly larger pool of women is being created who may, in the prime of their lives, ultimately develop chronic illness, disfigurement and disability because of the implants (silicone).'"[21] Dr. Wolfe began to publicly attack manufacturers and plastic surgeons for downplaying the potential health risks. Opponents of Dr. Wolfe agreed with Bruce Hansel, a biochemist and bioengineer at the Emergency Care Research Institute (ECRI), a watchdog group that had been tracking silicone-containing medical devices, who stated "'You can nit-pick anything to death. There will never be a perfect biomaterial,' but 'I would say that silicone in my view is probably the biomaterial of the 20th century. It is the best biomaterial we have going for us now.'" Manufacturers continue to deny a link between such illnesses of the human immune system and breast implants, but various doctors have concluded that such causation exists."[22]

As a result of conflicting expert medical data and opinions, the FDA once again became involved in the breast implant controversy. The agency announced, in November 1988, that although manufacturers could continue to produce breast implants, they would have to provide more detailed information on the safety concerns for a 1991 investigation. Unfortunately, the 1991 investigation proved uneventful. Although the FDA panel cited the overall lack of safety data, they did not move to ban the sale of breast implants. The panel noted testimony from cancer patients (and their psychological benefits from the implants) as an integral part of their decision.

Finally, in 1992, after Dow Corning was ordered to pay $6.5 million in punitive damages to a breast implant claimant, the FDA commissioner, David Kessler, announced a 45-day moratorium on the sale of silicone implants.[23] "Since April 1992, the FDA has banned breast implants for cosmetic purposes and allows them only for reconstructive breast surgery as part of the controlled clinical studies."[24] This was the last significant act by the federal government in the breast implant controversy.

As illustrated, the swirling controversy in the DCC case can be summarized as whether or not the silicone-gel breast implants cause medical disorders in women who have had implant surgery. By 1991, "the FDA had received 2,500 reports of illnesses or injuries associated with the implants, which have been used in one million women. But the degree of risk was unclear because extensive research had not been done."[25] As pressures mounted regarding the product safety, Dow adamantly "denied any link between the implants and illness." Moreover, "rather than wait for results from the [FDA] research, Dow undertook to determine the safety of silicone gel implants."[26] The Dow study of silicone implants in March 1993 "reported that the silicone gel in the implants altered the immune systems of laboratory rats . . . but they [rats] are more susceptible to inflammatory reactions than humans."[27]

The Controversy

Women who have had medical problems with their implants allege, with their doctors' support, the following medical disorders: autoimmune disease, breast cancer, arthritis, abnormal tissue growth, scleroderma, lupus erythematosus, fatigue, and nerve damage. Still, Dow Corning has maintained the safety of the implants, stating "plaintiffs [the women] claim that whatever injury, disease or illness from which they suffer is causally related to their implants."[28]

Numerous studies, including the Mayo Clinic Study, the University of Southern California Study, and a French International Study, all reported similar results. The French Ministry said that an analysis of international research "showed that the risk of contracting autoimmune diseases and cancer after the implantation of silicone breast implants was no greater than in the general public."[29] Scientists involved "noted that no study could completely dismiss the possibility that breast implants contributed to medical disorders." The degree of safety may never be completely known, but as of this writing, "about 5% of the two million American women with silicone implants have demanded compensation for side effects."[30]

The Right to Know

"Dow Corning has actively covered this issue up," Dr. Sydney Wolfe, director of the Public Citizen Health Research Group in Washington, said in 1992. "They are reckless and they have a reckless attitude about women.

". . . DCC was only thinking of themselves when they repeatedly assured women and their doctors that the implants were safe" while keeping "guard over hundreds of internal memos that suggested that some of Dow Corning's own employees have long been dissatisfied with the scientific data on implants."[31]

These internal memos, released in 1992, suggest that Dow long has known of major problems with the silicone implants it has marketed since 1975. The following are highlights from a sample of the memos to and from Dow scientists:

Jan. 28, 1975. Memo from Arthur H. Rathjen, chairman of the Dow implant task force, as Dow rushed a new implant to market: "A question not yet answered is whether or not there is excessive bleed (leakage) of the gel through the envelope. We must address ourselves to this question immediately. . . . The stakes are too high if a wrong decision is made."

Sept. 15, 1983. Memo from Bill Boley: "Only inferential data exists to substantiate the long-term safety of these gels for human implant applications."

April 10, 1987. Memo to Rathjen and others suggesting that Dow was considering a study to review 1,250 implant recipients: "The cost of this data is expected to be minimal, less than $10 million. The study never took place."[32]

In response to the release of these memos, Dow Corning stepped up an ad campaign it had started in the fall of 1991. In newspapers across the country, DCC urged women with questions about implants to call a company hot line. The ads said that instead of "half-truths," callers would receive information based on 30 years of valid scientific research. But when some women called, they were told the implants were "100 percent safe." Shortly afterward, the FDA warned Dow Corning that some of the information on its hot line was "false or used in a confusing or misleading context."[33]

An ethical issue at hand, however, is not only whether the implants do or do not cause harm to patients but also that DCC failed to inform stakeholders and clients that some of its employees felt the firm and the public had reason for concern about safety. Failure to accurately and timely inform consumers of questionable product uses violates the right of these women to know. "If you do not have data on the range of risks and problems, you are not free to choose, you are free to be ignorant. Informed consent requires both information and choice. Since the companies have not supplied the information, this is a dubious choice."[34]

Aftermath

In June of 1994, Dow Corning began to make announcements that it may have to declare bankruptcy if too many women opt out of the $4.25 billion settlement. These comments "led some financial analysts to suggest that the chairman [Keith McKennon made the statements] was trying to 'scare' women into joining the settlement, which could potentially save the company millions of dollars in litigation fees." DCC and the other manufacturers involved in the case have attempted to make the settlement appear generous on their part, but "it is hardly the simple and generous solution described. In reality, the payout to each woman would depend on the total number of claims filed and could decrease dramatically as the number of plaintiffs climbs. And the rights of women to drop out of the plan and seek their own settlements would actually be sharply curtailed. What's worse, thousands of sick women could lose their legal access to any compensation altogether. 'This is not insurance,' Norman D. Anderson, a Johns Hopkins University professor stated, who has treated hundreds of patients with problems related to silicone implants, 'This is pennies-on-the-dollar reimbursement.'"[35]

When DCC felt it had become financially overburdened with the trials, it followed through with its threat and filed Chapter 11. This was "a move that threatens to unravel a $4.25 billion breast implant settlement and has frozen thousands of individual lawsuits. The company's Chapter 11 filing was akin to protective bankruptcy-filing steps taken by big companies in other important product liability cases, which delayed payments to recipients for years. Under Chapter 11, a company gets a reprieve from bills while it works out a way to pay creditors and survive as a healthy business."[36]

Dow Corning may have modeled its behavior after Dow Chemical Corp. In an attempt to avoid litigation, Dow Chemical has maintained it was not aware of DCC's research activities in silicone. Dow Chemical initially was dismissed from the case until "a federal judge reinstated Dow Chemical as a defendant in thousands of breast implant lawsuits, raising the possibility of new negotiations in a landmark product liability settlement. . . . The ruling 'means Dow Chemical can no longer sit on the sidelines and pretend it is not a player in this litigation.'"[37]

Final Thoughts

Dow Corning's story and events regarding silicone breast implants occurred in a free-market, capitalist society. A free market encourages innovation, but it also may lead to corporate manipulation and to the introduction of dangerous products into the market. Marcia Angell, a physician and executive editor of *The New England Journal of Medicine*, concluded in her book *Science on Trial: The Clash of Medical Evidence and the Law in the Breast Implant Case* (New York: W.W. Norton & Co., 1996) that "Only by relying on scientific evidence can we hope to curb the greed, fear and self-indulgence that too often govern such disputes. This is the lesson of the breast implant story." Charles Rosenberg, professor of history and sociology of science at the University of Pennsylvania, argued in a *New York Times* review of Dr. Angell's book, "it is difficult to share her hope that scientific evidence can or will translate easily or naturally into social policy. She is dismayed, for example, that regulations 'should be influenced by political and social considerations.' Yet this is the way our system works. In most policy matters, scientific evidence is only one among a complex assortment of factors that interact to produce particular decisions."[38] A careful reading of the events, stakeholders, and outcomes in the silicone breast implants controversy reveals the social, economic, and political—as well as scientific—factors involved: "the practice of Federal regulation, the relationship between science and courts, the lack of consistently enforced professional standards in law, medicine and journalism."[39] The issues, along with the stakes and stakeholders, tell the story of the clash of medical evidence and the law in the breast implant case.

Questions for Discussion

1. Identify major stakeholders and stakes in this case. Who gained and who lost in this case?

2. Was the Dow Corning Corporation justified in considering bankruptcy? Why or why not?

3. What are the ethical issues and principles involved in this case? Who has acted the most responsibly? the least? Explain. Who in this case was at fault? Support you answer.

4. Evaluate Dr. Angell's statement: "Only by relying on scientific evidence can we hope to curb the greed, fear and self-indulgence that too often govern such disputes [referring to disputes raised in this case]. This is the lesson of the breast implant story." Do you agree? Is this the major or the only lesson from this case? Explain.

Notes

1. *Wall Street Journal*, 17 May 1995, A21.
2. Richard Carelli, "Justices Uphold Breast Implant Award," *Boston Globe*, 10 January 1995, 10.
3. *Maclean's*, 30 March 1992, 39.
4. *Facts on File*, 9 February 1995, 88.
5. *Boston Globe*, 10 January 1995, 10.
6. "Company Reinstated in Implant Lawsuit," Associated Press/*Boston Globe*, 26 April 1995, 7.
7. "Implant Makers Near a Deal," *Business Insurance*, 21 February 1994, 1. See also p. 51.
8. Ibid.
9. *Boston Globe*, 15 May 1992, 1.

10. *Boston Globe,* 22 January 1995, 9.

11. *Boston Globe,* 30 May 1995, 14.

12. Ibid.

13. Ibid.

14. *Boston Globe,* 16 April 1992, 3.

15. Elizabeth Neuffer, "Maker Quits Implant Market: Dow Corning Cites Drop in Sales, Sets Up Fund," *Boston Globe,* 20 March 1992, 1.

16. "Redrawing the Face of Cosmetic Surgery Procedures," *Washington Post,* 22 July 1986, 1.

17. *Boston Globe,* 21 May 1995, 48.

18. "Global Equity Research: Dow Chemical," *Merrill Lynch,* 24 July 1995, 2.

19. Ibid., 3.

20. Judy Foreman, "Safety of Solid Silicone at Issue," *Boston Globe,* 25 January 1992, 1.

21. "FDA Is Petitioned to Outlaw Saline-Filled Implants," Associated Press/*Boston Globe,* 5 August 1994, 17.

22. *The Progressive,* July 1994, 28–29.

23. *Wall Street Journal,* 7 January 1992, sec. B, 1.

24. *Chemical and Engineering News,* 21 February 1994, 4.

25. *Boston Globe,* 20 March 1992, 16.

26. Ibid.

27. *Boston Globe,* 5 May 1993, 13.

28. "France Readmits Breast Implants," Associated Press/*Boston Globe,* 1 March 1995, 4.

29. Daniel Q. Haney, "Harvard Doctors Quit Implant Study, Citing Conflict," *Boston Globe,* 21 December 1994, 35.

30. *Boston Globe,* 1 March 1995, 4.

31. *Maclean's,* 9 March 1992, 42, 43.

32. *Boston Globe,* 19 January 1992.

33. *Maclean's,* 9 March 1992, 43.

34. Judy Foreman, "Implants: Is Uniformed Consent a Woman's Right?" *Boston Globe,* 13 January 1992, 25. See also p. 1.

35. Thomas Burton, "Adding Insult to Injury," *The Progressive,* July 1994, 28.

36. *Boston Globe,* 21 May 1995, 48.

37. *Boston Globe,* 26 April 1995.

38. Charles Rosenberg, "The Silicon Papers," *New York Times Book Review,* 14 July 1996, 10.

39. Ibid., 9.

Additional Sources

"The Best-Laid Ethics Programs . . ." *Business Week,* 9 March 1992, 67–69.

"Breast Implant Makers Prepare $4B Settlement." *National Underwriter,* 7 March 1994, 6.

"Couple Wins $5.2M in Breast Implant Case: Dow Chemical Faulted." Associated Press/*Boston Globe,* 15 February 1995, 88.

"Dow Corning Announces Medical Silicone Resins." *Chemical and Engineering News,* 30 May 1994, 9.

"Dow Corning Mulls Over Filing for Bankruptcy." *Chemical and Engineering News,* 20 June 1994, 8.

"Dow Freed from Suit." Associated Press/*Boston Globe,* 29 March 1995, 14.

Facts on File, 31 December 1994, 992.

Facts on File, 2 March 1995, 154.

Facts on File, 30 March 30 1995.

"Firms May Face Thousand of Suits." Associated Press/*Boston Globe,* 21 July 1994, 19.

"5 Firms Join Implant Settlement." Associated Press/*Boston Globe,* 12 April 1994, 44.

Foreman, Judy. "Women and Silicone: A History of Risk." *Boston Globe,* 19 January 1992, 1.

———. *Boston Globe,* 15 May 1992, 25.

———. "Breast Implant Study Criticized Timing, Funding of Report at Issue." *Boston Globe,* 17 June 1994, 4.

———. "Dec. 1 Deadline to Join Implant Lawsuit." *Boston Globe,* 20 November 1994, 6.

Grimmer, Laura. "Silicone-Gel Implant Records Altered, Company Admits." *Boston Globe,* 3 November 1992, 3.

"Judge Finalizes $4.25B Settlement from Breast Implant Maker." Associated Press/*Boston Globe,* 2 September 1994, 3.

"Jury Selection Is Halted over an Implant Ad: Dow Corning Denies Trying to Influence Liability." Associated Press/*Boston Globe,* 11 May 1995, 14.

Lehr, Dick. "4.75B Accord Eyed on Breast Implant Plaintiffs: Manufacturers Agree on Compensation Fund." *Boston Globe,* 10 September 1993, 1.

McCarthy, Michael. "U.S. Breast Implant Agreement." *Lancet,* 2 April 1994, 7.

New York Times, 15 May 1995.

New York Times, 16 May 1995.

Strategic Withdrawal." *Time,* 30 March 1992, 51.

Wall Street Journal, 15 May 1995.

Wall Street Journal, 16 May 1995.

Warrick, Earl L. "Forty Years of Firsts: The Recollections of a Dow Corning Pioneer." New York: McGraw-Hill, 1990.

"Women Rejecting Implant Award." Associated Press/*Boston Globe,* 16 September 1994, 79.

CASE 2

THE "PENTIUM CHIP CRISIS"

Intel's Pentium Chip Problem

Intel Corporation develops, manufactures, and markets integrated circuit components. These complex components are constructed from small pieces of silicon composed of numerous transistors that perform electronic circuit functions. Silicon chips are the essential parts for processing information in computers worldwide. Intel began its venture in the microprocessing business when it was created in 1968 by Robert Noyce, Gordon Moore, and Andrew Grove.

Grove became the president and chief operating officer of Intel in 1979, at which time he focused Intel on a mission to take 2,000 new customers away from Motorola Inc. Intel surpassed this goal. One of the new customers, IBM, chose Intel's 8088 chip as the brain of its first personal computer (PC). Intel has not looked back since. It is at the top of the computer chip industry. Throughout the 1980s, Intel solidified its hold on the market. In 1987, Grove became the CEO. Intel has become an $16.2 billion corporation.

Intel has a progressive management philosophy that strives for success through an empowered team approach. Even the CEO occupies a cubicle sitting among staff at the Silicon Valley–based company. Intel prides in its ability to promote internal feedback flexibility. All employees can express opinions on any decision or action taken within the company by notifying the involved individual, including the CEO and upper management.

Currently, the company controls the computer microprocessing industry and has managed to remain ahead of its competitors in all facets of the chip-processing industry. Grove claims that the open, proactive environment Intel promotes has enabled the company to leap ahead of its competitors.

Chip Power

In March 1994, Intel released a microprocessor expected to bring the computer industry to the next level. It was labeled the Pentium chip. The goal was to replace the 486 microprocessor models by offering the fastest information processor in the market. Responding to the imminence of the IBM Power PC chip, Intel outpaced its competitors to the market with the

Pentium product by introducing this chip to the computer industry two months ahead of the projected release date.

Computer producers driven by the potential advantages of the new chip rushed to design and develop machines to accommodate it. Dell, AST, Hewlett-Packard, NEC, and Digital were some of the companies that launched computer processing units either to coincide with the Pentium introduction or to accommodate the chip shortly afterward. Noticeably, Compaq, an extremely important player in computer production, did not immediately meet this need and stated its belief that Intel's movement into this area was unnecessary and, at the very least, premature.

In a market where speed is a competitive advantage, Intel insisted that all PC software operated more effectively on a Pentium processor. Independent tests by the National Software Testing Labs (NSTL) confirmed the discernible speed advantages of the Pentium chip. NSTL ran tests on Windows applications such as Microsoft Word, Microsoft Excel, and Lotus 1-2-3. The Pentium processor outpaced 486 DX2s, the market's leading chip, by roughly 40 percent. Programs that relied on intensive graphics ran smoother and quicker on the Pentium chip. These programs took advantage of the Pentium's floating point unit (FPU). (The FPU is part of the microprocessor responsible for performing complicated mathematical functions.)

Intel pointed to the speed advantage of the Pentium chip by using the 3D Home Architect program from Brodebund as an example. With this program, Pentium users could bring up three-dimensional home designs twice as fast as those using a 486 processor.

Intel had planned to be the first into the market with its new chip in order to catch consumer fever for the newest technological advance. In an interview with America Online, Grove commented on the exponential need to be first into the market with an advanced processor in order to be successful. Intel commands 80 percent of the microprocessor market. Prior to the release of the Pentium chip, Intel's concern was growing over the impending introduction of the PowerPC chip produced collectively by IBM, Apple Computers, and Motorola. This chip would present the first significant challenge to Intel products—and its debut was to be headed by IBM, an important customer of Intel microprocessors. Realizing the consequences of the impending situation, Grove spearheaded an Intel effort to accelerate the Pentium chip's product development and to increase the manufacturing capacity to produce it. Intel began a new procedure of overlapping new product development to meet its needs for accelerated production. Grove stated and believed that "Products are what made this business."

The Race Began

Intel began rigorously testing the Pentium chip toward the end of 1993, with the hopes of releasing the chip early in the coming year. After the March 1994 rollout, the company continued testing, hoping to catch mistakes in order to correct future Pentium editions. The Intel labs were running tests 24 hours a day. Finally, in July 1994, after nearly 2 trillion random test calculations, Intel discovered a bug in the chip's FPU. The Pentium chip bug affected certain high-precision division problems and would not have an effect on the majority of Pentium users. The error occurred when dividing particular rare combinations of numbers and appeared in the 4th to the 19th decimal place. It seemed a minor problem, unless this chip were to be used for designing bridges and homes that count on accuracy to ensure safety.

The Hidden Flaw

Intel considered this flaw not serious enough to notify customers. The firm decided to continue to promote the chips, when on October 30, 1994, a mathematics professor from Lynchburg College, Thomas Nicely, sent an E-mail to several colleagues notifying them that answers provided through calculations on Pentium-based PCs were flawed. One of the corresponding colleagues posted the letter on CompuServe's online service. Eventually the letter was copied onto the Internet, the global computer network.

Intel's Crisis Management Strategy

The following week the first press release about the chip flaw was published in the *Electrical Engineering Times*. Intel attempted to parlay further development of this problem by offering to replace the chips to the customers, with one catch. The customers had to prove to Intel that they use the PC in a way that would be affected by the flaw. This crisis management strategy proved damaging. The home users were outraged by the arrogance Intel's attitude displayed with its insinuation the company understood their needs better than they did. Public outcry toward the company surfaced through numerous Internet communications and in thousands of phone calls complaining about the stance Intel took. Momentum built through the media. A feeding frenzy began on Intel's lack of concern for its customers.

Intel tried further damage control by explaining the rarity of this flaw's occurrence. According to Intel reports, the typical computer user would encounter a wrong answer once every 27,000 years from the flaw. At this juncture, Intel made the decision to withhold selling the defective chip. It attempted to calm computer producers by informing them it had corrected the Pentium. Consumers' concerns persisted, and published stories continued to surface about the Pentium chip.

IBM's Role

Intel's Pentium crisis reached its apex when IBM guaranteed replacement of Pentium chips for any customer that requested it. IBM went a step further toward promoting its image as a company that would respond to customers' needs by refusing to ship Pentium-based PCs. Researchers for IBM claimed the flaw could come into play once every 24 days for individuals who routinely used their PCs to make thousands of spreadsheet calculations a day. IBM said it would continue to make the Pentium-based computers and sell them to customers who insisted on operating the machines.

Many industry analysts believed IBM's concerns were based on its interest in providing an advantage for its efforts within the chip market. Following the IBM actions, the Gartner Group, a prominent consulting firm, recommended to its clients a delay in large-volume purchases of Pentium-based PCs. Reactions on Wall Street were negative as Intel stock dropped 2⅜ points.

Intel Concedes

Intel finally capitulated to customer anger over its restrictive replacement policy and promised to replace at no cost any Pentium chips—no questions asked. Intel added a public apology for problems the flawed chips had created and for the company's inappropriate actions.

Intel continued to sell the updated chip. The decision to bow to consumer demands was made on December 20, 1994, approximately two months after the first public discovery of the flaw. By that time, Intel's stock had fallen 3.6 percent since the onset of public awareness of this issue.

Intel recorded a loss resulting from the Pentium chip situation of $475 million within the fourth quarter of 1994. Profits were dramatically affected in the fourth quarter, and profit projections remained lower through the first quarter of 1995, compared to the previous level in the second quarter of 1994. However, profit projections showed a rise throughout 1995, beyond the first quarter. An estimated 1.5 million flawed chips were on inventory at the time Intel stopped selling them. These chips were transported to a warehouse where they remained until further notice. The cost of that inventory constituted nearly half of Intel's losses.

Andrew Grove conceded, "Sometimes you need a real jolt to realize a reality has kind of happened around you. We have to learn some skills that are second nature to others."

This episode certainly has taught Intel that the demographics within the PC market's customer base has moved away from businesses and toward the home user. PC sales passed car sales in 1993 and are gaining on television sales. The irony of the business today is that the more sophisticated technology becomes, the more likely it is to fall in the hands of a novice. A case in point is that in the last quarter of 1994 more PCs based on the Pentium chip were purchased by individual consumers than by businesses. The progression of the market into the future will test the ability of Intel to manage its customer base.

Aftermath

According to recent reports, Intel's business has survived the Pentium crisis, and the sales of the corrected chip have begun to flourish. Price cuts ranging from 7 to 40 percent have been implemented on all Pentium models in an attempt to win a larger stake in the market.

The return of the flawed microprocessors has been much lower than anticipated. Currently, only 1 to 3 percent of individual consumers have returned their defective chips. These consumers comprised approximately two-thirds of the estimated 5.5 million flawed-chip owners. The corporate customers have returned their faulty Pentium chips at a 25 percent rate. Overall, the returns have been close to 10 percent, or more than a half-million chips.

Lessons Learned

Based on the results of the returns to Intel, customers' concerns over the defect in the chips were not the driving force behind the Pentium crisis. It was more their anger at how they were treated. "They've had [PC makers] by the short hairs," management consultant Rich Bader, who ran Intel's small retail operation in Oregon in the mid-1980s, says of Intel. "They treat the consumers with a very similar philosophy."

Intel realized the change within the market structure and recognized that future dealings with individual customers must be handled differently from the past as compared to larger corporate clients. The overwhelming movement toward home computers and the crisis have awakened Intel's understanding of a changing customer base. Intel has begun to develop a customer service strategy and has made strides in areas that previously were foreign to the company. Its marketing strategy has further thrust the company closer to the customer base by concentrating on an advertisement campaign revolving around the slogan "Intel Inside." This approach is new for microprocessor producers and has surprised the computer producers. Most of Intel's rivals do not advertise in this manner and leave marketing to the manufacturer of the finished product. Intel also has recently begun to realize that closeness to customers at times can be frightening. The necessity of understanding the consumer point of view has caused Intel to create a phone hot line to answer any questions concerning the Pentium component.

The Pentium ordeal proved to be consumers' first major usage of the Internet to express dissatisfaction with a company and its product. The Internet currently has more than 30 million users (and is growing). It proved to be the accelerant of the Intel crisis. Andrew Grove got the message.

Questions for Discussion

1. What went wrong with the chip? What were the events and pressures that led to the Pentium chip crisis?

2. Describe Intel's crisis management strategy. Did it work? Explain.

3. Using one of the crisis management frameworks in Chapter 2, explain the events in this case.

4. What were the "lessons learned" in this case? Do you agree? (Were other lessons involved? If so, describe them.)

Sources

"Are You Ready for a Pentium Power Chip?" *Business Week,* 21 November 1994.

"Big Blue Chews Up Intel Chip." *Time,* 12 December 1994.

"Despite Furor, Most Keep Their Pentium Chips." *Wall Street Journal,* 13 April 1995, B1–2.

"The Education of Andrew Grove." *Business Week,* 16 January 1995.

Grove, Andrew. Interview. Computer network through Internet service provider. *America Online,* 29 June 1994.

Grove, Andrew. Interview. Computer network through Internet service provider. *America On Line,* December 20, 1994.

"Here's How." *PC World,* April 1995.

"Intel, Far beyond the Pentium." *Business Week,* February 20, 1995.

"Intel Takes a Bullet—And Barely Breaks Stride." *Business Week,* 30 January 1995.

"The Lurking 'Time Bomb' of the Silicon Valley." *Business Week,* 19 December 1994.

"Pentium: A House Divided." *PC World,* March 1995.

"Top of the News." *PC World,* June 1994.

CASE 3

WOMEN IN PUBLIC ACCOUNTING (AND OTHER PROFESSIONS)

Gender and Workplace Obstacles

The accounting profession has seen rapid growth in the percentage of women entering it over the past 15 years. However, this increase has not been appropriately reflected in the number of women who have penetrated the highest echelons of accounting firms, particularly the Big Six firms. Also, as the number of female entrants increases, a significant number of women leave the profession.

The retention of talented Certified Public Accountants (CPAs), many of whom are women, has become a critical issue for the Big Six. Firms allot a sizable expense to recruit, train, and develop CPAs. The CPA firm Deloitte & Touche notes that "companies that lose women employees recoup no long-term payback on their recruiting and training dollars, and there is no pot of gold at the end of the learning curve."[1] It is widely agreed that CPA firms that do not respond to the needs of increasing numbers of women will find themselves at a competitive disadvantage in the near future. As Joanne Alter observes, "Public accounting is a game of finding and keeping top talent. Half of that talent happens to be female. If we can keep these top people, we're at a competitive advantage."[2]

In 1977, 28 percent of all graduating accounting students were female. In 1991 that percentage increased to 50 percent.[3] Some observers predict that by A.D. 2000, 60 percent of the entrants into the accounting profession will be female. However, in 1983 only 1 percent of partners and principals in what was then the Big Nine were women.[4] In 1986, the percentage had increased only to 3 percent, and it is currently estimated to be about 5 percent in the Big Six.[5]

Initially, one might conclude that the lack of women at the top may be the result of a time lag. It generally takes 10 to 12 years to be promoted to a partner in the Big Six. Women began to permeate the profession just about 10 or 12 years ago. However, it does not appear that a time lag explains the low percentage of female partners. Accounting firms have hired men and women in equal ratios for the past decade, yet, after 6 to 8 years, only two women remain for every three men in the same accounting class.[6] In addition, the American Woman's Society of CPAs estimates that less than 20 percent of managerial positions are held by women; yet 40 percent of all women CPAs have been in the field for at least 10 years.[7] These statistics indicate the following: First, women are leaving the profession after only a few years; and, second, those who stay are not being promoted at the same rate as men.

Until recently, little was written on the issue of retention and promotion of women CPAs. However, during the past five years, an increasing number of surveys and articles have been published that address reasons why women are leaving the profession. Awareness of issues regarding this problem is also growing.

In 1984 the Accounting Institute of Certified Public Accountants (AICPA) Future Issues Committee identified the upward mobility of women in public accounting as one of the 14 major issues the profession faces. As a result, the Upward Mobility of Women Special Committee was formed and charged with identifying obstacles to the upward mobility of women CPAs and with recommending strategies to eliminate these obstacles. This report was submitted to the AICPA board of directors in March 1988. Since then, several articles and studies have been published. Most of the literature appears in the national trade journals, such as the *Journal of Accountancy* and the *Ohio CPA Journal*, as well as more regional publications.

Issues

The first issue raised is, of course, "Why are women leaving public accounting firms?" One theory is that women perceive the profession as irreconcilable with having a family. A 1989 New York Society study demonstrated that 45 percent of more than 800 women CPAs surveyed found family responsibilities incompatible with their career in their present firm under its current policies.[8] Additionally, a 1988 survey conducted by the American Women's Society of CPAs suggested that the main reason women leave public accounting is the scheduling demands that negatively impact their family life. Results from an industry survey showed that "about one third of the respondents indicated that their careers have had some adverse effect on either their marriages or on opportunities to marry. . . . [S]everal [respondents] indicated that job considerations (such as overtime and stress) had influenced the decision not to have children."[9]

When the Management of Accounting Practice Committee of the AICPA asked a staff sample if they believed they could simultaneously attain partnership and be a parent, the results were startling. Eighty-one percent of the men surveyed said yes, while only 41 percent of the women said yes.

Stress

Another factor thought to impact women CPAs' decision to leave public accounting is stress. A study published by the National Society of Public Accountants in 1983 found that women faced greater stress than men in the workplace. Women perceived they were constantly being scrutinized by upper management—mainly male—and consequently they felt they had to perform better than their male counterparts.[10] The New York Society Study found that an "estimated 49 percent of all women surveyed believed they were less accepted by partners than were males, while nearly half reported having fewer advancement opportunities than males."[11] This observation raises another two issues: "Are women in fact scrutinized more than their male counterparts, and are women discriminated against when considered for upper-level promotions?"

Other Obstacles

It is helpful to examine the results of the study the AICPA's Upward Mobility of Women Special Committee conducted. The committee was comprised of four men and four women. Their methodology included the following: a review of relevant literature, analysis of statistics, interviews, distribution of questionnaires, and communications with other professional organizations.[12]

As previously mentioned, the committee was charged with identifying the obstacles to women CPAs' upward mobility in public accounting. The committee stated that the seven obstacles identified were not unique to accounting but, rather, were universal obstacles confronting women in the workplace in general.[13] First, it was determined that outdated negative ideas about women still exist in organizations. Often women are seen as dependents, not colleagues. Women are still referred to as "girls" or "ladies," and they are criticized for displaying traits such as aggressiveness, which is viewed as a positive trait in men. Overall, management tends to judge women as a group while judging men as individuals.[14] The committee also identified a second obstacle, termed "the perception problem," in which employers denied such attitudes still exist.

The third identified obstacle involved awareness of success criteria by women. The committee felt women receive less advice from superiors about how to achieve success within an organization. Women can identify personal traits required to succeed but seem to have a hard time identifying the subtle criteria, such as visibility in the organization and projecting a successful self image.[15]

The fact women still bear most of the responsibility for child care is also viewed as an obstacle. Marriage and family are viewed as a social asset for men in an organization, yet these are considered a liability for women, and sometimes marriage and family can hinder advancement in a firm.

Some women sense these obstacles and abandon getting married and having a family, while others resent having to make such choices, so they leave public accounting instead.[16]

Networking

It was also noted that women do not participate as actively as men in professional organizations.[17] Such participation can further careers through contacts.

Another obstacle the committee presented was the fact some organizations appeared to have dating and marriage policies that discriminated unfairly against women.

Again, women face stress that results from facing all of the other obstacles. Women still experience more family pressures and organizational prejudice, and they maintain the perception that to succeed, their performance must exceed that of their male peers.

Women in Other Professions

Many of the issues women face in public accounting are not unique to the profession but are experienced by women in the workforce in general. Literature on the subject of retention and promotion addresses women in the law profession. In many ways, the accounting and law professions are similar with regard to partnership structures and the increased entry of women into these fields in the past 10 to 15 years. Many of the issues female lawyers face are related to those women in public accounting experience. Many top law firms are increasingly facing the issue of losing talented women and trying to address the situation.

Female professionals in general face a variety of challenges unique to their gender. Many of these are the result of generations of a male-dominated business world, a type of "old boy network." The passing of time is no longer an explanation for why women have not advanced in corporations. As one female executive in her mid-40s observed, "My generation came out of graduate school fifteen or twenty years ago. The men are now next in line to run major corporations. The women are not. Period."[18] A 1990 study by *Fortune* of the 1,000 largest U. S. industrial and service companies found that of the 4,012 people listed as the highest-paid officers and directors, only 19 were women.[19] This is less than one-half of 1 percent. Although this is slightly higher than a similar study done in 1978, the results are hardly encouraging.

Preconceptions and Power Differences

The primary barriers to professional women are stereotyping and preconceptions. In a 1990 *Fortune* poll of 1,000 CEOs, 81 percent listed these factors as the main impediments to women's professional advancement.

This is a subtle form of discrimination. For example, if one were to ask most male executives whether they were prejudiced against women, the answer likely would be no. However, when selecting an individual for a top job, males more frequently choose men.

Corporate males are often uncomfortable dealing with women in the workplace. Giving women negative feedback is often more difficult for men. One executive commented, "Men often worry women will run from the room in tears. . . . [T]hey think they are yelling at their mothers or their wives. . . . [T]hey just don't trust them as much as the guys with whom they talk football."[20] These stereotypes of women impede their success. For example, a strong male is seen as "aggressive" or "ambitious." An equally strong woman is often categorized as "abrasive" or even "bitchy." The same qualities in the different genders are regarded differently, especially by professional males in power.

The Part-Time Stigma

Difficulties and disadvantage in climbing the corporate ladder also are encountered by professional women who have chosen to work part-time for a period. One law firm believed that by promoting women who have worked part-time to partnership sent a message that the firm was not "demanding an equal commitment to the firm. . . . [It]would be telling all of [its] associates that [it] no longer values motivation and dedication."[21] However, the firm also realized that "the rules must change because the game has changed."[22] Firms need to "redefine the word commitment to mean whatever it takes to meet client needs—not a particular number of hours spent at the office."[23]

Some firms realize they need to recognize the value of their investment in female employees. As one CEO affirmed, "It seems idiotic if we're investing in people but making it impossible for them to advance. Are we sending out signals that women need not aspire to the top?" Another male executive noted:"

> [T]he question should not be what's wrong with a woman who doesn't want to work twelve-hour days, but what's wrong with a man who does— and a culture that applauds, glorifies, promotes people who put their jobs before their families. . . . This penchant for promotions via overtime reflects an assumption that those willing to work long hours are the best and the brightest, but maybe the ones willing to work long hours are just the ones willing to work long hours. . . . What if we discover the answer to moving American commerce and industry ahead is finding those smart enough not to work twelve-hour days and turning the reins of business over to them?"[24]

Recommendations for Change

Specific recommendations for the public accounting industry, in particular, are offered by the AICPA Special Committee. These recommendations also may apply to other professions. The committee suggested that employers establish a *mentoring process* to encourage the training and guidance of talented women. The committee also recommended that firms hold *open discussions* on the issue of upward mobility; that organizations rid their publications and policies of *sexist materials* and references; and that constructive steps to deal with *pregnancy* and *child care issues* be mandated.[25]

In addition, the committee's recommendations to women included *increasing participation* in the AICPA and state societies; that women become more involved in office activities, such as business luncheons and meetings with clients; and that women join support groups.

Recommendations to the AICPA itself include *monitoring trends and continuing to compile more information on the upward mobility of women CPAs.* Also, the committee suggested that *appointing more women to AICPA committees, boards, and the Council and studying and reporting on the effect of stress on female CPAs related to career advancement* should be priorities.

CPA Rebeka Joy Maupin, in her article "Why Are There So Few Women CPA Partners?" offers more in-depth explanations for women's problems in professions.[26] She presents two types of perspectives used to account for the scarcity of women in partnership positions: the person-centered perspective and the situation-centered perspective.

The Person-Centered Perspective

The person-centered perspective suggests that female socialization in U.S. culture "encourages the development of personality traits and/or behavior patterns that are contrary to the demands of a managerial role."[27] This view asserts that a man will be more committed to his work than a woman because a woman is socialized to choose her family if a conflict arises. Furthermore, even if a woman makes an equal initial commitment, the many demands she faces, with more intensity than her male counterpart, may encourage her incapability of maintaining her commitment. Because of extended socialization, women often lack the requisite managerial skills and traits and behave in a different manner than men in managerial positions.

The Situation-Centered Perspective

In contrast, the situation-centered perspective emphasizes that the characteristics of an organization shape and define women's behavior on jobs. For example, when women are viewed as a token group in an organization, three negative outcomes result: (1) visibility, which creates perceived performance pressures on the token group; (2) contrast, which exaggerates the differences between the groups and results in isolation of the token group from nonwork activities; and (3) assimilation, where the dominant group (males) assigns stereotypes to the token group to accept it.

Maupin administered a survey to 700 AICPA members (350 men and 350 women). She handed out a questionnaire describing the two separate explanations for the problem. The results illustrated that men disproportionately emphasized the person-centered perspective, assigning blame to women's personal and social traits. Women emphasized both perspectives, recognizing' their, as well as organizational, responsibility for the problem.

Those who subscribe to the person-centered explanation believe the solution lies with women. Women who aspire to top management might develop more "male-oriented" behavior patterns and suppress or eliminate attitudes and behaviors identified as "typically female." Women can be resocialized to compete with men on an equal basis if they are taught traditional male-oriented skills.

Disturbingly, some studies suggest that some women who have reached the upper echelons resemble males in power, demonstrating "old boy network" aggressiveness and dominance.

Maupin supports further exploration of the situation-centered hypothesis. She cites a need to "critically appraise current organizational barriers for women" and cautions that the idea of women conforming to the person-centered perspective and acquiring the appropriate skills and traits" may do nothing to reduce the hostility women face on the job or mitigate the fact they may be in token positions."[28]

Why Change?

In April 1993, Deloitte & Touche (D & T) issued a special report team bulletin titled "Women in the 90's: A Business Imperative." In it, Ellen Gabriel, D & T's National Director for the Advancement of Women, wrote that if firms do not see the ethical, legal, or moral arguments for advancing women, sheer business reasons should be enough. She stated that the combination of three factors should motivate firms to accommodate talented women and promote their retention: (1) The percentage of men available in the labor pool is declining; (2) global businesses will continue to prosper, creating labor needs; and (3) low birth rates in the 1970s will result in a growth in the population of less than 1 percent per year through the 1990s.[29]

Solutions?

First, it is imperative that firms recognize a problem exists and take steps to resolve it through formal programs. Much of the literature implies that the first step in creating a formal program is for firms to articulate a stated solid commitment to support women employees and seek solutions to their problems. The Management of Accounting Practice survey mentioned earlier found that although half of the staff respondents to the survey favored the implementation of flex-time and sabbaticals for parents who opt to take a slow path to partnership, they would hesitate to take advantage of such programs for fear the practices will still impact their advancement in the long run.[30] The message is that even if employers establish policies to address women professionals' problems, companies also must assure employees the organization supports them. Second, employers can survey employees to identify their needs and ask what would make it easier to continue working in the current organization. Third, flexible schedules such as part-time or work-at-home programs can be offered. Child care options can be provided. Concrete guidelines on advancement paths within the firm (such as partnership requirements) can be explicitly published. Mentor programs for women can be created. Delayed and nonpartnership tracks for those who may not be able to steadily meet or who do not choose the traditional partner-track advancement can be established.

Firms need to recognize the urgency of these problems and to take concrete steps to help women in need and at risk. Companies can address these issues openly and offer comprehensive goals for advancement. Firms can no longer address these problems on a piecemeal basis because if follow-through is lacking, expectations are raised and then dashed.[31]

The high turnover rate in public accounting is costing firms money and resources. As noted by the Big Six CPA firm Deloitte & Touche, "[C]ompanies willing to address these issues are finding the results worth the cost. . . . All the differences that now hold women back in the corporate workplace are remedial—and at a cost that is infinitesimal compared with the devastating cost of continuing to bury their talent."[32] As one female CPA quoted in her interview, "In a ferociously competitive global economy, no company can afford to waste valuable brainpower, simply because it's wearing a skirt."[33] However, in the meantime, in order to strive to achieve corporate advancements, women may have to follow what, unfortunately, has been the American 'woman's formula for success: "Look like a lady; act like a man; work like a dog."

Questions for Discussion

1. Why are so few women CPA partners? Is this a unique phenomenon in accounting firms only?

2. What are some major obstacles that prevent women in public accounting and other professions from advancing to top-level positions? Has the situation in major professions changed since this case was originally written in 1994? Explain.

3. Identify the "person-centered" and "situation-centered" perspectives regarding women's roles in the workplace. Comment on whether or not you find these perspectives of value. Why?

4. Discuss some solutions companies and women can use to help advance women's career paths to top-level positions.

5. Evaluate the validity of this statement as a success criterion from your perspective: "Look like a lady; act like a man; work like a dog."

Notes

1. Deloitte & Touche, "Women in the 90's: A Business Imperative," *Team Bulletin Special Report,* April 1993.
2. Joanne Alter, "Retaining Women CPA's: Firms Can Benefit through Programs That Help Keep Talented Female Professionals," *The Journal of Accountancy* (May 1991): 50–55.
3. Ibid.
4. Carl R. Borgia, "Promoting Women CPA's," *The CPA Journal* (June 1989): 38–45.
5. Karen I. Hooks and Shirley J. Cheramy, "Women Accountants—Current Status and Future Prospects," *The CPA Journal* (May 1988): 18–27.
6. Deloitte & Touche, "Women in the 90's."
7. Alter, "Retaining Women CPA's," 50–55.
8. Elaine Owen, "Women in Accounting: There Is Room at the Top," *The Ohio CPA Journal* (November/December 1991).
9. Teresa Tyson King and Jane B. Stockard, "The Women CPA: Career and Family, " *The CPA Journal* (June 1990): 22–28.
10. Borgia, "Promoting Women CPA's," 38–45.
11. Donald E. Parent, Clare DeAngelis, and Nancy R. Myers, "Parity for Women CPAs," *The Journal of Accountancy* (February 1989): 72–76.
12. Accounting Institute of Certified Public Accountants, "Upward Mobility of Women," *Upward Mobility of Women Special Committee Report to the AICPA Board of Directors,* March 1988.
13. Ibid.
14. Ibid.
15. Ibid.
16. Ibid.
17. Ibid.
18. Jaclyn Fierman, "Why Women Still Don't Hit the Top," *Fortune,* 30 July 1990, 40.
19. Ibid.
20. Ibid.
21. Gary W. Loveman, "The Case of the Part-Time Partner, " *Harvard Business Review* (September/October 1990): 12.
22. Ibid.
23. Ibid.
24. Fierman, "Why Women," 40.
25. Borgia, "Promoting Women CPAs," 38–45.
26. Rebeka Joy Maupin, "Why Are There So Few Women CPA Partners?" *The Ohio CPA Journal* (November/December 1991): 17–20.
27. Ibid.

28. Ibid.

29. Deloitte & Touche, "Women in the 90's."

30. Alter, "Retaining Women CPA's," 50–55.

31. Deloitte & Touche. "Women in the 90's."

32. Ibid.

33. Ibid.

Additional Sources

Marshall, Margaret H. "Not by Numbers Alone: A New Decade for Women in the Law."
The New England Journal of Public Policy: 107–18.

Sharpe, Rochelle. "Family Friendly Firms Don't Always Promote Females." *Wall Street
Journal*, 29 March 1994, sec. B.

CASE 4

TROUBLE IN PARIS

Euro Disney's Experiment

On January 1, 1994, Michael Eisner, Walt Disney (WD) Company's chairman and chief executive officer, discovered that he had become the latest casualty of Disney's European theme park, Euro Disney (ED). Excluding stock options, Eisner had averaged an annual income of $7.5 million per year since 1989, which included a $750,000 salary plus a bonus equal to 2 percent of the amount the company's net income exceeded a return on stockholders' equity of 11 percent. (Eisner did not receive a bonus for fiscal 1993, Disney's worst performance in years.)

Regarded as the unchallenged leader of WD, Eisner faced a demanding board of directors in 1994. Stockholders wanted answers on poor stock showings. Bondholders were threatening to take legal actions. For the first time since Eisner took over, the Disney magic and image was faltering and his job was on the line.

Eisner's problems stemmed from the failures of ED, which lost $900 million in fiscal year 1993. Moreover, ED's first-quarter 1994 estimates were worse than the previous year's. WD's 1993 net profit was $300 million with ED; without ED, WD's profit would have been $1.2 billion.

Eisner did not need his Harvard law degree to know he needed a solution to ED's financial crisis. In an effort to reach a solution, he threatened to close down ED if an agreement with creditor banks was not reached on a financial rescue plan by March 31, 1994. Eisner, WD, the French creditor banks, and the French government were braced for hard negotiations that would determine the future of this venture.

Background

Walt Disney, the founder of Disney, declared that his first park in Anaheim was "The happiest place on Earth." By the early 1980s, WD had maintained a squeaky clean image, consistent but mediocre earnings, and a growing presence abroad. It had built large additions to its domestic parks and studios and had successfully opened a profitable theme park in Japan.

In 1984, Disney hired a new CEO, Michael Eisner. Eisner and many of his own handpicked executives set out immediately to "remake" the company by increasing profits domestically.

Eisner's domestic strategy worked to the delight of shareholders. WD's stock soared every year (increasing by a 20 percent return on investment). The 1992 annual report to shareholders reflected management's pride in Disney's growth and earnings. Eisner pointed out the success stories in animations, films, and studios and the continued success of the theme parks in Orlando, Anaheim, and Japan. He even bragged about ED, opened in 1992, "the most beautiful park and hotels we have ever developed—somewhat expensive but still fantastic!" He stated "During a year of continued worldwide economic downturn, how many companies were fortunate to grow at 28 percent?"

Euro Disney Planning

Eisner was determined to exploit the European market by taking slim royalties. The ED plan called for a 5,000-acre lot, 5,200 hotel rooms, an amusement park and parking complex, a golf course, office space, 580 homes, and MGM studios. The projected cost was $4.5 billion. The creation of 11,000 jobs also was planned.

France won the bid to house ED over Spain late in 1985. France provided tax breaks and guaranteed the improvement of the surrounding infrastructure and the building of special rail lines. In addition, France provided the lowest-interest loans, along with a financial deal that largely insulated WD from risk. Access to large airports with a central European location also was offered. In return, the French Socialist government would prove, before its upcoming elections, that it was a "modern" government receptive to private enterprise—and 11,000 jobs. When the final contract was signed, the French government included a clause that constrained WD to respect the French culture.

WD planned on making ED a sister company. Stock was offered to finance its creation. WD planned on using the stock revenue along with bank capital to build phase one: everything but the MGM studios. WD then planned on issuing convertible bonds to finance phase two: building the MGM studios.

ED anticipated 11 million visitors in 1992, of which 50 percent were projected to be French. WD set the admission fee at $40 for adults and $27 for children—30 percent higher than the Disney World fee in Florida. ED estimated the average visitor would spend $33 per day on food and souvenirs. These numbers were based on the park's central location, vast and elegant hotels (such as the Newport Bay Club, which operated at above 76 percent occupancy), and—most important—the popular Disney name.

ED also used its Japanese park as a guide in planning the French venture. The elimination of trade and travel barriers during the anticipated unity of the European community further increased ED's optimistic expectations. Although an economic recession occurred after these optimistic projections—and before the park opened—still, the Disney corporation remained upbeat about meeting its projections.

ED supported its popularity and French cultural ties by pointing out that Le Journal de Mickey Mouse had been a long-running French story read by millions of French children since 1934. ED also enjoyed the top rating for family programming in France. In addition, Disney's video Jungle Book achieved world record sales in the European community. ED intended to use the current Disney theme that referenced the world of dreams and childhood. The cast of characters, led by Mickey Mouse, Donald Duck, and Snow White, remained the same.

Organization

ED was given status as an independent company. Banks and investors would put up approximately $3.6 billion to finance the private enterprise. Walt Disney would pay only $200 million, most of which was a 49 percent share of the new company. This 49 percent was bought at a fire-sale price of $1.50 per share—outside investors purchased shares at the offered price of $11.50 per share. ED chairman Robert Fitzpatrick, and a host of other Walt Disney management members, were assigned to the ED management team. The French and other Europeans comprised the remainder of the ED staff. With or without a profit, WD established for itself a 10 percent royalty of ticket sales and 5 percent of merchandise sales.

Cultural Context

Disneyland Paris is similar to its U.S. counterparts in Florida and California, but, because of critical press reviews, the Walt Disney Company carefully placed the park in a European cultural context. French was planned as the park's first language; English was the second language. Signs would be bilingual and multilingual. Some of the park's areas highlight French themes, such as Discoveryland, which is inspired by the work of the French science-fiction writer Jules Verne. Mickey Mouse and Donald Duck have French accents. The fairy-tale castle, the centerpiece of every Disney theme park, would be known as "Le Chateau de la Belle au Bois Dormant." Only the major attractions, such as the Pirates of the Caribbean and Adventureland, would be called by their English names.

Robert Fitzpatrick was promoted to the position of president of Disneyland Paris because of his knowledge of France, French, and French culture. Even Eisner said he "found himself explaining to French visitors that "'Snow White'" is a German fairy tale; "'Pinocchio'" was written by an Italian; "'Cinderella'" and "'Sleeping Beauty'" were both written by Frenchman Charles Perrault; the characters Mary Poppins and Peter Pan are English." Against French culture was the ban on wine and beer in the park.

Cultural Conflict

From the beginning, ED was plagued with problems. Months before the opening of the theme park, members of the French intelligentsia and the Socialist establishment blasted the park as the latest example of U.S. cultural imperialism. A Parisian theater director, Ariane Mnouchkine, was the first "to arms!"—"aux armes." "Disneyland Paris is a 'Cultural Chernobyl,'" she declared. Also, her colleague, Jean Cau of the Academie Francaise, wrote of "this horror of cardboard, plastic, atrocious colors, solidified chewing-gum constructions, and idiotic folk stories that come straight out of cartoon books for fat Americans. It is going to wipe out millions of children . . . mutilate their imaginations."

Only hours before the opening day (April 1992), saboteurs blew up an electricity pylon and plunged the entire complex into darkness. On opening day, a new railway station remained empty as the staff struck in hopes of damaging Disneyland Paris's reputation.

Intellectuals were not alone in their cultural protest. Disneyland Paris's employees had to accommodate a conservative, professional look. It was this clear, all-American, "'Disney look'" that brought scorn from the French. The French labor union, for example, complained that Disney's 13-page employee manual on dress and manners stripped the employees of their French individualism: "Men cannot have mustaches, beards or exposed tattoos, nor can they wear jeans. Women cannot wear any obtrusive jewelry (larger than two centimeters in diameter) nor have 'unusually colored' hair or long fingernails." Employees could not smoke or chew gum and had to use deodorant and wear "proper underwear." Workers were quoted as telling tales of being "spied on" by undercover management operatives. The Magic Kingdom was quickly labeled "Mouseschwitz." Leftist magazine editors of *Le Nouvelle Observateur* went so far as to assign a reporter to infiltrate the Euro Disney organization as a job trainee "to expose the rot of American Imperialism." (Not only was the reporter impressed and charmed by the operation but eventually wrote a positive article for Disneyland Paris. The story was published, suggesting the reporter had been "brainwashed.")

Despite rigid appearance codes, the cleanliness and friendliness requirements worked because of rigorous training. Disney executives apparently had worked magic. Even the French intellectuals noticed the curious phenomenon of smiling faces and conviviality that, they said, "unsettled, home-grown visitors." Jenny Rees, a writer for *The National Review* said, "I know France well; I have studied there and lived there. At Disneyland Paris, I heard uttered from French lips for the first time ever in my life, the words, 'You're welcome' and 'That's no trouble.'"

Hard Times

When in April 1992 ED opened its gates for the first time, $110 million in advertising was spent for this event. The opening-day ceremonies were broadcast to 30 countries. ED staged a giant parade before a soldout park. The stock price reached a high of $28.18 per share.

Attendance remained strong through the summer months. Hotel occupancy rates maintained a respectable 76 percent through September. However, merchandise sales had fallen more than 10 percent below expectations, and labor costs were almost 20 percent of revenue. In September 1992, Banque Paribus, the most influential bank in France, issued a "sell" recommendation for the ED stock, which then proceeded to nose-dive as the critical cold-weather season began in late September. ED was not attracting the volume of French visitors returning from their typical August vacations.

Travel agencies and potential visitors complained aloud about high prices, but ED president Fitzpatrick denied the claim. He publicly stated that ED represented a "good value," despite reports visitors were taking as many rides as possible to get the most out of the admission fee while spending less than expected on merchandise.

As attendance continued to plummet, the cast members' spirit deflated. Many jobs, both union and nonunion, were in jeopardy. The Newport Bay Club, the largest of the six hotels in Disneyland Paris and one of the largest in Europe, closed its 1,100 rooms until spring because of grim advance bookings. Park officials rationalized it was closed because it was a "summer theme" hotel. The lack of "a sunshine experience" for ED visitors contributed to the attendance problems.

Reactions: Financial and Cultural

In January 1993, Disney reacted to the dismally low occupancy rates at its six resort hotels by cutting room rates from $80 to $54 per night (for four people) at its least-expensive properties, the Hotel Cheyenne and the Hotel Santa Fe. Prices at the luxurious Disneyland Hotel, Sequoia Lodge, and Newport Bay Club ranged from $240 to $360 per night. In the first year of operation, Euro Disney's hotels operated at an occupancy rate of 55 percent against a forecasted 68 percent. Most analysts projected the company would not break even anytime prior to 1997. Restaurants were also slashing meal prices in an effort to compete with fast-food providers.

In Euro Disney's first year of operation, its stock fell more than 68 percent. Disney announced the delay of the Disney-MGM theme park in France until revenues were increased. The MGM park, similar to the one in Orlando, was projected to provide Euro Disney with a "second-gate appeal." Original plans for the Euro Disney complex project, a park, expanded to a size two-thirds that of Paris by 2017. Presently, all further expansion has been delayed indefinitely. Euro Disney continues discussion with creditor banks and its parent company over raising money to reduce debt and to begin the MGM Studios project.

In 1993, the proposed attraction already had been halved to a $1.6 billion investment by dropping plans for two hotels and a water park. The loss through delay was felt by the French government due to lack of tax revenue received from road construction. Euro Disney announced it was laying-off 950 employees to help balance the budget. Management blamed the European recession, high interest rates, and the decline of several currencies against the French franc.

A major cultural change that occurred in June 1993 was the offering of beer and wine by several park restaurants. (Selling alcoholic beverages is forbidden in all other Disney theme parks.) The typical 90-minute European sit-down lunch did not appeal to the park's diverse clientele. Unpredictably, European customers preferred a U.S.-style 20-minute eat-and-run lunch. Another unforeseen habit was that, unlike Americans who wander around with a hotdog in hand, Europeans eat at daily set times. Everyone converged on restaurants at 12:30 P.M. for lunch.

Disney hotels also were told Europeans did not prefer full breakfasts. Surprisingly, guests desired full-course American-style breakfasts. The restaurants were caught trying to serve 2,500 breakfasts in a 350-seat layout.

The November 1993 report for Euro Disney's first fiscal year showed the park lost more than $900 million and that its stock dropped to $7 per share—down from $30 prior to the park's opening. This move forced WD to call on its banks to restructure its debt. Eisner followed with a December statement stating the park might shut down while negotiations continued. Surprisingly, this rumor created a surge in bookings: People wanted to experience the park "before it closed."

In early February 1994, Moody's Investors Service Inc. lowered its rating on Disney's $1.8 billion of long-term debt securities from double-A-3 to single-A-1. The New York based rating service said the downgrades reflect expectations that operations at the Euro Disney theme park near Paris will remain 'under pressure' at least in the indeterminate term and that as a result, uncertainty over Walt Disney's future financial commitments to the project will increase its risk profile. Moody's cited that this price reduction would create difficulties in maintaining revenue levels. In February 1994, Euro Disney's first-quarter losses were 30 percent above those of the previous year. (See the Epilogue for a review of the next few years.)

Internally, the park operated more efficiently by decreasing the number of items available on the restaurant menus by half and by training staff who sell admission tickets in the morning also to sell T-shirts in the afternoon. The number of gift store items was reduced from 30,000 to 17,111, and more of the proceeds were directed to the parent Walt Disney Company. The years ahead are crucial to the future of this transplanted theme park, located in a small world with cultural diversity it is only beginning to understand.

Questions for Discussion

1. Evaluate the WD executives' strategic assumptions and planning process for the Paris theme park.

2. What cultural clashes were not foreseen or planned?

3. Explain how a corporation's strategy should consider the culture of a project, using this case as an example.

4. Who is responsible for this park's financial success? Who pays if the park is unsuccessful?

5. What specifically should have been done differently before the park was opened to the public? Why?

6. Disney is building themes parks in other countries. Has the company made similar cultural mistakes in other locations?

Sources

Cohen, Roger. "The French, Disneyed and Jurassick, Fear Erosion." *New York Times,* 21 November 1993, E2.

Gumbel, Peter. "Euro Disney Counts on Mary Poppins to Tidy Up Mess at French Resort." *Wall Street Journal,* 23 February 1994, A20.

Gumble, Peter, and Richard Turner. "Fans Like Euro Disney but Its Parent's Goofs Weigh the Park Down." *Wall Street Journal,* 10 March 1994, A1, A12.

Henderson, Jim, et al. "Euro Disney: Oui or non?" *Travel percent Leisure,* August 1992, 80, 114–15.

Liddle, Allan. "Vivre le Mouse! Mickey Takes on Europe." *Nation's Restaurant News,* 23 November 1992, 54.

Phillips, Andrew. "Where's the Magic? Problems Plague Euro Disney's First Year." *Maclean's*, 3 May 1993, 47.

Rees, Jenny. "The Mouse That Ate France." *National Review*, 11 May 1992, 57–61.

Revel, Jean-Francois. "Who's Afraid of Mickey Mouse?" *Current*, November 1992, 31.

Rudolf, Barbara. "Monsieur Mickey: Disneyland Paris Is on Schedule, but with a Distinctive French Accent." *Time*, 25 March 1991, 48–49.

Solomon, Julie. "Euro Disney's Attendance Is Disappointingly Mickey Mouse." *Journal of Commerce*, 10 August 1993, 9a.

———. "Mickey's Trip to Trouble." *Newsweek*, 14 February 1994, 34–39.

———. "When You Wish upon a Deficit." New York Times, 18 July 1993, 82.

———. "Walt Disney's Rating on Long-Term Debt Is Lowered by Moody's." *Wall Street Journal*, 11 February 1994, C16.

Vaughan, Vicki. "Euro Disney Designers Work to Avoid Culture Clash." *Orlando Sentinel*, 2 May 1991.

EPILOGUE

"Euro Disney Park Passes Five Years"

"Euro Disney's theme park on the edge of Paris, Europe's biggest single tourist attraction, celebrated its fifth anniversary yesterday.

"Decried from the outset by French intellectuals as a 'cultural Chernobyl,' Disneyland Paris, in Marne-la-Vallee, east of the French Capital, drew nearly 12 million people last year, twice as many as the Eiffel Tower and five times as many as the Tower of London.

"'Despite a difficult debut, the group's results have been improving constantly despite a poor tourism climate. In the 1996 fiscal year, turnover was up 9 percent to 5 billion francs, or $860 million,' chairman Gilles Pelissson told the daily newspaper Le Parisien. 'The number of visitors was on the same trend.'

"Euro Disney's $3.4 billion debt burden nearly drove it into the ground. It was saved by a financial restructuring that included a holiday on debt payments and royalty and management fees to The Walt Disney Co., the US-based group that owns 39 percent.

"Pelisson told Le Parisien that Euro Disney was still $2.5 billion in debt.

"A company spokesman said that since its opening, more than 50 million people had visited the park, which offers more than 40 attractions and includes the Space Mountain thrill ride.

"Despite French criticism that the Disney brand of entertainment was too American, one in five of the country's 56 million inhabitants has been to the park at least once.

"Admission prices have been slightly lowered, and in a concession to local taste, the park has dropped a ban on alcoholic drinks and agreed to serve wine.

"An eight-screen Gaumont movie theater is scheduled to open next month, a second convention center is under construction and should open in the autumn, and public authorities have approved the development of a commercial shopping center.

"As the park expands, Pelisson said it would be served by a second high speed TGV train station due to open by 2000 as well as by a second RER express commuter train station and a second motorway interchange."

SOURCE: *Boston Globe*, 13 April 1997, 14.

CASE 5

GENERAL MOTORS VERSUS THE MEDIA, *DATELINE NBC*

On Tuesday February 9, 1993, Harry Pearce, chief counsel at General Motors (GM), listened to coanchors Jane Pauley and Stone Phillips at *Dateline NBC* as they read a carefully worded statement to their viewers. The statement was an apology for withholding information and misrepresentations made in a story aired on the November 17, 1992, show titled "Waiting to Explode?" The statement was made as part of the settlement of a defamation suit GM brought against the National Broadcasting Company (NBC) on the previous day. The suit against NBC was a result of evidence gathered on a test crash the network aired in the November 17 segment. General Motors' lawyers had gathered significant evidence alleging that the crash had been rigged by the contractor, and Pearce presented this evidence in a 90-minute closed-circuit-television news conference from Detroit to a selected audience on February 8, 1993. The announcement of the damaging evidence sent NBC executives and those of its parent company, General Electric, scrambling.

Background

GM, a Big Three U.S. automaker, is based in Detroit, Michigan. Its sales for 1993 were $138 billion, which positioned the company as number one.[1] The design of the GM model C/K truck's fuel tank had been similar to those of Ford and Chrysler, which were mounted inside the cab, behind the seats, until federal regulations in 1973 forced the companies to relocate the tanks.[2] Ford and Chrysler responded by placing the fuel tank under the chassis within the steel frame. GM placed two 20-gallon fuel tanks on each side of the truck, outside the frame, in order to enlarge fuel capacity. The tanks were shielded only by the sheet metal of the body, instead of being protected by the truck's steel frame.

The first sign the new tank design might present high risks was an internal memo dated September 7, 1970. A GM safety engineer, George Carvill, issued the memo. He wrote, "Moving these side tanks inboard might eliminate most of these potential leakers."[3] A second memo dated December 15, 1983, written by GM product analyst Richard Monakaba, sent a message similar to Carvill's memo. GM responded 18 years later by changing the design of the tanks, beginning in 1988, for only some models. The new design placed a single 34-gallon tank within the frame.

Since GM deliberately did not act quickly, product liability cases began to mount against the firm. Side-impact crashes caused the pickups to explode. By late 1992, the company had been involved in 120 lawsuits stemming from the location of the gas tank. In the fall of 1992, consumer groups such as the Center for Auto Safety—founded by Ralph Nader in 1970—the Institute for Injury Reduction, and the Consumer Federation of America began to pressure the National Highway Traffic Safety Administration (NHTSA), a regulatory agency in the U.S. Department of Transportation, to order a recall on the trucks. Clarence Ditlow, executive director of the Center for Auto Safety, stated, "It's the Ford Pinto all over again, only worse."[4] Through November 1992, the company had paid more than $200 million to settle fuel-tank-related cases.[5]

The Media Ignites the Issue

Dateline NBC, a television investigative reporting program, was the first network to show a staged test crash of the GM C/K pickup. As noted, the film aired November 17, 1992. Robert Read was the story producer and Michele Gillen was the reporter for "Waiting to Explode?" The segment opened with the story of Shannon Mosely, a 17-year-old high school student who was killed in 1989 when his 1985 GMC pickup was hit by a drunk driver and burst into flames. Gillen then interviewed Byron Bloch, "Auto Safety Expert." Bloch stated, "The fuel bursts out of the tank and there is an immediate holocaust."[6] Clarence Ditlow stated in an interview, "These pickups are rolling fire bombs."[7] Additional statements on the danger of the truck were made by Ron Elwell, a former GM engineer, and Mick McBee, an attorney for a plaintiff in a lawsuit against GM. Representing GM in the story were Robert Sinkle Jr., GM's Director of Engineering Analysis, and Clinton Varner, an attorney for GM. Both noted that the general safety record of the C/K pickups was comparable to other models. The test crash footage then followed with Gillen delivering this narrative:

To see for ourselves what might happen in a side impact crash, DATE-LINE NBC hired the Institute for Safety Analysis to conduct unscientific crash demonstrations. In our demonstration, unlike GM tests, the fuel tank was filled with real gasoline. In one crash, at about 40 miles per hour, there was no leakage and no fire. But in the other, at around 30 miles per hour, look what happened. At impact, a small hole was punctured in the tank. According to our experts, the pressure of the collision and the crushing of the gas tank forced the gasoline to spew from the gas cap. The fuel then erupted into flames when ignited by the impacting car's headlight. The pickup's tank did not split open. If it had, the fire would have been much larger.[8]

The video of the crash was a dramatic illustration of a side-impact collision. The test crash was conducted on October 24, 1992, on a deserted road in Indiana. It was overseen by Bruce Enz, vice president of a company called The Institute for Safety Analysis (TISA). This company, which "specializes in investigating and testifying the causes of accidents and injuries," showed two driverless Chevy Citations that were sent into the side of two C/K pickups.[9] The first test crash resulted in a small fire; the second crash, at a higher speed, had no fire. "The NBC people were clearly disappointed" Enz says.[10] The show's producer presented a different version—a close view of the first crash showing a fiery crash and explosion, even at a slower-speed collision than the second. The NBC video segment was damaging to GM. Media attention regarding the safety of the pickup mounted. On December 8, 1992, NHTSA opened a formal investigation on the GM truck in an attempt to respond to pressure from consumer groups.

The Controversy Escalates

General Motors vigorously defended the safety of the pickup. The company noted that the trucks passed the Traffic Safety Administration's 20 mph side-impact crash tests and that GM also had conducted crash tests at 50 mph. GM argued that the risk of explosion from a side-impact crash with its pickups, though higher in crashes with some types of vehicles, was about average compared with most other vehicles. National Highway Traffic Safety Administration statistics showed that for each year a person drove a heavy pickup, the odds of dying in an accident were these:[11]

Dodge	1 in 8,606
Ford	1 in 6,916
GM	1 in 6,605
All Passenger Cars	1 in 6,053

Analysts estimated that if NHTSA had forced GM to recall its question-able trucks, the cost would be between $300 million and $1 billion to recall the 5 to 6 million C/K model pickups on the road.[12]

GM Responds

After the *Dateline NBC* story aired, GM, led by Pearce, began to vigorously respond to the critics. In addition to defending the truck's safety, GM im-mediately asked NBC for test data and a chance to examine the trucks used in the crash. NBC delayed giving the data. Its executives stated the vehicles "have subsequently been junked and are no longer available for inspection by anyone."[13]

On January 11, 1993, William O'Neill, head of North American Public Relations at GM, received a tip from a witness at the TISA test crash that the crash had been rigged. O'Neill began an investigation into the facts of the test crash. The trucks were subsequently found in a junkyard near the crash site. The tanks were missing. GM obtained video footage from wit-nesses of the crash that showed the planting of two model rocket motors next to the gas tank—rigged to ignite any fuel. GM also discovered that the tanks were overfilled with an extra five gallons over normal capacity. These facts, along with an improper gas cap the car's previous owner says in a sworn statement he used, caused the gas to spill from the tank. Using the wrecked trucks and the obtained video, GM contested the speed of the test and noted that what the program described as "around 30 mph" was at least 39 mph. Also, the test with an announced impact of "about 40 mph" was found to have been at least 47 mph.[14]

During the process of gathering evidence against NBC, GM lost the lawsuit the parents of Shannon Moseley filed (accident described in the *Dateline NBC* segment). On February 4, 1993, a jury in the Georgia court awarded the parents $4.2 million in compensatory damages and $101 mil-lion in punitive damages. As noted in the case opening, on February 8, 1993, Pearce, in a closed-circuit-television news conference, presented the evidence GM had gathered on the test crash to its employees, to dealers, and to NBC executives. On the same day, GM filed the defamation suit in Indiana against NBC. The initial response of NBC president Michael Gartner was to defend "the segment as 'fair and accurate' and [accuse] GM of trying to divert attention from its truck problem."[15] On February 9, 1993, faced with indisputable evidence and the possible loss of its share of GM's $500 million a year television advertising budget, NBC settled the suit by agreeing to issue an apology on *Dateline NBC* that night and to compensate GM $2 million for the cost of its investigation.

This fiasco by NBC is not an isolated incident. What happened with GM is not uncommon between the TV networks and automobile compa-nies, but the publicity and outcome are unprecedented. GM is, however, the first company to fight back against the so-called "expert" testing and to have won. Although GM won only an apology and a $2 million settlement, the victory would serve as a precedent and send a louder message to the media.

GM's Postscript

GM removed its advertising from NBC news programming on February 10, 1993. PR head O'Neil stated GM did "not feel we wanted to advertise in a negative environment. We believe the environment on NBC's news programs is negative."[16] Then on February 11, GM removed its ban and accepted NBC's apology.

On March 2, 1993, Gartner resigned under pressure from the *Dateline NBC* scandal. On March 11, 1993, GM filed for a retrial in the Shannon Moseley case. On March 22, 1993, the findings of an independent investigation conducted by attorneys Robert S. Warren and Lewis B. Kaden on the incident noted "that senior NBC News employees made 'serious flawed judgments' when producing "the story.[17] The report also blamed Gartner for failing to investigate the affair sufficiently. Also on March 22, Jeff Diamond, the executive producer of *Dateline NBC*; David Rummell, the senior producer; and Robert Read, the story producer, resigned under heavy pressure.

In April 1993, the NHTSA asked GM to voluntarily recall the pickups. GM refused, claiming the trucks were as safe as rivals' models. On November 3, 1993, a Texas state court cleared the way for a settlement with 650,000 GM truck owners in Texas. The settlement called for GM to issue $1,000 coupons toward the purchase of a new GM truck. On November 18, 1993, the Transportation Department announced that Transportation Secretary Federico Pena would decide on the government's next course of action. Finally, on December 16, 1993, "A Federal judge in Philadelphia approved a class-action settlement that required General Motors to give as much as $6 billion in coupons to owners of GM pickups with side-mounted gasoline tanks."[18]

Questions for Discussion

1. What are the major issues in this case? Why are these "issues"?

2. Who are the major stakeholders, and what are their stakes in this case?

3. Why did *NBC Dateline* act as it did in this case? What were its motives?

4. Was GM without fault? If not, why? If it was at fault, explain.

5. Was justice served to NBC in this case? Explain.

6. Did the federal judge in Philadelphia treat GM fairly? Why or why not?

Notes

1. Eric Hardey, "The Forbes 500's Annual Directory," *Forbes*, 25 April 1994, 196.

2. McCarroll, Thomas, "Was GM Reckless?" *Time*, 30 November 1992, 61.

3. Ibid.

4. Ibid.

5. Ibid.

6. *Dateline NBC*, transcript, 17 November 1992, 3.

7. Ibid., 4.

8. Ibid., 7.

9. David Greising, "A Safety Expert Under Fire," *Business Week*, 1 March 1993, 42.

10. Ibid.

11. Rich Thomas, "Just as Safe at Any Speed," *Newsweek*, 10 May 1993, 52.

12. James B. Treece, "Now, the Court of Public Opinion Has GM Worried," *Business Week*, 22 February 1993, 38.

13. Ken Zine, "Peacock Eats Crow," *Road and Track*, May 1993, 35.

14. *Dateline NBC*, transcript, 7.

15. Terry Eastland, "Keep on Trucking," *The American Spector*, May 1993, 54.

16. *Facts on File*, 11 February 1993.

17. *Facts on File*, 8 April 1993.

18. Douglas Lavin, "GM Settlement of Pickup Suit Backed by Court," *Wall Street Journal*, 17 December 1993, A5.

CASE 6

SOME DON'T LIKE IT SO HOT

Stella Liebeck vs. The McDonald's Corporation

In August 1992, 81-year-old Stella Liebeck pulled up to a McDonald's drive-through window in Albuquerque, New Mexico, to purchase a cup of coffee. Liebeck was a frequent customer of McDonald's, one of the largest fast-food franchises in the world—with more than 11,000 restaurants serving more than 22 million customers per day.

After buying a 49-cent cup of coffee, Liebeck placed the coffee container between her legs, removed the lid, and proceeded to pull away from the drive-through window. As she drove away, coffee spilled. She suffered from second- and third-degree burns on her inner thighs, buttocks, and groin area. Treatment of the injuries required hospitalization and surgery. Stella Liebeck asked McDonald's to reimburse her $11,000 for medical bills. McDonald's responded to Liebeck's request by presenting her with a counteroffer of a lesser amount. Dissatisfied with that offer, Liebeck sought legal representation from a personal-injury attorney, S. Reed Morgan and associates.

Morgan was familiar with this type of case and with the McDonald's Corporation. He previously had represented two other parties in separate lawsuits against McDonald's that involved injuries caused from hot-beverage burns. Morgan's first run-in with McDonald's occurred in 1988 when he represented a 29-year-old woman in a suit for injuries received from hot coffee. The jury ruled in favor of the woman, who was awarded $27,000. Also, in 1992, Morgan represented a Santa Monica, California, woman in a similar case against McDonald's; she won a settlement of $235,000.

S. Reed Morgan filed suit on behalf of Stella Liebeck (a former department store clerk who had never filed suit before) against the McDonald's Corporation, charging the company with "selling a defective product because it was unreasonably dangerous due to extreme temperatures, . . . failure to warn of extreme temperatures, . . . and breach of implied warranty of merchantability, because the coffee was not fit for human consumption."[1] Morgan and his associates sought an award of $300,000 for Stella for compensatory and punitive damages. In addition to the monetary award, Liebeck requested that McDonald's print warning labels on its hot-beverage containers.

During the trial, attorneys for Liebeck argued that McDonald's was negligent in its failure to reduce the temperature of its coffee. According to Morgan, "McDonald's officials have known about hundreds of java-related injuries dating back to 1978, and could easily have solved the problem by serving their coffee at a lower temperature."[2] Testimony from an array of "burn" experts supported this argument. Morgan also argued that coffee brewed by home coffeemakers had an average temperature of 140 degrees, while McDonald's served its coffee at an average of 180 to 190 degrees. The temperature of the coffee that injured Liebeck was estimated at approximately 170 degrees.

McDonald's countered by arguing that its coffee is served at between 180 and 190 degrees based on advice from a coffee consultant, who said the beverage tastes best at that temperature.[3] Further supporting arguments came from Terry Dort, executive director of the National Council of Chain Restaurants, who stated, "Coffee in our industry is served between 180 and 190 degrees. This is what our manufacturers recommend and this is what our customers want."[4] McDonald's also testified that safety is always its number-one priority and that the company had already printed warning labels on hot-beverage containers before Liebeck's incident.

As noted earlier, this was not the first time McDonald's had been sued for coffee burn injuries. The restaurant had received more than 700 reports of coffee burns ranging from mild to third degree. More than $500,000 in claims related to scalding injuries had been settled.

The Verdict

In August 1994, almost two years after Stella Liebeck had been burned, an Albuquerque, New Mexico, jury decided in favor of the plaintiff. The jury awarded Liebeck $2.7 million in punitive damages and $160,000 in compensatory damages—a sum almost ten times the $300,000 originally sought. According to jurors, the unusually high punitive award was decided not only for the injuries Liebeck suffered but also as a message to the fast-food industry to lower the temperature of the coffee. "The coffee's too hot out there, this (just) happened to be McDonald's," one juror said.[5] McDonald's had little to say after the decision but immediately filed an appeal, calling the punitive amount "excessive."

Stakeholders' Reactions

The response from the fast-food industry was mixed. The Popeye's fast-food franchise pulled coffee off its menus completely. Hardee's Restaurant, which was named two years earlier in a similar lawsuit and ordered to pay a plaintiff more than $150,000, announced it was considering issuing warning labels on containers and implementing more rigid training programs for employees on the safe handling of hot food and beverages.[6] "Because [of the jury's decision,] the public is more aware, [and] it is our belief that it will change the industry standard for serving coffee," Maurice Bridges, spokesperson for Hardee's Food Systems, Inc., said. "We are looking to raise the awareness internally and externally."[7] Wendy's International, Inc., temporarily removed hot chocolate from its menus as it tried to find a way to serve coffee at a reduced temperature. Wendy's said it felt that hot chocolate, which often ends up in the hands of children, did not require as high a temperature as coffee.[8]

Although these chains reacted almost immediately to the initial Liebeck decision, the majority of fast-food chains used a "wait and see" approach before taking any action. Burger King, Bruegger's Bagels, and Dunkin Donuts said they serve their product within the industry standard temperature range of 180 to 190 degrees and are likely to continue to do so. "It's a difficult issue," Steven Grover, assistant director of Technical Services, Public Health and Safety for the National Restaurant Association, said. "The expectation in our industry is that when customers order a hot cup of coffee, it should be hot. But then any beverage that is perceivably hot has the potential to hurt somebody. The restaurants are in a tough situation."[9]

The National Association of Trial Lawyers praised the jury's decision and the message it sent to fast-food restaurants. Russell F. Moran, an attorney and publisher of the *New York Jury Verdict Reporter*, stated that "People get upset when there are huge awards . . . like the woman burned by the McDonald's coffee . . . but you need to look beyond the facts, especially in this case. There were 700 incidents of prior notice. The fact is, the company was negligent . . . coffee doesn't have to be that hot."[10]

Punitive-reform activists spoke out against the decision, citing it as one of the many "excessive jury verdicts and frivolous lawsuits that continue to plague the U.S. civil justice system, inhibiting the competitiveness of corporate America."[11] "If ever a single incident shows how badly we need tort reform, this does," Dort said. "A $2.9 million decision points out how seriously flawed the (court) system is."[12] Still other reactions, such as one article written in the *Wall Street Journal*, questioned the common sense of the jurors. "We've often championed the common sense of the average citizen over a regulatory bureaucracy, but decisions like this make us scratch our heads."[13]

The decision came while at least two major pieces of legislation were being introduced to the Senate that would place strict limitations on punitive awards and would put product liability cases under federal jurisdiction. The Republican Party's controversial contract with America—led by Newt Gingritch—contained a proposal, supported by the National Association of Manufacturers, that would limit punitive damages in product liability cases to three times compensatory damages or to $250,000, whichever is the greater. Even more sweeping was the proposed Lawsuit Reform Act of 1995, which capped punitive damages in *all* civil cases to $250,000 or three times economic damages, whichever is greater.

Critics of product liability reform, such as Ralph Nader, have asserted that "[the proposed product liability] legislation would be a monumental rollback of consumer protections that have taken years to develop. Once the scaffolding of Federalism develops around product liability, there will be no stopping the downward erosion of individual rights."[14]

Follow-Up

McDonald's appeal of the $2.7 million punitive-damage award was heard in September 1994. State District Judge Robert Scott responded by lowering the punitive award to $480,000, a figure he calculated by tripling the $160,000 in compensatory damages the jury had previously awarded. The judge's ruling did not affect the compensatory damages. The total award was $640,000.[15] Judge Scott said the new amount was appropriate for the "willful, wanton, reckless, and what the court finds as callous" behavior on the part of the fast-food company.[16]

McDonald's said it believed the settlement was excessive and immediately followed with a statement announcing it would appeal the decision.

"Safety is always our first concern, and that is why we have 'hot contents' printed as reminder on our cups," Ann Connolly, a spokesperson for McDonald's, said. "We knew the initial damages awarded were excessive and unjustified, and yesterday the judge acknowledged that and agreed. But we feel they are still excessive, and will appeal this decision."[17] Attorneys for Stella Liebeck said they would appeal the judge's' decision to reduce the award.

Before a second appeal could be heard, both parties agreed to an out-of-court settlement of an undisclosed amount of money. As part of the settlement, however, McDonald's requested that neither Liebeck nor her attorney, Kenneth Wagner, speak about it.[18] Although the details of this request are unknown, attorneys for Liebeck subsequently have made public statements to the media following the agreement, and Liebeck appeared on the television news magazine show *20/20* on April 28, 1995, to discuss her ordeal.

The fast-food industry had found itself in an uncomfortable position from the attention paid to the Liebeck case. After the final decision, representatives of the industry seemed relieved and even showed support for McDonald's. "At this point, I'll probably get together with managers and take a strong look at putting [coffee] back in the stores," Greg Cutchall, president of Cutchall Management Co., which franchises five Popeye's stores, said. "I consider it a moral victory for McDonald's."[19]

The case caused some franchises to review their procedures. According to Don Perry, a spokesperson for the Atlanta-based Chik-fil-A Inc., "Something of that scale captures your attention. . . . We went through the process of doing some checks and going back to suppliers and asked them to advise us on their position for their own specifications and guidelines. . . . In keeping with one of our major tenets of operations of continuous improvements, we are analyzing the whole process from a viewpoint of safety."

For the "wait-and-see" franchises, business returned to normal. Although many of these restaurants now have labels cautioning consumers about the "hot" contents of their coffee, tea, and hot chocolate cups, the temperature of these beverages—including that of McDonald's coffee—continues to be served at the 180 to 190 degree industry standard.

Questions for Discussion

1. Was McDonald's fairly treated by the courts given all the facts in the case? Support your answer with case information.

2. Who are the stakeholders in this case? What are their stakes? Who won and who lost in this case?

3. Should the outcome of this case affect other beverage practices and standards of franchises such as McDonald's? Why or why not?

4. Does the McDonald's case signal that product liability law and tort reform are needed in the United States, *or* does this case prove that justice is fairly served in a democratic, capitalist society? Explain your answer.

5. Would consumers be better served if fewer or no standards existed regarding franchise beverage temperatures? Explain.

6. Was McDonald's just giving the customers what they wanted, *or* was McDonald's manipulating consumer tastes? Explain.

Notes

1. Theresa Howard, "Jury 'Burns' McD in $2.9M Verdict," *Nations Restaurant News*, 29 August 1994, 1, 55.

2. Eric Schine, "McDonalds's Hot Coffee Gets Her Cool Cash," *Business Week*, 5 September 1994, 38.

3. "Coffee Spill Burns Woman; Jury Awards $2.9 Million," *Wall Street Journal*, 19 August 1994, B3.

4. "Jury 'Burns' McD in $2.9M Verdict," *Nations Restaurant News*, 29 August 1994, 1,55.

5. "A Case for Iced Coffee," *Wall Street Journal*, 26 August 1994, A10.

6. "Jury 'Burns' McD."

7. Ibid.

8. Theresa Howard, "McD Settles Coffee Suit in Out-of-Court Agreement," *Nations Restaurant News*, 12 December 1994, 1, 59.

9. Theresa Howard, "Judge Slashes McD Settlement to $480,000," *Nations Restaurant News*, 26 September 1994, 4. See also p. 1.

10. Joanne Wojcik, "Excessive Punitive Awards a Matter of Debate," *Business Insurance*, 6 February 1995, 1, 49.

11. Ibid.

12. "Jury 'Burns' McD."

13. "A Case for Iced Coffee."

14. Stephen Labaton, "G.O.P. Preparing Bill to Overhaul Negligence Law," *New York Times*, 19 February 1995, 24. See also p. 1.

15. "McDonald's Coffee Award Reduced 75% by Judge," *Wall Street Journal*, 15 September 1994, A4.

16. Howard, "Judge Slashes McD Settlement," 1.

17. Ibid.

18. "McD Settles Coffee Suit," 1.

19. Howard, "Judge Slashes McD Settlement," 4.

Additional Sources

Jost, Kenneth. "A Changing Legal Landscape." *ABA Journal* (January 1995): 14.

McDonald's Settles Lawsuit over Burns from Coffee." *Wall Street Journal*, 2 December 1994, B6.

"Pick A Number, Any Number." *Legal Times*, 17 February 1992.

Sprunt, Hugh. "How Hot Is Coffee That's Not Too Hot?" *Wall Street Journal*, 2 September 1994, A9.

"When Risk Management Fails." *Business Insurance*, 12 September 1994, 8.

Accommodation stage The third phase in a firm's process for dealing with public crises related to unsafe products. In this stage the firm withdraws the product or defends its safety.

Acute crisis The second stage in a crisis during which actual damage is done and the crisis actually occurs.

Affirmative action A concept that focuses on active attempts by organizations to hire and promote individual members of groups that have been discriminated against in the past.

Agency stage The final phase in a firm's process for dealing with a public crisis related to unsafe products. In this stage the firm attempts to understand the safety issue and educate the public.

Altruist An ethical decision-making style based on providing benefits to others and contributing to the welfare of society.

Business strategy A level of corporate strategy formulation that deals with defining specific goals and business activities.

Capitalism An economic system governed by private and corporate ownership as opposed to governmental control.

Categorical imperative An ethical principle Immanuel Kant developed that contends individuals must act in ways they would universally wish all others to act in the same situation.

Chronic crisis The third stage in a crisis during which the firm undergoes a period of recovery, self-analysis, and healing.

Commercial speech A form of expression that refers to the type of language used in advertising and business interactions.

Compensatory justice A form of justice concerned with making amends to an individual for a past injustice.

Competitiveness The degree to which an individual or group can obtain or reach goals while engaging in rivalry with others in pursuit of the same goals.

Corporate internal decision structure The process for making corporate decisions about the organizational structure and the interpretation of established corporate policies.

Corporate strategy A level of corporate strategy formulation that deals with establishing broad goals to base corporate policies and plans on.

Covenantal ethic An ethical concept that focuses on the importance of social *relationships* among businesses, customers, and stakeholders.

Crisis management Methods presented in the text for identifying the stages of corporate crisis and ways for executives to responsibly manage these stages.

Crisis resolution The final stage in a crisis during which the firm focuses on managing and resolving the crisis.

Cultural relativism A form of ethical relativism that holds that moral standards vary from one culture to another and that individuals and firms should adhere to the moral standards of the culture where their actions occur.

Defense stage The second stage of crisis management during which a firm's image could be at stake as the firm deals with intense and widespread publicity.

Distributive justice A form of justice concerned with the fair and equitable distribution of benefits and burdens.

Due process A course of action that follows a society's established rules and laws.

Employment-at-will (EAW) doctrine A common-law principle that holds that the employer/employee relationship is strictly voluntary and that either party may end the relationship at any time.

Enterprise strategy A level of corporate strategy formulation that deals with the firm's broad role in society and identifies the values the firm wishes to represent.

Ethical idealism A view of corporate social responsibility that contends corporations can be responsible to society only if their actions are guided by a sense of moral duty toward stakeholder interests.

Ethical relativism An ethical framework that contends individuals have unique moral standards and that only these standards are relevant for judging their behavior. This framework dismisses the notion that universal rules for evaluating the morality of an action can exist.

Ethics code Corporate policies and rules of conduct that attempt to guide the behavior of employees with respect to acceptable work practices.

Free market theory An economic theory that contends that the primary objective of business is to maximize profits. The marketplace is seen as the mechanism that will protect and regulate both consumers and producers.

Functional strategy A level of corporate strategy formulation that deals with translating the business strategy into specific functional area goals.

Golden parachute Contracts between a firm and its high-level executives designed to protect and compensate these executives in the event of a takeover, merger, or restructuring.

Greenmail The practice of firms purchasing their own shares from corporate raiders at prices above market value in order to prevent a takeover.

Individualist An ethical decision-making style based on individual reasoning processes, self-interest, and self-preservation.

Infomercial A form of TV advertising characterized by a documentary format, an extended time frame, and more subtle sales techniques than conventional advertisements.

Insider trading The use of vital corporate information from a corporation member to obtain personal monetary gain.

Insight range The third stage in crisis management during which the firm must deal with the crisis and determine the extent the firm is at fault for the safety concerns relating to its product.

Issues management The frameworks presented in the text for guiding decision makers in identifying, prioritizing, and analyzing strategic issues and in evaluating the issues' effects on stakeholders. Also, the evolution and stages of issues at the societal level are presented.

Justice An ethical principle concerned with equal opportunities and equal access to them within society for all individuals. Moral judgments are based on the fair and equitable distribution of both opportunities and binders.

Keiretsu Financially interlocked groups or cartels of Japanese companies, banks, suppliers, and other commercial parties who work together to enhance each member firm's business activities.

Moral entitlement The belief that individuals or groups have inherent rights or privileges because they are members of society.

Multinational enterprise (MNE) A business whose operations are located in more than one country.

Myth A belief uncritically accepted by a group's members, especially in support of existing traditional practices and institutions.

Naive relativism A form of ethical relativism that holds that only the individual's self-interest and values are important for judging the morality of others' actions.

Neocapitalism A modified version of the traditional capitalist economic system characterized by strong interrelationships among political, corporate, and human capital resource strategies.

Nonconsequentialist ethic An ethical principle of not focusing on the outcome or consequences of an action when making a moral judgment.

Ombudsperson A third party located within a firm whose function is to hear and address employee grievances with respect to immoral behavior within the organization.

Pragmatist An ethical decision-making style based on justifiable actions determined by a combination of interests in a context of specific situations. Pragmatists make decisions based on the needs of the moment and on the specific consequences of those decisions.

Primary stakeholders Individuals or groups who are directly involved in an organization's operation and survival; for example, owners, suppliers, customers, employees.

Procedural justice A form of justice concerned with the fairness of the decision-making process, of practices, and of agreements.

Prodromal stage The first stage in a crisis during which the firm receives warnings or clues to a potential impending crisis.

Productionists Individuals who advocate corporate social responsibility with a focus on sharing corporate profits with less-fortunate members of society.

Progressivism A view of corporate social responsibility that holds that corporate actions should be guided by self-interest and a moral responsibility toward social change.

Pure speech A form of expression that refers to the general communication of ideas relating to politics, science, or art in the context of the marketplace.

Quality of work life (QWL) Employee benefit programs designed to improve the quality of the business environment by responding to employee needs and values.

Raider An individual who engages in corporate takeovers or takeover attempts. Raiders usually pursue hostile takeovers, which are strongly opposed by the target firm's managers.

Reaction stage The early stage of crisis management directly following the occurrence of a crisis. The firm must respond publicly to the crisis without the benefit of complete information or thorough analysis.

Retributive justice A form of justice concerned with punishing an individual or individuals for causing harm to another person.

Rights An ethical principle concerned with protecting the legal and moral rights of an individual or groups from being subjugated to the pursuit of societal well being.

Scientific management A management theory posed by Frederick Taylor that calls for the separation of management and labor, specifying the necessity for the division of labor and for formalized chains of command.

Secondary stakeholders Interested parties who are not directly related to a firm's daily operations and functioning.

Sexual harassment A form of sexual discrimination consisting of unwanted verbal or physical behavior toward an individual such that rejection of this behavior directly or indirectly affects the individual's employment or performance or creates a hostile work environment.

Social audit A method for measuring and evaluating the social responsibility performance of a firm with respect to its social goals, policies, and programs.

Social contract A philosophical concept that pertains to beliefs and assumptions that characterize relationships between various groups within society, such as the employer/employee relationship.

Special-interest groups Groups or organizations that focus media attention on corporations they believe pose a threat to public welfare.

Stakeholder analysis A form of analysis that focuses on observing and evaluating how business decisions as well as internal and external actions affect and are affected by constituencies.

Stakeholder approach An analytical approach concerned with the ways different constituencies impact and are affected by business decisions and actions.

Stakeholders Individuals or groups who have a vested interest or claim in a corporation.

Strategic business units (SBUs) Corporate divisions that focus on specific segments of the overall corporate product mix. They are primarily responsible for all business activity the firm undertakes within their market segment.

Takeover An attempt to gain control of a corporation by obtaining a majority share of its stock. Takeovers are characterized by stock purchases at a price much higher than the current market value.

Total ethics This concept is similar to the "zero defects" theory of organizational behavior. The basic premise of the concept is that businesses must understand their ethical responsibilities not as responses to external pressures or threats but as integral components of their ongoing activities.

Universalism An ethical principle that focuses on the means of taking an action, not on the consequences of that action. This view holds that an individual's actions should be guided by a sense of moral duty toward other individuals' humanity.

Utilitarianism An ethical principle that focuses on the consequences of an act to judge whether it is right or wrong. This principle seeks to maximize the benefits and minimize the costs for all parties the action affects.

Values Beliefs and principles individuals use to guide their actions, behaviors, and judgments of what is right and wrong.

Whistle-blowing The process whereby an employee reports to a third party about a known or suspected wrongdoing of his or her employer.

Zaibatsu A group of large Japanese corporations whose members own controlling blocks of shares in other member firms. Each member firm has its own keiretsu organized around it.

NAME INDEX

SUBJECT INDEX